St. Anne's Elementary School
12 Day Street - Box 818
Webster, MA 01570

MACMILLAN / McGRAW-HILL

LANGUAGE ARTS TODAY

Great literature is an inspiration. Isaac Asimov's *A Boy's Best Friend* inspired artist Don Daily to create the illustration on the cover of your book. The story begins on page 106. We hope that you enjoy the story and the illustration!

SENIOR AUTHORS

ANN McCALLUM   WILLIAM STRONG   TINA THOBURN   PEGGY WILLIAMS

Literature Consultant   Joan Glazer

Macmillan / McGraw-Hill School Publishing Company

New York   Chicago   Columbus

ACKNOWLEDGMENTS

The publisher gratefully acknowledges permission to reprint the following copyrighted material:

"A Boy's Best Friend" by Isaac Asimov. Copyright © 1975 by The Boy Scouts of America. Reprinted by permission of the author.

"The Case of the Uncooked Eggs" from *The Magic Orange Tree and Other Folktales* by Diane Wolkstein. Copyright © 1978 by Diane Wolkstein. Reprinted by permission of Alfred A. Knopf, Inc. and Curtis Brown, Ltd. Cassette permission by the author.

"Dear Mr. Henshaw" consists of Letters from January 12, 15, and 19 excerpted from *Dear Mr. Henshaw* by Beverly Cleary. Copyright © 1983 by Beverly Cleary. By permission of Morrow Junior Books (A Division of William Morrow and Company, Inc.) and Julia MacRae Books, London.

"Famous Caves Worldwide" is from *Caves* by George Laycock. Copyright © 1976 by George Laycock. Published by Four Winds Press. Reprinted and recorded by permission of the author.

"Is a Panda a Bear?" from *Project Panda Watch* by Miriam Schlein. Copyright © 1984 Miriam Schlein. Used with the permission of Atheneum Publishers, an imprint of Macmillan Publishing Company, and Janet Chenery for the author.

"My Love Affair with the Alphabet" by Natalie Babbitt from *Once Upon a Time*. Copyright © 1986 by G. P. Putnam's Sons. Reprinted by permission of the publisher.

"Morning—The Bird Perched for Flight' " from *Earth Shine* by Anne Morrow Lindbergh. Copyright © 1966, 1969 by Anne Morrow Lindbergh. Used by permission of Harcourt Brace Jovanovich, Inc. By permission also of Chatto and Windus and the Hogarth Press.

Poems, Brief Quotations, and Excerpts

"Dreams" from *The Dream Keeper and Other Poems* by Langston Hughes. Copyright 1932 by Alfred A. Knopf, Inc. and renewed 1960 by Langston Hughes. Reprinted by permission of the publisher and Harold Ober Associates, Inc.

Isaac Asimov quotation used by permission of the author.

Cover Design: Barnett-Brandt Design
Cover Illustration: Don Daily

Copyright © 1993 Macmillan/McGraw-Hill School Publishing Company

**Macmillan/McGraw-Hill School Division
10 Union Square East
New York, New York 10003**

Printed in the United States of America

ISBN: 0-02-244116-6

9 8 7 6 5 4 3

Excerpt from "For Laura" in *The Way Things Are and Other Poems* by Myra Cohn Livingston. Copyright © 1974 by Myra Cohn Livingston. Reprinted by permission of Marian Reiner for the author.

Jane Yolen quotation is copyright © Jane Yolen. Reprinted by permission of Curtis Brown, Ltd.

Natalie Babbitt quotation from *More Books by More People* by Lee Bennett Hopkins. Copyright © 1974 by Lee Bennett Hopkins. Reprinted by permission of Curtis Brown, Ltd.

Excerpt from "I Dreamed You Led Me" from *Eighty Poems of Antonio Machado*, translated by Willis Barnstone. Published by Las Americas Publishing Co. Reprinted by permission of Willis Barnstone.

Diane Wolkstein quotation is reprinted from *Fifth Book of Junior Authors and Illustrators* (Bronx, N.Y.: HW Wilson, 1983). All rights reserved. Used by permission.

Excerpt from "Little Gidding" in *Four Quartets* by T.S. Eliot. Copyright 1943 by T.S. Eliot, renewed 1971 by Esme Valerie Eliot. Reprinted by permission of Harcourt Brace Jovanovich, Inc. and Faber & Faber Ltd.

George Laycock quotation is from *Something About the Author*: Volume 5. Edited by Anne Commire. Copyright © 1973 by Gale Research Company. All rights reserved. Reprinted by permission of the publisher.

"Paula the Cat" from *Vacation Time* by Nikki Giovanni. Copyright © 1980 by Nikki Giovanni. By permission of William Morrow and Company, Inc.

Excerpt from "The Road Not Taken" from *You Come, Too* in *The Poetry of Robert Frost* edited by Edward Connery Lathem. Copyright © 1916 by Holt, Rinehart and Winston, Inc. Renewed 1944 by Robert Frost. By permission of Henry Holt and Company, Inc.

"The Sidewalk Racer, or On the Skateboard" from *The Sidewalk Racer and Other Poems of Sports and Motion* by Lillian Morrison. Copyright © 1977 by Lillian Morrison. Published by Lothrop, Lee & Shepard. Reprinted by permission of the author.

"Think Tank" and excerpt from "Landscape" (also the full poem) from *A Sky Full of Poems* by Eve Merriam. Copyright © 1964, 1970, 1973 by Eve Merriam. All rights reserved. Reprinted by permission of Marian Reiner for the author.

Excerpt from "To Look At Any Thing" from the volume *The Living Seed* by John Moffitt. Copyright © 1961 by John Moffitt. Reprinted by permission of Harcourt Brace Jovanovich, Inc.

"This Is Just To Say" from *Collected Poems, Volume I: 1909-1939* by William Carlos Williams. Copyright © 1986 by New Directions Publishing Corporation. By permission of New Directions. By permission also of Carcanet Press Limited.

"The Ways of Living Things" by Jack Prelutsky from *The Random House Book of Poetry for Children*. Selected by Jack Prelutsky. Copyright © 1983 by Random House, Inc. Reprinted by permission of the publisher.

Excerpt from "To James" from *Haverstraw* by Frank Horne. This originally appeared in *Letters Found Near a Suicide (1920-1930)* by Frank Horne.

Haiku by Basho is from *An Introduction to Haiku*,

(Acknowledgments continued on page 556.)

MACMILLAN / McGRAW-HILL

LANGUAGE ARTS TODAY

C O N T E N T S

THEME: *PATHWAYS*

THEME: *WONDERS*

Language Study

Writing

THEME: *DIRECTIONS*

THEME: *COMMUNICATIONS*

Language Study

Writing

AWARD WINNING
SELECTION

THEME: *OBSERVATIONS*

THEME: *CROSSROADS*

Language Study

Writing

AWARD WINNING
SELECTION

THEME: *EXPLORATIONS*

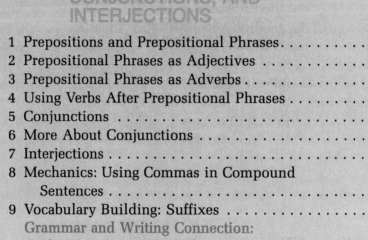

WRITER'S REFERENCE

How can I
get ideas
for writing?

This book can really help you there. There's great literature between these covers. I noticed that after reading a good story, biography, or poem, I wanted to respond. Sometimes I wanted to write about the same topic or in a similar style. Sometimes I wanted to write a journal entry.

Writers
are readers,
and readers
are writers!

I know that sometimes, no matter how hard I try, the ideas won't come. Reading a story doesn't work. Talking with my friends doesn't help. Then, I take a look at the **PICTURES** 📷 *SEEING LIKE A WRITER* section in this book, and presto! Ideas start to flow. The pictures turn up the volume on my imagination.

What will I write about today?

IMAGINE

Writers observe, and observers can find lots of ideas for writing.

How will I remember all my ideas?

 JOURNAL Personally, I don't know how I'd keep all my ideas straight without my journal. I write in it every day—facts, thoughts, feelings. I draw pictures, too. A journal is a great place to keep track of what you've learned.

A journal is a writer's best friend.

How does working with a group help?

Writing doesn't have to be something that you do alone. I get lots of ideas when I work with my classmates. During group writing, we write and conference together. When it's time to write on my own, I'm all warmed up and ready to go.

Writing together builds confidence; conferences get the ideas flowing.

How do thinking and writing go together?

I really give my brain a workout when I write. I can't help it. To write, you have to think about many things: sequence; main idea; beginning, middle, and end; likenesses and differences.

Writing is thinking on paper.

What is the writing process, and how will it help me?

Writing isn't something that just happens 1-2-3. It takes time to write. The writing process allows me the time I need.

MACMILLAN
LANGUAGE ARTS
TODAY

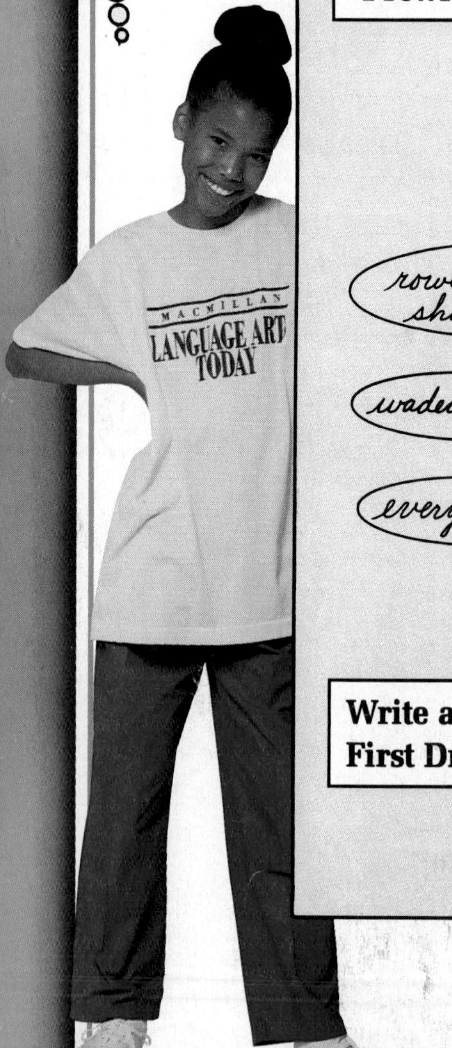

Prewrite

At this stage I can get ideas and plan my writing. I need to think about my purpose and audience. Graphic organizers can really help here.

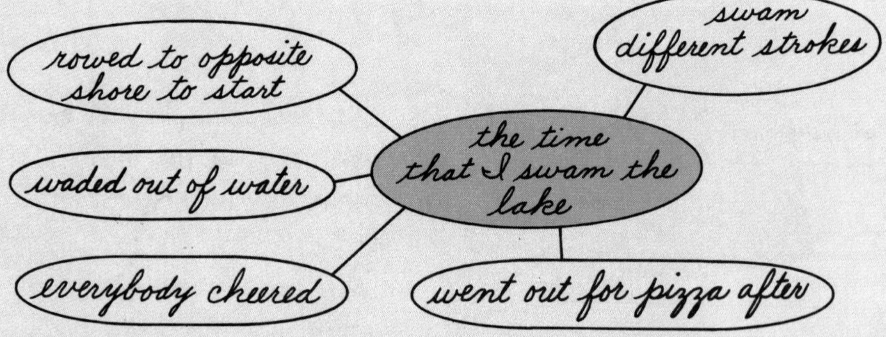

the time that I swam the lake
rowed to opposite shore to start
swam different strokes
waded out of water
everybody cheered
went out for pizza after

Write a First Draft

This is the stage when I overcome the "blank paper blues." I don't let small mistakes hold me up. I like this stage because I finally get to *see* what I think. I guess that's what it means to be a writer.

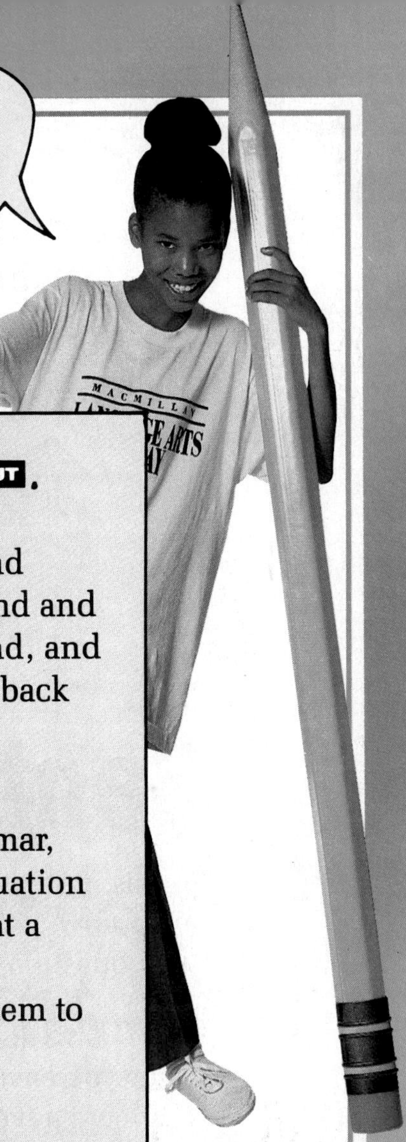

> Don't tell anyone, but this is when I feel most like a writer. It's such a thrill to be in control!

Revise

Before I revise, I take some **⏱ TIME-OUT**. I need to let my writing settle a bit. Then I read my writing to myself and to a friend. I then take pencil in hand and go to it. I add, take out, move around, and combine some sentences. I even go back to prewriting for more ideas.

Proofread

During this stage, I fix all my grammar, spelling, capitalization, and punctuation mistakes. I proofread for one error at a time. (Take my advice. Learn the proofreading marks. You can use them to make changes simply and easily.)

Publish

I knew I was an author when I saw the word "publish." Publishing can mean reading your writing out loud or taking it home to show your family—anything that involves sharing your writing with your audience.

Sentences

In this unit you will learn about kinds of sentences. You will learn how to express complete thoughts in different ways—with questions, statements, commands, and exclamations.

Discuss Read the poem on the opposite page. Think about paths you have followed. Talk with a partner about pathways you have traveled.

Creative Expression The unit theme is *Pathways.* Have you ever followed a difficult path? Write about an experience you had where you found your own way. Write your thoughts in your journal.

THEME: *PATHWAYS*

*I dreamed you led me
along a white footpath
through green fields,*

*toward the blue of the sierras,
toward the blue mountains,
one serene morning.*

—Antonio Machado, from ''I Dreamed You Led Me''

FOUR KINDS OF SENTENCES

A sentence is a group of words that expresses a complete thought.

The four kinds of sentences are listed below. Notice that every sentence begins with a capital letter and ends with a punctuation mark.

Declarative Sentence	Imperative Sentence
Purpose: makes a statement Example: I want to climb Mount Anvil. End Mark: period (.)	Purpose: gives a command or makes a request Examples: Come with me. Please climb high. End Mark: period (.)
Interrogative Sentence	**Exclamatory Sentence**
Purpose: asks a question Example: Who will come with me? End Mark: question mark (?)	Purpose: expresses strong feeling Examples: How silly I am! What wonderful friends I have! End Mark: exclamation mark (!)

Guided Practice

Tell whether each sentence is declarative, interrogative, imperative, or exclamatory.

Example: Clouds covered the mountaintop. *declarative*

1. Listen to my story.
2. Nobody would climb Mount Anvil with me.
3. Was it wise to climb the mountain alone?
4. The peak looked fairly high.
5. What a foolish decision I made!

THINK

- How would using different kinds of sentences make my writing more interesting?

REMEMBER

- A **declarative sentence** makes a statement.
- An **interrogative sentence** asks a question.
- An **imperative sentence** gives a command or makes a request.
- An **exclamatory sentence** expresses strong feeling.

More Practice

A. Write each sentence. Then write whether each sentence is **declarative, interrogative, imperative,** or **exclamatory.**

Example: The mountain stood in the distance. *declarative*

6. I decided to climb the mountain alone.

7. How easy the first two miles were!

8. Then I noticed the sky.

9. Were storm clouds beginning to form?

10. Turn back now.

11. Will my friends laugh at me?

12. Forget about your pride for once.

13. How I hate to quit halfway up the mountain!

B. Write each sentence. Use the correct end punctuation. Then write which of the four kinds of sentences it is.

Example: I was nervous   *I was nervous.*   *declarative*

14. By sundown I was lost, cold, wet, and frightened

15. Please travel with a companion or group

16. Where were my maps, compass, and trail mix

17. What I wouldn't have given for some matches

18. Did anyone even know of my plans

19. How miserable it was to sleep in that hollow tree

20. My friends found me first thing in the morning

Extra Practice, page 26

WRITING APPLICATION A Story

Write a brief story about a real-life adventure that you have had. Identify each of the four kinds of sentences you use. Then read your story to a classmate.

2 COMPLETE SUBJECTS AND COMPLETE PREDICATES

A sentence has two parts—the complete subject and the complete predicate. The **complete subject** includes all the words that tell whom or what the sentence is about. The **complete predicate** includes all the words that tell what the subject does or is. A sentence must have both parts to state a complete idea.

COMPLETE SUBJECT	COMPLETE PREDICATE
" I	never lost a passenger ."
" My train	never ran off the track ."
Those words	are Harriet Tubman's .
Her daring rescues	became famous in the 1850s .
Escape	was often difficult and dangerous .

Guided Practice

Identify the complete subject and the complete predicate of each sentence.

Example: Harriet Tubman led slaves to freedom.
      Complete subject   Harriet Tubman
      Complete predicate   led slaves to freedom.

1. Harriet Tubman was a "conductor" on the Underground Railroad.
2. This great woman guided runaway slaves.
3. The Underground Railroad showed the way to Canada.
4. Runaway slaves followed this route.
5. More than three hundred "passengers" traveled with Tubman.
6. Harriet Tubman escaped from slavery in 1849.

?! THINK

■ How can I tell the difference between the complete subject and the complete predicate of a sentence?

REMEMBER

- All the words that tell whom or what the sentence is about make up the **complete subject**.
- All the words that tell what the subject does or is make up the **complete predicate**.

More Practice

A. Copy the underlined words. Write **complete subject** or **complete predicate** next to each group of words.

Example: Harriet Tubman <u>was a slave</u>. *was a slave*
         complete predicate

  7. <u>Her first taste of freedom</u> led to a decision.
  8. "My family and friends <u>are still slaves</u>."
  9. "<u>Escape</u> is their only answer."
10. This woman <u>rescued her family and other slaves</u>.
11. <u>Angry slaveowners</u> offered rewards for her capture.
12. She <u>fooled these slaveowners each time</u>.
13. <u>Harriet's passengers</u> were never lost or caught.

B. Write each sentence. Draw a line between the complete subject and the complete predicate.

Example: Travelers|rode to freedom.

14. The Underground Railroad had many "tracks."
15. Difficult paths led through Ohio and Indiana.
16. A boat across Lake Erie carried many slaves.
17. The state of Pennsylvania helped these people.
18. Runaway slaves traveled from Philadelphia to Quebec.
19. Some slaves hid aboard ships in southern ports.
20. Large numbers of slaves reached Canada.

Extra Practice, page 27

WRITING APPLICATION A Diary Entry

Imagine that you are traveling with Harriet Tubman. Write a diary entry that tells about the problems you face. Draw a line between the complete subject and the complete predicate of each of your sentences.

The Granger Collection

3 SIMPLE SUBJECTS AND SIMPLE PREDICATES

The complete subject of a sentence includes all the words that tell whom or what the subject is about. The main word or words in the complete subject are called the **simple subject.**

The complete predicate is usually made up of several words, too. The main word or words in the complete predicate are called the **simple predicate.** The simple predicate is always a verb. A **verb** is a word that shows action.

SIMPLE SUBJECT	SIMPLE PREDICATE
My name	is Theseus.
I	am the prince of Athens.
Our nation	has conquered an enemy.
King Minos of Crete	was taking our warriors.
His terrible monster	threatened our people.

Guided Practice

Find the simple subject in each sentence. Then find the simple predicate.

Example: The horrible Minotaur lived in a maze.
          Simple subject   Minotaur
          Simple predicate   lived

1. Fourteen teenagers sailed for Crete.
2. The king's monster would devour them there!
3. Our people feared this evil Minotaur.
4. The time for action had come.
5. I can destroy this monstrous Minotaur!

THINK

■ How can I decide which words are the simple subject and the simple predicate in a sentence?

REMEMBER

- The **simple subject** is the main word or words in the complete subject.
- The **simple predicate** is the main word or words in the complete predicate.

More Practice

A. Write the simple subject and the simple predicate of each sentence.

Example: The trip to Crete was very exciting. *trip was*

6. I volunteered for the trip to Crete.
7. The cruel king threw me in prison.
8. The monster of Crete lived beneath me.
9. The Minotaur's home was a maze.
10. Nobody had escaped from this labyrinth.
11. The beautiful daughter of King Minos pitied me.
12. She gave me a gift of thread.
13. I tied one end of the thread to the entrance.

B. Write each sentence. Draw one line under each simple subject and two lines under each simple predicate.

Example: I unwound the thread behind me.

14. The maze had a hundred pathways.
15. The roars of the monster grew louder.
16. The shadow of the beast was now in sight.
17. I grabbed his ugly form.
18. The cruel Minotaur would kill no more!
19. The long thread led back to the entrance.
20. Finally I reached my ship.

Extra Practice, page 28

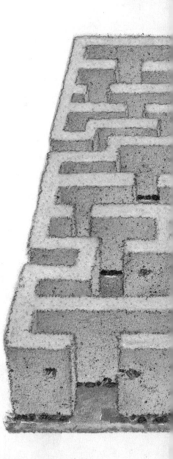

WRITING APPLICATION A Note

Imagine that you have a magic ball of thread that will lead you anywhere. Write a note that tells where you would go and why. Draw one line under the simple subject and two lines under the simple predicate of each sentence.

FINDING THE SUBJECT

The **subject** of a sentence tells whom or what the sentence is about. In a **declarative sentence,** or statement, the subject often comes first.

> Sleuth is my uncle's bloodhound.

In an **interrogative sentence** the subject often comes after the first word of the sentence. To find the subject, rearrange the question into a statement.

> Have I told you about my adventure with Sleuth?

> I have told you about my adventure with Sleuth.

The subject of an **imperative sentence** is always *you.* However, the word *you* is not stated. It is understood.

> (You) Listen to my story.

In sentences that begin with *Here* or *There* the subject comes after the verb.

> Here in the forest are searchers .

> There is a bloodhound with them.

Guided Practice

Identify the subject of each sentence.

Example: Did the boy follow
the path? *boy*

1. There was a lost child in the forest.
2. The searchers called my uncle immediately.
3. Can Sleuth find the little boy?
4. Take me on the search.
5. Sit in the car with Sleuth.

 THINK

■ How can I remember where to find the subject in each type of sentence?

REMEMBER

- The subject of an **interrogative sentence** often comes after the first word of the sentence.
- The subject of an **imperative sentence** is always *you*.
- *Here* and *There* are never the subject of a sentence.

More Practice

A. Write the subject of each sentence.

Example: Did you find the boy's parents? *You*

6. There are the boy's parents.
7. Have they searched everywhere?
8. Please find our son.
9. Give me an article of the boy's clothing.
10. Here is Jimmy's jacket.
11. Sleuth sniffs the jacket eagerly.
12. Can a bloodhound follow a three-day-old scent?
13. Follow Sleuth closely.

B. Write each sentence. Underline the subject.

Example: There is the bloodhound.
         There is the <u>bloodhound</u>.

14. Sleuth's nose picks up the scent.
15. Are bloodhounds dangerous in any way?
16. There is no gentler dog in the world.
17. Have we gone five miles already?
18. Look at that rocky stream bed.
19. Here is Jimmy at last!
20. Are there any dogs smarter than bloodhounds?

Extra Practice, page 29

WRITING APPLICATION A Letter

Write a letter about an animal that interests you. Ask the owner questions about the animal. Identify the subject of each of the interrogative and imperative sentences you write. Then share your letter with a small group of classmates.

COOPERATIVE
LEARNING

COMPOUND SUBJECTS AND COMPOUND PREDICATES

You know that every sentence has a simple subject and a simple predicate.

I spotted the tracks of wild animals.

Some sentences have two or more simple subjects. When a sentence has two or more simple subjects that have the same predicate, the subject is called a **compound subject.**

Uncle Al and I spotted the tracks of wild animals.

My uncle , a friend , and I followed these tracks.

Other sentences have two or more simple predicates. When a sentence has two or more simple predicates that have the same subject, the predicate is called a **compound predicate.**

I spotted and photographed the tracks of a deer.

I watched , waited , and listened for movement.

The word *and* or the word *or* joins the parts of a compound subject or the parts of a compound predicate.

Guided Practice

Identify the compound subject or compound predicate in each sentence.

Example: My uncle noticed and followed some tracks.
    Compound predicate   noticed   followed

1. My uncle and I hiked through a forest.
2. We found and examined some interesting tracks.
3. Mammals, birds, and reptiles live in wild places.
4. These animals usually run and hide from people.
5. Their tracks and droppings show us their whereabouts.
6. Uncle Al and I followed some tracks of animals.

Uncle Al and I

?! THINK

■ How can I decide if a sentence has a compound subject or a compound predicate?

REMEMBER

- A **compound subject** has two or more simple subjects that have the same predicate.
- A **compound predicate** has two or more simple predicates that have the same subject.

More Practice

A. Write and label the compound subject or compound predicate in each sentence.

Example: Animals scurried and twittered in the forest.
Compound predicate   scurried twittered

7. Stumps and wooden chips are signs of beaver.
8. Beavers store and eat the branches of trees.
9. Deer or moose were here this spring.
10. The skin of their antlers dried, split, and itched.
11. They rubbed and scraped their antlers on branches.
12. These maples and pines have bare spots on their trunks.

B. Write each sentence. Write whether each sentence has a **compound subject,** a **compound predicate,** or **no compound.**

Example: The forest is a wonderful place. *no compound*

13. A bobcat or fox lives in this hollow log.
14. Bones and feathers indicate a meat eater's home.
15. A woodchuck dug and inhabited this den.
16. The hidden entrances are eight inches across.
17. Playful otters slip and slide into the water here.
18. Their wet fur has worn the riverbank smooth.
19. I found and sketched the tracks of a skunk.
20. Uncle Al would not follow the tracks very far.

Extra Practice, page 30

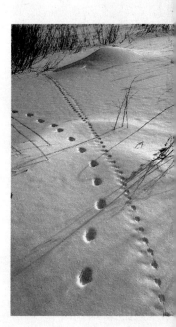

WRITING APPLICATION An Interview

Interview someone who knows a lot about wildlife. Use a question-and-answer format for your interview. Include a compound subject or a compound predicate in at least three of your sentences.

6 COMPOUND SENTENCES

The sentences you have studied so far in this unit have all been simple sentences. A simple sentence has one complete subject and one complete predicate. It expresses one complete thought.

Monarch butterflies are interesting insects.

Sometimes two simple sentences are combined to form a **compound sentence.** Pairs of simple sentences are joined by a comma and a connecting word. Such connecting words are *and, but,* and *or.*

Butterflies are interesting.
I study them in school.
Butterflies are interesting, **and**
I study them in school.

I find monarchs in the summer.
In the fall they disappear.
I find monarchs in the summer, **but**
in the fall they disappear.

Did the butterflies die? Did they fly away?
Did the butterflies die, **or** did they fly away?

Guided Practice

Tell whether each sentence is simple or compound.

Example: I study butterflies, but my sister studies birds.
    compound

1. I caught a monarch butterfly, and it had a tag.
2. The tag was tiny, but I read its message.
3. The tag gave the address of a Canadian professor.
4. I could write, or I could telephone her.
5. The professor studied monarchs and their habits.

THINK

- How can I decide if a sentence is a compound sentence or a simple sentence?

REMEMBER

■ A **compound sentence** contains two or more simple sentences that are joined by a comma and the word *and*, *but*, or *or*.

More Practice

A. Write **simple** or **compound** for each sentence.

Example: The professor was happy about my call. *simple*

6. The professor thanked me for my help.
7. Monarchs can live anywhere, but they need milkweed.
8. Most monarchs live six months, but some monarchs reach one year.
9. Young monarchs move south in August or September.
10. Often they fly in groups of three or more.
11. Do they fly, or do they drift on the wind?
12. The black and gold insects ride wind currents.
13. Monarchs fly long distances, and scientists study their flight paths.

B. Write each sentence. Underline the simple sentences that make up each compound sentence. Write **not compound** if the sentence is not compound.

Example: <u>Monarchs seem fragile</u>, but <u>they are strong</u>.

14. They can fly for five days or longer.
15. Many monarchs fly down the Pacific coast.
16. Some monarchs fly to California, but others go to Mexico.
17. Spring comes, and the monarchs head north.
18. They may go to New England or Canada.
19. The trip may take two weeks, or it may take longer.
20. Some monarchs fly to Australia.

Extra Practice, page 31

WRITING APPLICATION A Post Card

Imagine that you are a monarch butterfly. Write a post card that tells what you see as you make your journey in the spring. Exchange post cards with a classmate.

7 CORRECTING FRAGMENTS AND RUN-ON SENTENCES

A **sentence fragment** is a group of words that is only part of a sentence. It does not have both a subject and a predicate, and it does not express a complete thought. You can correct sentence fragments by supplying the missing parts.

INCORRECT: My father.

CORRECT: My father found an old photo.

A **run-on sentence** joins together two or more sentences that should be written separately. To correct a run-on sentence, separate each complete idea into a simple sentence or rewrite it as a compound sentence.

INCORRECT: The photo showed our road the road was unpaved.

CORRECT: The photo showed our road.
The road was unpaved.

CORRECT: The photo showed our road,
but the road was unpaved.

Guided Practice

Identify each item as a sentence fragment or a run-on sentence.

Example: Our road was only a path pioneers followed this path. *run-on*

1. The path was difficult even scouts had trouble.
2. From a feeding ground to a watering place.
3. Followed this trail in single file.
4. They had no vehicles the path remained narrow.
5. The pioneers with horses and wagons.

 **THINK**

■ How can I decide where to end a sentence?

REMEMBER

- A **sentence fragment** is a group of words that does not express a complete thought.
- A **run-on sentence** joins together sentences that should be written separately.

More Practice

A. Write **sentence fragment** or **run-on** for each item.

Example: The colonists were busy they worked hard. *run-on*

6. Widened the path with saws and axes.
7. Wagons got stuck in the mud tree roots tripped horses.
8. Travel best in winter in sleighs.
9. The road was paved with logs how bumpy it was!
10. Rotted after a while.
11. During the Revolution was part of a turnpike.
12. Gravel covered the road people paid by the mile.
13. For thirty years the turnpike.

B. Rewrite these sentence fragments and run-on sentences.

Example: The turnpike lost popularity it was not used.
The turnpike lost popularity. It was not used.

14. Later, people dug canals locomotives were invented.
15. Our road was slower than the railroad it was more expensive than the canal.
16. No one maintained the road it remained muddy.
17. Then along came the bicycle. And the automobile.
18. People needed better roads stronger materials were used.
19. Our road was paved in 1920 it has been widened twice.
20. The canals are gone traffic increases every year.

Extra Practice, Practice Plus, pages 32-33

WRITING APPLICATION Sentences

Imagine that you live in the year 3000. Write about how people travel. Have a partner point out any sentence fragments or run-on sentences in your writing.

GRAMMAR

MECHANICS: Capitalizing and Punctuating Sentences

Capitalize the first word of every sentence. The capital letter shows that a new sentence is beginning.

My great-great-great grandmother was a pioneer.

End each sentence with a period, a question mark, or an exclamation mark. These punctuation marks show the kind of sentence it is.

Type of Sentence	Punctuation Mark	Example
Declarative Sentence	period	This book is her diary**.**
Interrogative Sentence	question mark	When did she go west**?**
Imperative Sentence	period	Read this entry to me**.**
Exclamatory Sentence	exclamation mark	How brave she was!

Guided Practice

Tell how to begin and end each sentence.

Example: the pioneers headed for California
           The pioneers headed for California.

1. today we reached the Humboldt Sink
2. what a dry and empty part of Nevada this is
3. will we have enough water to cross this region
4. our oxen are already thin and weak
5. drive this wagon slowly
6. we traveled during the cool night hours

THINK

■ What would happen if sentences in books did not begin with capital letters and end with punctuation marks?

REMEMBER

- Capitalize the first word of every sentence.
- End each sentence with the correct punctuation mark—a period, a question mark, or an exclamation mark.

More Practice

A. Write these sentences. Add capital letters and punctuation marks correctly.

Example: the evenings were best for travel
The evenings *were best for travel.*

7. what a disaster our night journey was
8. three days ago we missed a turnoff
9. should we go back to find the turnoff or continue
10. the leaders of our party discussed the problem
11. look at the oxen
12. will they last another week
13. how awful this journey is

B. Write each sentence. Add the correct capitalization and punctuation marks. Then write whether each sentence is **declarative, interrogative, imperative,** or **exclamatory.**

Example: animals are very interesting
Animals are very interesting. declarative

14. can animals know more than people
15. please listen to what happened
16. our oxen refused to retrace their steps
17. they broke free from their yoke
18. what an amazing sight that was
19. why wouldn't the oxen turn around and go back
20. there was water and grass less than a mile ahead

Extra Practice, page 34

WRITING APPLICATION A Paragraph

Write a brief paragraph about a surprise you have had. Exchange your paragraph with a classmate. Identify each kind of sentence your classmate has used.

GRAMMAR

9 VOCABULARY BUILDING: Using Context Clues

Because of little rain this land is arid.

What do you do when you come across an unfamiliar word? First, look at the **context** of the word—the other words in the sentence. The context gives clues to the meaning of a word.

Sometimes a context clue might be a synonym or an antonym of an unfamiliar word. A **synonym** is a word that has the same or almost the same meaning as that of another word. An **antonym** is a word with an opposite meaning.

I built this model; it is an exact **replica** of that ship.

The Northwest Passage is **frigid,** even when it is warm here.

The context clue *model* is a synonym of the unfamiliar word *replica. Warm* is an antonym of the word *frigid.*

Guided Practice

Use context clues to tell the meaning of each underlined word.

Example: The <u>tranquil</u> ocean calmed the crew. *calm*

1. The explorers who followed Columbus were <u>disgruntled</u>. How disappointed they were that this land was not Asia!
2. They remained <u>optimistic</u>, though, certain that they would find Asia soon.
3. The <u>lure</u> of Asia's riches attracted them.
4. These explorers were <u>resolute</u>, not half-hearted.
5. They <u>diligently</u> searched lakes and rivers; they steadily explored water routes.

 THINK

■ How can I decide the meaning of an unfamiliar word?

REMEMBER

■ Context clues can help you find the meaning of a word.

More Practice

Use context clues to discover the meaning of each underlined word. Then write each meaning.

Example: The explorers were all in accord; they agreed that the passage had to exist. *agreement*

6. This short route would curtail the long voyage.
7. Where was this elusive route? That was the mystery.
8. The search for the route energized the crew; the sailors were active much of the time.
9. Heroes from many nations showed valor.
10. Explorers hazarded fortunes to take this great risk.
11. The explorers showed fervor; few lost their enthusiasm.
12. Henry Hudson made a disquieting discovery; the Northwest Passage would be frozen much of the year.
13. Despite the adverse conditions, exploration continued.
14. The search for the passage paid rich dividends.
15. The New World's bounty—fish and timber—was plentiful.
16. The ice did not deter later explorers; they continued their voyages.
17. What anguish they suffered—hunger and failure!
18. Cartographers could now map the New World.
19. The dream materialized in 1906; a ship actually sailed through the passage that year.
20. Today various vessels—submarines, tankers, and cutters— use the Northwest Passage.

Extra Practice, page 35

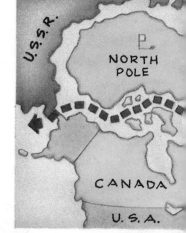

 WRITING APPLICATION Sentences

Find five difficult words in the dictionary. Read the definition of each word. Then use each word in a sentence. Include context clues. Have a classmate discover the meaning of each word from the context clues.

COOPERATIVE
LEARNING

G R A M M A R

GRAMMAR AND WRITING CONNECTION

Combining Sentences

When you write, often the details you give in two sentences are closely related. You can show the link between such sentences by using a comma and the connecting word *and*.

Separate: Lilly packed our gear in the car.
We drove to Greenville.

Combined: Lilly packed our gear in the car**, and** we drove to Greenville.

To point out a contrast between the ideas, use *but* instead of *and*.

Combined: Our map showed the way to the bandshell**, but** we took the wrong path.

If two sentences tell of a choice to be made, use the word *or*.

Combined: Would we find our way**, or** would we miss the concert?

Working Together

COOPERATIVE
LEARNING

Read each pair of sentences. Then tell how you would combine the two sentences into a single sentence.

Example: The musicians have arrived.
They are ready to play.
The musicians have arrived, and they are ready to play.

1. I play the bugle.
Lilly plays the drum.

2. We auditioned for the conductor.
He did not accept us.

Revising Sentences

Combine each pair of sentences into a single sentence. Use *and*, *but*, or *or* to show the connection between ideas.

3. Were we too young?
   Had we not studied long enough?
4. The band marches three times a week.
   Lilly and I watch every single parade.
5. Will we be old enough for membership next year?
   Will we have to wait longer to join the band?
6. All the concert uniforms are new.
   All the practice uniforms are old.
7. The buglers play the melody.
   The drummers keep the beat.
8. Will the next song be a modern one?
   Will the band play an old tune?
9. The buglers march to the left.
   The drummers march to the right.
10. The musicians then merge their marches.
    The leader calls a halt.

Imagine that you are at a fork in a road with two pathways ahead of you. Write a paragraph that tells which path you would choose and why.

When you revise, work with your partner to find pairs of sentences to combine. Use the connecting word that best fits the meaning.

UNIT CHECKUP

LESSON 1 Four Kinds of Sentences (page 2) Write each sentence. Add the correct punctuation mark. Label each sentence **declarative, interrogative, imperative,** or **exclamatory.**

1. Please study the circulatory system
2. What a wonderful system it is
3. How hard the heart works
4. Blood has many different jobs
5. What do arteries do

LESSONS 2-3 Complete Subjects and Complete Predicates and Simple Subjects and Simple Predicates (pages 4–7) Write each sentence. Draw a line between the complete subject and the complete predicate. Underline the simple subject once; underline the simple predicate twice.

6. Every organ needs blood.
7. Our arteries carry the blood away from the heart.
8. The veins return the blood to the heart.
9. The red blood cells carry oxygen.
10. White blood cells protect the body from disease.

LESSON 4 Finding the Subject (page 8) Write the simple subject of each sentence.

11. Study this plastic heart.
12. There are four chambers.
13. Do the valves control the flow?
14. Here is a diagram.
15. Please draw the veins.

LESSON 5 Compound Subjects and Compound Predicates (page 10) Write and label the **compound subject** or **compound predicate** of each sentence.

16. Arteries and veins carry the blood.
17. The heart muscle tightens and relaxes.
18. Each side of the heart collects and pumps blood.
19. Diet and exercise keep the heart healthy.
20. The heart and lungs are vital organs.

LESSON 6

Compound Sentences (page 12) Write each compound sentence. Underline the simple sentences that form it.

21. The heart is a muscle, but nerve cells control it.
22. The heart contracts, and blood flows quickly.
23. Arteries bulge with each beat of the heart.
24. You can feel your pulse in your wrist or your neck.
25. The heart is a powerful organ, but it needs care.

LESSON 7

Correcting Sentence Fragments and Run-on Sentences (page 14) Write each fragment or run-on sentence correctly.

26. Blood is a liquid it has many special cells.
27. More than 25 trillion red blood cells in the body.
28. Supplies cells with food and oxygen.
29. A red cell.
30. Travels through the bloodstream.

LESSON 8

Mechanics: Capitalizing and Punctuating Sentences (page 16) Write each sentence correctly.

31. white blood cells destroy bacteria
32. what an important job that is
33. are these cells white or red
34. read about the different types of cells
35. can cells pass through the walls of blood vessels

LESSON 9

Vocabulary Building: Using Context Clues (page 18) Use context clues to write the meaning of the underlined words.

36. Blood <u>coagulates</u> so that it is too thick to flow.
37. A blood clot, or <u>thrombus</u>, can form in an artery.
38. The <u>dire</u> outcome may be a heart attack.
39. Clots <u>obstruct</u> blood flow, blocking blood from the brain.
40. This serious <u>malady</u> is called a stroke.

Writing Application: Sentence Mechanics (pages 2–3, 12–17) The following paragraph contains 10 errors with sentences. Write the paragraph correctly.

41.–50.

   Medicine is interesting? Have you read about it! Medicine involves mathematics it involves science, too? Will you study medicine. Two friends will go to medical school the classes difficult! I will study medicine it may be difficult I will succeed?

DISCOVER THE MEANING

Reading is a good way to improve your vocabulary. When you come across a word you do not understand, think like a detective. Look for context clues in your search for the meaning of a word. Read the two sentences below and try to define the underlined words. Check your definitions in the dictionary. You will see these words again in the poem on the next page.

She was not aware of the surprise party. Her friends had made all the arrangements, <u>unbeknownst</u> to her.

I felt my spirits rise and my enthusiasm <u>surge</u> when my favorite band came onstage.

PARTS OF THE WHOLE

Play this game with a partner. First, look through some newspapers and magazines. Clip out an article that interests you. Next, read the article with your partner. Write down all the compound sentences you can find. Then compare your answers to see who has found more compound sentences.

ANIMALS ARE PEOPLE, TOO

Imagine that for a day you could be any animal in the world. Which animal would you be? Make a list of character traits that you would have as that animal. Then write a short paragraph that describes you and that tells how you feel about your life. Have a classmate guess which animal you are.

CREATIVE EXPRESSION

Paula the Cat

Paula the cat
not thin nor fat
is as happy as house cats can be

She reads and she writes
with all the delights
of intelligent cats up a tree

Tired of the view
she chose to pursue
a fate unbeknownst to the crowd

Finding a boat
locked up in a moat
she boarded and shouted out loud

I'm Paula the cat
not thin nor fat
as happy as house cats can be

But now I've the urge
for my spirit to surge
and I shall go off
to sea

— *Nikki Giovanni*

TRY IT OUT!

"Paula the Cat" is a musical poem that tells the story of a restless house cat. Look back at the paragraph you wrote for **Animals Are People, Too**. Rewrite your paragraph as a poem. Try adding some rhythm to it. If possible, end some of your lines with simple rhymes.

EXTRA PRACTICE

Three levels of practice

Four Kinds of Sentences (page 2)

LEVEL A. Write each sentence. Add the correct end punctuation.

1. I watched them tunnel beneath the river
2. What giant machinery they had
3. Look at that digging machine
4. Can it really cut through rock
5. The machine weighs more than six hundred tons
6. How difficult it is to move
7. Please stay behind the wooden guardrail
8. The guardrail will protect you
9. Did you see the machine
10. What an exciting day we had

LEVEL B. Write each sentence. Add the correct end punctuation. Then label each sentence **declarative, interrogative, imperative,** or **exclamatory.**

11. Is this a railroad tunnel
12. Many tunnels are dug to carry water
13. Read this article about tunnels
14. Tunnels provide convenient routes
15. Look at this ten-mile tunnel
16. How difficult it was to complete
17. Are there many tunnels beneath our city
18. Yes, there are many tunnels beneath our city

LEVEL C. Change each sentence to the type of sentence shown in parentheses.

19. This tunnel is very long. (interrogative)
20. Is it the world's longest tunnel? (declarative)
21. Can you find out where it is? (imperative)
22. The English have an amazing plan. (exclamatory)
23. They want to dig a tunnel to France. (interrogative)
24. Will they really do it? (declarative)
25. Will it be a success? (declarative)

EXTRA PRACTICE

Three levels of practice

Complete Subjects and Complete Predicates (page 4)

LEVEL A. Copy the underlined words. Write **complete subject** or **complete predicate** beside each group of words.

1. The Lewis and Clark expedition began in 1804.
2. About forty persons were in the group.
3. The leader was Meriwether Lewis.
4. William Clark became the co-leader.
5. The group left St. Louis, Missouri, in May.
6. The exploration of the Northwest was their goal.
7. The expedition spent the winter in North Dakota.
8. Sacajawea joined them there.
9. The westward journey resumed in April of 1805.

LEVEL B. Copy each sentence. Draw a line between the complete subject and the complete predicate.

10. The hardy explorers traveled mainly by canoe.
11. They reached the foothills of the Rocky Mountains.
12. Sacajawea's tribe helped the group.
13. The group paddled across the Columbia River.
14. The Pacific Ocean was a welcome sight.
15. The travelers built a fort for the winter.
16. The homeward journey began in March of 1806.
17. Many adventures occurred on the return trip.
18. The explorers gained valuable information.

LEVEL C. Write one sentence for each group of words.

19. horse/climbed
20. canoes/sped
21. adventures/occurred
22. Sacajawea/guided
23. explorers/wrote
24. crowds/cheered
25. Lewis and Clark/collected

GRAMMAR

Three levels of practice
Simple Subjects and Simple Predicates (page 6)

LEVEL A. Write the underlined words. Write **simple subject** or **simple predicate** next to each word.

1. My favorite <u>sport</u> is skiing.
2. Last winter I <u>competed</u> in some ski races.
3. The downhill races <u>test</u> high-speed skiing.
4. Top <u>racers</u> average more than 60 miles per hour!
5. The slalom <u>is</u> another popular race.
6. Many numbered gates <u>mark</u> the course.
7. Each <u>skier</u> must zigzag through the gates.
8. <u>Speed</u> is necessary for these skiers.
9. The skiers <u>race</u> down the hill.
10. The <u>tourists</u> watch the skiers.

LEVEL B. Write the simple subject and the simple predicate of each sentence.

11. The course of a cross-country race is long.
12. Ten-kilometer races are common.
13. The racers ski downhill for part of the time.
14. The course seems flat in some places.
15. The skiers travel uphill the rest of the way.
16. Experts reach a good speed.
17. Crowds cheer along the way.
18. The skiers finish the race.

LEVEL C. Write and complete the following sentences. Draw one line under each simple subject. Draw two lines under each simple predicate.

19. The snow _____.
20. _____ train for races.
21. The happy crowd _____.
22. _____ missed a gate in the slalom.
23. The winner of the downhill race _____.
24. _____ received a trophy.
25. The judge _____.

EXTRA PRACTICE

Three levels of practice
Finding the Subject (page 8)

LEVEL
A. Write the simple subject of each sentence.

1. Do you use a road map on trips?
2. There is useful information on a map.
3. Study the scale at the bottom.
4. Measure the number of miles to Houston.
5. Here is the legend on the map.
6. Can you see the different symbols?
7. Is there a large park in Houston?
8. Find the park on the map.
9. Here is the park.
10. Is the park large or small?

LEVEL
B. Write each sentence. Then underline the simple subject.

11. Is San Antonio southwest of Austin?
12. Look at the compass on the map.
13. There is a smudge on the compass.
14. Find Interstate Highway 20.
15. Look at the legend for the symbol of the highway.
16. Can you find Highway 52?
17. There is no Highway 52 on this map.

LEVEL
C. Write the simple subject of each sentence. Label each sentence
declarative, interrogative, or **imperative.**

18. Notice the numbers across the top.
19. There are also letters down the side.
20. Does this grid help you?
21. Find the index on the map.
22. Does the index list the cities and towns?
23. Can the numbers help me find Lubbock?
24. Here is the city of Lubbock.
25. Locate the city of Austin.

GRAMMAR

Three levels of practice
Compound Subjects and Compound Predicates (page 10)

LEVEL A. Write the compound subject or compound predicate in each sentence.

1. My friends and I jog each week.
2. Exercise strengthens and relaxes our bodies.
3. Our hearts and lungs benefit from exercise.
4. A track, park, or beach is safe for running.
5. Time and distance did not matter to us at first.
6. We ran, jogged, or walked around the track.
7. Weeks and months passed.
8. We practiced and improved.
9. Exercise and discipline are important.
10. We sprint and dash next.

LEVEL B. Write the sentences. Then write whether each sentence has a **compound subject** or a **compound predicate**.

11. The runners stood and waited.
12. Men and women participated in this ten-mile race.
13. Spectators cheered and waved all along the route.
14. A doctor and an ambulance stood by.
15. An African man and an American woman won the race.
16. Reporters interviewed and congratulated the winners.
17. Newscasters and fans applauded the runners.
18. The racers smiled and shook hands with the fans.

LEVEL C. Write the sentences. Complete each sentence with a compound subject or a compound predicate.

19. Running shoes and _____ should be comfortable.
20. Morning or _____ is a good time to run.
21. Exercises strengthen and _____ a runner's muscles.
22. Runners usually relax and _____ their run.
23. Rain or _____ need not stop a runner.
24. Joggers should not start too fast or _____ too hard.
25. The _____ and _____ will cheer the joggers.

EXTRA PRACTICE

Three levels of practice
Compound Sentences (page 12)

LEVEL A. Write **compound** or **not compound** to describe each sentence.

1. I read about the Chisholm Trail.
2. Texas ranchers and cattle traveled on this trail.
3. Cowboys used it, and their songs made it famous.
4. The trail stretched from Mexico to Abilene, Kansas.
5. The route was flat, but it had some wooded areas.
6. Jesse Chisholm used the trail first.
7. A railroad began in Abilene, and cattle were loaded onto boxcars there.
8. These cattle traveled to the East or Midwest.
9. The cattle were strong and hardy.
10. Cattle arrived at one stop on the trail and rested for a time.

LEVEL B. Write each sentence. Underline the simple sentences that make up each compound sentence. Write **not compound** if the sentence is not a compound sentence.

11. Trail drives were long, and they could be dangerous.
12. Crossings were hard, and stampedes were a problem.
13. The work was difficult, but there were some comforts.
14. Some cattle drives took days or even weeks.
15. Farmers planted crops, and barbed wire fences appeared.
16. Many people raised chickens and cattle.
17. Ranchers fought the settlers, and range wars were common.
18. The open range was gone, and the cattle boom ended.

LEVEL C. Write compound sentences. Use the subjects and predicates below. Use commas correctly and the words *and*, *or* and *but*.

19.	cowboy/threw	he/lassoed
20.	cattle/grazed	they/stampeded
21.	rustlers/stole	cowboys/chased
22.	wagons/arrived	pioneers/settled
23.	farmers/stayed	cattle/roamed
24.	ranchers/grew	sheep/were added
25.	workers/succeeded	farms/flourished

GRAMMAR

Three levels of practice

Correcting Sentence Fragments and Run-on Sentences (page 14)

LEVEL A. Label each group of words **sentence fragment** or **run-on sentence.**

1. Lemmings are little animals they look like mice.
2. About five inches long.
3. Have short tails.
4. Most lemmings are gray or brown they eat plants.
5. Lemmings like cold climates many live in Scandinavia.
6. Dig deep burrows for homes.
7. Networks of tunnels in some mountains.
8. Lemmings are interesting animals they are fun to observe.
9. Will watch them soon.
10. They are coming now get ready.

LEVEL B. Rewrite each fragment or run-on sentence correctly.

11. Lemmings make a strange journey they march to the sea.
12. The burrows get overcrowded food becomes scarce.
13. Leave their burrows in large numbers.
14. The trip to the sea is hard few lemmings survive.
15. Some lemmings starve other lemmings are eaten by birds.
16. Drown in rivers and lakes along the way.
17. Continue their journey.
18. With each step.

LEVEL C. Label each group of words **sentence fragment, run-on sentence, or sentence.** Rewrite each sentence fragment or run-on sentence.

19. Scientists study the behavior of lemmings.
20. Throw themselves into the sea and drown.
21. Some lemmings stay in the burrow there is plenty of food and space now.
22. Several years pass these lemmings have offspring.
23. Gets overcrowded.
24. The lemmings begin their strange march again.
25. How fascinating these little creatures are.

PRACTICE + PLUS

Three levels of additional practice for a difficult skill
Correcting Sentence Fragments and Run-on Sentences (page 14)

LEVEL A. Label each group of words **sentence fragment, run-on sentence,** or **sentence.**

1. I visited the source of the Rio Grande.
2. Usually begin high in the mountains or hills.
3. The source of the river may be snow it may be a lake.
4. The Rio Grande grows in size other streams flow into it.
5. Forms the boundary between our country and Mexico.
6. Spanish explorers named the river.
7. Mexicans call it *Río Bravo* that means "bold river."
8. The river is a magnificent sight.
9. Very powerful and mighty.
10. This river is on all the maps.

LEVEL B. Rewrite these sentence fragments. Add words to make each sentence fragment a complete sentence.

11. Flows south through New Mexico.
12. More than 1,800 miles long.
13. Reservoirs and dams along the river.
14. Water for household use and irrigation.
15. During the late summer, the river.
16. Few boats on this shallow river.
17. The bottom of the Rio Grande.
18. The Rio Grande, a magnificant sight.
19. Tourists with cameras.

LEVEL C. Rewrite each run-on sentence as two separate sentences or as a compound sentence.

20. People fish in the river they swim there.
21. Dams store water they prevent floods.
22. Floods kill people they damage buildings and soil.
23. A river drains land the drained region is called the drainage basin.
24. The bottom of a river is called the bed the edges are the banks.
25. Large rivers provide transportation they also generate power.

EXTRA PRACTICE

Three levels of practice
Mechanics: Capitalizing and Punctuating Sentences (page 16)

LEVEL
A. Rewrite each sentence correctly. Add capital letters and the necessary punctuation marks.

1. an eager Amelia Earhart climbed into the airplane
2. the date was May 20, 1932
3. was she the first woman to fly across the Atlantic
4. she left Canada in her tiny plane
5. what a dangerous flight it was
6. she could see nothing in the darkness
7. how far she flew above the water
8. she was a brave pilot
9. was she an American heroine
10. yes, she was an American heroine

LEVEL
B. Write each sentence correctly. Then write whether each sentence is **declarative, interrogative, imperative,** or **exclamatory.**

11. she landed successfully in Europe
12. read about her famous flight
13. how Americans loved their new heroine
14. what would Amelia Earhart do next
15. three months later she flew across the country
16. was hers the first solo flight across our nation
17. what a surprise it was
18. she also flew from Hawaii to California
19. what an outstanding example she was

LEVEL
C. Rewrite each run-on sentence as a compound sentence or as two separate sentences. Add capital letters and the necessary punctuation marks.

20. instantly Amelia became a heroine the whole world loved her
21. she tried a solo flight around the world her plane disappeared
22. at first the flight went well then there was trouble
23. ships searched everywhere they found no trace of her.
24. a brave pilot was lost her achievements remain
25. she will be remembered for her bravery we shall not forget her

EXTRA PRACTICE

Three levels of practice
Vocabulary Building: Using Context Clues (page 18)

LEVEL A. Use the context clues to discover the meaning of each underlined word. Then write the meaning of the word.

1. No plants grow well here; even trees are <u>stunted</u>.
2. Jolene often appears unfriendly, but she can be <u>cordial</u>.
3. <u>Enunciate</u> your words so that you can be understood.
4. Kevin <u>vows</u> to do his homework every night, but he often breaks his promise.
5. Her face showed she was not cheerful, but <u>despondent</u>.
6. A powerful <u>potentate</u> ruled the land harshly.
7. Rub oil into stiff leather to make it <u>pliant</u>.
8. Because of the flood, we were <u>evacuated</u> from our homes.

LEVEL B. Write the context clue or clues that help you know the meaning of the underlined word. Then write a synonym for the word.

9. The steak was black and <u>charred</u> outside, but raw inside.
10. By living <u>frugally</u>, I quickly repaid the debts.
11. Who could <u>perpetrate</u> such an awful crime?
12. John is <u>vying</u> with Dina for the top position.
13. The lawyer was convicted of <u>embezzling</u> his client's money and of using it to buy stocks.
14. I could see only a few inches into the <u>murky</u> water.
15. None of the artwork was special; it was <u>mundane</u>.

LEVEL C. Look up each word in the dictionary. Then use the word in a sentence. Include a context clue that shows the meaning of the word.

16. indispensable	21. wallow
17. glutton	22. avert
18. wary	23. barnacle
19. morose	24. rogue
20. vacillate	25. tardy

UNIT

2

Writing Personal Narratives

Read the quotation and look at the picture on the opposite page. How would you begin a story about yourself?

When you write a personal narrative, you will want to tell about a memorable event that will interest your audience.

Focus A personal narrative tells about a memorable incident in your life.

What experience would you like to write about? In this unit you will find a narrative and many photographs to help you to find ideas for writing a personal narrative.

With each new story, the pattern is much the same. It begins with a word or phrase that strikes some kind of sympathetic chord. . . .

—Natalie Babbitt

Do you remember what it felt like to learn to read? When did you first discover that the marks on a page *meant* something?

Natalie Babbitt recalls how learning to read felt to her. Everything about books and reading seemed magical, from the alphabet itself to the sound of the librarian's date stamp.

As you read the selection, look for the details and examples that Natalie Babbitt uses to tell about her experience of learning to read. How does her use of the word "I" make her writing more personal?

My *Love Affair* with the *Alphabet*

from *Once Upon a Time* by Natalie Babbitt

When I was in elementary school, during the last years of the 1930s and into the beginning of World War II, there were lots of things that I liked about learning to read besides the stories themselves. For one thing, we had, in the first and second grades, a big easel-like thing that stood in the front of the room and held a huge copy of our reading-lesson book. The pages turned over at the top instead of at the side, but otherwise they were exactly like the pages in our book, pictures and all, and they were made of thick, glossy paper. You got to go up front with a pointer and read out the words while you pointed to them, and everybody else would follow along in their books. I liked the feel of the pointer in my hand, and I liked tapping those shiny pages with its tip while I read out the Dick and Jane stories that we all learned on in those days.

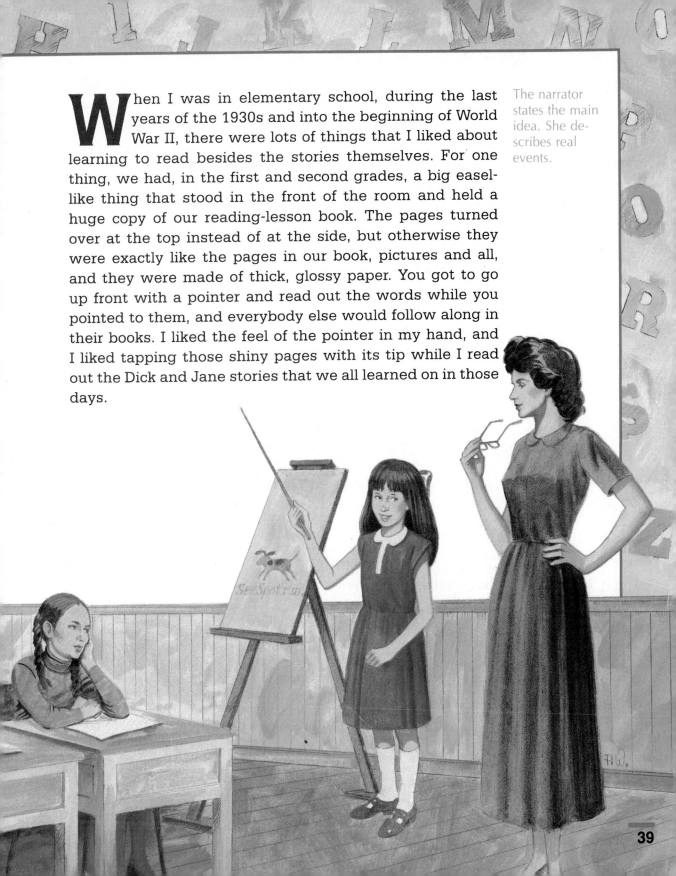

The narrator states the main idea. She describes real events.

I can remember my feeling of amazement and power when I began to recognize words in the magazines my mother and father had around the house. I had always liked looking at the pictures in those magazines, but the print had never been anything but a dense jumble of letters. And then one day I found that some of that jumble was beginning to form itself into words that I knew, words I'd learned in school. It was a little like bringing a blurry television picture into focus—suddenly things made sense. And I was hooked.

The alphabet is still a miracle to me—how those twenty-six funny shapes can group themselves in endlessly different ways to make words with endlessly different meanings. I still play alphabet games with myself, games like trying to think of five words that are exactly the same except for the vowels, like bAg, bEg, bIg, bOg, and bUg. Just by changing the vowels, you can utterly change the meaning. And another game I like is trying to find words that contain letters in alphabetical order. For instance, ABsConD and DEFoG, and my favorite, HIJacK.

My mother and I used to play a game called Anagrams where you made words out of letters printed on small, tidy squares of thick cardboard. Every once in a while, one would drop on the floor, and Dingo, our dog, would chew it. We didn't mind so much if it was a *J* or a *Q* because those were hard letters to use, but it was bad if an *E* or an *S* got chewed. Still, we just let them dry out and used them anyway, rumpled though they were with tooth marks.

Now my daughter, Lucy, and I play Boggle whenever we're together. The letters for this game are printed on wooden cubes, and Rosie, the dog we have now, isn't much

interested in them. I think dogs like the taste of paper better—Rosie always enjoys a paper napkin for a snack if she can sneak one. But whether they're printed on cardboard or wood or on the pages of a book, for me it's the same fascination over and over—those twenty-six funny shapes and the magical things they can do with each other.

Another reason why I was eager to learn to read was that I have a sister who is two years older than I am, so of course she learned first. And she was a very good reader who liked hard, heavy books. It was important to me to try to catch up with her. But it took a long time. In the beginning, when we went to the library, which was not in our elementary school but in the junior high school up the street, we got our books from different shelves. Hers were high up, while mine were on the very bottom so that I had to squat down to see what was there and make my choices.

Also, because of her constant reading, my sister had a truly amazing vocabulary at an early age. This made it possible for her to say what she said in ways that often struck me dumb. Once, playing jacks on the front porch, I impatiently reminded her that it was her turn, and she said, "I am fully cognizant of that fact." This is why Linus Van Pelt's manner of speaking in the *Peanuts* comic strip has always seemed perfectly reasonable to me. My sister talked that way, too.

For us in those days, the library was not another schoolroom, as it seems to be now. It was a place you went only if you wanted to. But a lot of us wanted to. You could check out as many as ten books a week and read them at your own speed, and if you didn't like one, you didn't have to finish it. I regularly dragged home the  whole ten, and it wasn't easy. They came in such a variety of shapes and sizes—square, tall, thin, fattish, large, small—and they always slipped and slid against one another. But this was part of their charm. The books my mother and father read all seemed to be exactly the same size and shape. I think I believed they all said exactly the same things inside.

Our librarian was a person I deeply admired, for she had polished the process of checking-out down to a fine little phrase of music. *Clump*—turning the book on its face. *Snap*—flinging open its back cover. *Whisk*—taking out the card from its paper pocket. *Thump*—the date stamp on the ink pad. *Thump thump*—stamping the book's card and my card. *Snick*—thrusting my card into the paper pocket. And *snap* again—flinging the book cover shut. The only thing

I've ever seen since to equal it was a graceful counterman at a White Tower diner years later who could turn the scrambling of two eggs into one long fluid movement from egg carton to serving plate without a single wasted gesture.

For a long time I wanted to be a librarian and used to practice with my own books at home, checking them in and out to imaginary patrons. But I didn't have the right kind of date stamp, so I could never make the right kind of music. And anyway, an older cousin came to live with us at about that time, and she had long fingernails that clicked when she played the piano, a sound of almost equal charm to those made by my librarian. So I quit biting my fingernails and concentrated on trying to click the way my cousin did.

But I didn't stop reading. More and more I was finding the charm, the excitement, the relief of sliding into the worlds of the stories I read, of escaping my own plain, ordinary life and becoming the hero I was reading about. So while my outer world stayed predictably the same, my

The narrator explains her thoughts and feelings.

inner world grew wider and wider, its possibilities infinite, the choices it suggested for how I *might* live, someday, multiplying with each new story.

Each of us has to live, finally, in her own little piece of the world, doing many things in the same way day after day, seeing the same old face in the mirror. But with books added to the day, you can be quite content. With books, your inner world has no walls. And in reading—and writing—stories, you can be many different people in many different places, doing things you would never have a chance to do in ordinary life. It's amazing that those twenty-six little marks of the alphabet can arrange themselves on the pages of a book and accomplish all that. Readers are lucky—they will never be bored or lonely.

Thinking Like a Reader

1. Why does Natalie Babbitt feel the way she does about the alphabet? Do you agree? Write your responses in your journal.

Thinking Like a Writer

2. The author tells her own story, using the word "I." What effect does the "I," or first-person point of view, have on you? Why does the author use it?

3. What details does Natalie Babbitt use to tell how she feels about reading and books?

4. What would you write about your experiences with books and the alphabet? Write your responses in your journal.

LITERATURE

Brainstorm *Vocabulary*

In "My Love Affair with the Alphabet," Natalie Babbitt writes of her sister's "truly amazing vocabulary," which came from reading. The words you choose say something about you, just as Natalie's sister's choice of words told something about her. Think of words you have met in your reading—words that you might use in writing about yourself. Write these words or phrases in your journal. Begin to create a personal vocabulary list. You can use these words and phrases in a personal narrative.

Talk It Over
Tell About an Event

When you *narrate*, you tell about something in the order in which it happened. In "My Love Affair with the Alphabet," Natalie Babbitt tells about learning to read. First, she looked at pictures. Next, she realized that the print was forming itself into words. Finally, she was reading. Think of something that you have learned, and tell in a few sentences how you learned it. Be sure to keep the details in the right order.

Quick Write *Write a Post Card*

Now try writing about an interesting thing that has happened to you. Imagine that you are writing a post card to a friend about it. For example, you might write about your first day in a new school.

Dear Wanda,

The first thing I did today was get lost! I thought I had found the locker room, but I was in the music room instead. The teacher told me to get a recorder. Since I didn't know what a recorder was, he knew that I was in the wrong place. Finally, someone led me to the locker room!

Your friend,
Darnell

Write your post card message on a separate sheet of paper.

Idea Corner
Think of Your Experiences

You probably already have some ideas for a good personal narrative. Write your ideas in your journal. You might begin each idea with the words "The time that I . . ."

PICTURES

SEEING LIKE A WRITER

Finding Ideas for Writing

Look at the photographs. Think about what you see.
What ideas for a personal narrative do the photographs
give you? Write your ideas in your journal.

1 GROUP WRITING: A Personal Narrative

COOPERATIVE LEARNING

You know that a personal narrative tells about something that happened to its writer, so that when you write a personal narrative you will be writing about yourself. What makes a personal narrative effective?

- A Focused Main Idea
- Strong Supporting Details
- Attention to Time Order

When you plan your writing, you should think about your **purpose,** or why you are writing. You should also consider your **audience,** or readers. Your audience can be your teacher, your classmates, your family, or yourself.

A Focused Main Idea

Read this paragraph of personal narrative. As you know, a paragraph is a group of sentences that develops one main idea.

One day last winter I learned that there is more than one way to get down a ski trail. I was skiing when suddenly I came to a steep turn in the trail. First, my skis hit a patch of ice and went out from under me. Next, I landed on my back and started to slide. I couldn't stop! Then, I slid down the trail head first. Finally, I came to a stop in a snowbank.

The underlined sentence gives the **main idea** of the paragraph. The other sentences tell more about the experience. These sentences are **detail sentences.**

Guided Practice: Stating the Main Idea

Working as a class, choose an incident from the following list, or think of another one. Then write one sentence that gives the main idea of the incident. Be sure that your main idea will serve as the focus of the paragraph.

Example: The first assembly was very confusing.

yesterday after school   the first assembly program
lunch in the cafeteria   the day the new _____ arrived

Strong Supporting Details

The middle of a personal narrative contains strong supporting, or detail, sentences that tell more about the incident or event. Each sentence gives specific information that tells what happened.

In the paragraph about skiing, the detail sentences tell what happened after the skier came to a steep turn in the trail. Look back at the paragraph.

■ Which sentences tell what happened?
■ Which sentence tells how the incident ended?

Attention to Time Order

Look again at the paragraph on page 48. Notice that the incident is told in **time order**—the order in which the events happened. Notice also that time-order words, such as *first, next, then,* and *finally,* are used. In a personal narrative the logical order of details is time order.

Guided Practice: Charting Details

Recall the incident you have chosen to tell about. Think of details that tell what happened. As a class, make a chart like this one. Remember to include specific details that tell more about the event or incident. Fill in the details.

Main Idea:	The first assembly was very confusing.
Details:	One class came in the wrong door. Not enough seats. People in wrong seats. Class monitors did not give good directions. Public address system failed.
Ending:	Principal sent us back to our rooms to try again.

Putting a Personal Narrative Together

With your classmates you have written an opening sentence that tells the main idea of your paragraph. Your opening sentence has expressed a focused main idea. You also have listed some details to include in your supporting sentences.

Think about your opening sentence. Then look at your chart of details. Which details support your main idea? Which details tell more about the event or incident? Those are the details you will want to include in your personal narrative.

Here are the details that one student chose. Read the opening sentence about the assembly. Then, look at the details that are checked.

> The first assembly was very confusing.
> ☐ One class found the correct seats right away.
> ☑ There were not enough seats for our class.
> ☑ The public address system failed.
> ☐ Most students followed directions calmly.
> ☑ Class monitors did not give good directions.

This student chose details that would tell more about the confusion at the first assembly than about the things that went right.

Guided Practice: Writing a Personal Narrative

Write several sentences, using details that support your main idea. Include details from your chart. Be sure to put the sentences in time order. Remember to use time-order words to make the organization clear.

Share your personal narrative with a friend. Ask this friend for suggestions that would help you to improve your paragraph.

Checklist: A Personal Narrative

When you write your personal narrative, you will want to keep some points in mind. A checklist will remind you of the things you need to include.

Look at this checklist. Some points are already there, but others need to be added. Make a copy of this checklist and complete it. Keep it in your writing folder. You can use it to check yourself when you write your personal narrative.

CHECKLIST

✔ Main idea

✔ Supporting details

✔ Time order

First

_____

_____

_____

✔ Purpose and _____

2 THINKING AND WRITING: Main Idea and Details

Think of what you have learned about writing a personal narrative. You know that narrative writing tells about an event or incident. You re-create that event for your audience by giving the details in the order in which they happened.

A writer shapes a narrative first by selecting a main idea and then by choosing the details that support it. A detail supports a main idea when it tells more about it, makes it clearer, or adds to it.

Look at this page from a writer's journal.

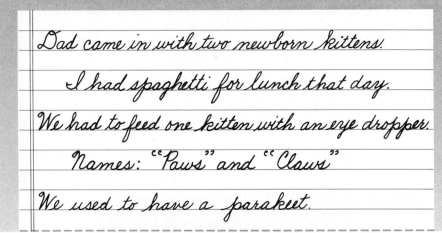

Dad came in with two newborn kittens.

I had spaghetti for lunch that day.

We had to feed one kitten with an eye dropper.

Names: "Paws" and "Claws"

We used to have a parakeet.

The writer plans to write about adopting two motherless kittens. She lists many details on the page.

Thinking Like a Writer

■ Which details do you think support the main idea?

The writer cannot use the details that do not support the main idea. Spaghetti and the parakeet do not support the main idea about adopting the kittens.

When you write a personal narrative, decide which details to include and which to omit because they do not support the main idea of your story.

THINKING APPLICATION Main Idea and Details

COOPERATIVE
LEARNING

Each of these writers is planning to write a personal narrative. Help each one decide which details to include. Write the details on a sheet of paper. You may wish to discuss your thinking with your classmates. In your discussions explain the reasons for your choices.

1. Keith's personal narrative will tell about teaching his brother to ride a bike. Which details should he include?

   My sister learned by herself.
   Cal kept falling off.
   I ran along, holding Cal up.
   Someday, I will learn to drive.

2. Winona will write a personal narrative about her first flight as a passenger in a small plane. Which details should she include?

   The pilot had to boost me into the plane.
   The plane felt like a toy.
   There are dozens of flights at a nearby airport.
   I could recognize houses and buildings.

3. Pedro's personal narrative will tell about the time the neighbor's dog got away while he was walking it. Which details should he include?

   The dog is eight years old.
   I make money by walking dogs.
   Silver jerked the leash out of my hand.
   I finally pretended I had a doggy treat.

4. Linda Jo will write a personal narrative about the time that she found an Indian arrowhead. Which details should she include?

   My brother and I were digging in the dirt.
   I unearthed a pointed object.
   Many new houses are being built on our street.
   My mother's professor said I had found a real Indian arrowhead.

3 INDEPENDENT WRITING: A Personal Narrative

Prewrite: Step 1

By now you know quite a bit about narrative writing. Now you are ready to choose a topic of your own for writing. Lisa, a student your age, chose a topic this way.

Choosing a Topic

First, Lisa wrote a list of incidents, beginning each one with the words "The time that I..." Next, she thought about the details of each incident. Last, she decided on the incident she thought was the most interesting.

Lisa chose her first idea, but she decided to narrow her topic to part of her visit—when she swam across the lake.

The time that I visited my aunt.

The time that I found a wallet.

The time that I rode on a roller coaster.

The time that I won the talent show.

Lisa explored her topic by making a **cluster**. Here is what Lisa's cluster looked like.

Exploring Ideas: Clustering Strategy

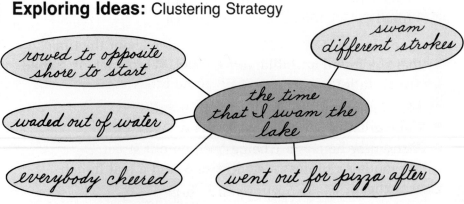

rowed to opposite shore to start

swam different strokes

waded out of water

the time that I swam the lake

everybody cheered

went out for pizza after

THE WRITING PROCESS: Prewriting

Lisa knew that her purpose for writing was to tell her incident so that her classmates would understand what it was like to swim across a lake.

Before beginning to write, Lisa reviewed in her mind what her experience had been like. She did this to recall details of how she had felt and what she had done. She even added more details to her cluster.

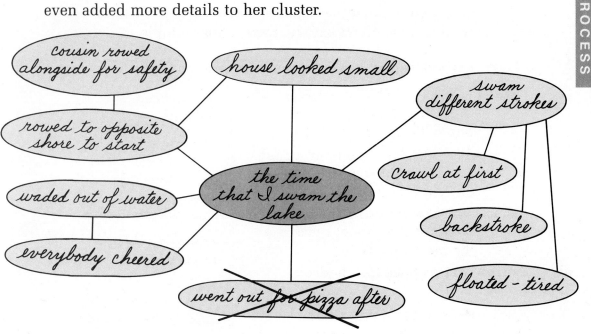

Thinking Like a Writer

- What did Lisa add?
- What did she decide to cross out?
- Why do you think she made the changes she did?

YOUR TURN

Think of an incident that you would like to narrate. Look at **Pictures** or your journal to find some ideas. Follow these steps.

- Make a list of possible incidents or events.
- Choose the one you like best.
- Narrow the topic if it is too broad.
- Think about your purpose and audience.

Write a First Draft: Step 2

Lisa knows what a personal narrative should include. She has made a planning checklist.

Lisa is now ready to write her first draft.

Lisa's First Draft

Last summer I had my goal. It was to swim acrost the Lake one morning the water was pretty still. After breakfast my cousin rowed me to the shore opposite. I waded into the cold water. I started out at a fast crawl to warm up. My cousin rowed alongside. He stayed with me for safety. When I got tired, I did the backstroke or sometimes I just floated. Finally sand under my feet and waded out of the water. All my cousins cheered.

While Lisa was writing her first draft, she did not worry about making mistakes. She knew she could go back later to revise and correct her work.

YOUR TURN

Write your first draft. As you prepare to write, ask yourself these questions:

- What is my main idea? How can I best explain it?
- Which details should I include? How can time-order words help me present these details?

TIME-OUT You might want to take some time out before you revise. That way you will be able to revise your writing with a fresh eye.

Planning Checklist
- Remember purpose and audience.
- Include a main idea.
- Use supporting details.
- Use time order.

Revise: Step 3

After Lisa had taken a moment to relax, she reread her personal narrative. Then she shared her writing with a classmate. She wanted some suggestions for improvement.

Would you really like to know that? Okay, I'll add it. Thanks.

I like your paragraph, but I've never swum across a lake. Can you tell more about how you felt?

Lisa then looked back at her planning checklist. She noticed that she had forgotten one point. She checked it off so that she would remember it when she revised her writing. Lisa now has a checklist to use as she revises her draft.

Lisa made the changes in her paragraph. Notice that she did not correct small errors. She knew that she could fix them later.

The revisions Lisa made changed her paragraph. Turn the page to see Lisa's revised draft.

Revising Checklist
- ■ Remember purpose and audience.
- ■ Include a main idea.
- ✔ ■ Use supporting details.
- ■ Use time order.

Last summer ~~I had~~ my goal. It was to swim acrost the Lake
as smooth as glass.
one morning the water was ~~pretty still~~. After breakfast my
slowly
cousin rowed me to the shore opposite. I waded into the
and shivered   *brisk*
cold water. I started out at a ~~fast~~ crawl to warm up. My

cousin rowed alongside. He stayed with me for safety.

When I got tired, I did the backstroke or ~~sometimes~~ I just
I felt
floated. Finally sand under my feet and waded out of the
on rubbery legs
water. All my cousins cheered. *I felt happy and proud.*

WISE
WORD
CHOICE

Thinking Like a Writer

- Which specific details did Lisa add? How do they improve her paragraph?
- Which sentences did she combine? How does combining them improve her paragraph?
- Which sentence did she add? How does it help her paragraph?

YOUR TURN

Read your first draft. Ask yourself these questions:

- What will my audience want to know?
- What is the main idea of my paragraph?
- How do the details support the main idea?
- Why is time order effective in my paragraph?
- Which sentences can I combine?

If you wish, ask a friend to read your paragraph and to make suggestions. Then revise your paragraph.

Proofread: Step 4

Lisa knew that her work was not complete until she proofread her paragraph. Although she had made important changes in what her paragraph said, she needed to check her work for errors in grammar and mechanics. Lisa used the checklist below.

Lisa's Proofread Draft

¶Last summer I ~~had~~ my goal. It was to swim ⓐcross the Lake⊙

one morning the water was ~~pretty still~~. *as smooth as glass.* After breakfast my

cousin rowed me to the shore opposite. I waded *slowly* into the

cold water *and shivered*. I started out at a *brisk* ~~fast~~ crawl to warm up. My

cousin rowed alongside. He stayed with me for safety.

When I got tired, I did the backstroke or ~~sometimes~~ I just

floated. Finally *I felt* sand under my feet and waded out of the

water *on rubbery legs*. All my cousins cheered. *I felt happy and proud.*

YOUR TURN

Proofreading Practice

Below is a paragraph that you can use to practice your proofreading skills. Use the proofreading marks to correct any mistakes. Write the paragraph correctly on a separate sheet of paper.

Saturday Morning looked perfect for a hike, the sun was shinning. Cool with a light breeze. i didn't even think about taking rain gear. Who would have thought it would rain. My first mistake. I had gone about two miles when the sky clouded over, I soon felt raindrops. Then a downpour. I had to race home in a cold drizzle. What a miserable day.

Proofreading Checklist
- Did I indent my paragraph?
- Did I spell all my words correctly?
- What punctuation errors do I need to correct?
- What capitalization errors do I need to fix?

THE WRITING PROCESS: Proofreading

Applying Your Proofreading Skills

Now proofread your personal narrative. Read your checklist one last time. Review the **Grammar Connection** and the **Mechanics Connection,** too. Use the proofreading marks to show changes.

THE GRAMMAR CONNECTION

Remember these rules about correcting sentence fragments and run-on sentences.

■ To correct a **sentence fragment,** add a subject part or a predicate part.

My friend. My friend swam the lake.

■ To correct a **run-on sentence,** separate each complete idea into a simple sentence of its own, or write a compound sentence.

We swam the lake it was cold.
We swam the lake. It was cold.
We swam the lake, but it was cold.

THE MECHANICS CONNECTION

Remember these rules about using punctuation marks.

■ Use a **period** at the end of a sentence that makes a statement or a request or that gives a command.
■ Use a **question mark** at the end of a sentence that asks a question.
■ Use an **exclamation mark** at the end of a sentence that expresses strong feeling.

Lisa swam the lake.   Please swim.   Swim quickly.
Can you swim?   What a great swimmer you are!

Proofreading Marks

¶ Indent
∧ Add
⅄ Add a comma
⅋⅋ Add quotation marks
⋎ Add a period
⏄ Take out
≡ Capitalize
/ Make a small letter
∿ Reverse the order

Publish: Step 5

Lisa decided that she wanted to share her personal narrative with her friends in class. She made a neat final copy and posted it on the class bulletin board. Several of her classmates asked questions about her narrative. Many wanted to know more about what it was like to swim across a lake.

YOUR TURN

Make a neat, final copy of your personal narrative. Think of a way to share your narrative. You might find some ideas in the **Sharing Suggestions** box below.

SHARING SUGGESTIONS

Create a class book of personal narratives. Illustrate the book with photographs or your own drawings.	Form a small group and read your personal narratives aloud. If you wish, tape-record these readings.	Make your narrative into a diary entry. Place the date at the top of the page and address the entry to "Dear Diary." Share your entry with a friend.

4 SPEAKING AND LISTENING: A Class Discussion

You have just written a personal narrative. In your narrative you have told about an experience from your own life. Now you will have an opportunity to listen to and discuss the experiences and ideas of other people. In a class discussion you and your classmates exchange ideas or opinions about a particular subject.

You often hold a discussion to solve a problem or to decide on an action. When you discuss something, you should be prepared with ideas, details, and examples. You may want to jot down your ideas before you discuss them with your classmates. Making notes will help you remember all the points you want to discuss. Then, during the discussion, you can check off your ideas as they are mentioned to make sure you have not skipped any of them.

Look at these notes that one student wrote. This student thought it might be a good idea to invite Mrs. Chen to speak to his class on International Day. Mrs. Chen had grown up in China and could tell about her experiences there.

> *Notes for a Class Discussion*
>
> *Who should be the speaker on International Day?*
> *Mrs. Chen—grew up in China. Friendly, tells interesting stories. Are people interested in China?*

Notice that the student who wrote these notes has a suggestion that he wants to contribute. What else has he included?

When you have a class discussion, it will help if you keep some guidelines in mind. These guidelines will help focus your discussion.

SPEAKING AND LISTENING GUIDELINES

1. Contribute your ideas and give reasons for them.
2. Listen for the main idea. Ask yourself, do I agree?
3. Stick to the subject. Discuss each idea thoroughly.
4. Ask questions to get more information.
5. Speak in a loud, clear voice.
6. Be courteous.

■ Why is understanding the main idea during a class discussion important?

■ How do supporting details help my listeners?

SPEAKING APPLICATION A Discussion

Work with two or three classmates to discuss one of the following topics. Try to reach a group decision within ten minutes.

1. Your class is inviting people to tell about interesting personal experiences. Whom should your class invite?
2. Your group will choose a topic on which to write a personal narrative. What will your topic be?
3. Your class is in charge of entertainment for the next school assembly. What entertainment will you need to provide?

5 WRITER'S RESOURCES: The Dictionary

In this unit, your main resource for writing has been your life. The dictionary and the thesaurus are also useful resources. Both books can help you find the right word.

A **dictionary** gives meanings, pronunciations, and other information about words. The words in a dictionary are called **entry words.** Look at the sample pronunciation key and entry word below.

Pronunciation Key

at; **ā**pe; **fä**r; **câ**re; **e**nd; **m**ē; **i**t; **ī**ce; **pî**erce; **ho**t **ō**ld; **sô**ng, **fô**rk; **oi**l; **ou**t; **u**p; **ū**se; **rü**le; **pu̇**ll; **tû**rn; **ch**in; **si**ng; **sh**op; **th**in; <u>th</u>is; **hw** in **wh**its; **zh** in trea**s**ure. The symbol **ə** stands for the unstressed vowel sound heard in **a**bout, tak**e**n, penc**i**l, lem**o**n, and circ**u**s.

Sample Entry Word

Respelling Part of speech

Entry word — **cop.y** (kop′ē) *n.,pl.* **cop.ies.** — Plural form

1. a reproduction of an original: *a copy of a picture.* **2.** one of a number of books, or the like: *He bought two copies of the book.* **3.** material to be set in type for printing in a newspaper, or the like. —*v.,* **cop.ied, cop.y.ing.** —*v.t.* **1.** to make a copy of (something): *to copy a letter* **2.** to do something in imitation of: *Jean copied her sister's style of dressing.* — Example sentence
v.i. to make a copy or copies. [Old French *copie* transcript, plenty, going back to Latin *cōpia* plenty; the meaning "transcript" developed from the sense of a plentiful supply of copies.] — Word history
—**Syn.** *n.* **1.** see **duplicate.** *v.t.* **1.** see **imitate.** — Synonym

Definitions —

The **entry word** shows how the word is spelled and how it may be divided into syllables at the end of a line.
The **respelling** tells how to say the word. The **pronunciation key** tells the sound for each symbol. Accent marks show which syllable stressed.
The **part of speech** is labeled with an abbreviation, such as *v.* for *verb.*
The **plural form** is shown when the spelling of the base word changes.
The **definitions,** or meanings, of a word are numbered.
Example sentences show how the word is used.
Some entries include a **word history** in brackets.
Some entries include a **synonym** or an **antonym,** labeled with the abbreviation *Syn.* or *Ant.*

The words in a dictionary are arranged in alphabetical order. On each page **guide words** at the top tell you the first and last word on that page.

Practice

Use the entry word **detail** to answer these questions. Look at the entry below. Write your answers on a separate sheet of paper.

> **de·tail** (di tāl′, dē′tāl) *n.***1.** a small or secondary part of a whole; item; particular: *Modern scholars know few details of the life of Shakespeare.* **2.** treatment of matters item by item; attention to particulars: *The detail in the portrait was painted with great care.* **3.** a small group of people assigned to some special duty: *A detail of policemen patrolled the troubled area* —*v.t.* **1.** to tell or describe item by item: *He detailed his camping experiences to the class.* **2.** to assign to or send on special duty: *Troops were detailed to guard the frontier.*

1. How many ways can **detail** be pronounced?
2. Which two parts of speech can the word **detail** be?
3. In the following sentence is **detail** a noun or a verb? Support your idea with at least one **detail.**
4. Which definition of the word would apply to this sentence?
   The saleswoman had to **detail** all the expenses in her report.
5. How many different definitions are shown for **detail** in this entry?
6. Write an example sentence of your own for each definition of **detail.**

WRITING APPLICATION Sentences

Use a dictionary to look up the meaning of a familiar word, such as *run*, *play*, *fast*, or *go*. Write a sentence for each new meaning you find. Then, with a classmate, read and compare each other's sentences. Check to see that the meaning of the dictionary words is clear and that the words have been used correctly.

WRITING EXTENSION

6 WRITER'S RESOURCES: The Thesaurus

A **thesaurus** can help you find synonyms or antonyms for words you use in your writing. Lisa, who wrote about swimming across the lake, found the word *brisk* in a thesaurus and used it to replace *fast*. She thought *brisk* better described her energy at the beginning of her swim.

Your thesaurus may be one of two types. One type is arranged like a dictionary. The entry words are shown in alphabetical order. After each entry word a list of synonyms, or words with similar meanings, is given. Sometimes antonyms, or words with opposite meanings, are also included. Here is an example:

Sample from Thesaurus Arranged like a Dictionary

small *adj.* **1.** *Are you small enough to squeeze through this hole?:* little, tiny, petite; diminutive, undersized, slight. **2.** *The business made only a small profit this year:* meager, scant, not great. **3.** *Even the small details should be checked thoroughly:* minor, inconsequential, trivial, superficial, unimportant. **4.** *Someone with a small mind usually believes the worst:* mean, petty, narrow, opinionated, bigoted; **5.** *The kitten uttered a small cry:* feeble, weak, fragile, faint.

Another type of thesaurus groups similar words together. An index at the back of the book lists all the entries alphabetically. To find a word, you must use the index. *Roget's Thesaurus* is an example of this kind of thesaurus.

Sample from Thesaurus with an Index

small
small 33 *adj.*
weak 163 *adj.*
little 196 *adj.*
unimportant 639 *adj.*

33. small
  moderate, modest, not much
163. weak
  delicate, fragile, puny
196. little
  petite, dainty, wee, tiny, teeny
639. unimportant
  insignificant, minor, trivial, nothing

Practice

A. Use the sample from the thesaurus that is arranged like a dictionary. Replace the word **small** with a synonym from the sample.

1. We heard a **small** scratching noise.
2. This detail may seem **small** to you, but it can make a big difference.
3. Louise has very **small** hands and feet.
4. It was **small** of him to refuse to accept the apology.
5. There was only a **small** amount of food in the cabinet.

B. Use the sample from the thesaurus that has an index. Each word listed has a different meaning for **small**. First tell which word you would look up to find a synonym for **small** in each sentence. Then write the sentence, using one of the synonyms listed.

6. From the time he was **small**, Makoto loved music.
7. Please skip the **small** details and come to the point.
8. She answered in a **small** voice.
9. Lem receives a **small** allowance from his grandmother.

WRITING APPLICATION Sentences

Use the thesaurus in the back of this book to find a synonym for one word you have used in your personal narrative. Rewrite your sentence, using the synonym. Compare the two sentences and decide which one better expresses your thoughts.

THE CURRICULUM CONNECTION

Writing About Social Studies

Social studies is the study of people and their world. From social studies we learn how people have lived in the past and how they live today.

One of the ways in which we can learn about people and their times is by reading published diaries, autobiographies, and other narratives that people have written to tell about their experiences. Many social studies books include primary sources—first-person accounts of moments in history—that help to make social studies come alive.

ACTIVITIES

Make a Story Board In your social studies book find a narrative—a short account of an incident. Imagine that you were there. Make a three-frame story board that illustrates the incident in time order. Under each frame write captions that explain what is happening at that moment.

Tell About a Photograph Look at the photograph on the opposite page. Think of how you might narrate an incident or event that could occur in that setting. Imagine that you are in the picture. Write a personal narrative about the incident or event. Start by giving the main idea. Remember to present the details in time order and to use your imagination for the details you present.

Respond to Literature The following narrative by the Polish writer Esther Hautzig tells about her childhood after she and her family were deported to Siberia during World War II. After reading the narrative, write a response. Your response may be a narrative about a time of change in your own life, a letter to Ms. Hautzig, or a summary of her experience and what you thought about it.

The Endless Steppe
by Esther Hautzig (haut'zik)

My first lesson in school in Siberia was memorable for being a chilly one. Not only did Krylov (kry'lof) evade me, lost as he was in a sea of Cyrillic (si ril'ik) [Russian] letters, but so did the book itself—literally. My classmate somehow managed to keep slipping it out of my field of vision, which forced me to strain, squirm, and nudge her to bring the book closer. Naturally, I had barely read the first paragraph when Raisa Nikitovna (rī ē'sa ni kē'tov na) began to quiz the class. To my horror, one question was directed at me. Fortunately—or with more humanity than I was giving that severe-faced woman credit for—it concerned the opening of the fable. As I began to answer in my halting Russian, all the children turned to stare at me; I braced myself against the derisive laughter I expected. But no one laughed. As I was to learn, discipline was no problem in the Siberian classroom, none whatsoever. In that harsh country, going to school was a privilege no one wanted to monkey with.

LESSON 1

Group Writing: A Personal Narrative (page 48) Read this paragraph. On a separate sheet of paper, write the sentence that states the main idea.

Last summer I learned that honesty is the best policy. The day I found somebody's wallet, my first thought was about how lucky I was. My second thought, though, was about how the owner must feel. Therefore, I called him. He was so happy that I knew I had done the right thing. That made me feel happy, too.

LESSON 2

Thinking: Main Idea and Details (page 52) Imagine that you are planning to write a personal narrative. Your main idea is that skateboarding is a great sport. Which of the following details support your main idea? Write those details on a separate sheet of paper.

I fell many times. Skateboarding improves balance. It is a good means of transportation. It provides good exercise.

LESSON 3

Writing a Personal Narrative (page 54) Imagine that you are grown-up and famous. A magazine has asked you to write about an incident from your childhood. Write a short personal-narrative article.

LESSON 4

Speaking and Listening: A Class Discussion (page 62) Work with a small group of classmates. Discuss the theme of this unit—Pathways. You might discuss experiences involving sports. Remember to listen for the main ideas.

LESSONS 5-6

The Dictionary/The Thesaurus (pages 64–67) Choose one of the following words: *narrative, idea, support.* Use a dictionary to discover the meanings of the word. Then use a thesaurus to find synonyms for it. Write a short summary of the information.

THEME PROJECT

A *TV SCRIPT*

You have been learning about pathways—the many different and interesting roads on which people travel in their lives. In writing a personal narrative you have been exploring the pathways you are taking in your life.

Think about the other kinds of personal writing that you know. These may include autobiographies, diaries, magazine articles about important events in people's lives, movies, plays, and television programs. Each of these forms of personal writing shows you something about the different paths that people have taken in their lives.

Look at the picture below.

- Think back on your life so far. Imagine that your life will be the basis of a pilot for a television program. You will need only one short incident from your life for the first script.
- Ask yourself what kind of story it will be—an adventure? a situation comedy? a drama? A cluster diagram may help you to find ideas and to add details.
- Then write about the incident. If you wish, work with a group of your classmates to act out the incident for the class.

UNIT

3

Nouns

In Unit 3 you will learn about nouns. You can name people, places, things, or ideas by using nouns. When you choose exact nouns, you make your writing clear and precise.

Discuss Read the poem on the opposite page. Think about wonders that you know. Talk with a partner about the things you find wonderful.

Creative Expression The unit theme is *Wonders*. A place or thing that causes you to feel amazement and curiosity can be called a wonder. Describe an event in your life in which you experienced something wonderful. Write your sentences in your journal.

JOURNAL

There is wonder past all wonder
in the ways of living things,
in a worm's intrepid wriggling,
in the song a blackbird sings. . . .

—Jack Prelutsky,
from "The Ways of Living Things"

1 COMMON AND PROPER NOUNS

A noun names a person, place, thing, or idea.
The chart below shows some examples of nouns.

	Common Nouns	Proper Nouns
Person	man	Old Dan Canyon
Place	state	Arizona
Thing	river	Colorado River

A **common noun** names any person, place, thing, or idea. The nouns *man* and *state*, for example, name any man or any state.

A **proper noun** names a particular person, place, thing, or idea. The nouns *Old Dan Canyon* and *Arizona* are proper nouns. They name a particular person and state. All proper nouns begin with a capital letter.

Most nouns name things you can see or touch. However, nouns also name ideas. Names of ideas, such as *democracy, hope,* or *friendship,* are nouns, too.

Guided Practice

Tell which words in each sentence are nouns.

Example: Rangers tell the story of Old Dan Canyon.

               Rangers   story   Old Dan Canyon

1. Listen to the legend of Old Dan Canyon.
2. According to the legend, Old Dan has lived in the Grand Canyon for years.
3. Hardly any tourists see the hermit anymore.
4. Long ago, Dan colored the walls of the canyon.
5. The hero painted a rainbow in the sky.

 THINK

■ How can I tell the difference between a common noun and a proper noun?

REMEMBER

- A **common noun** names any person, place, thing, or idea.
- A **proper noun** names a particular person, place, thing, or idea and always begins with a capital letter.

More Practice

A. Write each sentence. Draw one line under each noun.

Example: Many <u>stories</u> surround the <u>Grand Canyon</u>.

6. The rangers at the Grand Canyon tell a legend.
7. The hero of their story is Old Dan Canyon.
8. Old Dan takes tourists across the canyon.
9. These visitors fly on a bolt of lightning.
10. What joy these people feel on his tours!
11. Dan remembers the birth of this natural wonder.
12. The Colorado River created this marvel.
13. Heavy wind and rain formed the walls of this gorge.

B. Copy each sentence. Draw one line under each noun. Write **CN** above the noun if it is a common noun. Write **PN** if it is a proper noun.

Example: The <u>walls</u> of the <u>Grand Canyon</u> are steep.

14. The steep hills are a home to Old Dan Canyon.
15. Some people say Dan lives at Mohave Point.
16. The walls of his house are of brown and red rock.
17. In May, Dan moves to Orphan Mine.
18. The burros of Navaho Bridge lead the way.
19. In summer, Dan travels to Hermit's Rest.
20. A ranger says Old Dan lives at Phantom Ranch.

Extra Practice, page 94

WRITING APPLICATION A Post Card

Imagine that Old Dan Canyon gave you a tour of the Grand Canyon. Write a post card that tells about the adventure. Label the nouns you use as **common** or **proper**. Then read your post card to a partner.

GRAMMAR

2 SINGULAR AND PLURAL NOUNS

A **singular noun** names one person, place, thing, or idea. A **plural noun** names more than one.

The chart below shows how to form plural nouns.

Singular Nouns	To Form Plural	Examples	
most singular nouns	add **s**	dream	dream**s**
nouns ending in *s, ss, x, ch, sh*	add **es**	bus buses	dress dresses
nouns ending in a consonant and *y*	change **y** to **i** and add **es**	city cit**ies**	baby bab**ies**
nouns ending in a vowel and *y*	add **s**	day day**s**	turkey turkey**s**
nouns ending in *f* or *fe*	most add **s**; some change **f** to **v** and add **es**	chief chiefs	calf cal**ves**
nouns ending in a vowel and *o*	add **s**	rodeo rodeo**s**	studio studio**s**
nouns ending in a consonant and *o*	most add **es**; some add **s**	echo echo**es**	banjo banjo**s**
some irregular nouns	change their spelling	man **men**	tooth **teeth**
a few irregular nouns	keep the same spelling	sheep trout	deer moose

Guided Practice

Tell the plural of each underlined noun.

Example: The <u>lake</u> and <u>river</u> were dry. *lakes   rivers*

1. The <u>sky</u> had been cloudless.
2. Even the <u>stream</u> and <u>brook</u> had no water.
3. The <u>leaf</u> turned brown and dropped from the <u>branch</u>.

 THINK

■ How can I learn to spell each kind of plural form correctly?

REMEMBER

- Add **s** or **es** to form the plural of most nouns.
- Some nouns are spelled differently in the plural. Other nouns have the same singular and plural form.

More Practice

A. Write the plural form of each noun.

Example: bush *bushes*

4. sandwich   **7.** country   **10.** cameo
5. foot   **8.** potato   **11.** key
6. life   **9.** boy   **12.** sheep

B. Write each sentence. Use the plural form of the underlined nouns.

Example: The Indian faced difficulty. *Indians   difficulties*

13. Turkey and goose left in search of water.
14. The Shoshone man and woman felt great sadness.
15. A snake heard the cry of the Indian.
16. "I have magic power and ability," it said.
17. "Throw me up, and I will make the raindrop fall."
18. The Shoshone chief and hero threw the snake upward.
19. As the warrior watched, the snake's body filled the heaven.
20. Its scale magically turned all the color of the rainbow.
21. The snake melted the cliff and valley of the sky.
22. Torrent of rain poured down on the man.
23. Bush turned green, and flower bloomed.
24. The child sang praise to this rainbow snake.
25. The deer, moose, and other animals returned.

Extra Practice, page 95

WRITING APPLICATION A Folk Tale

COOPERATIVE LEARNING

The folk tale you have just read explains rainbows. Write a folk tale that explains something about nature—for example, why bees sting. Underline the plural nouns you use. Share your folk tale with a small group of classmates.

3 POSSESSIVE NOUNS

Nouns have special forms to show ownership, or possession. **Possessive nouns** are nouns that name who or what has or owns something.

The chart below shows how to form possessive nouns.

Noun	To Form Possessive	Examples
most singular nouns	add an **apostrophe** (') and **s** ('s)	Pat has a new history book. Pat**'s** new history book James also has a new book. James**'s** new book
plural nouns ending in *s*	add only an **apostrophe** (')	The girls have a guidebook. The girls' guidebook
plural nouns not ending in *s*	add an **apostrophe** (') and **s** ('s)	Two women own cameras. Two women**'s** cameras

Remember that possessive nouns have apostrophes. Plural nouns do not.

Guided Practice

Tell which noun in each sentence is possessive. Then tell whether the noun is singular or plural.

Example: Paul's book has pictures of the seven wonders.
Paul's   singular

1. Six of the ancient world's seven wonders are gone.
2. Egypt's Great Pyramid remains.
3. The engineers' skills were truly great.
4. The men's tools were coarse and rough.
5. Now, imagine the world's other six wonders.
6. Some books tell of Asia's seven ancient wonders.

THINK

■ How do I decide how to form a possessive noun?

REMEMBER

- To form the possessive of a singular noun, add **'s**.
- To form the possessive of a plural noun that ends in *s*, add only an **apostrophe (')**.
- To form the possessive of a plural noun that does not end in *s*, add **'s**.

More Practice

A. Write the possessive noun in each sentence. Label it *S* if it is singular and *P* if it is plural.

Example: There are many books in the <u>school's</u> library. *S*

  7. Few describe Babylon's Hanging Gardens.

  8. The king's gardens were built for his princess.

  9. His gardeners' efforts made her feel at home.

10. Greece's first wonder was the Temple of Artemis.

11. An army's invasion destroyed it by fire.

12. Several writers' books tell of the other wonders.

B. Write each sentence. Use the possessive form of each underlined noun.

Example: <u>Egypt</u> pyramids are another wonder. *Egypt's*

13. <u>Zeus</u> statue is the fourth wonder of the world.

14. This <u>god</u> likeness was made of gold and ivory.

15. A <u>ruler</u> tomb is the next marvel to admire.

16. An earthquake toppled this <u>emperor</u> tomb.

17. A Greek <u>sculptor</u> huge statue is the sixth wonder.

18. Many <u>nations</u> artists still copy this Colossus of Rhodes.

19. <u>Alexandria</u> lighthouse is the last marvel.

20. This magnificent lighthouse guided <u>men</u> ships.

Extra Practice, page 96

WRITING APPLICATION A Travel Poster

Make a travel poster about the seven wonders of the ancient world. Draw the wonders and write a sentence about each one.

4 APPOSITIVES

An **appositive** is a word or group of words that follows a noun. An appositive identifies or tells more about the noun it follows.

China's first ruler, an emperor , is worried.
His northern neighbors, Mongols , might invade his land.

Sometimes an appositive contains several words.

The emperor begins work on a structure, a high wall .

Notice that commas are used to set off an appositive from the rest of the sentence.

The Great Wall of China, the largest wall of all time , is the result.

Good writers often use appositives to combine two choppy sentences into one longer sentence.

The Great Wall is almost a perfect structure. The wall is strong.

The Great Wall, almost a perfect structure , is strong.

Guided Practice

Identify the appositive in each sentence. Then tell which noun it identifies.

Ch'in, a cruel emperor, punishes his workers.
Appositive: a cruel emperor   Noun: Ch'in

1. Workers build the entire length, four thousand miles, by hand.
2. The workers, a million people, labor for years.
3. Ch'in, a strong ruler, does not like delays.
4. Nearby hills supply the foundation, granite.
5. Workers pound the core, loose earth, until it is firm.
6. Builders work on the Great Wall, a twenty-five-foot barrier.

THINK

■ How do I decide if a word or a group of words is an appositive?

REMEMBER

■ An **appositive** is a word or group of words that follows a noun. It identifies or explains the noun it follows.

More Practice

A. Write the appositive in each sentence. Then write the noun it identifies.

Example: The workers, poor peasants, work long hours.
     Appositive: poor peasants Noun: workers

  7. They build watchtowers, tall stone structures.

  8. The towers, lookout posts, occur every six hundred feet.

  9. Many construction workers, poorly fed slaves, die.

10. Thousands are buried in the wall, a kind of cemetery.

11. Soldiers patrol the top, a road.

12. The cavalry, soldiers on horseback, ride back and forth.

B. Write each sentence. Add a comma or commas to set off the appositive from the rest of the sentence.

Example: Khan the Mongol leader attacks the wall.
     Khan, the Mongol leader, attacks the wall.

13. Archers men with bows and arrows watch the wall.

14. They stand behind the parapet a protective structure.

15. For a while the Chinese attain their purpose peace.

16. In time, the wall no longer a great structure crumbles.

17. Mongols invaders from the north cross the wall.

18. Their leader a great warrior conquers China.

19. Later, the wall a ruin is rebuilt.

20. The wall now a tourist attraction is still a wonder.

Extra Practice, page 97

WRITING APPLICATION A Paragraph

Imagine that you are a tour guide. Explain the history of the Great Wall in a paragraph. Use at least three appositives. Share your paragraph with a classmate.

5 MECHANICS:
Capitalizing Proper Nouns

A **proper noun** names a particular person, place, thing, or idea. It begins with a capital letter.

Types of Proper Nouns	
names, initials, and titles of people	Jan, Mr. B. W. Inouye, Captain Floyd McCarthy
cities, states, countries, and geographic features	Dallas, Indiana, Mexico, Painted Desert
months, days, and holidays	July, Sunday, Labor Day
businesses, clubs, and organizations	Data Company, Girl Scouts, Valley Fire Department
buildings, bridges, and monuments	White House, Bay Bridge, Lincoln Memorial
languages, nationalities	English, Vietnamese
titles of books, movies, and other works	*Heidi, The Sound of Music,* "America, the Beautiful"

For proper nouns made up of several words, the first word and each important word are capitalized. However, short words—*and, of,* and *the*—are not capitalized.

Guided Practice

Tell the proper nouns in these sentences. Tell which letter or letters should be capitalized.

Example: The statue stood on bedloe's island. *Bedloe's Island*

1. This wonder now stands on liberty island.
2. Its real name is *liberty enlightening the world.*
3. A frenchman, frédéric bartholdi, designed it.

 THINK

■ How do I decide which words to capitalize in the titles of works?

REMEMBER

■ A **proper noun** begins with a capital letter.

More Practice

A. Write and capitalize the proper nouns in these sentences.

Example: The french wanted to give a gift.   *French*

   4. The story of the statue of liberty begins.
   5. The french presented the statue on july 4, 1884.
   6. Two years passed before the statue arrived in new york city.
   7. Packed in crates, this statue left france in 1885.
   8. In 1886 president grover cleveland dedicated it.
   9. Many americans attended the ceremony.
  10. From the decks of ships, immigrants from europe saw the statue.
  11. A poem by emma lazarus was carved on the pedestal.
  12. This poem, titled "the new colossus," welcomed all immigrants.

B. Write a proper noun for each common noun below. Then write one sentence, using the proper noun you wrote.

Example: ocean   *Atlantic Ocean*

  13. book
  14. person
  15. lake
  16. state
  17. holiday
  18. nationality
  19. club
  20. language

Extra Practice, page 98

WRITING APPLICATION Sentences

Imagine that you are a proper noun—an ocean, a city, a holiday, a monument. Write eight to ten sentences that tell about yourself. Give your name and describe what you think, feel, and see. Circle the proper nouns in your sentences.

G R A M M A R

MECHANICS: Apostrophes with Possessive Nouns

You know that **possessive nouns** name who or what has or owns something. You also have learned that an apostrophe (**'**) is used to form a possessive noun.

the boy's home = the home of the boy
the settlers' food = the food of the settlers
the mice's squeaking = the squeaking of the mice

The chart below shows how to use an apostrophe with possessive nouns.

Rules for Using Apostrophes with Possessive Nouns	
most singular nouns: add **'s**	our **country's** bison Mr. **Jones's** land
plural nouns ending in *s*: add only an **apostrophe (')**	many **countries'** wildlife the **Joneses'** ranch the **animals'** skins
plural nouns not ending in *s*: add **'s**	the **men's** wagons the **children's** school the **geese's** noises

Guided Practice

Tell the possessive form of each of these words. Remember to use an apostrophe and an *s* (**'s**) or an apostrophe alone (**'**).

Example: hunter   *hunter's*

MRS. CHARLES'S CLASS MEETS IN THE LIBRARY TODAY.

1. man   **2.** women   **3.** the Douglases   **4.** boys   **5.** girl

?! THINK

■ How do I decide where to use an apostrophe with a possessive noun?

REMEMBER

- Add **'s** to form the possessive of most singular nouns.
- Add only an **apostrophe (')** to form the possessive of a plural noun that ends in *s*.
- Add **'s** to form the possessive of a plural noun that does not end in *s*.

More Practice

A. Write the possessive form of each underlined noun.

Example: Bison roamed <u>America</u> plains.   *America's*

6. This is the story of our <u>country</u> bison.
7. In 1850 our <u>nation</u> bison numbered 20 million.
8. The <u>settlers</u> arrival soon destroyed the herds.
9. <u>Hunters</u> records show many bison were killed.
10. Often an <u>animal</u> hide was taken.
11. By 1900 <u>America</u> bison numbered only twenty!
12. <u>People</u> outrage at the slaughter of the bison grew.
13. <u>Lawmakers</u> actions ended the hunting of bison.

B. Write each sentence. Use the possessive form of the noun in parentheses. Add apostrophes correctly.

Example: The _____ future was assured. (bison)   *bison's*

14. _____ response was to set up game preserves. (Congress)
15. These preserves were fenced for the _____ safety. (animals)
16. Because of our _____ concern, the bison multiplied. (citizens)
17. The _____ future is now secure. (bison)
18. Today, _____ small herd roams freely. (Yellowstone Park)
19. _____ zoos even contain bison. (Children)
20. Many of the _____ animals now live in safety. (world)

Extra Practice, Practice Plus, pages 99-100

WRITING APPLICATION A Letter

Imagine that you belong to a pioneer family. Write a letter to a member of Congress about the slaughter of bison. Use possessive nouns in some of your sentences.

7 VOCABULARY BUILDING: How Language Changes

Our language changes to meet the needs of people. New discoveries and ideas create a need for new words. These new words are formed in different ways.

Many new words are made by joining together two words that already exist. These new words are called compound words. **Compound words** can be written as one or two words.

air + port = airport   control + tower = control tower

Some new words are short forms of old words. People often cut off parts of frequently used words. A word formed in this way is called a **clipped word.**

airplane→plane   bicycle→bike   champion→champ

Blended words are formed by combining two words. As a result, some letters are dropped.

smoke + fog = smog   breakfast + lunch = brunch

Borrowed words come from other languages. For example, *ranch*, *corral*, and *rodeo* are only three of the many Spanish words adopted into English.

Guided Practice

Tell whether each underlined word is a **compound**, **clipped**, **blended**, or **borrowed word**.

Example: A <u>plane</u> has just landed. *clipped word*

1. Let's visit a busy international <u>airport</u>.
2. Sometimes <u>smog</u> delays the landings.
3. Parking garages hold thousands of <u>autos</u>.
4. Helicopters fly to <u>heliports</u> nearby.
5. Hungry travelers on the run gobble <u>tacos</u>.

sea + coast

 THINK

■ Why are so many new words nouns?

REMEMBER

- A **compound word** is formed from two words.
- A **clipped word** is a shortened form of a word.
- A **blended word** is a combination of two words.
- A **borrowed word** comes from another language.

More Practice

A. Write each underlined word. Next to each, write **compound**, **clipped**, or **blended**.

Example: A <u>taxi</u> brings us to the airport.

        taxi   clipped

6. Jumbo jet airplanes roar down the <u>runways</u>.

7. A <u>pro</u> team arrives in its own special jet.

8. <u>Loudspeakers</u> announce arrivals and departures.

9. Long lines snake toward the <u>ticket counter</u>.

10. The <u>waiting room</u> is full of tired people.

11. Airport <u>limos</u> hurry to nearby cities.

12. Dozens of <u>motels</u> are just a short drive away.

B. Blend each pair of words. Write the new word.

Example: documentary + drama   *docudrama*

13. smoke + fog

14. motor + pedal

15. television + marathon

16. camera + recorder

C. Write the clipped word that comes from each word.

Example: telephone   *phone*

17. gymnasium

18. laboratory

19. champion

20. mathematics

Extra Practice, page 101

WRITING APPLICATION Lists

List at least three words for each of the four types of words in this lesson. Then write a sentence for three words on each list. Exchange papers and have a partner suggest other sentences.

COOPERATIVE
LEARNING

GRAMMAR —AND WRITING CONNECTION

Combining Sentences

When you write a story, one way to keep your readers interested is to avoid writing short, choppy sentences.

Choppy: Ben told scary stories. Laura told scary stories.

Better: Ben **and** Laura told scary stories.

Sentence parts can be joined with *and* or *or*, depending on the meaning.

Separate: Did Val scare you? Did Mike scare you?
Combined: Did Val **and** Mike scare you?
Did Val **or** Mike scare you?

You can combine two or more sentence parts in either the subject or the predicate part of a sentence.

The children told stories to Val, Mike, **and** Tom.

Working Together

Tell how you would combine each pair of sentences.

COOPERATIVE LEARNING

Example: People like scary stories.
People like surprising stories.
People like scary and surprising stories.

1. Ben told a story about goblins.
   Ben told a story about elves.
2. Something moved across the hall.
   Something moved into a secret room.
3. Did Jim slam the door?
   Did Lisa slam the door?

Revising Sentences

Rewrite these pairs of sentences by combining them. Use **and** or **or** to show the connection between sentence parts.

4. Laura told a scary story.
   Laura told a silly joke.
5. The story delighted Val.
   The story delighted Tom.
6. Did Mike feel wonder?
   Did Mike feel fear?
7. The storytellers met at school.
   The listeners met at school.
8. Scary stories should be told at a fire.
   Scary stories should be told in a darkened room.
9. At the party, the friends dressed as pirates.
   At the party, the friends dressed as skeletons.
   At the party, the friends dressed as clowns.
10. Ben learned many stories from his uncle.
    Ben learned many stories from his aunt.
    Ben learned many stories from his cousin.

Write a scary story to read aloud to a group of friends. When you revise, work with a classmate to find sentence parts to combine or to put into a series. Use the connecting words that best fit your meaning. Be sure to add commas where needed.

UNIT CHECKUP

LESSON 1

Common and Proper Nouns (page 74) Write each noun. Label each common noun **CN** and each proper noun **PN**.

1. Last August the Smiths visited Mount Rushmore.
2. The family traveled to the Black Hills of South Dakota.
3. Faces of presidents are carved into a mountain.
4. The head of George Washington is very big.
5. The heads of Jefferson and Lincoln are also quite large.
6. Gutzon Borglum designed this beautiful memorial.

LESSON 2

Singular and Plural Nouns (page 76) Write each sentence. Use the plural form of each noun in parentheses.

7. (Man), (woman), and (child) enjoy the state fair.
8. People exhibit (calf), (sheep), and (pony).
9. You can see (goose), (turkey), and (chicken), too.
10. Local (business) and farm (society) have displays.
11. The best (tomato), (peach), and (jelly) win prizes.
12. (Race) and (dance) are all part of the fun.

LESSON 3

Possessive Nouns (page 78) Write the possessive form of each noun in parentheses.

13. Yellowstone is our (country) oldest national park.
14. Most (people) favorite sight is Old Faithful.
15. All (visitors) eyes watch the geyser spurt water.
16. Most (guests) first impression is one of amazement.
17. During my (family) visit, the geyser erupted.
18. Some (tourists) favorite activity is timing the eruptions.

LESSON 4

Appositives (page 80) Write each sentence correctly.

19. The White House the home of the president has 132 rooms.
20. The address 1600 Pennsylvania Avenue is famous.
21. The site about eighteen acres is well landscaped.
22. The British once our enemies burned this house.
23. The house was rebuilt for James Monroe the fifth president.

LESSON 5

Mechanics: Capitalizing Proper Nouns (page 82) Correctly write the proper nouns in each sentence.

24. The grand coulee dam is the largest in our country.

25. The dam is in washington, northwest of spokane.

26. Almost a mile long, it stands across the columbia river.

27. The river originates in british columbia.

28. This province is not in the united states.

29. It is in the country of canada.

30. The columbia flows into the pacific ocean.

31. Behind the dam is the franklin d. roosevelt lake.

LESSON 6

Mechanics: Apostrophes with Possessive Nouns (page 84) Write the possessive form of each underlined noun. Use apostrophes correctly.

32. California Sierra Nevada is the home of Yosemite.

33. Much of the park spectacular scenery is in the Yosemite Valley.

34. The Yosemite Indians name was given to this valley.

35. A Yosemite chief raids made the valley famous.

36. John Muir reports of the valley interested Congress.

LESSON 7

Vocabulary Building: How Language Changes (page 86) Copy each group of words. Then write whether the words are **compound**, **clipped**, **blended**, or **borrowed**.

37. wiener, waltz, noodle

38. caribou, skunk, totem

39. photo, auto, lab

40. motel, brunch, smog

41. spaceship, campsite, bedroom

42. pancake, headache, bedspread

Writing Application: Noun Usage (pages 74–85) The following paragraph contains 8 errors with nouns. Rewrite the paragraph correctly.

43.–50.

Niagara Falls a leading tourist attraction is a natural wonder. Geologists' think niagara falls was formed about 10,000 years ago. Above the falles the rivers width is nearly a mile. Below the falls the river flows through deep cliffes.

WHAT'S IN A NAME?

Play this game with a partner. Bring to class pictures, photographs, and actual objects. Ask your partner to name these objects by calling out common nouns, such as *beach* or *flowers*. Then switch places. This time have your partner act out a scene involving a proper noun. Give the special name of this noun when you guess it.

IT'S WONDERFUL

Make a list of things (nouns) that you think are wonderful. For example, you might list things you find wonderful in nature. For each item (noun) on your list, write a phrase telling what is wonderful about it. For instance, you might write this: *peaches, juicy fruit of summer*. Illustrate the most wonderful noun and phrase on your list.

WHAT A WONDER!

Think of a place you would like to explore. Imagine the wonderful things you might see there. Refer to the list of wonderful nouns you made earlier. Write a poem that narrates your adventure.

Rhyme Away

With a small group, write rhyming possessives. Think of some zany combinations and some realistic ones. Try to think of as many as possible. Then, list them on a poster, illustrating a few of them. Here are some examples of rhyming possessives.

mouse's houses	Fred's shed
the bee's knees	the pig's wig

WHERE WORDS COME FROM

Hundreds of years ago, people in England spoke Middle English. Middle English sounded something like the modern English we speak today, but many of its words were spelled differently.

Work with a partner. Write each word below in modern English.

1. brothor
2. fyve
3. berye

4. speake
5. tretee
6. trouthe

GRAMMAR

Three levels of practice
Common and Proper Nouns (page 74)

LEVEL
A. Write each sentence. Underline the nouns.

1. Long ago, there were few paved highways.
2. Good maps of roads were rare, too.
3. A trip across the country by car could be dangerous.
4. Still, Alice Ramsay made the long journey.
5. In June she started from New York City.
6. Alice drove every inch of the way.
7. Turnpikes were best in the eastern United States.
8. Ramsay reached Chicago in just two weeks.

LEVEL
B. Write the nouns in each sentence. Label them **CN** for common noun and **PN** for proper noun.

9. Alice continued west through Illinois.
10. There was a bridge across the Mississippi River.
11. Ramsay drove onto the rolling plains of the Midwest.
12. Heavy rains turned roads in Iowa into mud.
13. Deep potholes were a serious danger.
14. Twelve flat tires did not stop the brave motorist.
15. A farmer had to pull the car from a ditch.
16. In Nebraska the axles and springs broke.
17. Roads without signs made guesswork necessary.
18. Ramsay's determination never weakened.

LEVEL
C. Rewrite the sentences by correctly capitalizing the proper nouns.

19. The car, a maxwell, crossed the rocky mountains.
20. Then, this woman headed toward california.
21. Finally, ramsay reached san francisco.
22. On august 7, 1909, she completed her journey.
23. She became the first woman to drive from new york to the pacific ocean.
24. Today, highways stretch from bangor, maine, to burbank, california.
25. The highways from new york to florida are filled with cars.

EXTRA PRACTICE

Three levels of practice
Singular and Plural Nouns (page 76)

LEVEL A. One noun in each sentence is plural. Write the plural noun.

1. Imagine a forest without any leaves.
2. Each tree lost its branches long ago.
3. This strange forest is made up of logs.
4. Most amazing of all, the trees are solid rock!
5. A visit to the Petrified Forest fascinates people.
6. This forest is one of nature's strangest stories.
7. This site was once covered with many living pines.
8. Some shrubs were also very tall.
9. In time, each tree died from natural causes.
10. Hot ash from volcanoes buried everything.

LEVEL B. Write the plural form of the noun in parentheses.

11. The wood decayed and escaped in the form of (gas).
12. Mud and sand destroyed the (life) of some trees.
13. (Mineral) from the water took the place of the wood.
14. (Slide) under a microscope show the original wood.
15. The stone logs lay buried for many (century).
16. Finally, (flood) uncovered the logs.
17. In the light the stone logs have many (color).
18. Thousands of men and (woman) visit the site.
19. They spend their (day) in awe of the trees.
20. (Echo) from the distant past hover over this forest.

LEVEL C. Write one sentence for each pair of nouns. Use the plural form for both nouns.

21. deer/park
22. child/class
23. mouse/shelf
24. bus/factory
25. brush/box

EXTRA PRACTICE

Three levels of practice
Possessive Nouns (page 78)

LEVEL A. Write each possessive noun, and label it **singular** or **plural**.

1. Athena was Zeus's daughter.
2. She sprang fully grown from her father's head.
3. In wartime, Greece's need for Athena was great.
4. Athena helped when the army's causes were just.
5. A famous sculptor's skills came from Athena.
6. All artists' works were inspired by her.
7. The Greeks' artwork frequently pictures her.
8. Athena's gift to a city was the first olive tree.
9. The city's name was then changed to Athens.
10. The Parthenon was the citizens' temple to Athena.

LEVEL B. Write the possessive form of each underlined noun.

11. <u>Athena</u> wisdom was greater than her beauty.
12. <u>Aphrodite</u> beauty was well known, however.
13. A <u>shepherd</u> decision angered Athena.
14. In a beauty contest this <u>man</u> vote went to Aphrodite.
15. <u>Greece</u> war with Troy was the result of this contest.
16. <u>Homer</u> *Iliad* tells this story.
17. One of the <u>story</u> heroes was Hector.
18. The story of <u>Hector</u> death was also told by Homer.

LEVEL C. Write each sentence. Use the possessive form of each underlined noun.

19. Different <u>gods</u> skills were well known.
20. <u>Athena</u> skill in the art of weaving was famous.
21. However, she accepted <u>Arachne</u> challenge to weave.
22. In a contest these <u>weavers</u> skills were tested.
23. Angered by the skill shown by Arachne, Athena changed this <u>woman</u> body into that of a spider.
24. Today, <u>scientists</u> name for the spider family is *arachnid*.
25. Many science <u>words</u> origins are in the ancient Greek language.

EXTRA PRACTICE

Three levels of practice
Appositives (page 80)

LEVEL A. Write the appositive in each sentence.

1. Tall tales, wildly exaggerated stories, are humorous.
2. Mythical characters, imaginary beings, were created by lumberjacks in Minnesota.
3. The Roperite, a small beast, has a ropelike beak.
4. This beak, a kind of lasso, is used to catch rabbits.
5. The Upland Trout, a flying fish, nests in trees.
6. This trout is afraid of only one thing, water.
7. The Goofang, another strange fish, swims backward.
8. The Axhandle Hound, a small dog, eats ax handles.
9. Its head, a square with a deep notch, is like a hatchet.
10. Its teeth, sharp needles, can cut through wood.

LEVEL B. Write each sentence, punctuating correctly.

11. The Goofus a mythical bird always flies backward.
12. It always searches for one thing the past.
13. Its nest an unsafe place is built upside down.
14. The Gillygaloo another bird lays square eggs.
15. These eggs square blocks cannot roll away.
16. Lumberjacks famous gamblers used the eggs as dice.
17. The Hidebehind a shy creature is hard to describe.
18. Its favorite activity hiding keeps it safe.

LEVEL C. Rewrite each sentence. Use the appositive in parentheses.

19. There are many other mythological animals. (fantastic creatures)
20. Lumberjacks exchange their tales in the bunkhouse. (their living quarters)
21. At the end of the workday they tell their tales. (7:00 P.M.)
22. The Pinnacle Grouse is their favorite. (a one-winged bird)
23. The Pinnacle Grouse flies in only one direction. (east)
24. For two months its feathers change colors. (October and November)
25. One lumberjack is the subject of many tall tales. (Paul Bunyan)

EXTRA PRACTICE

Three levels of practice

Mechanics: Capitalizing Proper Nouns (page 82)

LEVEL A. Write all the proper nouns in each sentence.

1. The Illinois Indians named the Mississippi River.
2. Hernando de Soto of Spain reached the river.
3. This explorer came from the continent of Europe.
4. Some explorers from France claimed the Mississippi Valley.
5. The United States bought the territory in 1803.
6. This was known as the Louisiana Purchase.
7. The territory was sold by Napoleon.
8. He needed the money for his war against England.
9. New Orleans is a major city in Louisiana.
10. It is named after the city Orléans in France.

LEVEL B. Write the sentences. Capitalize the proper nouns.

11. The mississippi river begins in minnesota.
12. The river widens as it flows through iowa and missouri.
13. The author mark twain described this river.
14. One of his books is called *life on the mississippi.*
15. The *natchez* was a famous riverboat.
16. The illinois river and the missouri river join the mississippi above st. louis.
17. Water from the rocky mountains reaches this river.
18. From new orleans the river flows into the gulf of mexico.

LEVEL C. Write a proper noun for each common noun below.

19. bridge
20. weekday
21. actor
22. business
23. mountain
24. book
25. country

GRAMMAR

EXTRA PRACTICE

Three levels of practice

Mechanics: Apostrophes with Possessive Nouns (page 84)

LEVEL A. Write the possessive noun in each sentence.

1. Ayers Rock is the world's biggest boulder.
2. This rock is located in Australia's outback.
3. According to scientists' studies, it is over a thousand feet tall.
4. The lower slopes of the boulder serve as some families' homes.
5. These native Australians' homes are really caves.
6. These people's myths tell the story of the great rock.
7. Some caves were discovered in France's south.
8. These caves were some boys' accidental discovery.
9. The caves' walls have paintings of animals.
10. These pictures are cavemen's art.

LEVEL B. Write the possessive form of each underlined noun. Use apostrophes correctly.

11. Long ago, a meteorite entered <u>earth</u> atmosphere.
12. This fiery ball crashed into <u>Arizona</u> desert.
13. Our <u>nation</u> Coon Butte Crater was the result.
14. One of the <u>world</u> natural wonders, this crater is a mile wide.
15. <u>Children</u> eyes widen as they look down six hundred feet.
16. According to some <u>men</u> studies, this crater was once much deeper.
17. Some <u>miners</u> stories tell of diamonds inside the rim.
18. The <u>diamonds</u> location has never been found.

LEVEL C. Write each sentence. Use the possessive form of the noun in parentheses. Add apostrophes correctly.

19. Carlsbad Caverns is our _____ greatest system of caves. (country)
20. These caverns are _____ pride. (New Mexico)
21. _____ records mentioned these caves. (Cattlemen)
22. Today, _____ feet tire as they walk through the caves. (tourists)
23. A _____ elevator descends into the caverns. (visitor)
24. _____ homes are found in one part of the cave. (Bats)
25. A _____ journey from the cave is made in warm weather. (bat)

PRACTICE + PLUS

Three levels of additional practice for a difficult skill
Mechanics: Apostrophes with Possessive Nouns (page 84)

LEVEL A. Write the possessive noun in each sentence. Write **S** if the possessive noun is singular and **P** if it is plural.

1. Camouflage is one of nature's wonders.
2. Many animals' hiding techniques depend on color.
3. The colors of some birds' feathers help them hide.
4. Their feathers blend with the forest's colors.
5. Some foxes' use of color is dramatic.
6. A hare's use of color is interesting, too.
7. These creatures' coats turn snow white in winter.
8. An enemy's hungry eyes cannot spot them.

LEVEL B. Write the possessive form of each underlined noun. Use apostrophes correctly.

9. The shapes of some <u>animals</u> bodies protect them.
10. <u>People</u> nickname for the bittern is "invisible bird."
11. These <u>birds</u> slender bodies look like reeds.
12. Hungry birds are scared away by a <u>treehopper</u> shape.
13. This <u>insect</u> form resembles a thorn.
14. Stick <u>insects</u> bodies look like twigs.
15. Another <u>bug</u> survival depends on its looking like a leaf.
16. At an <u>enemy</u> approach these animals remain still.
17. Color and shape are these <u>creatures</u> best defenses.

LEVEL C. Correctly write the possessive form of each noun. Then write a sentence for each possessive noun.

18. child
19. children
20. pony
21. geese
22. country
23. girls
24. horses
25. class

EXTRA PRACTICE

Three levels of practice
Vocabulary Building: How Language Changes (page 86)

LEVEL A. Write the original word from which each clipped word was made. Write each borrowed word and the language from which it came. Use a dictionary if needed.

1. bazaar
2. bike
3. raccoon
4. gym
5. plaza

6. igloo
7. graffiti
8. sophomore
9. moccasin
10. opera

LEVEL B. Match the words in the two columns to form blended words. Then write a sentence for each blended word you form.

11. breakfast
12. simultaneous
13. motor
14. camera
15. parachute
16. smoke

hotel
trooper
lunch
fog
recorder
broadcast

LEVEL C. Write the separate words used to form each compound. Then write the definition of each compound word. Use a dictionary if needed.

17. horsepower
18. windmill
19. stovepipe
20. grandstand
21. campground
22. heartbeat
23. eyepiece
24. skylight
25. cloudburst

M A I N T E N A N C E

UNIT 1: Sentences

Four Kinds of Sentences (page 2) Copy each sentence. Add the correct end punctuation.

1. Is that a red-tailed hawk
2. The bird lives on that hill
3. Listen to its strange call
4. How gracefully the hawk soars

Complete Subjects and Complete Predicates (page 4) Write each sentence. Draw one line between the complete subject and the complete predicate.

5. Some loons live on the lake.
6. The large gray birds eat fish.
7. They stay underwater for a long time.
8. A loon's call is like a laugh.

Simple Subjects and Simple Predicates (page 6) Write each simple subject and simple predicate.

9. That tall tree is an oak.
10. Most oaks live about two hundred years.
11. This book lists many oak trees.
12. These acorns are oak seeds.

Compound Sentences (page 12) Label each sentence **simple** or **compound**.

13. Mount Saint Helens erupted in 1980.
14. Hot ash started fires, and snow melted.
15. Mud slides occurred, and houses slid down hills.
16. The destruction was enormous.

Correcting Sentence Fragments and Run-on Sentences (page 14) Correctly rewrite each fragment or run-on sentence.

17. Last spring a terrible tornado.
18. We hid in the cellar we heard a roar.
19. Cars were overturned houses were destroyed.
20. Lasted less than an hour.

Mechanics: Capitalizing and Punctuating Sentences (page 16) Write these sentences. Add capitals and end marks.

21. have you seen Niagara Falls
22. what a spectacular sight it is
23. there are two waterfalls here
24. point to the Horseshoe Falls

Vocabulary Building: Context Clues (page 18) Use context clues to find the meaning of each underlined word. Then write the meaning of the word.

25. The ship landed at the <u>quay</u>.

26. The mountain climbers finally reached the <u>pinnacle</u>.

27. I <u>guffawed</u> loudly at the funny joke.

28. Do not <u>procrastinate</u>; do the job now.

UNIT 3: Nouns

Common and Proper Nouns (page 74) Write each noun. Label the noun **CN** if it is a common noun and **PN** if it is a proper noun.

29. Mount McKinley is located in Alaska.

30. The summit is the highest in North America.

31. The mountain got its name from William McKinley.

32. The peak is the main attraction of Denali National Park.

Singular and Plural Nouns (page 76) Write the plural form of each noun.

33. calf
34. brush
35. donkey
36. woman
37. potato
38. berry
39. deer
40. rodeo

Possessive Nouns (page 78) Write the possessive form of each underlined noun.

41. <u>Grandma</u> artwork is famous nationwide.

42. This <u>woman</u> first painting was a landscape.

43. Her paintings now show <u>people</u> lives in cities.

44. Other <u>artists</u> paintings are not as bright.

45. My <u>teacher</u> art collection has works by my grandmother.

Appositives (page 80) Write each sentence. Add a comma or commas to set off the appositive from the rest of the sentence.

46. Mount Vernon the home of George Washington is in Virginia.

47. The estate once thousands of acres is located on the Potomac River.

48. The house a well-proportioned wooden structure has nineteen rooms.

49. The grounds lawns and garden add to the beauty.

50. Washington's burial place a tomb is on the grounds of the estate.

4

Writing Stories

Read the quotation and look at the picture on the opposite page. Isaac Asimov has written many stories about strange and wonderful places. When did you write your first story?

Your own imagination and your audience are important ingredients for creating a story. A good story needs a setting and characters and a plot that will interest and excite your audience.

Focus A story has a beginning, a middle, and an end. It provides enjoyment for its audience.

What do you imagine would make a good story? You can use the story and the photographs on the following pages to find ideas for writing.

THEME: *WONDERS*

I imagine there must be such a thing as a born writer. At least, I can't remember when I wasn't on fire to write. At the age of twelve (possibly earlier), I was filling a nickel notebook with scrawlings, divided into chapters. . . .

—Isaac Asimov

Have you ever had a pet? How did you feel toward it? Would another pet—even the same kind of pet—have done just as well?

Jimmy lives on the moon. Since there are no real dogs on the moon, Jimmy has a mechanical dog named Robutt. Jimmy loves his pet dog. However, his father decides to surprise him with another dog—one that is real!

As you read the selection, notice how the author has woven together details that are real and unreal to create the people, places, and events in this story.

A BOY'S BEST FRIEND

by Isaac Asimov

Mr. Anderson said, "Where's Jimmy, dear?"

"Out on the crater," said Mrs. Anderson. "He'll be all right. Robutt is with him. Did he arrive?"

"Yes. He's at the rocket station, going through the tests. Actually, I can hardly wait to see him myself. I haven't really seen one since I left Earth 15 years ago. You can't count films."

"Jimmy has never seen one," said Mrs. Anderson.

"Because he's Moonborn and can't visit Earth. That's why I'm bringing one here. I think it's the first one ever on the Moon."

"It cost enough," said Mrs. Anderson, with a small sigh.

"Maintaining Robutt isn't cheap, either," said Mr. Anderson.

The main characters are introduced immediately, and the problem is stated.

Jimmy was out on the crater, as his mother had said. By Earth standards, he was spindly. His arms and legs were long and agile. He looked thicker and stubbier with his space suit on, but he could handle the lunar gravity as no Earthborn human being could. His father couldn't begin to keep up with him when Jimmy stretched his legs and went into the kangaroo hop.

The setting is described.

The outer side of the crater sloped southward and the Earth, which was low in the southern sky (where it always was, as seen from Lunar City), was nearly full, so that the entire crater-slope was brightly lit.

The slope was a gentle one, and even the weight of the space suit couldn't keep Jimmy from racing up it in a floating hop that made the gravity seem nonexistent.

"Come on, Robutt," he shouted.

Robutt, who could hear him by radio, squeaked and bounded after.

Jimmy, expert though he was, couldn't outrace Robutt, who didn't need a space suit, and had four legs and tendons of steel. Robutt sailed over Jimmy's head, somersaulting and landing almost under his feet.

"Don't show off, Robutt," said Jimmy, "and stay in sight."

Robutt squeaked again, the special squeak that meant "Yes."

"I don't trust you, you faker," shouted Jimmy, and up he went in one last bound that carried him over the curved upper edge of the crater wall and down onto the inner slope.

The Earth sank below the top of the crater wall and at once it was pitch-dark around him. A warm, friendly darkness that wiped out the difference between ground and sky except for the glitter of stars.

Actually, Jimmy wasn't supposed to exercise along the dark side of the crater wall. The grown-ups said it was dangerous, but that was because they were never there. The ground was smooth and crunchy and Jimmy knew the exact location of every one of the few rocks.

Besides, how could it be dangerous racing through the dark when Robutt was right there with him, bouncing around and squeaking and glowing? Even without the glow, Robutt could tell where he was, and where Jimmy was, by radar. Jimmy couldn't go wrong while Robutt was around, tripping him when he was too near a rock, or jumping on him to show how much he loved him, or circling around and squeaking low and scared when Jimmy hid behind a rock, when all the time Robutt knew well enough where he was. Once Jimmy had lain still and pretended he was hurt and Robutt had sounded the radio alarm and people from Lunar City got there in a hurry. Jimmy's father had let him hear about that little trick, and Jimmy never tried it again.

Just as he was remembering that, he heard his father's voice on his private wavelength. "Jimmy, come back. I have something to tell you."

The story is told in time order.

Jimmy was out of his space suit now and washed up. You always had to wash up after coming in from outside. Even Robutt had to be sprayed, but he loved it. He stood there on all fours, his little foot-long body quivering and glowing just a tiny bit, and his small head, with no mouth, with two large glassed-in eyes, and with a bump where the brain was. He squeaked until Mr. Anderson said, "Quiet, Robutt."

Mr. Anderson was smiling. "We have something for you, Jimmy. It's at the rocket station now, but we'll have it tomorrow after all the tests are over. I thought I'd tell you now."

"From Earth, Dad?"

"A *dog* from Earth, son. A real dog. A Scotch terrier puppy. The first dog on the Moon. You won't need Robutt anymore. We can't keep them both, you know, and some other boy or girl will have Robutt." He seemed to be waiting for Jimmy to say something, then he said, "You know what a dog is, Jimmy. It's the real thing. Robutt's only a mechanical imitation, a robot-mutt. That's how he got his name."

Jimmy frowned. "Robutt isn't an imitation, Dad. He's my dog."

"Not a real one, Jimmy. Robutt's just steel and wiring and a simple positronic brain. It's not alive."

"He does everything I want him to do, Dad. He understands me. Sure, he's alive."

"No, son. Robutt is just a machine. It's just programmed to act the way it does. A dog *is* alive. You won't want Robutt after you have the dog."

"The dog will need a space suit, won't he?"

"Yes, of course. But it will be worth the money and he'll get used to it. And he won't need one in the City. You'll see the difference once he gets here."

Jimmy looked at Robutt, who was squeaking again, a very low, slow squeak, that seemed frightened. Jimmy held out his arms and Robutt was in them in one bound. Jimmy said, "What will the difference be between Robutt and the dog?"

"It's hard to explain," said Mr. Anderson, "but it will be easy to see. The dog will *really* love you. Robutt is just adjusted to act as though it loves you."

"But Dad, we don't know what's inside the dog, or what its feelings are. Maybe it's just acting, too."

Mr. Anderson frowned. "Jimmy, you'll *know* the difference when you experience the love of a living thing."

Jimmy held Robutt tightly. He was frowning, too, and the desperate look on his face meant that he wouldn't change his mind. He said, "But what's the difference how *they* act? How about how *I* feel? I love Robutt and *that's* what counts."

And the little robot-mutt, which had never been held so tightly in all its existence, squeaked high and rapid squeaks —happy squeaks.

Thinking Like a Reader

1. What special relationship does Jimmy have with Robutt? How do you know?
Write your response in your journal.

Thinking Like a Writer

2. As you know, every story is told from a particular point of view. Often an author uses the third-person point of view—"he said" or "she said"—to tell a story. What other point of view could a writer use?

3. How does the author let you know where and when the story takes place? What details does he use? Why is the setting, or place, important to the story?

4. If you were writing a story that took place on the moon, how would you introduce it? What details could you include in your story? How would you describe the setting? What characters would you include?
Write your responses in your journal.

Brainstorm *Vocabulary*

In "A Boy's Best Friend," the characters talk naturally about the places and objects they see around them—lunar craters, space suits, and a robot dog with a positronic brain. These words help you imagine life on the moon. Think of a time and a place where a story might happen. It might be a city, a school, a house of the future, or a country town of the past. In your journal write all the words and phrases that would describe that place. You can use these words and phrases in your writing.

Talk It Over *Tell a Story*

When you tell a story, you are narrating—telling the details of an incident in the order in which they happen. Imagine that you are writing the next chapter of the story, "A Boy's Best Friend." What will happen? Work with a partner. Tell the story of what happens next to Jimmy and Robutt. Remember to use lively details. Also, use time order to help your listener keep track of the story. Ask your partner for a response to your story.

Quick Write
Write Some Dialogue

You have been thinking about parts of a story, such as where the story takes place and what happens in it. Now, think about the people in the story. Imagine that Jimmy wants to persuade his father to let him keep Robutt. What might Jimmy say? What might his father say?

Jimmy: Dad, I know you want me to have a live dog, but nothing could be better than Robutt.

Dad: I know you feel that way now, but you haven't met the dog from Earth.

Jimmy: But Dad, a real dog won't have an electronic signal.

Write another dialogue between two people in the story. Keep your dialogue in your folder.

Idea Corner *Expand Your Ideas*

Perhaps you already have some ideas for a story. In your journal, expand on these ideas. For example, you may have ideas about a situation or a problem, or about a person who would make an interesting character. Add to any story ideas that you have already written.

PICTURES

SEEING LIKE A WRITER

Finding Ideas for Writing

Look at the photographs. Think about what you see.
What ideas for a story do the photographs give you?
Write your ideas in your journal.

COOPERATIVE
LEARNING

1 GROUP WRITING: A Story

A story is a narrative that comes from a writer's imagination or life. What are the important parts of a story?

- An Introduction and a Plot, with a Problem and a Solution
- The Characters and the Setting
- Sequential Order

An Introduction and a Plot, with a Problem and a Solution

When you plan a story, your **purpose** usually is to entertain. The **audience** for your story can be your teacher, your classmates, your family, or even yourself. A story has a beginning, a middle, and an end. This sequence of events is called the **plot**. Most plots revolve around a problem that is solved at the end. Read the following passage. Can you tell what the problem will be?

> Jason stared at his homework—ten word-problems. So far, he had done only two. Then his eye fell on his computer. Maybe a quick video game would clear his brain. He flipped on the computer. The screen glowed, and an unfamiliar pattern appeared. "Hey," Jason said aloud, to nobody in particular. "What's going on?"
>
> The computer replied, "Look—do you want my help?"

This passage sets up the **introduction** or beginning of a story. It introduces the characters and suggests that the problem will be how they get along.

Guided Practice: Developing Plot

As a class, think of a problem around which to develop a plot for a story. Choose an idea from this list or from your journal, or think of a new idea. Then, write a short beginning that presents the problem of the story.

Example: Curtis had been sitting on the bench all season. He knew he wasn't good, but this was the last game. Suddenly the coach pointed to him and said, "Curtis—you're in."

a contest   a spaceship without radio contact
getting lost on a hike   a missing letter

The Characters and the Setting

The **characters** are the people in the story. Their actions create the plot. One way to show characters is through their own words, or **dialogue.** The **setting** of a story is its time and place. A setting can be realistic or imaginary. Within a story, the setting may remain the same or it may change with the events of the story.

Look back at the passage on page 116.

■ Who will the characters be?

■ Is the setting in the present, the past, or the future? Where will most of the action take place?

Guided Practice: Charting Narrative Details

Recall the plot you have chosen to write about. As a class, make a chart like this one. Fill in the narrative details.

Situation/Problem	Characters	Setting	Resolution
last game; team losing; Curtis goes in.	Curtis, Coach, Kyle	baseball field	Curtis helps win the game.

Sequential Order

A story is told in sequential order. The beginning of the story introduces the problem. The middle of the story leads to the climax, or high point, of the story, and the end shows the resolution, or outcome. Look at the passage on page 116. Notice how it introduces the problem in the story, including the setting and main characters.

When you write a story, you should arrange the details in sequential order: problem, climax, and resolution. Often, sequential order and time order will be the same.

Putting a Story Together

With your classmates you have written a beginning that introduces a problem in a story. You also have thought about characters and setting.

Now it is time to develop the plot. To do this, you must add details. Here is a type of story outline that one student made to tell her story.

Beginning:
(introduction of problem)

It is the last inning, and the score is 5-3 with 2 outs. The left fielder sprains his thumb. Coach sends in Curtis.

Middle:
(climax)

Curtis shuts his eyes and swings. He hears a *thunk*. The ball rolls toward third base and stays fair. Curtis is safe. The next batter walks. Kyle hits a home run. The team wins.

End:
(resolution)

Everyone praises Kyle. Kyle points out that it was Curtis who kept the game alive.

This student added realistic details about the game. She wanted the story to end well for Curtis. She also put these details in the order in which they happened.

Guided Practice: Writing a Short Story

Write a brief middle and ending to add to the story beginning that you wrote earlier. In the middle of your story, use details that make the events clear and that lead up to the ending you want. Be sure to write these details in the order in which they took place. Also be sure to use details that tell more about the characters and the setting. Remember to describe the characters' actions, using narrative details.

Also try to include some dialogue to help to bring your characters to life. As you write, remember to describe a new setting if the setting of the story changes—in place or in time.

Share your story with a friend. Ask your friend if he or she thinks your story is interesting and exciting.

Checklist: A Story

You have been learning about writing stories. When you write a story, a checklist will remind you of the things you need to include in your story.

Look at this checklist. Some points need to be added. Make a copy of the checklist and complete it. Keep it in your writing folder. You can use it whenever you write a story.

CHECKLIST

- ✔ Introduction
- ✔ Characters
- ✔ Setting
- ✔ Plot

_____ (beginning)
_____ (middle)
_____ (end)

- ✔ Purpose and _____
- ✔ _____ order

2 THINKING AND WRITING: Understanding Sequence

Think of what you have learned about narrative writing. You know that narrative writing tells a story. You also know that it follows a particular order, or **sequence.**

When you put things in sequence, you arrange them in a logical order. The logical order for a story usually is **chronological.** This means that the story is told in time order—from the first to the last event. Writers use time-order words to help their readers follow the order of events in a story.

Look at this time line of events.

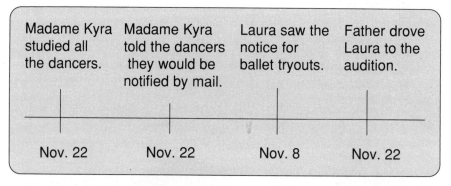

Madame Kyra studied all the dancers.	Madame Kyra told the dancers they would be notified by mail.	Laura saw the notice for ballet tryouts.	Father drove Laura to the audition.
Nov. 22	Nov. 22	Nov. 8	Nov. 22

The writer plans to write about a girl who auditions for a ballet company. On the time line, many details are listed.

Thinking Like a Writer

- What do you think would be the best order, or sequence, for these details?

The writer needs to rearrange her details so that they are in the right sequence. Here, the details are out of order. Laura's seeing the notice for ballet tryouts should be the first event. Father's driving Laura to the auditorium should be the second event. What are given as the first and second details become the third and fourth details.

When you write a story, you will have to remember to keep the details in the right sequence.

THINKING APPLICATION Sequencing

Each of the writers named below is planning to write a story. Help each writer to decide on the proper sequence. Write the details in the best order on a separate sheet of paper. You may wish to discuss your thinking with your classmates. In these discussions explain the reasons for choosing the order you did.

1. Nadia's story will be about a girl who travels back in a time machine to the days of the California Gold Rush to stake a claim and look for gold. What is the best order for her details?

   She traveled to California by wagon.
   She returned home on the time machine.
   She found only one tiny nugget of gold.
   She staked a claim near a river.

2. Rashad's story will be about a basketball game. What is the best order for his details?

   With seconds to play, the team needed one more basket.
   The ball hung on the rim and finally went in.
   The star player fouled out early in the third period.
   With six minutes left, the team was losing.

3. Sarah's story will be about the first sixth grader to fly a spaceship to the moon on her own. What is the best order for her details?

   The spaceship leaves the launching pad.
   She takes over the controls.
   She successfully lands on the moon.
   No one is on board except her.

4. Larry's story will be about a forest fire caused by a campfire that burns out of control, destroying large sections of a forest. What is the best order for his details?

   A forest ranger spots smoke.
   A family forgets to pour water on its campfire.
   Animals return to the forest.
   Volunteer firefighters arrive.

3 INDEPENDENT WRITING: A Story

Prewrite: Step 1

You have been learning about narrative writing. Now you are ready to choose a topic for your own story. Matt, a student your age, chose a topic this way.

Choosing a Topic

First, Matt thought about interesting events, both from his own life and those he had heard about. Next, he thought about characters and settings. Last, he decided what he would enjoy writing about.

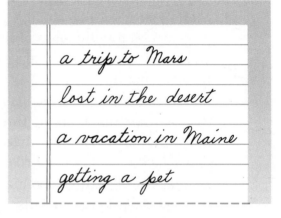

a trip to Mars

lost in the desert

a vacation in Maine

getting a pet

Matt liked his third idea best, although he decided he would focus on seeing the Northern Lights.

Matt explored his idea by making a question-and-answer chart. Here is what Matt's chart looked like.

Exploring Ideas: Charting Strategy

Questions for Exploring the Events of a Story	Sample Answers
1. What is the setting?	Maine, in the summer
2. Who are the characters?	Jim and his cousin Ted
3. What is the problem?	Jim doesn't like Maine.
4. What events lead to the climax?	Jim doesn't like anything Ted likes to do. Ted shows Jim the Northern Lights.
5. How does the story end?	Jim realizes he has had a good time after all.

Matt decided that his partner would be his **audience.** His **purpose** for writing was to entertain his partner.

Before he began to write, Matt tried role-playing the characters to discover what they were like and what they might say. Then he turned his chart into a simple outline.

STORY OUTLINE

I. **Beginning**
- A. **Describe the setting.** Maine in the summer
- B. **Who are the characters?** Jim and his cousin Ted
- C. **What is the problem?** Jim does not like Maine.

II. **Middle**
- A. **What happens?** Ted takes Jim hiking and sailing, but Jim does not have a good time.
- B. **What is the climax?** Ted shows Jim the Northern Lights.

III. **End**
- A. **What is the solution?** Jim likes the Northern Lights.
- B. **How does the story end?** Jim realizes he has had a good time.

Thinking Like a Writer

- Which details did Matt put at the beginning?
- Which details did he put in the middle?
- How does Matt's story end?

Think of a story you would like to tell. Use **Pictures** or your journal for ideas. Follow these steps.

- Think about situations and events.
- Choose the one you like best.
- Decide on a problem.
- Think about characters and setting.
- Think about your purpose and audience.

Make a story outline. Remember, you can add to or take away from your outline at any time.

Write a First Draft: Step 2

Matt has made a planning checklist to remind himself of what a story should include. Look at his checklist. Matt is now ready to write his first draft.

Matt's First Draft

Jim went to Maine on his Vacation. Jim didn't liked maine much. Maine was chilly and cold—not like home in Georgea. there was his cousin Ted Who didn't seem to like him much. Ted him took for a hike. Jims heels got a blister. They went saleing, which Jim didn't like.

At last the week was over. Jim packed and went to bed. An hour later, Ted got him up to see the Northern Lights.

The Northern Lights were pink and green. Jim was amazed.

While Matt was writing his first draft, he did not worry about making mistakes. He knew he could go back later to revise and correct his work.

YOUR TURN

Write your first draft. Ask yourself these questions.

- What will my audience want to know?
- What is the problem in my story? How can I solve it?

TIME-OUT You might want to take some time out before you revise. That way you will be able to revise your writing with a fresh eye.

Planning Checklist
- Remember purpose and audience.
- Have a plot, characters, and setting.
- Include an introduction, a problem, and a climax.
- Have a resolution.
- Use sequence.

Revise: Step 3

Matt read his finished draft to himself. Then he shared his story with a classmate. He wanted some suggestions for improvement.

I like your story, but I'd like to see the characters' own words.

That's a good idea. It would make my story seem more real. Thanks.

Matt then looked back at his planning checklist. He noticed that he had forgotten one point. He checked it off so that he would remember it when he revised his writing. Matt now has a checklist to use as he revises.

Matt made changes in his story. Notice that he did not correct small errors. He knew he could fix them later.

The revisions Matt made changed his story. Look at Matt's revised draft.

Revising Checklist
- ■ Remember purpose and audience.
- ■ Have a plot, characters, and setting.
- ■ Include an introduction, a problem, and a climax.
- ✔ ■ Have a resolution.
- ■ Use sequence.

Matt's Revised Draft

~~Jim went to Maine~~ on his Vacation Jim didn't liked maine

~~much~~ Maine was ~~chilly and~~ cold—not like home in Georgea.

there was his cousin Ted Who didn't seem to like him

First,
much. Ted him took for a hike, Jims heels got a blister.
and

Then,   *was boring and made Jim feel seasick.*
They went saleing, which ~~Jim didn't like~~

At last the week was over. Jim packed and went to bed.

shook him. "Get up," he said. "It's
An hour later, Ted ~~got him up~~ to see the Northern Lights.

like   jewels
The Northern Lights were pink and green. Jim was amazed.

He and Ted grinned happily at each other.

Thinking Like a Writer

WISE
WORD
CHOICE

- Which phrases and sentences did Matt add? What effect do they have on the story?
- Which sentences did he combine? How does combining them improve his story?
- How did Matt change the ending? Why did he do this?

YOUR TURN

Read your first draft. Ask yourself these questions.

- Does my story have a beginning, a middle, and an end?
- Does it have a problem and a solution?
- Have I used enough dialogue?

If you wish, ask a friend to read your story and to make suggestions. Then revise your story.

Proofread: Step 4

Matt knew that his story was not finished. He had made changes, but he still needed to proofread it. In proofreading, he would check his work for errors in grammar and mechanics. Matt made a proofreading checklist.

Matt's Proofread Draft

¶ Jim went to Maine on his vacation. Jim didn't liked maine much. Maine was chilly and cold--not like home in Georgea *Georgia*. there was his cousin Ted, Who didn't seem to like him *First,* much. Ted him took for a hike, *and* Jims heels got a blister. *Then,* They went saleing, which Jim didn't like. *sailing was boring and made Jim feel seasick.*

At last the week was over. Jim packed and went to bed. An hour later, Ted got him up to see the Northern Lights. *shook him. "Get up," he said. "It's*

The Northern Lights were pink and green. Jim was amazed. *like* *jewels*

He and Ted grinned happily at each other.

YOUR TURN

Proofreading Practice

Below is a paragraph that you can use to practice your proofreading skills. Write the paragraph correctly on a separate sheet of paper.

Ever since Sallys Great-grandmother had died, everyone who came to the johnsons house asked What became of her ruby pin? Sally had seen the pin once. It was her great-grandmothers proudest possession. Sally knew that day one this beutiful pin would be hers.

Proofreading Checklist
- Did I indent my paragraphs?
- Did I spell all words correctly?
- Which punctuation errors do I need to correct?
- Which capitalization errors do I need to correct?

Applying Your Proofreading Skills

Now proofread your story. Read your checklist again. Review **The Grammar Connection** and **The Mechanics Connection**, too. In addition, check and correct any errors you made in subject-verb agreement. Use the proofreading marks to show changes.

THE GRAMMAR CONNECTION

Remember these rules about forming possessive nouns.

- To form the possessive of most singular nouns, add *'s*.
- To form the possessive of a plural noun ending in *s,* add only *'*.
- To form the possessive of a plural noun not ending in *s,* add *'s*.

my friend**'s** house

our friend**s'** houses   the children**'s** books

Check your story. Have you formed singular and plural possessive nouns correctly?

Proofreading Marks

- ¶ Indent
- ∧ Add
- ⋏ Add a comma
- ⅍ ⅍ Add quotation marks
- ⦾ Add a period
- ⌫ Take out
- ≡ Capitalize
- / Make a small letter
- ∿ Reverse the order

THE MECHANICS CONNECTION

Remember these rules about using quotation marks.

- Use **quotation marks** before and after the words of a direct quotation.
- Begin a new paragraph and use a separate set of quotation marks each time the speaker changes in a dialogue.

"The lights are out," said Peter.

"It must be the storm," Lance replied.

Check your story. Have you used quotation marks correctly?

Publish: Step 5

Matt decided that he wanted to share his story with his classmates. He made a final, neat copy of his story and put it in a folder in the reading corner. Several of his classmates told him they had enjoyed reading it. Some asked him questions about the Northern Lights and the state of Maine.

YOUR TURN

Make a final copy of your story. Use your best handwriting. Think of a way to share your story. Look in the **Sharing Suggestions** box below for ideas.

SHARING SUGGESTIONS

Illustrate your story and make it into a booklet. Present it to a younger class or to the children's ward of a local hospital.

Submit your story to the school magazine. If your school has no magazine, work with your classmates to produce one.

Create a book of stories. Collect stories from classmates. Make a title page, a table of contents, and a cover. Display the book in your classroom or in the school library.

4 SPEAKING AND LISTENING: Telling a Story

You have just written a story. Your story focused on a problem and a solution, and it had a beginning, a middle, and an end. It also had characters and a setting. Now you can use what you have learned about writing a story to tell a story orally.

First, you will want to make a note card to use when you tell your story. You do not have to write the whole story on your note card. Your note card should include only the main points and a few details.

Look at the note card that Stephanie wrote.

> Notes for Telling a Story
>
> 1. Maria moves to Los Angeles.
> 2. She has a hard time making new friends.
> 3. Then her father gets a job at Disneyland.
> 4. All her classmates but Sonia want to be her friend now.
> 5. She learns that Sonia is the only one who doesn't want to take advantage of her.
> 6. She and Sonia become good friends.

Notice that the beginning, middle, and end are written on the note card. In what order are the details listed?

Stephanie's note card does not include many details, so she must remember to elaborate and add details as she tells her story. What kinds of details do you think she should add?

When you tell a story, remember to use these speaking guidelines.

> **SPEAKING GUIDELINES:** A Story
>
> 1. Remember that your **purpose** is to entertain.
> 2. Try to catch your listeners' interest with the first sentence. Then develop your plot in sequential order.
> 3. Make a note card. Practice using it.
> 4. Look at your listeners.
> 5. Speak slowly, clearly, and loudly enough to be heard.

- Why are narrative details important when I am telling a story?
- How does telling a story in sequence help my listeners to understand the events?

SPEAKING APPLICATION A Story

Think of a story you could tell. Develop a setting, characters, and a plot. Use the speaking guidelines to help you prepare your notes. Your classmates will be using the following guidelines as they listen to your story.

> **LISTENING GUIDELINES:** A Story
>
> 1. Listen for the order of events.
> 2. Listen for narrative details.
> 3. Listen for the problem and its solution.

5 WRITER'S RESOURCES: The Atlas

In this unit you have written a story. One important resource for your story has been your imagination. However, real facts and figures can help make a story seem more true to life.

One useful resource for a writer is the atlas. Matt, who wrote about Maine, used an atlas to help him choose his setting. An **atlas** is a book of maps. The maps provide information about countries. Most atlases also have an index.

Look at this sample map.

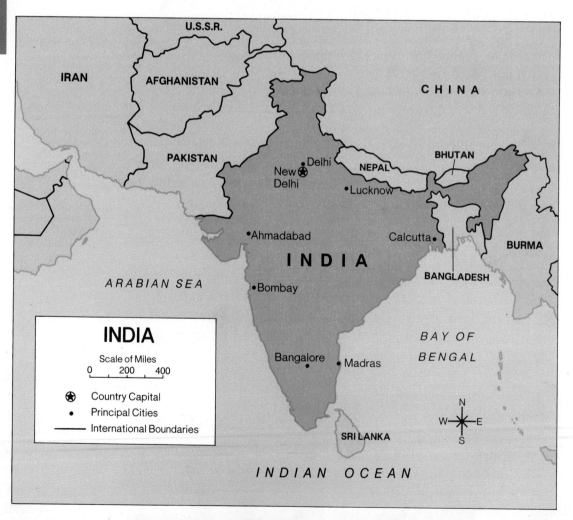

Notice the map key. It helps you to read the information on the map by explaining what the symbols mean. For example, by using the key you can distinguish between the symbols for a capital city and a principal city. The key includes the scale of miles, which helps you to figure out the size of the countries and the distances between cities. The compass rose shows the directions of the compass: north, south, east, and west.

Practice

Use the sample atlas map on the opposite page to answer each question below.

1. How can you tell where south is on this map?
2. Which country is India's neighbor to the south?
3. Which bodies of water are off India's coast?
4. In which direction would you travel to go from New Delhi to Bombay?
5. Which major city is on India's west coast?
6. Which symbol shows that a city is the national capital?
7. Which symbol shows the principal cities?
8. What is India's capital?
9. How could you figure out the distance from Calcutta to Madras?
10. Is Nepal part of India or a separate country?

WRITING APPLICATION Notes

Use an atlas to look up information about a place that interests you. When you choose a place, try to choose one that is the setting for a book—either a book that you know, or one that you would like to read. Remember to use the index of the atlas to help you locate the right map, if necessary.

Make notes about the information the atlas gives you. As you work, also jot down notes about any new map symbols you come across in the map key. Keep your notes in your writing folder. You will use them in **The Curriculum Connection** on page 136.

WRITER'S RESOURCES: The Almanac

Another helpful writer's resource is the almanac. An **almanac** contains current information about important people, places, and events. An almanac is usually published each year so that its facts and figures are always up-to-date. The information in an almanac often appears in a table or a chart. Look at this sample taken from an almanac.

Population of the World's Largest Cities

City	Population
Bangkok, Thailand (1984 estimate)	5,174,682
Beijing, China, metro (1981 estimate)	8,500,000
Bombay, India, metro (1981 census)	8,202,759
Cairo, Egypt (1983 estimate)	5,881,000
Calcutta, India (1981 estimate)	9,165,640
Canton, China (1981 estimate)	5,200,000
Delhi, India, metro (1981 census)	5,277,730
Hong Kong (1985 estimate)	5,415,000
Jakarta, Indonesia (1983 estimate)	7,636,000
Karachi, Pakistan, metro (1981 estimate)	5,100,000
London, England, greater (1983 estimate)	6,756,000
Mexico City, Mexico (1978 estimate)	8,988,230
Moscow, USSR (1984 estimate)	8,500,000
New York City, USA (1982 estimate)	7,086,096
São Paulo, Brazil (1980 census)	7,033,529
Seoul, South Korea (1983 estimate)	9,204,300
Shanghai, China, metro (1981 estimate)	12,000,000
Teheran, Iran (1982 estimate)	5,734,199
Tianjin, China, metro (1981 estimate)	7,200,000
Tokyo, Japan (1985 estimate)	8,500,000

Like an atlas, an almanac has an index. The index for an almanac is usually found in the front of the book, not in the back. However, you may find an abbreviated index in the back, in addition to a main index. The index gives you all the references to the subject for which you are looking in the almanac. It may also mention other subjects under which you can look to find related information. When you use an almanac, check the index to be sure you have found all the information about your subject.

Practice

Use the sample from the almanac on the opposite page to answer each question. Write your answers on a separate sheet of paper.

1. What information does the table present?
2. How many of the world's cities have 7 million people or more?
3. How many Indian cities have populations of more than 5 million people?
4. Which Indian city has the greatest population?
5. What is the population of Bombay, India?
6. Which Indian cities are larger than New York City?
7. How many people live in the world's largest city?
8. How many cities have more than 8 million people?
9. Which country has more of the world's largest cities than any other?
10. Which of the world's largest cities is in the United States?

WRITING APPLICATION Notes

Use an almanac to find information about the same place you looked up in the atlas. Make notes about the information you find. Then use your notes from the atlas and the almanac to write a brief description of the place you chose. Keep your notes and description in your writing folder. You will use them in **The Curriculum Connection** on page 136.

Writing About Literature

Reading literature is a way to expand your world without ever having to leave home. For example, through literature you can discover what life on the moon might be like. The characters in books can even help you understand real people better.

After Anh, a girl in Matt's class, read "A Boy's Best Friend," she decided to read another story about a person's love for a pet. Anh's teacher assigned a book report to the class. Anh wanted to read a book that was set in California. She had looked up information about California in an atlas and an almanac. Anh chose *The Red Pony* by John Steinbeck for her book report.

INTRODUCTION

BODY

CONCLUSION

THE RED PONY by John Steinbeck

How would you feel if you were given a red pony for a gift? Would you feel proud? Would you know how to care for it? How would you feel if the pony were taken away from you? Jody, in the novel *The Red Pony*, experiences many different feelings when he is suddenly given the responsibility of caring for a horse of his own.

Jody, a ten-year-old boy in Salinas, California, is given the chance of proving himself when his parents present him with the horse of his dreams. With the help of the ranch hand Billy Buck, Jody cares for his pony by feeding and training it. Jody loves his new horse, but one day the horse gets soaked in the rain and dies. For the first time in his life, Jody faces a great loss. Later, Jody's father makes a bargain with him. He will give him a new horse if Jody promises to work hard.

If you want to know if Jody earns his new horse, read *The Red Pony*. I recommend this book because the characters are warm and interesting. Although the characters in the book may not be real, you will probably find that Jody's feelings are much like your own.

Writing a Book Report A book report provides a "guided tour" of a work of literature. It should contain the following information.

1. **The title and the author**
2. **The introduction** Your introduction should include
   - whether the book is fiction or nonfiction
   - an opening sentence that will grab your reader's attention
3. **The body of the report** The body should include
   - information about the setting and main characters
   - a summary of the plot that does not tell the whole story
4. **The conclusion** Your conclusion should include
   - a clue about the ending of the book
   - your opinion of the book
   - your recommendation to read or not to read the book

ACTIVITIES

Write a Book Report Choose a book you would like to read. Be sure that the book has the same setting as the place you looked up in the atlas and the almanac. Now, read the book and write a book report. Follow the model above.

Make a Map You have already looked in an atlas and an almanac to find information about the setting of your book. Now, use that information to make a map of the setting of the book.

UNIT CHECKUP

LESSON

1

Group Writing: A Story (page 116) Read this story starter. On a separate sheet of paper, write a sentence that explains the problem.

Mr. McClusky pulled the car off the road to check the suitcases on top, and Bobby got out to stretch. Neither of them noticed when Angus, their little dog, hopped out, too. Almost immediately, Mr. McClusky called, "OK—let's go!" and started the car. Too late, Angus burst through the bushes. The car had already pulled away.

LESSON

2

Thinking: Understanding Sequence (page 120) Imagine that you are planning to write a story about two girls who are marooned on an island. Below are your notes. What would be the best sequence of events? On a separate sheet of paper, write the details in order.

They tied the canoe to some bushes.
When they returned, the canoe was gone.
They had a picnic on the island.
It took them two hours to canoe to the island.

LESSON

3

Writing a Story (page 122) Write a science-fiction story that takes place on Earth. For example, your story could be about a robot that does household chores. Include a strong setting and an interesting main character and plot.

LESSON
4

Speaking and Listening: A Story (page 130) Imagine that you have been invited to tell a story on the radio. Think about the **Speaking Guidelines** for telling a story. Then make the notes for the note card you will use to guide you.

LESSONS

5-6

The Atlas and The Almanac (pages 132–135) Select a city, a state, or a country. Use an atlas and an almanac to find information about it, and then write a short summary.

THEME PROJECT

A DIORAMA

You probably know all about wonders. Space travel, for example, is a wonder. The Northern Lights and the Grand Canyon are natural wonders. Perhaps the human mind is the greatest wonder of all.

Talk with your classmates about what makes something a wonder. What would be a good way to explain a wonder to someone who had never seen one? Would a story be good? How might a picture help? Look at the picture below.

This picture shows a diorama. A diorama is a model of a scene or an event. It uses small, three-dimensional figures.

- Brainstorm your own list of wonders. Choose your favorite. Make a diorama to illustrate your wonder.
- To make a diorama, use a box with the side cut out and add scenery made of different materials. Small dolls or pipe-cleaner figures can represent people.
- As you work on your diorama, think of a story that focuses on your wonder.
- When you complete your diorama, use it as a visual aid to tell your story to the class.

UNIT

5

Verbs

In this unit you will learn about verbs. You can use verbs in your writing to make it lively and vivid. Choosing the correct verb is very important.

Discuss Read the poem on the opposite page. The poet tells a racer how to get ready for a race. Talk with a partner about the things you know how to do.

Creative Expression The unit theme is *Directions*. What directions have you given or received lately? Write a set of directions. You could write a list or a paragraph. Write your set of directions in your journal.

*Dig your starting holes
deep and firm
lurch out of them
into the straightaway*

*with all the power
that is in you
look straight ahead
to the finish line . . .*

—Frank Horne, from "To James"

1 ACTION VERBS

An action verb is a word that expresses action. It tells what the subject of the sentence does.

Verbs express many of the actions people perform every day.

Celia **types** faster than Manny.

Manny **writes** better than Maria.

Most verbs express physical actions. Some verbs, however, express mental actions.

Manny **thought** about computers.

Guided Practice

Find the action verb in each of these sentences.

Example: Manny received a new computer.   *received*

1. Manny's father brought home a package.
2. He called Manny downstairs.
3. Manny dreamed about this day.
4. He unwrapped his new computer.
5. Then Manny read the directions.

 THINK

■ How can I decide if a word is an action verb?

REMEMBER

■ An **action verb** is a word that expresses action. It tells you what the subject does.

More Practice

A. Write each sentence. Draw a line under the action verb in each sentence.

Example: Manny <u>bought</u> a computer.

6. Manny uses a computer for his homework.
7. The computer works faster than a typewriter.
8. It shows Manny's sentences on a screen.
9. Manny finds his mistakes quickly.
10. He corrects his errors immediately.
11. Then the computer prints a perfect copy.
12. This machine saves him time and effort.

B. Write each sentence. Complete each sentence with a different action verb.

Example: The computer _____ little electricity.
The computer uses little electricity.

13. At first Manny _____ little about computers.
14. He also _____ the directions in the manual.
15. The manual _____ him the basic directions.
16. It _____ him all the commands.
17. His friend, Celia, _____ about computers.
18. Celia _____ Manny some easy steps.
19. She _____ the function keys to him.
20. Now Manny _____ commands to the computer.

Extra Practice, page 174

WRITING APPLICATION A Paragraph of Directions

Think of something you can do well, such as using a typewriter or a computer. Write a paragraph of directions that explains how to do this activity. Exchange papers with a partner. Ask your partner to underline the action verbs.

2 MAIN VERBS AND HELPING VERBS

Sometimes a verb is made up of several words.

Our class **will report** on the Old West.

A verb that contains more than one word is called a **verb phrase**. The last word in a verb phrase is the **main verb**. All the other words are **helping verbs**.

Common Helping Verbs					
have	am	be	do	will	can
has	are	being	does	would	could
had	is	been	did	shall	may
	was			should	might
	were				must

Some verbs can be used as both main verbs and helping verbs. These verbs are **main verbs** if they stand alone or if they come last in a verb phrase.

MAIN VERB: Buffalo Bill **had** many skills as a scout.
HELPING VERB: Buffalo Bill **had** gained fame as a scout.

Guided Practice

Find the verb phrase in each sentence. Identify the main verb and the helping verb or verbs.

Example: Buffalo Bill has earned great fame.
           earned   main verb   has   helping verb

1. The class has started small group projects.
2. Two groups have chosen the Old West.
3. One group will give a report about Buffalo Bill.
4. Another group might discuss Wild Bill Hickok.
5. The groups will be reading books about the West.

 THINK

■ How can I decide if a word is a main verb or a helping verb?

REMEMBER

- A **verb phrase** consists of a main verb and all of its helping verbs. The main verb is the last word in a verb phrase.
- A **helping verb** helps the main verb to show an action or make a statement.

More Practice

A. Write the verb phrase in each sentence. Draw one line under each helping verb and two lines under each main verb.

Example: His story has become a legend.   <u>has</u> <u><u>become</u></u>

6. Buffalo Bill was named William Frederick Cody.
7. He must have been born before the Civil War.
8. He had earned his nickname by age 31.
9. He was performing great deeds by that time.
10. Cody had ridden for the Pony Express.
11. He must have served as a scout in the Indian wars.
12. Yes, he did take his Wild West show to Europe.

B. Write the following sentences. Draw one line under each helping verb and two lines under each main verb.

Example: Cody may have made cowboys famous.
       Cody <u>may have</u> <u><u>made</u></u> cowboys famous.

13. Other scouts have been compared to Cody.
14. Perhaps only one has proved as great.
15. Wild Bill Hickok was born in Illinois.
16. By age 30, Wild Bill had worked at several jobs.
17. He was working as a scout during the Civil War.
18. After the war he was made a marshal in Kansas.
19. Later Hickok and Cody would work together.
20. Hickok may have directed Buffalo Bill's first Wild West show.

Extra Practice, page 175

WRITING APPLICATION A Letter

Write a letter to a famous person from the Old West. Underline the main verbs and helping verbs that you use. Then read your letter to a small group of classmates.

COOPERATIVE
LEARNING

DIRECT AND INDIRECT OBJECTS

3

In many sentences you write, you add words after the verb to complete the action named by the verb. A **direct object** receives the action of the verb. It answers the question *whom?* or *what?* after an action verb.

Ellen called **Miki**. (Ellen called **whom**?)

Miki answered the **phone**. (Miki answered **what**?)

Some verbs may have an indirect object as well. An **indirect object** answers the question *to whom?*, *for whom?*, *to what?*, or *for what?* after an action verb.

She gave **me** a kitten. (She gave a kitten **to whom**?)
He showed **her** a book. (He showed a book **to whom**?)

An indirect object always comes before a direct object. To decide if a word is an indirect object, rearrange the sentence to see if the word can be placed elsewhere in the sentence after the word *to* or *for*.

She gave a kitten **to me**. He showed a book **to her**.

Guided Practice

Tell whether each underlined word is a direct or an indirect object.

Example: Ellen brought <u>her</u> a <u>gift</u>. *her   indirect object,*
gift   direct object

1. Ellen gave Miki a <u>kitten</u>.
2. Ellen also gave <u>Miki</u> directions.
3. Miki offered her kitten <u>water</u>.
4. She also left <u>it</u> food.
5. Miki sent her <u>friend</u> a thank-you note.
6. Ellen ignores her <u>cat</u>.
7. The cat gives <u>Ellen</u> much love, however.

THINK

- How do I decide if a word is a direct object or an indirect object?

REMEMBER

- A **direct object** is a noun or pronoun in the predicate that receives the action of the verb.
- An **indirect object** is a noun or pronoun in the predicate that answers the question *to whom?*, *for whom?*, *to what?*, or *for what?* after an action verb.

More Practice

A. Copy the underlined word in each sentence. Correctly label it **direct object** or **indirect object**.

Example: Miki gave <u>Ellen</u> a cat.   *Ellen   indirect object*

8. Miki feeds her cat <u>vitamins</u>.
9. She offers <u>it</u> food once a day.
10. Her cat often shows <u>everyone</u> its bad temper.
11. The cat gave <u>Miki</u> a nasty scratch.
12. That scratch taught Miki a <u>lesson</u>.
13. Now she prefers Ellen's <u>cat</u> to her own.

B. Copy the following sentences. Correctly label each **direct object** and **indirect object**.

Example: Ellen gave the dog a bath.   *bath   direct object,*
                   dog   indirect object

14. Ellen bought Miki a dog.
15. The dog gives Miki affection.
16. Miki teaches her pet many tricks.
17. She gives it a good diet.
18. Miki bought her pet a soup bone.
19. Soup bones give dogs much pleasure.
20. Other bones cause them serious injuries.

Extra Practice, page 176

WRITING APPLICATION An Interview

Interview someone who has two different kinds of pets. Ask questions about feeding and training. Write the interview in a question-and-answer form. Label each direct object and indirect object.

4 TRANSITIVE AND INTRANSITIVE VERBS

You have learned that a direct object is a word that answers the question *whom?* or *what?* after an action verb. A verb that takes a direct object is called a **transitive verb**.

> Liz **bought** a bike.

Not every verb has a direct object. An **intransitive verb** has no direct object.

> Liz **laughed**. Frank **arrived** on time.

Some action verbs, such as *hit* and *receive*, are always transitive. Other action verbs, such as *laugh* and *arrive*, are always intransitive. Many verbs, however, can be used either way.

Verb	Transitive	Intransitive
accept	Frank **accepted the invitation.**	Frank **accepted** happily.
paint	Liz **paints pictures.**	Liz **paints** well.

Guided Practice

Identify the verb in each sentence. Tell whether the verb is transitive or intransitive.

Example: Frank rides his bike.

> *rides   transitive*

1. Frank bought his bike at a store.
2. Liz borrowed her bike from her friend, Elena.
3. Frank sings during his ride.
4. Liz rides more often than Frank.
5. Yesterday Frank fixed a flat tire.

 THINK

■ How can I decide if a verb is transitive or intransitive?

REMEMBER

- A **transitive verb** is a verb that has a direct object.
- An **intransitive verb** is a verb that does not have a direct object.

More Practice

A. Copy the underlined verb in each sentence. Write **transitive** or **intransitive** to show the kind of verb it is.

Example: Liz and Frank <u>love</u> their bikes. *love   transitive*

  6. Liz and Frank <u>took</u> a tour last summer.
  7. They <u>traveled</u> on bikes through Massachusetts.
  8. They <u>rode</u> far each day.
  9. Frank <u>climbed</u> long hills easily.
  10. Liz <u>balanced</u> heavy loads well.
  11. She <u>maneuvered</u> with great skill.
  12. She also <u>repaired</u> the flat tires.

B. Write the following sentences. Underline the verb in each sentence and label it **transitive** or **intransitive**.

Example: Liz and Frank <u>biked</u> all summer. *intransitive*

  13. Liz and Frank met their group in the Berkshires.
  14. The members loaded their gear.
  15. The leaders guided them along the route.
  16. They biked south through the Berkshires.
  17. Then they rode toward Cape Cod.
  18. They lost their way once.
  19. Luckily, a man gave directions to the group.
  20. The cyclists traveled with great happiness.

Extra Practice, page 177

✏️ WRITING APPLICATION Sentences

Write eight to ten sentences about a trip you have taken. When you have finished, exchange papers with a classmate. Label the verbs in each other's paragraphs as transitive or intransitive.

LINKING VERBS

Some verbs do not express action. Such verbs are called **linking verbs**.

The map **is** a guide.   The directions **seem** clear.

Common Linking Verbs				
am	was	being	feel	smell
are	were	been	appear	stay
is	be	seem	become	taste

A **linking verb** links the subject with a word in the predicate. This word can be a **predicate noun** or a **predicate adjective**. A **predicate noun** renames or identifies the subject. A **predicate adjective** describes the subject.

PREDICATE NOUN: Vera is a **scout**.
PREDICATE ADJECTIVE: She seems **brave**.

Some verbs can be either action verbs or linking verbs.

Vera **sounded** nervous. (linking verb)
She **sounded** the alarm. (action verb)

Guided Practice

Identify the linking verb and the predicate noun or the predicate adjective in each sentence.

Example: Vera remained calm.

remained, calm   predicate adjective

1. The girls became curious.
2. Their map looked real.
3. The directions seemed clear.
4. Perhaps the treasure was a chest.
5. The trail appeared crooked most of the way.

The treasure is round.

THINK

- How can I recognize a linking verb?

REMEMBER

- A **linking verb** is a verb that links the subject of a sentence to a noun or adjective in the predicate.
- A **predicate noun** follows a linking verb and renames or identifies the subject.
- A **predicate adjective** follows a linking verb and describes the subject.

More Practice

Write these sentences. Underline the verbs and label them **action verb** or **linking verb**. Then label any **predicate noun** or **predicate adjective**.

Example: The class read a story.   *action verb*

6. Vera and Nan became happy.
7. They found an old map.
8. The map looked genuine.
9. The paper felt heavy.
10. The writing appeared faint.
11. The directions seemed familiar.
12. The girls followed a trail into the woods.
13. The treasure was three marbles in a squirrel hole.
14. Vera's teacher assigned a book report.
15. *Treasure Island* was Vera's choice.
16. She remembered the story from the movie.
17. The young hero's name is Jim.
18. Jim grows curious about an old sea captain.
19. The captain's map reveals the secret.
20. The treasure's fate remains a mystery.

Extra Practice, page 178

WRITING APPLICATION A Map

In your classroom, hide a treasure such as a dime. Draw a map and write directions for finding the treasure. Exchange papers with a partner. Then hunt for each other's treasure.

6 PRESENT, PAST, AND FUTURE TENSES

Verbs do more than express actions. They also help you to tell **when** these actions take place. Verbs show time by changes in tense.

The **present tense** tells that something is happening now.

> Michael **works** on his project.
> Victor **appears** happy.
> Karlene **is** a clever student.

The **past tense** shows that something has already happened.

> Michael **worked** on his project.
> Victor **appeared** happy.
> Karlene **was** a clever student.

The **future tense** shows that something is going to happen.

> Michael **will work** on his project.
> Victor **will appear** happy.
> Karlene **will be** a clever student.

Guided Practice

Identify the verb in each sentence. Tell whether it is in the present, past, or future tense.

Example: Yesterday the class studied a book.

> *studied   past tense*

1. Last year Michael studied a book about the Babylonians.
2. Now Victor wants a book about Egypt.
3. Next term the boys will learn about printing.
4. Karlene already knows more than Richard.
5. Tomorrow the boys will ask her for help.
6. Babylonian scribes wrote on clay tablets.

THINK

■ How can I decide whether a verb is in the present, the past, or the future tense?

REMEMBER

- A verb in the **present tense** tells that something is happening now.
- A verb in the **past tense** shows an action that has already happened.
- A verb in the **future tense** shows an action that will take place in the future.

More Practice

A. Write the underlined verb. Write **present, past,** or **future** to show which tense it is.

Example: People <u>developed</u> writing.   *developed*   *past*

7. Egyptian papyrus <u>will crumble</u> if touched.
8. Medieval scribes <u>copied</u> books by hand.
9. This method <u>takes</u> months or even years.
10. Today, publishers <u>print</u> books by the thousands.
11. Some books <u>survived</u> for hundreds of years.
12. People in the next century <u>will read</u> them.

B. Write the sentences. Underline each verb. Then write **present, past,** or **future** to show its tense.

Example: Books <u>appeared</u> much later.   *past*

13. Karlene showed Victor the method.
14. Victor will make his own book.
15. First, she folded a single sheet in half.
16. Now, she places several folds together.
17. She usually sews the sheets along the fold.
18. With several sheets she will make a booklet.
19. Then, she stitched the booklet to a piece of cloth.
20. She glues the cloth inside a cover.

Extra Practice, page 179

The Granger Collection

WRITING APPLICATION A How-to Paragraph

Think about a skill you have, such as making models or clothes. Write a paragraph about how to perform the skill. Identify the verb tenses in a classmate's paragraph.

PRINCIPAL PARTS OF VERBS

All the ways a verb can be changed to show the time of an action come from four basic forms. These forms are called the **principal parts** of the verb.

	Principal Parts of Verbs		
Verb	**Present Participle**	**Past**	**Past Participle**
walk	(is) walking	walked	(has) walked
live	(is) living	lived	(has) lived
try	(is) trying	tried	(has) tried
slip	(is) slipping	slipped	(has) slipped

The present participle is sometimes the main verb in a sentence. It is always used with *is*, *was*, or some other form of the helping verb *be*. The helping verbs *has*, *have*, or *had* are used when the past participle is the main verb.

LeRoy **is visiting** England. He **has visited** London.

Regular verbs form the past and the past participle by adding *d* or *ed*. When a regular verb ends with a consonant preceded by *y*, you change the *y* to *i* before adding *ed*. When a one-syllable verb ends with a consonant preceded by a vowel, double the consonant before adding *ed*.

try tried   drop dropped

Guided Practice

Tell the present participle, the past tense, and the past participle of the following verbs.

Example: help *(is) helping* *helped* *(has) helped*

1. look **2.** share **3.** skip **4.** learn **5.** dry

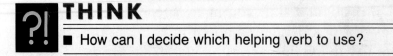

THINK

■ How can I decide which helping verb to use?

REMEMBER

- Use a form of the verb *be* with the present participle.
- Use a form of the verb *have* with the past participle.

More Practice

A. Write the underlined verb form in each sentence. Label it **present participle**, **past**, or **past participle**.

Example: We have <u>traveled</u> every summer.
         traveled   past participle

  6. We are <u>enjoying</u> our trip to England.
  7. No one in the class had <u>visited</u> England before.
  8. Today we are <u>touring</u> the Tower of London.
  9. This castle once <u>served</u> as a prison.
10. The guide is <u>describing</u> the crown jewels.
11. LeRoy and Mary Kay are <u>gasping</u> in amazement.
12. The tour also <u>included</u> a bus ride.
13. The bus was <u>traveling</u> on the left side of the road.

B. Rewrite each sentence. Use the correct form of the verb in parentheses.

Example: Our trip is _____ us busy. (keep)
        Our trip is keeping us busy.

14. Yesterday we _____ Buckingham Palace. (visit)
15. It _____ larger than the White House. (seem)
16. Today we are _____ the Houses of Parliament. (view)
17. The members are _____ a new law. (discuss)
18. A guide was _____ Parliament with Congress. (contrast)
19. She has _____ the American system. (study)
20. She has _____ the differences clearly. (explain)

Extra Practice, page 180

WRITING APPLICATION A Post Card

Imagine that you are on vacation. Write a post card that compares two sights. Then, find an example of each of the principal parts of a verb in a classmate's post card.

IRREGULAR VERBS I

Irregular verbs do not form the past and past participle by adding *d* or *ed*. The best way to learn the principal parts of irregular verbs is to memorize them.

Principal Parts of Some Irregular Verbs			
Verb	**Present Participle**	**Past**	**Past Participle**
catch	(is) catching	caught	(has) caught
do	(is) doing	did	(has) done
drive	(is) driving	drove	(has) driven
give	(is) giving	gave	(has) given
grow	(is) growing	grew	(has) grown
know	(is) known	knew	(has) known
make	(is) making	made	(has) made
say	(is) saying	said	(has) said
see	(is) seeing	saw	(has) seen
sink	(is) sinking	sank	(has) sunk
speak	(is) speaking	spoke	(has) spoken
take	(is) taking	took	(has) taken
teach	(is) teaching	taught	(has) taught
tear	(is) tearing	tore	(has) torn
throw	(is) throwing	threw	(has) thrown
write	(is) writing	wrote	(has) written

Guided Practice

Give the principal parts of the following verbs.

Example: drive *is driving* *drove* *has driven*

1. do **2.** see **3.** tear **4.** sink **5.** know

 THINK

■ How can I decide if a verb is an irregular verb?

REMEMBER

- **Regular verbs** add *d* or *ed* to form the past and the past participle.
- **Irregular verbs** do not add *d* or *ed* to form the past and the past participle.

More Practice

A. Write the correct verb in parentheses for each sentence.

Example: Alison (gave, given) her dog lessons.   *gave*

6. Alison has (teach, taught) her dog new tricks.
7. Yesterday she (threw, thrown) the dog a ball.
8. Her dog (catch, caught) the ball in its mouth.
9. The dog has (grew, grown) a bit this past month.
10. Alison's cat was (driven, driving) her crazy.
11. The cat has (taken, taking) all the dog's toys.
12. Once, Alison (spoke, spoken) harshly to her cat.
13. Overall, her pets have (make, made) her happy.

B. Write each sentence. Use the past or the past participle of the verb in parentheses.

Example: The project _____ a mess. (become)   *became*

14. Alison's brother has _____ a model ship. (make)
15. He _____ the model in a store window. (see)
16. The directions _____ him mad, however. (drive)
17. They _____ incorrect information. (give)
18. They _____ few things that made sense. (say)
19. In anger, he _____ away the directions. (throw)
20. He has _____ to ask for a refund. (write)

Extra Practice, page 181

WRITING APPLICATION A Story

Write about a surprising experience you have had. You might write about a gift or a visit you received. Exchange papers with a classmate. Have your classmate list the principal parts of the verbs you used.

IRREGULAR VERBS II

Learn the principal parts of the following irregular verbs.

Principal Parts of More Irregular Verbs			
Verb	**Present Participle**	**Past**	**Past Participle**
blow	(is) blowing	blew	(has) blown
break	(is) breaking	broke	(has) broken
bring	(is) bringing	brought	(has) brought
come	(is) coming	came	(has) come
draw	(is) drawing	drew	(has) drawn
drink	(is) drinking	drank	(has) drunk
eat	(is) eating	ate	(has) eaten
fly	(is) flying	flew	(has) flown
freeze	(is) freezing	froze	(has) frozen
go	(is) going	went	(has) gone
ride	(is) riding	rode	(has) ridden
run	(is) running	ran	(has) run
sing	(is) singing	sang	(has) sung
sit	(is) sitting	sat	(has) sat
swim	(is) swimming	swam	(has) swum
think	(is) thinking	thought	(has) thought
wear	(is) wearing	wore	(has) worn

Guided Practice

Give the principal parts of the following verbs.

Example: run *is running* *ran* *has run*

1. swim **2.** fly **3.** think **4.** wear **5.** blow

THINK

■ How can I learn the different forms of irregular verbs?

REMEMBER

- All verbs form the present participle by using a form of the verb *be* plus *ing*.
- Memorize irregular past and past participle forms.

More Practice

A. Write each sentence. Use the correct past-tense form of the verb in parentheses.

Example: We (take) an extra ticket for Roberto. *took*

6. Janet's father (bring) us to the theater.
7. We (go) at six o'clock in the evening.
8. Three of us (ride) in the back of the van.
9. Janet (sit) in the front.
10. We (sing) silly songs on the way to town.
11. Suddenly the van (come) to a stop.
12. We (run) to our seats just before seven o'clock.

B. Write each sentence. Use the present participle or the past participle form of the verb in parentheses.

Example: Luckily we have _____ good seats. (buy)
  Luckily we have bought good seats.

13. Now we are _____ in the theater. (sit)
14. We have _____ all the popcorn already. (eat)
15. The feature has _____ on the screen. (come)
16. We have _____ in fear. (freeze)
17. Waves have _____ a ship into pieces. (break)
18. The lifeboats have _____ these waves to shore. (ride)
19. A helicopter has _____ to the beach. (fly)
20. Rescuers have _____ the survivors to safety. (bring)

Extra Practice, page 182

WRITING APPLICATION A Review

Write a paragraph reviewing a movie you have seen recently. Present your review to your classmates. Ask your classmates to identify any irregular verbs in your review.

COOPERATIVE LEARNING

10 SUBJECT-VERB AGREEMENT

A verb must **agree** with its subject. A singular subject takes a singular verb, and a plural subject takes a plural verb.

SINGULAR:
Jennie **plays** soccer.
Dora **skates** well.

PLURAL:
The girls **play** soccer.
Her friends **skate** well.

Present-tense verbs that are singular usually end in *s* or *es*. However, when the singular subject is *I* or *you* the singular verb does not end with *s* or *es*.

SINGULAR:
I **steal** the ball.   You **score** a goal.

The verb *be* is irregular. Study this chart.

Subject	Verb	Example
I	am (present) was (past)	I **am** happy today. I **was** sad yesterday.
he, she, it, and singular nouns	is (present) was (past)	She **is** the captain. The game **was** close.
we, you, they, and plural nouns	are (present) were (past)	We **are** teammates. The boys **were** helpful.

Guided Practice

Tell which verb in parentheses agrees with the subject.

Example: The players (pass, passes) the ball.   *pass*

1. Jennie (drive, drives) the ball toward the goal.
2. The players (kick, kicks) it down the field.
3. Ricardo (play, plays) today.
4. The cheerleaders (is, are) absent.
5. Damon (own, owns) this ball.

THINK

■ How can I tell when to use a singular or a plural verb?

REMEMBER

- Verbs must agree with their subjects.
- A singular subject takes a singular verb.
- A plural subject takes a plural verb.

More Practice

A. Write the present-tense form of the verb that agrees with the underlined subject.

Example: The <u>coach</u> (tell, tells) us the rules.   *tells*

6. <u>Jennie</u> (play, plays) soccer after school.
7. The <u>teammates</u> (arrive, arrives) together.
8. The <u>girls</u> (practice, practices) almost every day.
9. <u>Mr. Mitrakis</u> (serve, serves) as the coach.
10. His <u>suggestions</u> (make, makes) them better players.
11. The <u>coach</u> (is, are) never late.
12. Rosa's <u>father</u> (help, helps) with the equipment.
13. Rosa's <u>mother</u> (bring, brings) refreshments.

B. Write each sentence. Use the correct form of the verb in parentheses. Be sure the subjects and verbs agree.

Example: The two sports _____ practice. (require)
          The two sports require practice.

14. I _____ soccer and tennis. (like)
15. Both sports _____ the heart and lungs fit. (keep)
16. Soccer _____ a team sport. (be)
17. Tennis _____ an individual sport. (be)
18. Jennie _____ injuries. (avoid)
19. The girls _____ to the coach's directions. (listen)
20. The coach _____ the rules. (explain)

Extra Practice, Practice Plus, pages 183-184

WRITING APPLICATION A Rule Book

Make up a game or a sport and explain its rules. Exchange rule books with another student. Check to be sure that all subjects and verbs agree.

11 MORE ABOUT SUBJECT-VERB AGREEMENT

You have learned that a verb must agree with its subject. When the subject of a sentence has more than one part, it is called a **compound subject**. When the parts of a compound subject are joined by *and*, use a plural verb.

Archery and golf **are** precision sports.

When the parts of a compound subject are joined by *or*, *either . . . or*, or *neither . . . nor*, the verb agrees with the subject that is nearer to it.

Luck or chance **is** seldom a factor.
Either professionals or amateurs **play** here often.
Neither luck nor distractions **help** the player.
Noises or anxiety **works** against your skill.

When a sentence begins with *There* or *Here*, the verb must still agree with the subject. The words *there* and *here* are never the subject. You can find the subject by asking *Who or what is there?* or *Who or what is here?*

Here **is** an excellent *bow*.   (What is here?)
Here **are** the *golfers*.   (Who is here?)

Guided Practice

Tell which verb in parentheses agrees with the subject.

Example: There (is, are) a golf course nearby.   *is*

1. Skill and concentration (bring, brings) success.
2. Here (is, are) some tips.
3. Either archery or golf (provide, provides) a challenge.
4. There (is, are) new bows in that rack.
5. Neither Rick nor his friends (practice, practices) very often.

 THINK

- How can I decide whether a compound subject takes a singular verb or a plural verb?

REMEMBER

- When a compound subject is joined by *and*, use a plural verb.
- When a compound subject is joined by *or, either...or,* or *neither...nor,* the verb agrees with the subject that is closer to it.

More Practice

A. For each sentence, write the form of the verb in parentheses that agrees with the subject.

Example: Rick and Beth (have, has) new bows. *have*

6. Rick and Beth (take, takes) archery lessons.
7. Beth or her friends (carry, carries) the target.
8. There (is, are) four circles on this target.
9. There (is, are) a different color for each circle.
10. Either a coach or a parent (supervise, supervises).
11. Neither Rick nor his parents (own, owns) this gear.
12. Here (is, are) the method for stringing a bow.
13. Either Beth or Rick (do, does) the job.

B. Write each sentence. Use the form of the verb in parentheses that agrees with the subject.

Example: Here _____ the secret of success. (be) *is*

14. There _____ many strategies in these sports. (be)
15. Either winds or spinning _____ a ball. (affect)
16. This golf club and golf ball _____ to me. (belong)
17. There _____ also a target in golf. (be)
18. Neither Rick nor Beth _____ in archery. (miss)
19. Here _____ a new set of arrows. (be)
20. Neither rain nor clouds _____ us from playing. (keep)

Extra Practice, page 185

WRITING APPLICATION A Story

Write a brief story in which two friends try out for a sports team. Check that each verb agrees with its subject.

12 MECHANICS: Using Commas in a Series

You have often written sentences that tell about two different actions.

Cindy **planned** a picnic and **invited** her friends.

When you want to tell about more than two actions, use commas and the word *and* to write the words in a series.

Cindy **washed, dressed, and went** to the park.

A series contains three or more items. Many kinds of words can be written as a series. Use commas to separate each item. Include a comma before *and*.

Glenn ate **a hamburger, beans, and a peach.**
The runner ran **long, hard, and fast.**
Wesley ate a **red, ripe, and tasty** apple.
I ran **out the door, down the street, through the gate, and into the park.**

Guided Practice

Tell where you would use commas in order to separate the items in each series.

Example: We planned a party a dance and a picnic.
We planned a party, a dance, and a picnic.

1. The students walked ran and drove to the picnic.
2. The afternoon was warm sunny and lovely.
3. Timothy barbecued hamburgers corn chicken and ribs.
4. Mrs. Riggs prepared the salad quickly beautifully and expertly.
5. Some friends ran around the track played baseball and swam in the lake.

?! THINK

■ How do I decide where to use commas to separate words in a series?

REMEMBER

- Use commas to separate words or phrases used in a series.
- Include a comma before the word *and* in a series.

More Practice

Write the sentences. Add commas where they are needed.

Example: We could choose a trip a fair or a picnic.
We could choose a trip, a fair, or a picnic.

  6. Cindy Glenn and Pablo voted to have a picnic.
  7. Their energy eagerness and enthusiasm persuaded us.
  8. Students planned the games transportation and food.
  9. We needed a time a menu and directions.
 10. The lake chosen for the location of the picnic was small distant and hard to find.
 11. Students came by bus by bike and by car.
 12. "I know the way," said a voice timidly faintly and cautiously.
 13. We cheered clapped and followed our guide.
 14. Roy Pam and David had planned the picnic.
 15. David fell broke his arm and left the committee.
 16. Roy and Pam compared plans ideas and strategies for the picnic.
 17. Roy worked days weeks and even months.
 18. Pam also worked long hard and often.
 19. Both students were bright clever and creative.
 20. However, they could not give clear exact and correct directions.

Extra Practice, page 186

WRITING APPLICATION Lists

Prepare lists of games, food, and equipment that you would need for a class outing. Include at least three items in each list. Discuss your lists with a partner and have him or her add items and any missing commas.

13 VOCABULARY BUILDING: Word Choice

Good **word choice**, or **diction**, depends on knowing many words. It also depends on knowing the differences between words. Many words have synonyms. A **synonym** is a word that has the same or almost the same meaning as that of another word. Be sure to choose the synonym that best expresses your meaning.

One way to choose between synonyms is by their **connotations**. Besides its meaning, each word carries its own feelings and overtones, or shades of meaning. For example, you would rather wear *inexpensive* sneakers than *cheap* ones. The word *inexpensive* carries a more positive connotation.

Positive connotations	lively	slender	amusing
Negative connotations	rowdy	bony	silly

antique

Guided Practice

Tell which word in each pair has the positive connotation. Be prepared to explain your answer.

Example: mob *or* crowd *crowd*

1. curious *or* nosy
2. loaf *or* relax
3. antique *or* old-fashioned
4. tricky *or* clever
5. careful *or* timid
6. talk *or* chatter

old-fashioned

 THINK

■ How can I decide which synonym to use in my writing?

REMEMBER

■ Many synonyms have different **connotations**—the feelings and shades of meaning suggested by a word.

More Practice

A. Write the word in parentheses that better fits the meaning of each sentence.

Example: The hero's action was very (bold, rash). *bold*

7. That tightwad Mr. Crenshaw is (thrifty, stingy).
8. Marilyn saves money by being (thrifty, stingy).
9. Some perfumes have a wonderful (odor, fragrance).
10. Ripe garbage has a horrible (odor, fragrance).
11. A hard worker deserves to (loaf, relax) a while.
12. The lazybones likes to (loaf, relax) on the job.
13. Good actors like to (show off, perform) on stage.
14. Silly Elliot likes to (show off, perform) in class.

B. Write these sentences. Use the word in parentheses that better fits each sentence.

Example: The beautiful vase was quite (delicate, frail). *delicate*

15. That dancer has a (slender, bony) body.
16. Underweight people develop a (slender, bony) look.
17. (Amusing, Silly) comedians tell witty stories.
18. One (amusing, silly) student can disrupt a class.
19. A (crowd, mob) of rioters took over the train.
20. An orderly (crowd, mob) gathered at the box office.

Extra Practice, page 187

WRITING APPLICATION A List

Think of four other pairs of synonyms that can be used in a positive and negative way. Use one word in a complete sentence with a positive connotation. Then, exchange your paper with a classmate. Use the remaining word in each pair in a sentence with a negative connotation.

GRAMMAR —AND— WRITING CONNECTION

Keeping the Same Tense

Verb tenses show **when** an action happens. In a paragraph about a single event, all the tenses should be the same. Changing tenses in a paragraph can confuse the reader. Read these paragraphs about making popcorn.

Different Tenses: Fred will combine the corn kernels with the oil in the pan. He watched the heat carefully. He removes the pan from the stove after ten minutes.

Same Tense: Fred combines the corn kernels with the oil in the pan. He watches the heat carefully. He removes the pan from the stove after ten minutes.

Working Together

COOPERATIVE
LEARNING

Think about each group of sentences. Then tell how you would change each group to keep the verbs in the same tense.

Example: At summer camp everyone will do various jobs. Marcia <u>filled</u> the water glasses for the first week.
will fill

1. Last year Marcia attended art class.
   She makes a beautiful stained-glass lamp.
   Marcia will enjoy that class.
2. Next year the camp will offer an acting class.
   The campers performed in a play.
   There are daily rehearsals.

Revising Sentences

Rewrite each group of sentences, keeping the verbs in the same tense. Before you revise, determine which tense works best.

3. At camp, good swimmers teach the younger campers.
   They taught the butterfly stroke first.
   The good swimmers will learn different strokes easily.

4. Marcia and some campers want a volleyball court.
   A flat area on the beach made a good court.
   Marcia will smooth a large area of sand.

5. The volleyball net was a real challenge.
   The girls buy the net in town.
   They will insist on material of the finest quality.

6. A small group will choose members for the team.
   The girls wanted tall players.
   They select some members from the basketball team.

7. Everyone gets a turn at the net.
   Tall players were valuable.
   All team members will rotate positions, however.

Think of a sport you would like to learn. Look up information about this sport. Then write a paragraph that explains how this game is played.

When you revise, work with a partner to correct any sentences in your paragraph that have not kept the same tense and that may be confusing as a result.

UNIT CHECKUP

LESSON 1

Action Verbs (page 142) Write the action verb in each sentence.

1. Archaeologists use shovels and picks.
2. Often they uncover ancient objects.
3. They examine these items carefully.
4. They write informative reports about the past.

LESSON 2

Main Verbs and Helping Verbs (page 144) Write each verb phrase. Draw one line under the helping verb and two lines under the main verb.

5. Many thousands of people have visited the famous Luray Caverns.
6. Underground water has formed these caves.
7. Someone had discovered them by accident.
8. The visit will have made a big impression on this group of visitors.

LESSONS 3-4

Direct and Indirect Objects and Transitive and Intransitive Verbs (pages 146–149) Write each verb. Label it **transitive** or **intransitive**. Then write and label each **direct object** and **indirect object**.

9. Mrs. Murasaki gave Warren a book.
10. The book read well.
11. His sister enjoyed the story, too.
12. The story described a voyage.
13. Warren returned the book to Mrs. Murasaki.

LESSONS 5-6

Linking Verbs and Present, Past, and Future Tenses (pages 150–153) Write each verb. Label it **action** or **linking** and identify the tense as **present**, **past**, or **future**.

14. Corey seems tired and sleepy.
15. He probably has a case of the flu.
16. He was unwell yesterday.
17. His fever will remain high for a while.

LESSON 7 Principal Parts of Verbs (page 154) Write the main verb. Label it **present participle** or **past participle**.

18. Dawn is working at the bike shop.
19. She was delivering papers last month.
20. She has worked hard in both jobs.
21. Dawn had earned a week's vacation.

LESSONS 8-9 Irregular Verbs and More Irregular Verbs (pages 156–159) Write the present participle, past, and past participle.

| 22. give | 24. do | 26. grow | 28. take | 30. see |
| 23. choose | 25. say | 27. speak | 29. teach | 31. make |

LESSONS 10-11 Subject-Verb Agreement and More About Subject-Verb Agreement (pages 160–163) Write each sentence correctly.

32. Many students (join, joins) the sports club.
33. They (play, plays) baseball or tennis after school.
34. Several teachers (coach, coaches) our teams.
35. Soccer (is, are) also a popular game.

LESSON 12 Mechanics: Using Commas in a Series (page 164) Write each sentence, puncutating correctly.

36. Tina campaigned gave a speech and won the election.
37. She had energy experience and intelligence.
38. Mary Chuck and Alice also won.
39. They cheered laughed and hugged each other.

LESSON 13 Vocabulary Building: Word Choice (page 166) Write each sentence, choosing the appropriate word in parentheses.

40. The game plan had a (clever, tricky) strategy.
41. The first question on that crazy test was (clever, tricky).
42. A (mob, crowd) of players nearly tackled him.
43. The (mob, crowd) in the theater applauded.

44.-50. Writing Application: Verb Usage (pages 142–163) This paragraph contains 7 verb errors. Rewrite it correctly.

The earth are a sphere. Its surfaces is curved. This have created a problem for mapmakers. There is several ways to solve the problem. Mapmakers have drew accurate maps by bending the dimensions. The lines curves to show how the dimensions have been bended.

PLEASED TO MEET YOU, MR. OR MS. MACHINE!

Think about the different machines that play a part in your daily life. Choose one that you find especially interesting. Then, imagine that it is alive and can speak. Create a personality for the machine. Give it a name. Then write a character sketch that describes your machine.

A VARIETY OF VERBS

Play this game with a partner. Choose a verb. Then, ask your partner to think of a synonym for it. Next, you think of an antonym for that verb. Then your partner names a synonym for the verb, you again name an antonym, and so on. For example,

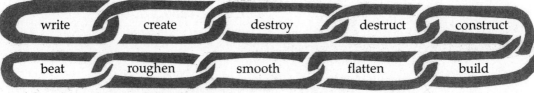

write   create   destroy   destruct   construct

beat   roughen   smooth   flatten   build

See how long a list of verbs you can make. If you like, illustrate your list when you have finished.

VERBS IN MOTION

The ways in which people and animals move can be described by action verbs. For example, runners *jog*. Read these action verbs that describe motion.

dart	wiggle	soar	hop	stalk	bounce
slide	glide	creep	leap	pounce	gallop

Match a creature with each verb. Then think of other animals and match them with verbs that describe their actions. For example, elephants *lumber*.

A FANTASY

Use your imagination and your knowledge of verb tenses to write a story that does not make sense!

Think of a topic—a science fiction story, a funny incident, an episode from history—and retell it. In the retelling, mix your tenses, using past, future, present participles, and past participles. Write out your story and read it to the class.

PANTOMIME TIME

Think of an action verb that you can show by acting it. Plan how you will represent the verb, making sure you will show the direct object of the verb. Then, form a small group of classmates. Taking turns, pantomime the verb to the group. Your classmates can guess both the action verb and the direct object of the verb.

For example, you might choose to pantomime giving someone a book, riding a bike, or baking a cake.

THE MOON IS . . .

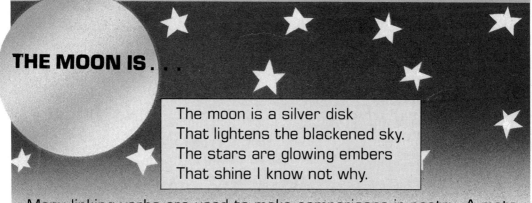

The moon is a silver disk
That lightens the blackened sky.
The stars are glowing embers
That shine I know not why.

Many linking verbs are used to make comparisons in poetry. A metaphor describes something by comparing it to something else without using the word *like* or *as*; for example, *The sea was a mirror*. Write a brief poem that contains at least two linking verbs. Above is an example.

GRAMMAR

Three levels of practice
Action Verbs (page 142)

LEVEL A. Write the action verb in each sentence.

1. Newspapers print the latest events.
2. Television also brings us news reports.
3. Newspapers carry long articles.
4. Newscasters report stories.
5. Newscasters show us pictures on television.
6. They interview people on camera.
7. Newspapers treat stories in more depth.
8. We learn more details about each story.

LEVEL B. Write each sentence. Underline each action verb.

9. Television news lasts only half an hour.
10. Commercials often interrupt the program.
11. Sound and pictures make the news exciting.
12. Newspapers contain many pages.
13. The articles offer us a great deal of information.
14. Reporters often describe events in detail.
15. They explore the reasons for current events.
16. Good reporters provide the background of news stories.

LEVEL C. Write a different action verb to complete each sentence. Use each verb only once.

17. Television _____ many entertaining programs.
18. Newspapers also _____ entertainment features.
19. My brother _____ the puzzles and comics.
20. Newspapers _____ articles about famous people.
21. However, television _____ us life in action.
22. We _____ sports programs rather than variety shows.
23. More and more people _____ television these days.
24. Probably fewer people _____ newspapers.
25. We still _____ newspapers for information, however.

EXTRA PRACTICE

Three levels of practice
Main Verbs and Helping Verbs (page 144)

LEVEL A. Write the verb phrase in each sentence. Underline the main verb in each phrase.

1. Inventors were designing airships before airplanes.
2. The first airplane flight had changed history.
3. The Wright brothers have created a legend.
4. Since 1903 everyone has known about them.
5. The first airship flight had occurred in 1852.
6. We may think of airships as cigar-shaped balloons.
7. Airships were kept in the air by gas.
8. Airplanes must depend on wings and motors.
9. Airships can hover in the air.
10. Airplanes must maintain a certain speed.

LEVEL B. Write the verb phrase in each sentence. Draw one line under each helping verb and two lines under each main verb.

11. Few people have used airships for transportation.
12. Airplanes are employed today for this purpose.
13. Airships had moved very slowly.
14. They were used occasionally in wartime.
15. Size and slowness may have made them easy targets.
16. The gas had caused another problem.
17. Pilots were using hydrogen gas in airships.
18. The hydrogen could cause an explosion.
19. The explosion of the Hindenburg has changed our thoughts.
20. Now blimps are lifted by helium.

LEVEL C. Write a sentence with each of these verb phrases.

21. should have
22. will be working
23. has gone
24. may have succeeded
25. could have flown

EXTRA PRACTICE

Three levels of practice

Direct and Indirect Objects (page 146)

Write each sentence. Underline the direct object.

1. Stories about Amazons fascinate readers.
2. The ancient Greeks told these legends.
3. In ancient Greece the men usually gave orders.
4. Among the Amazons, women ruled men.
5. Amazon women formed armies.
6. They trained their troops well.
7. They rode their horses with great skill.
8. Some legendary heroes challenged them.
9. These heroes started a war.

Write the underlined word in each sentence. Label it **direct object** or **indirect object**.

10. This challenge finally hurt <u>Athens</u>.
11. The Athenians showed the <u>Amazons</u> no mercy.
12. Then the Athenians offered their enemies <u>peace</u>.
13. Greek men gave their <u>wives</u> little freedom.
14. Stories of the Amazons taught women a <u>lesson</u>.
15. These stories showed <u>them</u> an example of courage.
16. The stories gave the <u>women</u> an ideal.
17. This ideal fueled their <u>struggle</u>.

Write the following sentences. Label the **direct object** and the **indirect object** in each sentence.

18. Greek myths offer us stories about the past.
19. These stories show people many truths.
20. Our teacher read us several Greek myths.
21. She gave the class some modern examples.
22. Susan B. Anthony showed women their rights.
23. She promised them the vote.
24. Eventually Anthony won women more freedom.
25. Many states guaranteed women equality.

GRAMMAR

EXTRA PRACTICE

Three levels of practice
Transitive and Intransitive Verbs (page 148)

LEVEL A.

Write the underlined verb. Label it **transitive** or **intransitive**.

1. In 1887 Gottlieb Daimler <u>produced</u> the first car.
2. The event <u>happened</u> in Germany.
3. Daimler <u>removed</u> the horse from a buggy.
4. He <u>installed</u> a gasoline engine in the buggy.
5. The engine <u>spluttered</u>.
6. It <u>frightened</u> horses and people.
7. Henry Ford <u>developed</u> cars in America.
8. He <u>gave</u> the cars his name.

LEVEL B.

Find and write each verb. Label each verb **transitive** or **intransitive**.

9. Eventually, in America cars succeeded.
10. At first, people preferred buggies with horses.
11. Later, cars gained more appeal.
12. Horses cost money.
13. They needed stables.
14. They ate grain.
15. They required grooms and equipment.
16. Most cars also needed shelter.
17. However, they ran smoothly.
18. They still needed repairs occasionally.
19. Cars worked better than horses.
20. They traveled faster and farther.

LEVEL C.

Write these sentences. Complete each sentence with a verb. Label each verb **transitive** or **intransitive**.

21. Henry Ford _____ the Model T.
22. Workers _____ the car on an assembly line.
23. Usually the cars _____ without problems.
24. They even _____ on time.
25. Many Americans _____ Ford's car.

Three levels of practice
Linking Verbs (page 150)

LEVEL
 A. Label the underlined verbs **action** or **linking**.

1. Jason Wing <u>took</u> a music class.
2. He <u>was</u> curious about musical instruments.
3. Two instruments <u>became</u> his favorites.
4. Both <u>were</u> very loud.
5. The drums <u>looked</u> easy.
6. He <u>tapped</u> a rhythm.
7. Jason <u>loved</u> the beat of the drums.
8. However, the trumpet <u>sounded</u> beautiful.
9. He <u>played</u> wonderful music.

LEVEL
 B. Write these sentences. Underline the verbs and label them **action** or **linking verb**.

10. Jason played melodies on the trumpet.
11. The trumpet sounded silvery.
12. It seemed simple.
13. The drums exercised his arms.
14. The trumpet was good for his breathing.
15. Drums are percussion instruments.
16. The trumpet is a brass instrument.
17. Finally, Jason chose the trumpet.

LEVEL
C. Write these sentences. Label the word or phrase after the verb **predicate noun** or **predicate adjective.**

18. Jason is a musician.
19. His choice of instruments was difficult.
20. On parade, the drum was heavy.
21. The trumpet is a delight.
22. The drum is a unique instrument.
23. However, the trumpet was beautiful.
24. In time, Jason grew fond of the trumpet.
25. The trumpet became Jason's instrument.

EXTRA PRACTICE

Three levels of practice
Present, Past, and Future Tenses (page 152)

LEVEL
A. Label each underlined verb **present**, **past**, or **future**.

1. Our art teacher <u>assigned</u> projects.
2. Last month Len <u>admired</u> some mobiles.
3. The mobiles <u>gave</u> him an idea for his project.
4. Len <u>will build</u> a simple mobile.
5. Mr. Lopez <u>helps</u> him with some directions.
6. Len <u>cuts</u> a length of string.
7. He <u>designed</u> shapes on construction paper.
8. Now he <u>will use</u> scissors.

LEVEL
B. Write each sentence. Underline each verb and write **present**, **past**, or **future** to show its tense.

9. Len added some shells to the pieces of paper.
10. He also uses some stiff, lightweight wires.
11. He will tie the wires to the string.
12. Then, he will attach the shells to the wires.
13. His classmates praised Len's work.
14. Teresa will mount one of her photographs.
15. She read directions in her photography book.
16. She assembles all the materials.

LEVEL
C. Write each sentence. Change each underlined verb to the tense named in parentheses.

17. First Teresa <u>needs</u> a mat board. (past)
18. Then she <u>found</u> an iron. (future)
19. She <u>placed</u> the photograph on the mat board. (present)
20. Then she <u>will cover</u> it with wrapping paper. (present)
21. Teresa also <u>uses</u> a ruler and a knife. (past)
22. She <u>glues</u> the photograph to the mat board. (past)
23. Then she <u>will iron</u> the photo gently. (past)
24. Now she <u>trimmed</u> the mat to the right size. (present)
25. Teresa <u>displays</u> her photo on the bulletin board. (future)

GRAMMAR

Three levels of practice
Principal Parts of Verbs (page 154)

LEVEL A. Write the present participle, the past, and the past participle of the following regular verbs. Be sure to include the helping verbs *is* or *has* when they are needed.

1. open
2. carry
3. cry
4. praise
5. walk
6. laugh
7. rub
8. pick
9. jog
10. rinse
11. slip
12. doze

LEVEL B. Write the underlined verb phrase in each sentence. Then write **present participle** or **past participle** to identify the main verb.

13. Engines <u>have powered</u> airplanes.
14. People <u>have compared</u> them to huge fans.
15. Those propellers <u>are pushing</u> the air backward.
16. They <u>are pulling</u> the airplane forward.
17. The Germans first <u>had experimented</u> with jets.
18. Jet airplanes <u>have traveled</u> faster than propeller planes.
19. Almost all airlines <u>are using</u> jet planes today.

LEVEL C. Write the verb phrase in each sentence. Then underline the main verb and label it **present participle** or **past participle**.

20. Jet planes have consumed more fuel than propeller planes.
21. Some jets have broken the sound barrier.
22. Airlines have used jets for many years.
23. Today, jet engines are powering most big planes.
24. Now engineers are designing faster planes.
25. Travel time between distant points is becoming shorter.

EXTRA PRACTICE

Three levels of practice
Irregular Verbs I (page 156)

LEVEL
A. Write the present participle, the past, and the past participle of the following irregular verbs. Be sure to include the helping verbs *is* or *has* where they are needed.

1. make   **4.** say   **7.** catch
2. do   **5.** grow   **8.** see
3. speak   **6.** take

LEVEL
B. Write the correct past or past participle of the verb in parentheses.

  9. Ben has (write) a report about astronomy.
10. Last week he (speak) to the class.
11. Ben (do) a good job.
12. He had (choose) his main points well.
13. His first sentence (catch) our attention.
14. Ben (speak) loudly and clearly.
15. The report had (make) a good impression.
16. Ben had (do) his research well.
17. His report (teach) us many interesting facts.

LEVEL
C. Write each sentence. Use the correct past or past participle form of the verb in parentheses.

18. Belief in astrology _____ in ancient times. (grow)
19. Many authors had _____ about the stars. (write)
20. People _____ omens in the sky. (see)
21. They _____ comets and eclipses as signs. (take)
22. Ancient astrologers _____ maps of the sky. (make)
23. They _____ the location of important stars. (know)
24. They _____ the movements of the planets. (teach)
25. The science of astronomy has _____ from astrology. (grow)

EXTRA PRACTICE

Three levels of practice
Irregular Verbs II (page 158)

LEVEL A. Write these sentences. Complete each sentence with the past tense of the irregular verb in parentheses.

1. Sandy and her family _____ to the beach. (go)
2. They _____ blankets and towels. (bring)
3. During the ride they all _____ songs. (sing)
4. Mr. Jordan _____ under an umbrella. (sit)
5. Sandy's brothers _____ into the ocean. (run)
6. The boys nearly _____ in the chilly water. (freeze)
7. The waves _____ quite far from shore. (break)
8. Charlie and Jim _____ the big waves. (ride)

LEVEL B. Write the sentences. Complete each sentence with the correct past-tense form or past participle of the verb in parentheses.

9. The Campbell family (go) north for their vacation.
10. They (come) to the Adirondack Mountains.
11. They had (bring) skis, boots, and poles.
12. During the ride they (drink) hot chocolate.
13. Ice had (freeze) the windshield.
14. Jeff (break) the ice with a scraper.
15. The car (draw) to a stop at the motel.
16. The children had (wear) heavy coats and scarves.
17. Then they (bring) their gear to the ski area.

LEVEL C. Write a sentence that uses the past or past participle of each irregular verb below. Label the verb as **past** or **past participle**.

18. wear
19. sing
20. break
21. sit
22. draw
23. ride
24. think
25. blow

EXTRA PRACTICE

Three levels of practice
Subject-Verb Agreement (page 160)

LEVEL A. Write the present-tense form of the verb in parentheses that agrees with the underlined subject.

1. Many <u>hobbies</u> (is, are) interesting.
2. <u>Irene</u> (buy, buys) stamps at a store.
3. <u>They</u> (has, have) stamps from many countries.
4. Irene's <u>father</u> (help, helps) with the collection.
5. The <u>girls</u> (compare, compares) stamps once a week.
6. <u>Beth</u> (bring, brings) the album.
7. <u>They</u> (locate, locates) the countries in an atlas.
8. Then the <u>girls</u> (paste, pastes) stamps in the album.

LEVEL B. Write each sentence. Use the correct verb in parentheses.

9. Phil (prefer, prefers) photography.
10. The boys (use, uses) Phil's new camera.
11. They (develop, develops) pictures in Ken's darkroom.
12. Landscapes (is, are) their favorite subjects.
13. Ken (choose, chooses) the correct film.
14. Both boys (select, selects) the shutter speed.
15. Phil (take, takes) the pictures.
16. Both friends (love, loves) photography.

LEVEL C. Write each sentence. Use the correct present-tense form of the verb in parentheses.

17. Fred (make) his own prints.
18. Polly (gather) leaves and feathers.
19. They (find) leaves with interesting textures.
20. Both friends (brush) the leaves with ink.
21. Fred (press) them between two sheets of paper.
22. Sometimes Polly (smudge) the ink.
23. Often they (use) light ink on dark paper.
24. A leaf (make) a beautiful design.
25. The friends' posters (be) works of art.

PRACTICE + PLUS

Three levels of additional practice for a difficult skill
Subject-Verb Agreement (page 160)

LEVEL A. Write the verb in parentheses that correctly completes each sentence.

1. Emma (raise, raises) sheep on her family's farm.
2. Sheep (requires, require) regular care.
3. Plants (is, are) the animals' diet.
4. All sheep (produce, produces) wool.
5. Their winter coats (give, gives) them a different appearance.
6. Emma's parents (shear, shears) the sheep in spring.
7. A large mill (buy, buys) the wool.
8. Emma's neighbors (recognize, recognizes) the sheep.

LEVEL B. Write these sentences. Use the verb in parentheses that correctly completes each sentence.

9. A sheep (yield, yields) wool, meat, and leather.
10. It (furnish, furnishes) raw materials for glue and soap.
11. Goats (is, are) different from sheep in some ways.
12. Most wild goats (live, lives) in Asia.
13. A goat (provide, provides) people with wool, meat, and milk.
14. Mohair (come, comes) from goats.
15. A goat's teeth (is, are) sharper than a sheep's teeth.
16. Both animals (walk, walks) on hooves, however.

LEVEL C. Complete each sentence with a different verb in the present tense. Make sure that the subjects and verbs agree.

17. A sheep _____ fresh water daily.
18. Emma _____ hay in the summer.
19. Her father _____ the hay.
20. Cuddly lambs _____ in late spring.
21. Then Emma _____ the hardest.
22. A lamb _____ a baby goat.
23. Goats _____ any vegetable in sight!
24. A lamb _____ indoors.
25. These animals _____ the pastures.

EXTRA PRACTICE

Three levels of practice
More About Subject-Verb Agreement (page 162)

LEVEL
A. Write the verb that correctly completes each sentence.

1. Every summer Jed's mother and father (rent, rents) a beach cottage.
2. Jed and his sister Sue (go, goes) with them.
3. The dunes on the trail (are, is) my favorite spot.
4. Trees and bushes (surround, surrounds) the dunes.
5. There (are, is) a lake along the trail.
6. Neither Sue nor Jed (swim, swims) well.
7. Luckily, there (are, is) lifeguards at the beaches.

LEVEL
B. Write these sentences. Use the correct present-tense form of the verb in parentheses.

8. There (be) a canal on the peninsula.
9. Tom or his brother (use) the bridge every day.
10. Quaint towns and villages (delight) visitors.
11. The museum or the historical society (give) tourists information.
12. There (be) miles of sandy beaches.
13. Artists and naturalists (admire) the landscape.
14. The forests or the beach (draw) them to the area.
15. Either the fishing industry or tourism (provide) most of the income.
16. Cranberries and strawberries (grow) in many areas.
17. Neither factories nor pollution (spoil) the beauty.

LEVEL
C. Complete each sentence with a verb in the present tense. Make sure that the subject and verb agree.

18. Jed or his sister _____ strawberries.
19. Neither Jed nor his parents _____ cranberries.
20. Jed's mother and father _____ on the beach.
21. There _____ seashells everywhere.
22. There _____ a cool breeze along the shore.
23. The wind and the waves _____ a soft sound.
24. Jed and Sue _____ their parents on the beach.
25. Neither Jed nor his sister _____ to leave.

GRAMMAR

Three levels of practice

Using Commas to Separate Words in a Series (page 164)

LEVEL A. Write these sentences. Use commas to separate words in a series.

1. Norm Mitch and Pat are friends.
2. They like baseball soccer and hockey.
3. Mitch's birthday is in one month one week and two days.
4. He gave a list to his father mother and sister.
5. He wants new skates a puck and a hockey stick.
6. Mitch knows the rules regulations and penalties of hockey.
7. Pat Norm and Ray are on his hockey team.
8. Parents teachers and friends attend the games.

LEVEL B. Write these sentences. Use commas to separate words in a series.

9. Carla Joy and Fran are best friends.
10. They love computers calculators and video games.
11. They eat sleep and breathe electronics.
12. Carla designed built and displayed a calculator.
13. This machine adds subtracts and multiplies.
14. She read understood and followed the directions.
15. She explained everything to her close intelligent and creative friends.
16. Mr. Donoso Mrs. Levine and Ms. Coe praised her.

LEVEL C. Write these sentences. Use commas to separate words in a series.

17. Ms. Ross campaigned in Ohio Indiana and Illinois.
18. She spoke at factories at colleges and at shopping malls.
19. Then she headed west toward Iowa Kansas and Nebraska.
20. There she saw farms villages and small towns.
21. She was interviewed by rude sharp and pushy reporters.
22. She answered questions clearly firmly and accurately.
23. She stressed social economic and political issues.
24. Many voters encouraged cheered and congratulated her.
25. Ms. Ross organized managed and directed her own campaign.

Three levels of practice
Vocabulary Building: Word Choice (page 166)

LEVEL
A. Write the word in parentheses that better fits the meaning of each sentence.

1. Roses have a wonderful (odor, fragrance).
2. Rotten eggs have a terrible (odor, fragrance).
3. That (cheap, inexpensive) jalopy needs many repairs.
4. We bought Dad that (cheap, inexpensive) silk tie.
5. Our favorite candidate gave a (pushy, forceful) speech.
6. Opponents criticized her (pushy, forceful) behavior.
7. My stupid jokes seemed (amusing, silly).
8. Her charming stories were (amusing, silly).

LEVEL
B. Use the word in parentheses that better fits each sentence.

9. The actors can (loaf, relax) after the audition.
10. Did that lazybones (loaf, relax) all weekend?
11. My (thrifty, stingy) brother did not lend me a dime.
12. The bank rewards (thrifty, stingy) depositors.
13. Small groups (chat, gossip) politely at the party.
14. The Kearns often (chat, gossip) about their neighbors.
15. The fair was (choked, crowded) with vacationers.
16. The main avenues were (choked, crowded) with traffic.

LEVEL
C. Write these sentences. Label the connotation of each underlined word **positive** or **negative**.

17. The coach thoughtfully encouraged us.
18. A forceful salesperson pressured you.
19. A moderate shower is forecast for today.
20. Despite the heavy downpour, we went outside.
21. The explorer carried cheap trinkets as gifts.
22. The jewelry went well with her elegant dress.
23. The speaker praised the graduates.
24. Ambitious persons flattered the king.
25. The boss complimented her assistant on his promotion.

6

Writing Explanations

Read the quotation and look at the picture on the opposite page. To what does Jane Yolen compare writing?

When you write an explanation, you will want to make your meaning plain and understandable. Your audience must be able to understand exactly what you mean.

Focus An explanation makes something clear. It may provide clear, concise directions about how to do something.

What would you like to explain? In this unit you will read an explanation and look at many photographs that will help you find ideas for writing an explanation.

THEME: *DIRECTIONS*

I have two pieces of advice for young people interested in writing. Read and read and read. Write every day because writing is like a muscle that needs to be flexed.

—Jane Yolen

Have you ever a seen a picture of a panda? Can you name some ways in which a panda looks like a bear? What other animals do you think are similar to a panda?

Pandas and bears share many features. However, these two animals are also very different. In some important ways pandas are more like raccoons than they are like bears!

As you read "Is a Panda a Bear?" look for information that the author gives to compare and contrast pandas with bears and raccoons.

IS A PANDA A BEAR?

from *Project Panda Watch*
by Miriam Schlein

The panda was not always known by the name "panda." The Chinese had always thought it was a kind of bear. Sometimes they called it the clawed bear or the bamboo bear. Other names for it were the harlequin bear, the speckled bear, and the cat-bear. Most often, it was called "bei-shung"—the white bear.

Is the panda a kind of bear?

In size and shape, it looks a lot like a bear. It climbs trees like a bear. And it moves and sits in a bearlike way. There is another way it resembles a bear. Its young are unusually small at birth as compared to the size of an adult. A mother grizzly bear may weigh 500 pounds (226 kilograms). Her newborn cub weighs about a pound (less than half a kilogram).

When Père David discovered the panda in 1879, he also thought it was some kind of bear. Since the person who discovers a new species has the honor of naming it, Père David gave it the name *Ursus melanoleucus*. This means, in Latin, "black and white bear."

Excited by his discovery, he sent a specimen of the animal—a skin and skeleton—to his friend, Professor Alphonse Milne-Edwards, in Paris. There, at the natural history museum, the new specimen was eagerly examined. Soon they saw things that made them disagree with Père David. They did not think the animal was a bear.

Important points of comparison and contrast are noted.

When scientists try and decide which animals are in the same "family" and are most closely related to each other, they don't just go by what the animal looks like, or by its behavior. There are other things they consider more basic. A similarity in the bone structure is considered important, especially foot and leg bones. Teeth and skull are also important. (Thus, for example, the hippo is considered more closely related to the giraffe than it is to the rhino, even though a hippo and rhino *look* more alike.)

Examining the remains of the panda, this is what Milne-Edwards and the others saw:

The skull did not resemble that of a bear. It was different in shape; shorter in the muzzle, and also heavier and more solid than a bear skull.

The jaws and teeth were not like those of a bear, either. Nor were the feet and legs. The skeleton in general was not really bearlike.

Then, examining the foot and leg bones more carefully, they saw the most telling feature of all—that extension of the wrist bone, creating the unusual sixth claw, or "panda's thumb."

No bear has anything like that. But they knew another animal that did; it was called the red panda. It was a small animal with reddish fur, a bushy, ringed tail, and a fox-like

bear

panda

raccoon

red panda

white face. It was in the raccoon family. Its scientific name was *Ailurus fulgens*, meaning "fire-colored cat."

Certainly Père David's animal and the red panda did not *look* alike. One was large and bearlike, the other small and raccoon-like. But they did have other important things in common. Their skulls were both short-muzzled and similar in shape. Their jaws and teeth were also quite similar. They were alike in another curious way: they both ate bamboo. (*Panda* is a Nepalese word meaning "bamboo-eater.")

As the scientists examined Père David's new specimen, they became more and more convinced that these two animals were closely related. If so, since the red panda was in the raccoon family, they felt the newly discovered animal must also be in the raccoon family. It was not a bear at all!

This meant it could not keep the name *Ursus* (bear) given to it by Père David. Its name was changed to *Ailuropoda melanoleucus*—meaning "black and white cat-foot."

Comparison and contrast is organized point by point. The points are linked by transition words.

As time went on, the larger panda was known as the Great Panda, and the small, fire-colored one called the Lesser Panda. We now call the large one the Giant Panda.

But the change in name did not settle the argument. Through the years, many scientists have felt that Père David *was* right, and that the giant panda does belong in the bear family. In their view, the fact that both kinds of pandas have the "panda's thumb" doesn't prove the giant panda is in the raccoon family, or even that the two animals are closely related. They feel that the red panda and the giant panda may simply have developed this unusual feature independently.

They feel the similarity in the two animals' teeth doesn't prove a close relationship, either. It is possible, they say, that both animals developed the same type of teeth because they both eat the same diet—bamboo.

They feel the two pandas are not in the same family, but belong in two different families: the giant panda in the bear family, and the lesser panda in the raccoon family.

New lab techniques developed in recent years have provided evidence for both sides of the panda argument. Blood can now be analyzed. The blood of the giant panda has been found to be more like bear blood than red panda blood.

That doesn't prove anything, say the people who believe the giant panda is a member of the raccoon family, because they have another new fact on *their* side. The giant panda has the same number of chromosomes as the raccoon (42). Different kinds of bears have been shown to have either 56 or 74 chromosomes.

Chromosomes are that part of the cell that carry the genes, which determine an animal's qualities. So this would seem to be an important point. We also know the stomach, liver, and intestines of the giant panda are more like that of a raccoon than that of a bear.

So, although the giant panda was discovered more than 100 years ago, the argument about it is still going on:

Is the giant panda a super-huge raccoon-type animal? Or is it a rather unusual bear-type animal?

George Schaller and many Chinese scientists do not agree with either side. They have a different point of view altogether. A giant panda is not a raccoon, they say. And it is not a bear. They feel the panda is a sufficiently different kind of animal to be in a family of its own. "A panda is a panda," says George Schaller.

Thinking Like a Reader

1. In what important ways are pandas like bears?
2. In what ways are pandas more like raccoons?
3. Do you think pandas are more like bears or raccoons?

Write your responses in your journal.

Thinking Like a Writer

4. How does the author compare and contrast pandas and bears? Does she first tell everything about pandas and then tell everything about bears? Or does she go back and forth between the two animals, point by point, telling how they are alike and how they are different?
5. Why do you think the author chose the technique she did to write the selection?
6. If you were going to compare and contrast two animals, what method would you use?

Write your responses in your journal.

Brainstorm *Vocabulary*

Clawed bear, bamboo bear, speckled bear, cat-bear, and *white bear*—the Chinese had many descriptive words for *panda*. Descriptive words add color and variety to your language. Think of some people, places, and things that you see every day—your friends, your house, or the family car. In your journal write one or more descriptive words for each person, place, or thing. Try to think of words that are a part of your everyday language. You can use your vocabulary list when you write.

Talk It Over
Hold a Debate

When you debate, you present arguments for or against something. Debate this question with a partner: Is a panda a bear? One partner should argue that a panda is a member of the bear family. The other partner should argue that the panda is a raccoon or that the panda is neither a bear nor a raccoon. Use details from the selection to support your positions. After a few minutes change positions and argue from the opposite point of view.

Quick Write
Writing Directions

Work with a partner. Think of two similar games or activities that you and your partner both enjoy. For example, you both might enjoy playing backgammon and Chinese checkers or swimming the backstroke and the crawl. On a sheet of paper, your partner will write the directions for how to do one item of the pair. On another sheet of paper, you will write the directions for doing the other item. When you are finished, compare the two sets of written directions. How many similarities do you find? What differences do you see?

Idea Corner
Think of Writing Topics

Comparing is showing how things are alike. Contrasting is telling how they are different. In your journal write any ideas that you might have for comparing and contrasting two people, places, or things. Under each idea write the headings *Similar* and *Different*. Then write down any points that you could compare and contrast for this idea.

Finding Ideas for Writing

Look at the pictures. Think about what you see.
What ideas about what to compare and contrast do these pictures
give you? Write your ideas in your journal.

1 GROUP WRITING:
Comparison and Contrast

COOPERATIVE LEARNING

Comparison and contrast writing shows how two things are alike and how they are different. When you plan this type of writing, your **purpose** usually is to inform your **audience**. Remember these elements in comparison and contrast writing.

- Topic Sentence
- Order of Details
- Transition Words

Topic Sentence

The underlined sentence below is important because it is the topic sentence. The **topic sentence** states the main idea of a paragraph. It lets the reader know what will be compared and contrasted in the sentences that follow.

> <u>The flutter kick and the dolphin kick are swimming kicks that are alike and different in some important ways.</u> In the flutter kick, first one leg and then the other leg is rapidly moved up and down in the water. By contrast, in the dolphin kick, both legs move up and down together. Swimmers use the flutter kick in two swimming strokes—the front crawl and the backstroke. The dolphin kick, however, is used in the butterfly stroke. For both the flutter kick and the dolphin kick, the legs must be straight and close together. Despite some differences, both kicks are useful and easy to perform while swimming.

Guided Practice: Stating a Topic Sentence

As a class, choose one pair from the list that follows. Then write different topic sentences for a paragraph that would compare and contrast the two items.

Example: Although they have some features in common, hurricanes and tornadoes are very different.

Venus and Earth   dogs and wolves   soccer and football

Order of Details

The **point-by-point** method is one way to order details in comparison and contrast writing. Using this method, a writer moves back and forth between two items, comparing and contrasting details of each. The paragraph about the two swimming kicks is ordered point by point. The writer could have organized the paragraph by first giving all the details about the flutter kick and then all the details about the dolphin kick. This method of ordering is called **item-by-item.**

Transition Words

Transition words help writers to compare and contrast. Words such as *similarly,* *both,* and *like* show comparisons. Words such as *however,* *but,* *by contrast,* *yet,* and *unlike* show contrast. Look back at the paragraph on page 200.

- Which points does the writer compare and contrast in the paragraph?
- Which transition words does the writer use to show comparison and contrast?

Guided Practice: Making a Comparison Chart

Recall the pair of items that you named in your topic sentence. As a class, make a chart like the one below. List the points that you could compare and contrast.

Points to compare and contrast	Flutter kick	Dolphin kick
How legs move	Legs alternate in up-and-down movement.	Legs move up and down at same time.
Swimming strokes	front crawl; backstroke	butterfly stroke
Position of legs	straight; close together	straight; close together

Putting a Comparison and Contrast Together

With your classmates you have written a topic sentence for a paragraph of comparison and contrast. You also have listed some points to compare and contrast.

Reread your topic sentence and look over your comparison chart. Will the points in the chart develop the main idea stated in the topic sentence? Should you add or remove any points from your comparison chart?

Look at one class's topic sentence and comparison chart.

Set shots and lay-ups are both common basketball shots that are similar, yet different.

Points to compare and contrast	Set shot	Lay-up
Player's location	usually far out on court	close to basket
Player's stance	standing with feet together	jumping off one foot
Grip on ball	two hands next to each other	ball lifted with both hands but shot with one hand

Notice that the topic sentence includes both items that are being compared and contrasted and mentions that they are both similar and different.

Guided Practice: Writing a Comparison and Contrast

As a group, write sentences that compare and contrast at least three points in your chart. Order the details point by point. Make sure that details are presented in a clear and orderly way. Remember to move back and forth between two items, comparing and contrasting details. Choose transition words that will help your readers see the similarities and differences.

Checklist: Comparison and Contrast

When you write a comparison and contrast, you will want to keep certain writing skills in mind. A checklist will remind you of the things to include in your writing.

Look at the checklist below. Make a copy of the checklist, complete it, and put it in your writing folder. Check off each item as you write.

CHECKLIST

✔ Purpose and audience

✔ Topic sentence

✔ _____

✔ Transition words

2 THINKING AND WRITING: Comparing and Contrasting

You have learned that you can use comparison and contrast writing to point out similarities and differences between people or things. In order to appreciate differences between two things, there have to be a number of similarities. For example, you could compare and contrast a ten-speed bike and a moped because both are two-wheeled vehicles. However, it would not be meaningful to compare a bike with a walking stick. They do not have enough points in common.

It is also important to choose topics that do not have too many differences. For example, you could compare and contrast a soccer ball and a basketball in one paragraph. However, you would not be able to compare the games of soccer and basketball in one paragraph. There are just too many ways in which they are different.

On the following journal page a writer has jotted down some possible pairs of topics to compare and contrast in a paragraph.

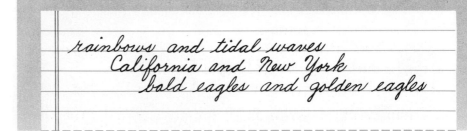

rainbows and tidal waves
California and New York
bald eagles and golden eagles

Thinking Like a Writer

- Which pair of topics do you think could be compared and contrasted in one paragraph? Why?

The best topic is bald eagles and golden eagles. The two birds have much in common, but they also have a few important differences. Also, unlike the others, the topic is narrow enough to be explained in one paragraph.

When you write, you will have to make choices, too. You will have to choose suitable items to compare and contrast.

COOPERATIVE
LEARNING

THINKING APPLICATION Comparing and Contrasting

Each of the writers below is planning to write a paragraph of comparison and contrast. Help each writer to choose a topic. You may wish to discuss your thinking with a small group of classmates. In your discussions explain your choices.

1. Seth wants to write about his new ten-speed bicycle. With which item could he best compare and contrast it?

   his old three-speed bicycle   his new roller skates
   the family station wagon   his sister's wagon

2. Kumiko wants to describe her violin. If you were Kumiko, to which item would you compare and contrast your violin?

   the radio   a guitar
   a set of drums   bird songs

3. Kristie recently moved from Texas to Wisconsin. She wants to compare her two homes. Which topics might be best for her paragraph?
   Texas and Wisconsin   Houston and Milwaukee
   life in the Southwest and life in the Midwest
   Los Robles Avenue, Houston and Hope Street, Milwaukee

4. Gavin wants to write about his pet parakeet. To which animal could he best compare and contrast it?

   a goldfish   an eagle
   a parrot   a garter snake

5. Carmella is intending to write about one of her favorite kinds of food—chili. To which item below could she best compare her topic?

   salad   stew
   soup   sauce

3 INDEPENDENT WRITING: Comparison and Contrast

Prewrite: Step 1

By now you know enough about comparing and contrasting to choose a writing topic. Raynell chose her topic in the following way.

Choosing a Topic

First, Raynell made a list of topics that were alike in some ways but different in others. Next, she thought about each pair of topics. Last, she decided on the best topic for her paragraph.

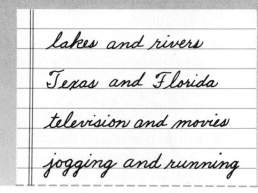

lakes and rivers

Texas and Florida

television and movies

jogging and running

Raynell thought the last topic might be best. The other topics seemed too broad.

Raynell explored the last topic by quickly jotting down some similarities and differences. She then checked her notes to make sure this topic was suitable to compare and contrast.

Exploring Ideas: Charting Strategy

Raynell decided that jogging and running would be good topics to compare and contrast. Many of her classmates also liked these sports. Her classmates would be a good **audience** for her writing. Raynell reminded herself of her **purpose** for writing. Her paragraph of comparison and contrast should explain to readers how jogging and running are alike and how they are different.

Before beginning to write, Raynell talked to some friends about jogging and running. They gave her some other ideas. At this point she made a comparison chart for her ideas.

Comparision Chart		
Points to compare and contrast	**Jogging**	**Running**
Purpose	relaxing exercise	competitive recreation
Benefits	physical fitness	physical fitness
Equipment	running shoes; shorts; T-shirt	running shoes; shorts; T-shirt
Speed	slower, but how slow?	faster; concerned with time/distance
Style	short strides; land heel first	longer strides? land toe first?

Thinking Like a Writer

- Which points on the chart show similarities?
- Which points show differences?
- Which points on the chart is Raynell unsure about?

YOUR TURN

Think of some pairs of things that you might like to compare and contrast. You may wish to refer to **Pictures** or to your journal for ideas. Follow these steps.

- List pairs of items that are alike and different.
- Choose the pair that interests you most. If necessary, narrow your topic.
- Quickly write down some similarities and differences.
- Decide whether you still think your topic is a good one.
- Think about your purpose and audience.

Make a comparison chart for your topic. You can add to or take away from your chart at any time.

Write a First Draft: Step 2

Raynell knows what comparison and contrast writing should include. She used a planning checklist. Raynell is now ready to write her first draft.

Raynell's First Draft

Jogging and Running seem the same. They are different. they are good ways to stay strong healthy and fit by moving the legs fast. Joggers do not compete with other people. They run to relax. Runners often races in competishuns They are concerned with speed and distance. Joggers take short steps and land flat on their feet. Runners takes longer steps and land differently. A jog is anything slower than eight miles an hour. A run is anything faster than that pace.

While Raynell was writing her draft, she did not worry about making errors. She wanted to put her ideas down on paper. She could go back to revise and correct her work later.

YOUR TURN

Write your first draft. Ask yourself these questions.

- What will my audience need to know?
- Are the points on my comparison chart the most important ones?
- How can I best arrange my information?

TIME-OUT You might want to take some time out before you revise. That way you will be able to revise your writing with a fresh eye.

Planning Checklist
- Remember purpose and audience.
- Include a topic sentence.
- Order details clearly.
- Use transition words.

Revise: Step 3

Raynell reread her first draft. Then she shared her paragraph with a classmate. She wanted some suggestions for improvements.

Raynell then looked back at her planning checklist. She noticed that she had forgotten one point. She checked it off so that she would remember it when she revised. Now Raynell has a checklist to use as she revises.

Raynell made the changes in her paragraph. She found additional information at the library. Notice that she did not correct small errors. She knew she could fix them later.

Turn the page. Look at Raynell's revised draft.

Revising Checklist
- ■ Remember purpose and audience.
- ■ Include a topic sentence.
- ■ Order details clearly.
- ✔■ Use transition words.

Jogging and Running seem the same. They are different. ~~they~~ *,but* *Both*
are good ways to stay strong healthy and fit by moving the
legs fast. Joggers do not compete with other people. They
run to relax. Runners often races in competishuns They are *By contrast,*
concerned with speed and distance. Joggers take short steps
and land flat on their feet. Runners takes longer steps and
land ~~differently~~. A jog is anything slower than eight miles *on their toes.*
an hour. A run is anything faster than that pace. *Although*
jogging and running are somewhat different,
both provide good exercise.

Thinking Like a Writer

WISE
WORD
CHOICE

- Which transition words did Raynell add? How do they improve her paragraph?
- Which sentences did Raynell combine? How did combining them improve her writing?
- What information did Raynell add? Do you think this information is important?

YOUR TURN

Read your first draft. Make a checklist. Ask yourself these questions.

- How can I improve my topic sentence?
- How can I state the similarities and differences more clearly?
- Have I ordered the information in a logical way?

  If you wish, ask a classmate to read your paragraph and to make suggestions. Then revise your writing.

Proofread: Step 4

Raynell knew that her work was not complete until she proofread her paragraph. She used a checklist.

Part of Raynell's Proofread Draft

¶Jogging and ⁁Running seem the same⁁ ᵇᵘᵗ They are different. ~~they~~ Both ⁀ are good ways to stay strong⁁ healthy⁁and fit by moving the legs fast. Joggers do not compete with other people. They run to relax. *By contrast,* Runners often races⁁ in ~~competishuns~~ *competitions*⊙ They are concerned with speed and distance. Joggers take short steps and land flat on their feet. Runners takes⁁ longer steps and land ~~differently~~ *on their toes.* A jog is anything slower than eight miles

YOUR TURN

Proofreading Practice

Use the paragraph below to practice your proofreading skills. Find the errors. Then, write the paragraph correctly on a separate sheet of paper.

Shuffling and overstriding is two problems runners face. shuffling occur becauz you don't lift your Thighs high enough. When you bring your foot forward, they scrape against the ground. This could cause you to stumble and hurt yourself Overstriders raise their thighs too high. they try to cover too much ground. This unnatural pace put too much strain on the leg mussels.

Proofreading Checklist
- Did I indent my paragraph?
- Did I spell all words correctly?
- Do subjects and verbs agree?
- Which punctuation errors do I need to correct?
- Which capitalization errors do I need to correct?

Applying Your Proofreading Skills

Now proofread your paragraph of comparison and contrast. Read your checklist again. Also review **The Grammar Connection** and **The Mechanics Connection**. Use the proofreading marks to make changes.

THE GRAMMAR CONNECTION

Remember these rules about making subjects and verbs agree.

- When the subject is a singular noun or pronoun, use the present-tense verb ending in *s* or *es*.

   That runner **takes** long strides. She **lands** on her toes.

- When the subject is a plural noun or pronoun, use a present-tense verb without the *s* or *es* ending.

   Runners **take** long strides. They **land** on their toes.

Check the sentences in your writing. Do all subjects and verbs agree?

THE MECHANICS CONNECTION

Remember this rule about using commas.

- Use a comma to separate words or groups of words in a series. A series contains three or more items.

   Joggers wear running shoes, shorts, and T-shirts.
   Runners are strong, healthy, and fast.

Check your writing. Have you used commas to separate items in a series?

Proofreading Marks

- ⁊ Indent
- ∧ Add
- ⩙ Add a comma
- ᵛᵛ Add quotation marks
- ⦵ Add a period
- ℓ Take out
- ≡ Capitalize
- / Make a small letter
- ∿ Reverse the order

Publish: Step 5

Raynell decided to share her paragraph of comparison and contrast. She carefully retyped her final paragraph and posted it on the bulletin board in the gym. The gym teacher and several classmates read it. Then they discussed other differences between jogging and running.

YOUR TURN

Make a final, neat copy of your paragraph. Think of a way to share your work. You might find some ideas in the **Sharing Suggestions** box below.

SHARING SUGGESTIONS

Make a diagram or poster that shows the two things that you have compared and contrasted. Display it with your paragraph on the bulletin board.	With your classmates, assemble your paragraphs to form a book called *Alike and Different*. Place it in the classroom library.	Read your paragraph to your classmates. Answer questions they may have about the similarities and differences you described.

4 SPEAKING AND LISTENING: Giving Instructions

In her paragraph of comparison and contrast, Raynell explained facts about jogging and running. After reading Raynell's paragraph, her classmate Wayne joined a track team and learned how to sprint. When the teacher asked Wayne to give oral directions for how to do something, Wayne explained how to start a sprint.

A good speaker uses note cards to help to recall the points he or she will make. The note cards list key words and phrases. They do not include oral instructions written word for word. Look at Wayne's note card.

Notes   How to Start a Sprint

1. "Take Your Mark" -- squat down on foot or knee; put soles against starting blocks; spread fingers; lean forward.
(display set of starting blocks)

2. "Set!" -- raise hips; shift weight forward

3. "Go!" -- push off rear foot; pump arms

Notice that the notes start with what the speaker will explain how to do. The actual steps of the instructions are listed in the order in which he will discuss them. There is also a reminder to show an object to illustrate his talk.

When you have to explain orally how to do something, it will help to keep some guidelines in mind. These speaking guidelines will help you to focus your talk.

SPEAKING GUIDELINES: Giving Instructions

1. Begin by clearly stating what you are going to explain.
2. Use transition words such as *first, next,* and *finally* to order the steps of the instructions.
3. Use illustrations, objects, or demonstrations to clarify or to add interest to your instructions.
4. Summarize the explanation in a closing sentence.

- Why is using logical order especially important when I am giving a set of directions or instructions?
- How do clear and precise details help my audience?

SPEAKING APPLICATION Giving Instructions

Choose something that you know how to do well. Perhaps you know how to make pizza or how to fix a flat tire. On a note card list the steps of the process that you will explain. Use the speaking guidelines to help you prepare. When you are ready, tell your classmates your instructions. Your classmates will use these guidelines as they listen to your explanation.

LISTENING GUIDELINES: Instructions

1. Listen for the order of the steps.
2. Listen for transition words.
3. Listen for a summary or closing sentence.

5 WRITER'S RESOURCES: The Library

The library is a useful resource for a writer. For example, Raynell went to the library to find out some of the differences between jogging and running. She knew that adding facts and details to her explanation would improve her writing.

In the library Raynell passed by the fiction section. Works of **fiction,** such as novels and short stories, are created from an author's imagination. These books are arranged alphabetically by the author's last name. To find the book *Charlotte's Web* by E.B. White, you would look among the books whose authors' last names begin with W.

Raynell went to the nonfiction section to look for a book about running. **Nonfiction** books contain factual information about real people, places, and events. They tell about subjects such as biology and baseball. Nonfiction books are numbered and arranged on shelves by subjects. The number of each book appears on the spine below the title.

Biographies and autobiographies are nonfiction. They tell about the lives of real people. Libraries alphabetize these types of books by the last name of the person whom a book is about.

The **reference** section is another important part of the library. In this section you will find encyclopedias, dictionaries, atlases, and almanacs.

Newspapers and magazines are **periodicals.** The *Readers' Guide to Periodical Literature* will help you to find magazine articles on particular subjects.

Practice

A. Arrange these fiction books in the order in which they would appear on the shelves of a library.

	Title	Author
1.	*My Side of the Mountain*	Jean George
2.	*Zia*	Scott O'Dell
3.	*Charlotte's Web*	E.B. White
4.	*The Witch of Blackbird Pond*	Elizabeth George Speare
5.	*The Summer of the Swan*	Betsy Byars
6.	*Rabbit Hill*	Robert Lawson
7.	*The Call of the Wild*	Jack London

B. Write whether each book could be found in the **fiction, nonfiction,** or **reference** section of the library.

8. *The Story of My Life* is an autobiography of Helen Keller.

9. *The Canadian Encyclopedia* is a three-volume set.

10. *Diving Basics* explains how to perform many dives.

11. *A Crown of Olives* is a novel set in Greece.

12. *Scientific American* is a monthly magazine.

13. *The World Almanac* contains information about education and transportation, for example.

14. *USA Today* is a national newspaper.

15. *Goode's School Atlas* has maps of the world.

WRITING APPLICATION A Comparison

Write a brief paragraph that compares and contrasts fiction books with nonfiction books. Be sure to tell how the library organizes each type of book.

6 WRITER'S RESOURCES: The Card Catalog

Raynell used the card catalog to find books about running. Each drawer of the card catalog is labeled with a range of letters. The cards inside each drawer are alphabetized by the information listed on the top line of each card.

Each library book usually has three cards: the **author card,** the **title card,** and the **subject card.** All three cards give the same information about the book, but in a different order. Notice that each card has the number of the book in the upper left-hand corner. This number is the **call number** and tells how the book is classified. For example, books about sports have call numbers in the 790s.

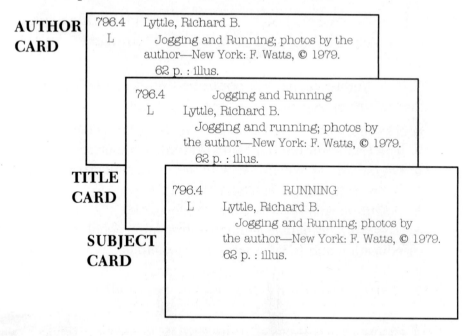

AUTHOR CARD

796.4 | Lyttle, Richard B.
L | Jogging and Running; photos by the author—New York: F. Watts, © 1979.
62 p. : illus.

TITLE CARD

796.4 | Jogging and Running
L | Lyttle, Richard B.
Jogging and running; photos by the author—New York: F. Watts, © 1979.
62 p. : illus.

SUBJECT CARD

796.4 | RUNNING
L | Lyttle, Richard B.
Jogging and Running; photos by the author—New York: F. Watts, © 1979.
62 p. : illus.

Use the author card when you know the author but not the title. Below the author's name are the title and more information about the book. Title cards are filed alphabetically by the first word in the title. If the first word is *A, An,* or *The,* the card is filed by the second word of the title.

Raynell was looking for a book on a particular topic—running. However, she did not have any authors or titles in mind. Therefore, Raynell looked in the card catalog under the heading *RUNNING*. There, she found a subject card for each book in the library about this topic.

Practice

A. Use the cards on page 218 to answer these questions.

    1. What is the title of the book?

    2. Who is the author?

    3. When was the book published?

    4. What is the name of the publisher?

    5. How many pages are there in the book?

    6. How is the book illustrated?

    7. How would you use the number in the upper left-hand corner?

B. Tell whether you would use an author card, a title card, or a subject card to answer each of the following questions.

    8. How many books in the library are by Jean Fritz?

    9. Who is the author of *April Morning*?

    10. Which books about tennis does the library have?

    11. Is there a biography of Marie Curie in the library?

    12. Besides *Stuart Little*, which books are by E. B. White?

    13. Who wrote *Hear the Wind Blow*?

    14. Is there a book in the library by Beth Day?

    15. Does the library have any books about polo?

WRITING APPLICATION Taking Notes

Use the card catalog in the library to look for books about health and physical fitness. List the titles and call numbers of three such nonfiction books. Then, find the books on the library shelves and take notes on how a person who is physically fit differs from someone who is out of shape.

Writing About Health

Raynell wrote about two different forms of exercise because she was interested in fitness and health.

What does the word *health* mean to you? Perhaps you think of being free of disease or of feeling good. You might think of health as being well adjusted or of getting along well with others. Health might consist of eating certain foods or exercising.

Physical fitness is a key to good health. When you are physically fit, you look better and feel better. You are also less likely to get sick. Fit people even seem to get along better with their families and friends. To keep fit, people all across the country are jogging and running, working out in gyms, and doing aerobics.

ACTIVITIES

Draw "Before and After" Cartoons   Use the information you have found in the library about physical fitness to draw two cartoons. In the first cartoon, draw an out-of-shape young American who is totally unconcerned about diet or exercise. In the second cartoon, show the same student after he or she has become a health-and-fitness enthusiast. In a paragraph, contrast the two cartoons, point by point, describing ways in which this person is different from the way he or she was before.

Tell How to Do It   Find a diagram that shows an athlete doing a pole vault or some other move in a sport. Study each step of the process. Then, write an explanation telling how to perform the move.

Respond to Literature   Althea Gibson is one of the greatest tennis champions that the United States has produced. This excerpt from a biography about her compares fourteen-year-old Althea with the other players at a local tennis club. After reading the excerpt, write a response. Your response might be a conversation between Althea and another member of the club that brings out the differences between them.

Althea Gibson

Now in those days the Cosmopolitan Tennis Club was, in Althea's words, "*the* ritzy tennis club in Harlem. All the Sugar Hill society people belonged to it." And Althea's family was definitely not Sugar Hill. Her father worked in a garage, where he earned just about enough to support his wife and Althea, her brother, and three sisters. In any case, Althea wasn't exactly the sort of girl one found on the Cosmopolitan courts. A tough street kid, she would probably have been more at home, she reflected later, training in Stillman's Gym than playing tennis amidst Harlem's elite on the carefully kept courts of the Cosmopolitan Club. But she could hit the ball. Oh, how she could hit it! So the members of the club, hoping they were nourishing a future champion, chipped in to buy Althea a junior membership and provide her with lessons . . .

UNIT CHECKUP

LESSON 1

Group Writing: Comparison and Contrast (page 200) Read the following paragraph of comparison and contrast. On a sheet of paper, write a topic sentence for the paragraph.

Runners find the morning a pleasant time to run. By contrast, they find the afternoon to be tiring. The morning is quiet and cool. Traffic makes running in the afternoon less relaxing. It is easy to run in the morning. However, running in the afternoon is harder to schedule. Still, all running is good exercise.

LESSON 2

Thinking: Comparing and Contrasting (page 204) Imagine that you are writing a paragraph of comparison and contrast. Explain why each pair of topics would or would not be a good choice for a paragraph.

1. tennis and scuba diving
2. skateboards and roller skates
3. the U.S. and Canada
4. balloons and blimps

LESSON 3

Writing to Compare and Contrast (page 206) Think of two different routes from your house to a local shopping center. Write a paragraph that compares the two routes.

LESSON 4

Speaking and Listening: Giving Instructions (page 214) Imagine you will give oral directions on how to get from school to your home. Make a note card to recall your points.

LESSON 5

Writer's Resources: The Library (page 216) Write the names of five books you would find in each of these sections of a library: fiction, nonfiction, and reference.

LESSON 6

Writer's Resources: The Card Catalog (page 218) Think of a topic for a nonfiction book that you would like to write. On a separate sheet of paper, make up an author card, a title card, and a subject card for your book that might appear in the card catalog of the library.

THEME PROJECT  DIRECTIONS

Directions can tell how to find places, how to make things, or how to play sports. You also have learned that directions must be given in logical order.

Now have some fun with directions. Look at this ridiculous contraption. It was designed to help an out-of-shape person start jogging. All that is missing is an explanation of how it works. Study the picture and discuss it with a small group of classmates. Explain to one another how you think this machine functions. You might compare and contrast it with other, more familiar machines.

Choose one of the following activities.

- Try to imagine a better exercise machine than the one in the picture. Your invention can be serious or silly. Draw a picture of the exercise machine and write an explanation of how it works.

- Think of a new sport that would be fun to play and that would promote physical fitness at the same time. Write directions that explain how to play this sport.

- Compare and contrast two similar sports.

UNIT

7

Pronouns

In Unit 7 you will learn about pronouns. Using pronouns is a convenient way to avoid repeating nouns in your writing.

Discuss Read the poem on the opposite page. How do you think the writer in the picture is feeling?

JOURNAL

Creative Expression The unit theme is *Communications*. How could you communicate with people in the future? One way would be to write a message and then preserve it. What would you tell the people of tomorrow about our world? You might write your message as a poem or as song lyrics. Write your thoughts in your journal.

I have to stop writing now.
I have to go. You see
I am writing because
I am lonesome without you seeing me.

—Myra Cohn Livingston, from "For Laura"

1 PERSONAL PRONOUNS

A pronoun is a word that takes the place of one or more nouns and the words that go with the nouns.

To avoid repeating nouns, you can replace nouns with **pronouns**. **Personal pronouns** usually refer to persons.

Joanna studied the script. **She** studied at home.

Some pronouns are used as the subject of a sentence. A pronoun used as a subject is called a **subject pronoun.**

The lines are difficult. **They** are hard to learn.

An **object pronoun** is used as the object of a verb or as the object of a preposition, such as *to*, *in*, or *at*.

Roberto's teacher helped **him.**
The teacher gave the script to **him.**

Subject Pronouns		Object Pronouns	
Singular	Plural	Singular	Plural
I	we	me	us
you	you	you	you
he, she, it	they	him, her, it	them

Guided Practice

Name the pronoun in each sentence.

Example: She was in the play.   *She*

1. I asked Roberto for help.
2. He and Dan are working backstage.
3. They volunteered for the Stage Club.
4. The director handed us a script.
5. Mrs. Rios gave voice lessons to them.

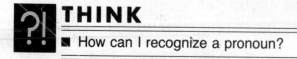

THINK

■ How can I recognize a pronoun?

REMEMBER

- A **pronoun** takes the place of one or more nouns and the words that go with the nouns.
- A **subject pronoun** is used as the subject of a sentence. An **object pronoun** is used as the object of a verb or as the object of a preposition.

More Practice

A. Write the personal pronoun in each sentence.

Example: The director asked her about the role.   *her*

6. The students asked if they could put on a play.
7. The principal said he wanted a good performance.
8. Mrs. Rios chose a play and said it was a comedy.
9. Joanna said that she wanted a leading role.
10. Roberto said that he would work backstage.
11. Mrs. Rios looked at Roberto and thanked him.
12. "Roberto, you will have to stay after school."
13. Roberto replied, "I don't mind working late."

B. Write each sentence. Draw one line under each personal pronoun. Label each pronoun **subject** or **object.**

Example: Every day <u>we</u> rehearsed after school.   *subject*

14. The students worked hard, and they finished rehearsals.
15. Joanna had many lines, but she memorized them.
16. She remembered all the lines on opening night.
17. The whole school applauded her.
18. Joanna ran off the stage and hugged me.
19. We were both happy.
20. Joanna wrote to Tom to tell him the good news.

Extra Practice, page 250

WRITING APPLICATION A Personal Narrative

Write a brief paragraph that describes a satisfying experience that you have had. Exchange papers with a classmate and identify the pronouns in each other's work.

2 PRONOUNS AND ANTECEDENTS

Remember that pronouns take the place of nouns. The noun that a pronoun refers to is called the **antecedent**. The antecedent includes any words that go with the noun. Make sure that you have a clear antecedent for every pronoun, or the meaning of your writing will be unclear.

Emily wanted a good grade, and **she** worked hard.

Pronouns and antecedents must agree in number. Always use a singular pronoun to refer to a singular antecedent. Use a plural pronoun to refer to a plural antecedent.

SINGULAR: **Emily** went to the library, where **she** wrote a report.
Dad read the **report** and liked **it**.

PLURAL: The **students** cheered because **they** were happy.
When **Emily and I** write good reports, **we** feel proud.

Guided Practice

Tell which word in each sentence is a pronoun. Then name its antecedent.

Example: Dad missed Emily and called her often.
        her   pronoun   Emily   antecedent

1. Emily called Bill and then wrote him a letter.
2. The student wrote a report and enclosed it.
3. Emily wrote to Dad and told him of the report.
4. Emily wrote to her parents because they were out of town.
5. Dad likes Emily's reports and always reads them aloud.
6. Emily went to the library, and she looked up Alexander Graham Bell.
7. Illness brought Bell to Canada, where he lived for years.

 THINK

■ How can I decide which noun is the antecedent of a pronoun?

REMEMBER

■ The **antecedent** of a pronoun is the word or group of words
to which the pronoun refers.

More Practice

A. Write each pronoun and its antecedent.

Example: The teacher asked the class to read to her.

her pronoun   teacher antecedent

8. The students asked the librarian for her help.
9. The librarian said, "Please come to me for any book."
10. The librarian was helpful, and Emily said, "Thanks, you
   have really helped."
11. Emily admired Bell and wrote about him.
12. Bell taught deaf pupils because they wanted to learn to speak.
13. Bell used "Visible Speech" because it helped the deaf.

B. Write each of the pronouns and its antecedent.

Example: Bell met Watson in 1875. He asked Watson for
   help.   *He pronoun   Bell antecedent*

14. Watson and Bell worked together. They carried out
   experiments on electricity.
15. Watson spoke into the telephone. It carried the sound to Bell.
16. Bell had invented the telephone. People congratulated him.
17. Later, other people claimed the invention. They took Bell to
   court.
18. Bell was angry. He fought the case.
19. The Supreme Court ruled in favor of Bell. It upheld that he
   had invented the first telephone.
20. Bell invented other devices. He hoped they would help the deaf.

Extra Practice, page 251

WRITING APPLICATION A Diary Entry

Imagine that you are Bell's assistant, Watson. Write a
diary entry that tells how you helped with the invention.
Identify the antecedent of each pronoun you use.

3 USING PRONOUNS CORRECTLY

You know that pronouns can be used as subjects or objects in sentences.

SUBJECT PRONOUN	OBJECT PRONOUN
She needs a pencil.	Tod lent **her** one.

Use a subject pronoun as the subject of a sentence.

CORRECT: **They** are new pencils.

INCORRECT: **Them** are new pencils.

Use an object pronoun when the pronoun is the object of a verb or the object of a preposition. Use an object pronoun even when the pronoun is part of a compound object.

CORRECT: Tod spoke with **her**.

INCORRECT: Tod spoke with **she**.

CORRECT: The teacher helped **Tod and me**.

INCORRECT: The teacher helped **Tod and I**.

Check your usage by saying the sentence aloud with only the pronoun in it. Your ear will be your guide.

CORRECT: The teacher helped **me**.

INCORRECT: The teacher helped **I**.

Guided Practice

Choose the correct pronoun to replace the underlined noun or nouns.

Example: Melissa likes <u>Amy</u> very much. (she, her)   *her*

1. <u>Tod</u> wrote a letter to his friend. (He, Him)
2. He told <u>Rob</u> about camp. (he, him)
3. Tod also wrote to <u>Amy</u>. (she, her)
4. <u>Amy</u> met Tod at camp. (She, Her)
5. Tod and <u>Amy and Melissa</u> are friends. (they, them)

THINK

- How can I decide whether to use a subject pronoun or an object pronoun?

REMEMBER

- Use a subject pronoun when the pronoun is the subject of a sentence.
- Use an object pronoun when the pronoun is the object of a verb or the object of a preposition.

More Practice

A. Write the pronoun that could replace the underlined word or words.

Example: Amy met <u>Melissa</u> at school. (she, her)   *her*

6. Tod met <u>Amy and Melissa</u> at Camp Dune. (they, them)
7. <u>Tod, Amy, and Melissa</u> liked each other. (They, Them)
8. <u>Melissa</u> planned some bike trips. (She, Her)
9. Melissa wrote <u>Tod</u> a note. (he, him)
10. "<u>Amy and I</u> will see you on Sunday morning." (We, Us)
11. Tod answered <u>Amy and Melissa</u>. (they, them)
12. "Look for <u>Rob and me</u> at the lake." (we, us)

B. Write each sentence, using the correct pronoun.

Example: Rob told (I, me) about archery class.
          Rob told me about archery class.

13. TOD: Rob and (I, me) are ready for archery class.
14. AMY: Do you want Melissa and (I, me) in your class?
15. TOD: Yes, (we, us) could all take it together.
16. AMY: Doesn't (she, her) hate archery?
17. TOD: No, she taught (I, me) all about archery.
18. AMY: Maybe I misunderstood (she, her).
19. TOD: Ask (she, her) again.
20. AMY: (She, Her) and (I, me) will take crafts instead.

Extra Practice, page 252, **Practice Plus,** page 253

WRITING APPLICATION A Dialogue

COOPERATIVE LEARNING

With a small group of classmates, write a dialogue that describes a summer experience, for example, camping. Check for the correct usage of object and subject pronouns.

4 PRONOUNS IN COMPOUND SUBJECTS AND OBJECTS

Sometimes you use a pronoun as part of a compound subject. A compound subject is two or more simple subjects that are joined by *and* or *or* and that have the same predicate. Always use a subject pronoun when the pronoun is part of a compound subject.

Amy and John wrote often.   Amy and **he** wrote often.

Use an object pronoun when the pronoun is part of a compound direct object or a compound object of a preposition.

She missed John and Amy.   She missed John and **her**.
Sue wrote to Amy and John.   Sue wrote to Amy and **him**.

If you use the pronoun *I* or *me* in a compound subject or compound object, it is polite to put it last.

Amy and **I** wrote often.
Pat wrote to Amy and **me**.

Guided Practice

Choose the correct pronoun for each sentence.

Example: John sent a letter to Anita and (I, me).   me

1. John and (I, me) have never met.
2. (He, Him) and his parents live in England.
3. John writes to Anita and (I, me).
4. He tells our friends and (we, us) about his life.
5. In return, we tell (he, him) and his friends about life here in the United States.

 THINK

■ How do I decide which pronoun to use in a compound subject or object?

She and he wrote often.

REMEMBER

- Use a subject pronoun in a compound subject.
- Use an object pronoun in a compound object.

More Practice

A. Choose the correct word in parentheses to complete each sentence. Write the sentences.

Example: My friends and (I, me) have pen pals.

My friends and I have pen pals.

6. Ms. Liu told my friends and (I, me) about pen pals.
7. (She, Her) and Mr. Green talked about letter writing.
8. (Anita and I, I and Anita) want to write good letters.
9. (Her, She) and I make lists of ideas to include.
10. Will my ideas interest John's friends and (he, him)?
11. Mr. Green encouraged my classmates and (we, us).
12. John and (they, them) are unfamiliar with our land.
13. Our use of the language might confuse (they, them) and their friends.
14. The teachers and (us, we) discussed our rough drafts.
15. They helped (Anita and me, me and Anita) to write better.

B. Write each sentence with a pronoun that completes it.

Example: My friends and _____ enjoy John's letters.

My friends and I enjoy John's letters.

16. John shows them to Anita and _____.
17. The British and _____ have much in common.
18. Nevertheless, John's letters surprise our teachers and _____.
19. _____ and his friends eat foods with names like "toad in a hole."
20. They eat _____ with beans at a meal called "tea."

Extra Practice, page 254

WRITING APPLICATION A Summary

Write a summary of several things that you would like to tell a pen pal in a foreign country. Check a partner's summary to see if pronouns have been used correctly.

POSSESSIVE PRONOUNS

Possessive pronouns show who or what owns something.

Mary Chen's books were on the table.
Her books were on the table.

There are two forms of possessive pronouns. One form is used before nouns. The other always stands alone.

Their rulers were missing.   **Theirs** were missing.

Possessive Pronouns			
Used before nouns		**Used alone**	
my	our	mine	ours
your	your	yours	yours
his, her, its	their	his, hers, its	theirs

Remember that, unlike contractions, possessive pronouns do not have apostrophes.

Possessive Pronouns	your	its	their
Contractions	you're (you are)	it's (it is)	they're (they are)

Guided Practice

Choose the pronoun that correctly completes each sentence.

Example: Mary discussed (her, hers) subject with Juan. *her*

1. Juan's topic is smoke signals, but (her, hers) is not.
2. Your topic is easy, but (my, mine) is difficult.
3. (Their, They're) topic is the telegraph.
4. (Her, Hers) teacher wants oral, not written, reports.

 THINK

■ How can I tell the difference between a possessive pronoun and a contraction?

REMEMBER

- A **possessive pronoun** is a pronoun that shows who or what owns something.
- Possessive pronouns never contain an apostrophe.

More Practice

A. Write the possessive pronoun in each sentence and indicate whether it comes **before a noun** or **stands alone**.

Example: Ours is a history project.　　*Ours*　　*stands alone*

5. His project requires a lot of research.
6. The Pony Express is the subject of my report.
7. I think that mine is the most interesting topic.
8. The Pony Express had a major role in our mail service.
9. Its purpose was to carry mail to California.
10. A rider changed his horse in two minutes.
11. The responsibility for the mailbag was his.
12. Young riders rode their horses at top speed.
13. Theirs was an important mission.

B. Write each sentence. Use the correct word in parentheses.

Example: Mary wrote a letter to (her, hers) brother.
　　　　Mary wrote a letter to her brother.

14. (Her, Hers) was a long letter.
15. (He's, His) response came quickly.
16. "(Your, You're) topic sounds interesting," he replied.
17. "Perhaps (our, ours) neighborhood library can help."
18. "(It's, Its) collection on history is excellent."
19. "(Our, Ours) is not a big library," Mary thought.
20. "(Your, Yours) is much better than (our, ours)."

Extra Practice, page 255

WRITING APPLICATION A Comparison

Look up an early means of communication. Write a paragraph that compares such a method to modern methods. Identify the possessive pronouns in a classmate's work.

USING *WHO*, *WHOM*, AND *WHOSE*

Some pronouns help you to ask questions. The pronoun **who** has three forms—**who, whom,** and **whose.**

Use **who** as a subject pronoun.

> **Who** invented the telegraph?

Use **whom** as an object pronoun.

> **Whom** did you telegraph?

You can often tell whether to use *who* or *whom* by replacing it with a different subject or object pronoun.

SUBJECT	DIRECT OBJECT
Who invented the telegraph?	**Whom** did you telegraph?
He invented the telegraph.	Did you telegraph **him**?

Whose is a possessive pronoun. It asks about ownership.

> **Whose** telegram is this?

Do not confuse *whose* with the word *who's*, which is a contraction for *who is*. Remember that, like all possessive pronouns, *whose* never has an apostrophe.

POSSESSIVE	CONTRACTION
Whose invention came first?	**Who's** the inventor?
His invention came first.	**He's** the inventor.

Guided Practice

Choose the correct word for each sentence.

Example: (Whose, Who's) idea was the Morse code? *Whose*

1. (Who, Whom) used the first telegraphs in the 1840s?
2. (Who, Whom) did Samuel Morse help with his invention?
3. (Who, Whom) linked cities with telegraph wires?
4. (Who, Whom) does the telegraph serve today?
5. (Whose, Who's) lives were changed by this device?

?! THINK

- How can I decide whether to use *who, whom,* or *whose*?

REMEMBER

- Use the pronoun *who* as a subject.
- Use the pronoun *whom* as an object.
- Use the possessive pronoun *whose* to show ownership.

More Practice

A. Write the word that correctly completes each sentence.

Example: (Who, Whom) invented the typewriter?   *Who*

6. (Who, Whom) did he work with on the typewriter?
7. (Whose, Who's) work on it was most important?
8. (Who, Whom) would this invention affect the most?
9. (Who, Whom) in your class types the fastest?
10. (Whose, Who's) the inventor of the radio?
11. (Who, Whom) did Marconi hope to serve with it?
12. (Whose, Who's) new scientific ideas did Marconi use?
13. (Who, Whom) improved upon Marconi's early radio?

B. Write **who, whom, whose,** or **who's** to complete each sentence correctly.

Example: _____ likes television?   *Who*

14. _____ is the inventor of television?
15. _____ did John Baird impress with his experimental TV?
16. _____ homes received the first telecasts in 1936?
17. _____ did President Truman address in the first nation-wide telecast?
18. _____ inventions made color TV possible in 1953?
19. _____ uses TV today to broadcast messages?
20. _____ your favorite TV character?

Extra Practice, page 256

WRITING APPLICATION An Interview

Imagine that you are about to interview an inventor. Prepare a list of questions for the interview. Concentrate on asking who did what. Then, compare your questions with a partner's.

---

7 INDEFINITE PRONOUNS

You know that the noun referred to by a pronoun is called the antecedent of the pronoun. An **indefinite pronoun**, however, does not refer to a particular person, place, or thing.

Someone left the window open.
Anybody could have done that.

Some indefinite pronouns are singular; others are plural.

no one
Memorize

Indefinite Pronouns				
Singular			**Plural**	
anybody	everybody	nothing	all	most
anyone	everyone	somebody	both	others
anything	everything	someone	few	several
each	nobody	something	many	some

Remember that when an indefinite pronoun is used as a subject, the verb must agree with it.

SINGULAR: **Everyone** is cold.
PLURAL: **Some** are shivering.

Guided Practice

For each sentence, tell which word is the indefinite pronoun and which verb agrees with it.

Example: Many (has, have) helped us.   *Many have*

1. Someone (has, have) left the tent flap open.
2. Everybody (is, are) freezing in here.
3. Few (has, have) warm enough clothing.
4. Everything outside (is, are) covered with snow.
5. Both my feet (was, were) icy cold.

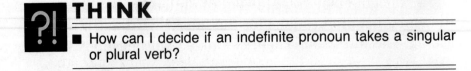

THINK

■ How can I decide if an indefinite pronoun takes a singular or plural verb?

REMEMBER

- Use a singular verb with a singular indefinite pronoun.
- Use a plural verb with a plural indefinite pronoun.

More Practice

A. Write the verb that agrees with each underlined indefinite pronoun.

Example: <u>Someone</u> (has, have) sent me three notes.   *has*

6. <u>All</u> (was, were) addressed, "Dearest Nicole."
7. <u>One</u> (was, were) decorated with *X*'s and *O*'s.
8. <u>Others</u> (was, were) decorated with hearts.
9. <u>Something</u> (tells, tell) me I have a secret admirer.
10. In the tent at camp <u>everyone</u> (wonder, wonders).
11. <u>Several</u> of the campers (guess, guesses) about it.
12. <u>Someone</u> (says, say) Kyle wrote the note.
13. <u>All</u> (enjoys, enjoy) the guessing game.

B. Write each sentence and underline the indefinite pronoun. Use the correct verb form.

Example: Everyone (is, are) ready for the camping trip.
    <u>Everyone</u> is ready for the camping trip.

14. Someone (is, are) going to lead us up the mountain.
15. Last time, somebody (was, were) hurt in a fall.
16. Everyone (was, were) nearly frozen on the mountain.
17. Most of us (seem, seems) willing to go.
18. But some of us (has, have) doubts about this trip.
19. Both of our counselors (is, are) a little upset.
20. However, everything (is, are) packed already.

Extra Practice, page 257

WRITING APPLICATION A Story

Think of an outdoor adventure that you have had, like camping in cold weather. Write a brief story that tells what happened. Have a classmate check that you have used indefinite pronouns correctly. Then share your story.

GRAMMAR

MECHANICS: Abbreviations

Some words are abbreviated, or shortened, to make writing them simpler. Many **abbreviations** begin with a capital letter and end with a period. Abbreviations for the names of the states are in the **Handbook** on page 506.

Abbreviations						
Titles	Mister	Mr.	Doctor	Dr.	Governor	Gov.
Days	Monday	Mon.	Thursday	Thurs.	Saturday	Sat.
	Tuesday	Tues.	Friday	Fri.	Sunday	Sun.
	Wednesday	Wed.				
Months	January	Jan.	April	Apr.	October	Oct.
	February	Feb.	August	Aug.	November	Nov.
	March	Mar.	September	Sept.	December	Dec.
Streets	Street	St.	Avenue	Ave.	Drive	Dr.
	Road	Rd.	Place	Pl.	Boulevard	Blvd.

Abbreviations for time use capital letters and periods.

9:30 **A.M.** (ante meridiem) 5:30 **P.M.** (post meridiem)

Abbreviations for agencies use capital letters and no periods.

FBI (Federal Bureau of Investigation)

Guided Practice

Tell the abbreviation for each underlined item.

Example: <u>Sunday</u>, May 10   Sun.

1. <u>Doctor</u> Maria Narvaez
2. <u>October</u> 25, 1988
3. <u>Environmental Protection Agency</u>
4. 3456 Kennedy <u>Boulevard</u>
5. Chicago, <u>Illinois</u>

 **THINK**

■ How do I decide how to abbreviate a word?

REMEMBER

- An **abbreviation** is the shortened form of a word.
- Most abbreviations begin with a capital letter and end with a period.

More Practice

A. Write the abbreviation for each underlined item.

Example: <u>Governor</u> Olga Funes   *Gov.*

6. 84 Los Alamos <u>Drive</u>
7. 1:30 <u>ante meridiem</u>
8. <u>Tuesday</u>
9. <u>Columbia Broadcasting System</u>
10. <u>Representative</u> Sam Hill
11. <u>February</u>
12. St. Louis, <u>Missouri</u>
13. <u>Reverend</u> Molly Paris
14. <u>Federal Deposit Insurance Corporation</u>

B. Find one item to abbreviate in each sentence. Write the item and its abbreviation.

Example: The Federal Communications Commission regulates radio and television stations.
          Federal Communications Commission   FCC

15. It is based in Washington, District of Columbia.
16. The commission contacted Mister Thomas Hicks recently.
17. He has a new radio station on Steele Avenue.
18. In April the station was assigned a radio frequency.
19. Senator Jackson has described the commission's work.
20. Last Thursday the commission approved rate increases.

Extra Practice, page 258

WRITING APPLICATION A Chart

With a partner, create a chart of words that can be abbreviated, along with their abbreviations. Have other classmates add items to your chart.

COOPERATIVE LEARNING

---

9 VOCABULARY BUILDING: Homophones and Homographs

Sometimes words are confused because they sound alike or are spelled alike. Be careful to choose the exact word you mean.

Homophones are words that sound alike but have different spellings and different meanings. Use a dictionary to help you decide which homophone to use.

right	correct	**sew**	do needlework
write	send a letter	**so**	very, extremely
		sow	plant seeds

Homographs are words that are spelled the same but have different meanings and may have different pronunciations.

roll	a kind of bread	**stand**	to endure
roll	to turn over	**stand**	to hold oneself upright

To understand the correct meaning of a homograph, look at the context in which it appears—that is, the other words in the sentence.

I cannot **stand** having my picture taken.

Stand still while I take your picture.

Guided Practice

Tell which word in parentheses correctly completes each sentence.

Example: Do (not, knot) leave the path.   *not*

1. Last year a guide (led, lead) us through these woods.
2. We did not (no, know) what to expect.
3. He asked us not to (brake, break) any branches.
4. The sky was a (pail, pale) shade of gray.
5. The wind (blue, blew) around us all day.

 THINK

■ How can I decide the correct spelling of a homophone?

REMEMBER

- **Homophones** are words that sound alike but have different spellings and different meanings.
- **Homographs** are words that are spelled the same but have different meanings and sometimes different pronunciations.

More Practice

A. Write each sentence, choosing the correct word in parentheses.

Example: Rosa is (sew, so) angry.   *so*

6. Did Rosa find a misleading (ad, add)?
7. The advertisement seemed (plane, plain) enough.
8. It offered a choice of (to, two) horses.
9. The horses looked quite (real, reel).
10. She wanted the one with the silky red (mane, main).
11. Rosa sent her money by (male, mail).
12. The horse came in a box with postage (due, do).
13. It was a stuffed horse with (course, coarse) hair.
14. "(It's, Its) not real!" she cried.
15. She exclaimed, "I cannot (bare, bear) this deception!"

B. Read each homograph below. Write two definitions for each. Use a dictionary if needed.

Example: wind   *1. to turn   2. air in motion*

16. roll
17. stand
18. hide
19. mean

20. tear
21. fine
22. duck
23. bear

24. mine
25. saw

Extra Practice, page 259

WRITING APPLICATION Sentences

Select three pairs of homophones and three pairs of homographs from this lesson. Write six sentences, each using one of the pairs you have selected. Identify the homophones and homographs in a partner's sentences.

GRAMMAR —AND— WRITING CONNECTION

Combining Sentences

One way to make your writing flow more smoothly is to combine sentences. Look especially for sentences with pronouns. Sometimes a sentence with a pronoun can be combined with another sentence. Make sure that subject and object pronouns are used correctly in the combined sentence.

Separate: **Marta** will organize a stamp club.
I will organize a stamp club.
Combined: **Marta and I** will organize a stamp club.
Separate: Marta asked **my brother** for names of interested people.
Marta asked **me** for names of interested people.
Combined: Marta asked **my brother and me** for names of interested people.

Working Together

COOPERATIVE
LEARNING

Combine each pair of sentences.

Example: Marta talked to other stamp collectors.
Marta talked to us.
Marta talked to other stamp collectors and us.

1. Marta got advice from our local post office.
   I got advice from our local post office.
2. Eric told Marta about a place for our first meeting.
   Eric told me about a place for our first meeting.
3. Marta visited the place with some classmates.
   Marta visited the place with me.

1928 Locomobile — USA 25

1931 Cord — USA 25

1929 Pierce-Arrow — USA 25

1932 Packard — USA 25

1931 Cord — USA 25

1935 Duesenberg — USA 25

Revising Sentences

Inez wrote these sentences for a composition. Help Inez revise her sentences. Try to make the writing flow more smoothly. Combine each pair of sentences by using a pronoun.

4. The other students liked the place.
   I liked the place.
5. They agreed to a meeting date.
   We agreed to a meeting date.
6. A postal employee will meet with them.
   A postal employee will meet with us.
7. The postal employee told Marta about communication through the mail service.
   The postal employee told me about communication through the mail service.
8. She gave some club supplies to my brother.
   She gave some club supplies to me.
9. Marta had collected stamps for more than two years.
   I had collected stamps for more than two years.
10. Marta traded many stamps with another collector.
    Marta traded many stamps with me.

WRITER AT WORK

Think about some group activity in which you have participated. Write a friendly letter to someone you know, telling about your work with others in the group.

When you revise your letter, work with a classmate to find pairs of sentences that can be combined.

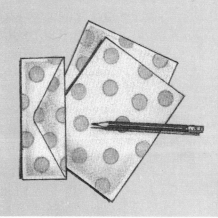

UNIT CHECKUP

LESSONS **Personal Pronouns and Pronouns and Antecedents** (pages 226–229) Write each sentence. Draw one line under the pronoun and label it **subject** or **object**. Draw two lines under its antecedent.

1. Joanna remembered all the lines, and she felt good.
2. Roberto hugged Joanna and gave her encouragement.
3. Mrs. Rios shook hands with Roberto and thanked him.
4. Encouragement is important because it helps people.
5. Gloria recited some lines, and the class encouraged her.

LESSON **Using Pronouns Correctly** (page 230) Write each sentence. Replace each underlined word with the correct pronoun.

6. After camp, Tod wrote to <u>Amy</u> often. (she, her)
7. Amy would write Al and <u>Tod</u> letters, too. (he, him)
8. <u>Tod</u> and Al showed the letters to Rob. (He, Him)
9. Rob wrote to Amy and <u>Melissa</u>. (she, her)
10. Tod and <u>Rob</u> both wrote to their friends. (he, him)

LESSON **Pronouns in Compound Subjects and Objects** (page 232) Write each sentence with the pronoun that completes it.

11. John writes to Anita and (him, he) about British sports.
12. His friends and (she, her) watch British football.
13. At first, I faulted (he, him) for his spelling.
14. Then someone told my classmates and (I, me) about British spelling.
15. My friends and (I, me) are finally learning English!

LESSON **Possessive Pronouns** (page 234) Write each sentence using the correct possessive pronoun.

16. Gloria invited us to (her, hers) party.
17. The next day So Yun invited us to (her, hers).
18. They planned (their, they're) parties for the weekend.
19. We had planned (our, ours) for Friday.
20. Maybe I'll have (my, mine) party next week.

LESSON 6

Using *who*, *whom*, and *whose* (page 236) Complete each sentence with **who**, **whom**, or **whose**. Write the sentence.

21. _____ did Marconi aid with his new invention?
22. _____ theories did Marconi follow?
23. _____ developed the transistor?
24. _____ did smaller radios benefit?
25. _____ radio show do you like best?

LESSON 7

Indefinite Pronouns (page 238) Write each sentence using the correct verb form.

26. Nobody (likes, like) to sleep out in cold weather.
27. No one (remember, remembers) to bring matches.
28. Somebody always (lets, let) the fire die.
29. Some (thinks, think) camping in winter is fun.
30. Few (agrees, agree) with them.

LESSON 8

Mechanics: Abbreviations (page 240) Write the abbreviation for each underlined word or group of words.

31. April 10, 1990
32. New York, New York
33. Saturday, June 12
34. Food and Drug Administration
35. Governor Thomas Kean
36. Varick Street

LESSON 9

Vocabulary Building: Homophones and Homographs (page 242) Write each sentence correctly.

37. Randy (red, read) more about communication.
38. We communicate (threw, through) signs.
39. Parents listen to (here, hear) their baby's cries.
40. Communicating without words is a (real, reel) challenge.

Writing Application: Pronoun Usage (pages 226–239) The following paragraph contains 10 errors with pronouns. Rewrite the paragraph correctly.

41.–50. The students wanted a school newsletter, and she planned them carefully. The teachers and them prepared the newsletter together. The teachers approved theirs ideas. Whom can do the best illustrations, the students wondered. Everyone were excited about the project. Then everyone were sad. The art was finished, and they did not look good. Most of they despaired. Finally, the students agreed—he needed to postpone the issue.

ENRICHMENT

WHAT DID YOU DO?

Play this game with a partner. Begin a sentence with a phrase made up of a pronoun and a verb or verb phrase. For example, you might start with the phrase "I have hidden." Tell your partner the phrase, and ask him or her to complete the sentence by adding another phrase, such as "the bananas in the bathtub." Take turns starting and completing sentences. Try to make your sentences humorous.

THE SAME BUT DIFFERENT

Read the words listed here. For each word write a homophone. Then choose a set of these homophones. Write at least five sentences that use the set of homophones in each sentence.

know	made
son	read

RETELL A FABLE

Think of a fable or a folk tale that you have read and enjoyed. Then retell the fable by using a pronoun in each sentence of your new version. A retelling of the folk tale, "The North Wind and the Sun," might begin in the following way.

The North Wind and the Sun could not settle an argument about who was stronger. The North Wind saw a chance to prove that it was the champ.

CREATIVE EXPRESSION

This Is Just to Say
I have eaten
the plums
that were in
the icebox

and which
you were probably
saving
for breakfast

Forgive me
they were delicious
so sweet
and so cold

—*William Carlos Williams*

TRY IT OUT!

"This Is Just to Say" is an example of free verse—it sounds like ordinary speech and has no regular rhythm or rhyme. As you read the poem, you can imagine that the speaker has written a quick note to a friend and left it on the kitchen table. Write a short "letter" poem of your own. Like William Carlos Williams, you might apologize for something, even though you were really glad that you did it.

EXTRA PRACTICE

Three levels of practice
Personal Pronouns (page 226)

LEVEL A. Write the personal pronoun in each sentence.

1. "I must try the role again," Doris said.
2. A group of people asked her why.
3. She wanted to make up for her mistakes.
4. Doris reminded them of the play's importance.
5. The students should see it.
6. They should understand the message about fires.
7. It was an important message.
8. Doris said she did not want to run from the challenge.

LEVEL B. Write each sentence. Draw one line under each pronoun. Then label each pronoun **subject** or **object**.

9. When given these reasons, the students accepted them.
10. The actors said they would try again.
11. Doris studied one speech and memorized it.
12. Soon Doris knew the lines without saying them.
13. Bert even said some lines while he was asleep.
14. Doris's letter to Bert had affected him.
15. The class read the parts, and we helped Doris.
16. Doris's classmates cheered her.

LEVEL C. Write each sentence, replacing the underlined word or words with the correct pronoun. Write whether you used a **subject** or **object** pronoun.

17. Doris even read a telegram sent by Mrs. Diaz.
18. "You will be great!" the telegram said.
19. The actors gathered near the stage, ready to walk onto the stage.
20. The actors were all excited.
21. All of the actors had prepared hard.
22. The play began, and the audience liked the play.
23. Enrico and I watched happily.
24. People in the audience cheered and finally people shouted.
25. Doris looked at Enrico and me and smiled.

EXTRA PRACTICE

Three levels of practice
Pronouns and Antecedents (page 228)

LEVEL
A. Write the antecedent for each underlined pronoun.

1. Emily did research for the report she wrote.
2. The report was about communication, and it was for school.
3. Emily went to two libraries, and they had good information.
4. Messengers once carried information with them.
5. Messengers used drums and pounded on them to send messages.
6. Smoke was a good means of communication because it could be seen for miles.
7. Later people wrote letters, and they were carried by hand.
8. Mail carriers work hard, and we appreciate them.

LEVEL
B. Write each sentence. Draw one line under the pronoun. Then draw two lines under the antecedent.

9. Telegraph operators send messages by typing them.
10. A message is relayed quickly, and it is readable.
11. Teleprinters have keyboards, and they look like regular typewriters.
12. *Telegraph* comes from Greek, and it means "to write from afar."
13. Morse invented the telegraph and the code it uses.
14. Edison also developed a system so that he could send four messages at once.
15. Edison worked on a telegraph, and it led to his first invention.
16. Edison patented 1,093 inventions, and they changed many lives..

LEVEL
C. Read each noun and pronoun below. Write a sentence that contains the pronoun and uses the noun as the antecedent of the pronoun.

17. Maria, she
18. man, he
19. people, they
20. letter, it
21. mother, her

22. Mark, him
23. words, them
24. book, it
25. paragraphs, them

EXTRA PRACTICE

Three levels of practice
Using Pronouns Correctly (page 230)

LEVEL A. Read this telephone conversation. Then write the correct pronoun that is enclosed in parentheses.

1. AMY: Melissa and (I, me) are going on a trip.
2. TOD: Perhaps (I, me) can guess where you're going.
3. AMY: Melissa's parents are taking (we, us) to California.
4. TOD: Are (they, them) taking both of you?
5. AMY: Yes, and (we, us) are going to San Francisco.
6. TOD: Rob and (I, me) have been there.
7. AMY: Did you and (he, him) ride on a cable car?
8. TOD: (I, me) took one to Fisherman's Wharf.

LEVEL B. Read this conversation. Write the pronoun that could replace the underlined word or words.

9. AMY: Missy invited Amy to her grandparents' house.
10. TOD: Do the grandparents live in San Francisco?
11. AMY: Yes, the grandparents do live there.
12. TOD: Does Missy visit often?
13. AMY: Amy got a post card from her last year.
14. TOD: Will Missy be away for a long time?
15. AMY: My friend and I will be away for two weeks.
16. TOD: I will miss Amy.

LEVEL C. Write this dialogue. Fill in each blank with a pronoun that fits the meaning of the sentence.

17. AMY: Missy will take _____ around the city.
18. TOD: Did she say _____ would take you sightseeing?
19. AMY: She will show _____ the Golden Gate Bridge.
20. TOD: _____ should show you Coit Tower.
21. AMY: _____ may not go there.
22. TOD: Ask _____ for a good guidebook.
23. AMY: Tell _____ the name of one.
24. TOD: Missy can tell _____ that.
25. AMY: Are _____ sure?

PRACTICE + PLUS

G R A M M A R

Three levels of additional practice for a difficult skill
Using Pronouns Correctly (page 230)

A. Write the pronoun that correctly completes each sentence.

1. My class and (I, me) visited a newspaper office.
2. Newspaper workers met with (we, us) there.
3. A reporter showed our teacher and (we, us) around.
4. Our teacher asked (she, her) about reporters.
5. "(We, Us) are the news gatherers," the reporter said.
6. A man entered and the reporter spoke to (he, him).
7. "This gentleman has really helped (I, me)," she said.
8. "(He, Him) is Mr. Rand, the editor of the paper."

B. Write the pronoun that could replace the underlined word or words.

9. The reporter showed the students a large machine.
10. "The workers rely on this photo-composition machine to type stories on photographic paper," she said.
11. "Mr. Rand knew the machine would help us," she added.
12. The reporter smiled at Mr. Rand as she said that.
13. "Follow your teacher and me into the press room," she said.
14. The reporter described how the printers make printing plates.
15. The class discussed the process with the reporter.
16. My teacher and I were surprised at the giant presses.

C. Complete each sentence, using a subject or object pronoun.

17. _____ enjoyed their trip to the newspaper office.
18. It showed _____ how a newspaper is run.
19. Sue said, "Now _____ want to be a reporter."
20. "Mr. Rand talked to _____ about being a reporter," said Lea.
21. "I also spoke to _____ about studying journalism," said Sam.
22. "The reporter said we could send _____ a story," said Pat.
23. "_____ gave us a good tour," said Mike.
24. "She sat with _____ at lunch," said Tina and Jan.
25. "Did _____ learn a lot?" asked Frank.

PRACTICE PLUS: Lesson 3

253

Three levels of practice
Pronouns in Compound Subjects and Objects (page 232)

LEVEL A. Write the compound subject or compound object in each sentence. Underline each subject or object pronoun.

1. American sign language interests Sara and me.
2. She and I have hearing-impaired parents.
3. Our parents and we communicate with hand gestures.
4. My sister and I know the signs for most ideas.
5. Other hearing-impaired people understand her and me.
6. The finger alphabet also aids our parents and us.
7. Sara and I know the finger positions for each letter.
8. Regular practice helps my parents and me.

LEVEL B. Write the pronoun or phrase that completes each sentence.

9. Jacob and (I, me) know some braille.
10. Grandma told my cousin and (I, me) about this code.
11. (She, Her) and her friends communicate in braille.
12. (Jacob and I, I and Jacob) read about Louis Braille.
13. Over 100 years ago (he, him) and some other teachers first used braille to teach blind French students.
14. Grandma's braillewriter interests (I and Jacob, Jacob and me).
15. Her friends and (she, her) write letters on it.
16. My cousin and (I, me) can use this six-key machine.

LEVEL C. Write a pronoun that completes each sentence correctly. Label each pronoun **subject pronoun** or **object pronoun**.

17. Arne met my guide dog Duke and _____.
18. _____ walked with us.
19. Duke led _____ and me through the streets.
20. Duke impressed Arne and _____ with his responsibility.
21. Duke led my friend and _____ away from obstacles.
22. Along the way, neighbors greeted Duke and _____.
23. Duke and I greeted _____ and their children.
24. _____ and their friends think Duke is great.
25. Duke and _____ are good friends.

EXTRA PRACTICE

Three levels of practice
Possessive Pronouns (page 234)

LEVEL A. Write the possessive pronoun from each sentence.

1. LIANA: Maybe we can work together on letters for our school.
2. SUSAN: Rob and a friend wrote theirs yesterday.
3. LIANA: It's your turn to ask the teacher.
4. SUSAN: She already gave us her permission.
5. LIANA: Okay, let's start our letter.
6. SUSAN: Here is my first draft.
7. LIANA: Your first draft is good, but it seems too informal.
8. SUSAN: That's always my trouble.

LEVEL B. Write the correct pronoun in parentheses to complete each item of the dialogue.

9. LIANA: My little sister wants (my, mine) help.
10. SUSAN: What is (her, hers) problem?
11. LIANA: She needs help with (her, hers) friendly letter.
12. SUSAN: I need (your, yours) help, too.
13. LIANA: Why? Is (your, yours) problem the same?
14. SUSAN: I have to write (my, mine) business letter.
15. LIANA: Well, I have to write (my, mine), also.
16. SUSAN: But (your, you're) letters are always good.

LEVEL C. Write each sentence. Correctly fill in each blank with one of these pronouns: **my, mine, your, yours, her,** or **hers**.

17. LIANA: _____ are well written, too.
18. SUSAN: I work so hard at _____.
19. LIANA: That is _____ friendly letter.
20. SUSAN: Isn't it addressed to _____ sister?
21. LIANA: Yes, it is _____.
22. SUSAN: She clearly doesn't need _____ help.
23. LIANA: No, I need _____ most of the time.
24. SUSAN: You can depend on _____ help, too.
25. LIANA: Thanks for _____ assistance.

EXTRA PRACTICE

Three levels of practice
Using *who*, *whom*, and *whose* (page 236)

LEVEL A. Write the word in parentheses that correctly completes each sentence.

1. (Who, Whom) communicates at a baseball game?
2. (Whose, Who's) messages are on the giant billboards?
3. (Who's, Whose) singing the national anthem?
4. (Who, Whom) does the announcer address over the P.A. system?
5. (Who, Whom) does the crowd cheer the most?
6. (Whom, Who) received the loudest boo?
7. (Who, Whom) gives signals to the pitcher?
8. (Whose, Who's) gestures show balls and strikes?

LEVEL B. Write **who, whom, whose,** or **who's** to complete each sentence.

9. _____ told the runner to steal a base?
10. _____ did the umpire throw out of the game?
11. _____ building up excitement with that organ music.
12. _____ home run was celebrated with fireworks?
13. _____ bowed and waved to the happy crowd?
14. _____ did the manager call in from the bullpen?
15. _____ opinions about the game are broadcast on TV?
16. _____ designed the graphics on the scoreboard?

LEVEL C. Write a question that each sentence below might answer. Begin each question with **who, whom,** or **whose**.

17. The center fielder autographed this scorecard.
18. Those are posters made by fans.
19. The third-base coach signals to the batter.
20. The vendor is shouting, "Popcorn and peanuts."
21. I want the Wrens to win tonight.
22. A sportswriter is interviewing the manager.
23. The umpire called the runner out at third.
24. The Wrens' fans are roaring with delight.
25. Sam will watch the next game with us.

EXTRA PRACTICE

Three levels of practice
Indefinite Pronouns (page 238)

LEVEL A. Write the indefinite pronoun in each sentence.

1. No one has heard from Bob.
2. He writes letters, but few arrive.
3. Everybody asks about him.
4. Has anybody called him?
5. Somebody should call.
6. Something could have happened to him.
7. All of us are concerned about him.
8. Each of us is eager for news of Bob.

LEVEL B. Write the verb that agrees with each underlined indefinite pronoun.

9. Everyone (expects, expect) a letter from Bob.
10. Few (arrives, arrive) on time.
11. "Everything (is, are) all right," his father says.
12. "Someone (calls, call) if there is trouble."
13. Most of us (agree, agrees) with him.
14. Several of us (checks, check) the mailbox each day.
15. Others (talks, talk) to Bob's father.
16. Many (was, were) happy when a letter arrived.

LEVEL C. Write each sentence. Underline each indefinite pronoun. Then use the correct verb in parentheses that agrees with each indefinite pronoun.

17. Some of us in camp (has, have) overheard two counselors.
18. Both of them (discusses, discuss) a new building.
19. Nothing definite (is, are) said about the building.
20. One of us (wants, want) a new dining hall.
21. Nobody really (knows, know) a great deal about it.
22. Much certainly (was, were) discussed by the campers.
23. Anything at all (starts, start) a new rumor.
24. Everyone here (has, have) a vivid imagination.
25. No one (lack, lacks) interest in the matter.

Three levels of practice
Mechanics: Abbreviations (page 240)

LEVEL

A. Write the abbreviation from the box that has the same meaning as the underlined word or words.

1. Denton <u>Lane</u>
2. <u>Reverend</u> Tim Daly
3. <u>United Nations</u>
4. <u>American Medical Association</u>
5. 8:45 <u>ante meridiem</u>

6. <u>Doctor</u> Mu Lan
7. <u>United States Information Agency</u>
8. <u>Louisiana</u>
9. <u>Sunday</u>
10. <u>August</u>

| Dr. | LA | La. | Aug. | USIA |
| A.M. | Sun. | U.N. | Rev. | AMA |

LEVEL

B. Write the abbreviation for the underlined word or words.

11. <u>Internal Revenue Service</u>
12. <u>Mister</u> Richard Gallo
13. Tallahassee, <u>Florida</u>
14. <u>December</u> 11, 1990
15. 500 Sunset <u>Boulevard</u>
16. <u>Professor</u> Susanne Donaldson
17. <u>American Library Association</u>

LEVEL
C. Read the note below. Each numbered item contains one or more incorrect abbreviations. Write the abbreviations correctly.

18. 11 Milton aven.
19. Millville, N. Jer. 07960
20. Decem. 11, 1990
21. Dear Doc. Addams:
22. I won't be able to keep my appointment on Tuesd.,
23. Janu. 5, at 11:30 am. Mstr. Shannon is taking our
24. class to the Uni. Nat. on that day. He says we
25. won't be back until after 5 Pm.

EXTRA PRACTICE

Three levels of practice
Homophones and Homographs (page 242)

LEVEL A. Choose the correct meaning for each underlined homograph. Write **a** or **b**.

1. Please <u>pick</u> the best stationery.   a. tool   b. select
2. Did they <u>coat</u> this paper with perfume?   a. jacket   b. cover
3. Put my name at the <u>top</u>.   a. toy   b. head
4. The tent <u>pole</u> broke.   a. unit of measurement   b. rod
5. She has a slender <u>figure</u>.   a. number   b. shape
6. The lawyer is in <u>court</u>.   a. sports area   b. judicial assembly
7. We will <u>comb</u> the area for the book.   a. search   b. arrange
8. Many call my grandmother a <u>sage</u>.   a. wise person   b. herb

LEVEL B. Write these sentences, using the correct homophone.

9. (There, Their) is a long history of making paper.
10. Papyrus is a (coarse, course) paper.
11. The Egyptians (maid, made) papyrus from a plant.
12. They did so by a very (crewed, crude) method.
13. (There, Their) method was to cut strips of reed.
14. They matted the stems (through, threw) pressure.
15. The mats were then dried in the (son, sun).
16. People (rote, wrote) on papyrus in ancient times.

LEVEL C. Write each sentence, using the correct homophone from the box.

17. Paper was invented _____ the Chinese.
18. They _____ plant strips into a pulp.
19. The fibers _____ mat together.
20. The pulp was _____ to dry.
21. The secret came _____ Europe from Arabia.
22. Paper was never _____ to make.
23. Paper is now _____ by machine.
24. Both _____ and fancy types of paper are made.
25. Which _____ do you prefer?

aloud/allowed
cheap/cheep
by/buy
plain/plane
one/won
beat/beet
wood/would
to/too
made/maid

MAINTENANCE

UNIT 1: Sentences

Four Kinds of Sentences (page 2) Write each sentence. Add the correct end mark. Label each sentence **declarative, interrogative, imperative,** or **exclamatory**.

1. Daffodils bloom early in spring
2. Please rake the whole lawn
3. Will the lawn mower never start
4. What a glorious summer day it is
5. Please water the lawn immediately

Complete Subjects and Complete Predicates (page 4) Copy each sentence. Draw one line under the complete subject and two lines under the complete predicate.

6. A long hot summer day begins.
7. Clouds of insects buzz in the trees.
8. The old dog rests in the cool shade.
9. The leaves of plants wilt.
10. Sounds echo for miles in the dry air.

Simple Subjects and Simple Predicates (page 6) Copy each sentence. Draw one line under the simple subject and two lines under the simple predicate of each sentence.

11. The winds of autumn blow from the north.
12. All the leaves turn red and brown.
13. The squirrels on the lawn gather acorns.
14. Large orange pumpkins appear on porches.
15. We smell smoke in the air from burning leaves.

Correcting Sentence Fragments and Run-on Sentences (page 14) Correctly rewrite each run-on sentence or sentence fragment.

16. The wind howled last night all the leaves scattered.
17. An inch or two of light, even snow.
18. Tiny rabbit tracks in the deep snow.
19. Stay away from that pond the ice is not thick.
20. The sky is gray the sun seems so far away.

UNIT 3: Nouns

Common and Proper Nouns

(page 74) Write each noun. Label it **common** or **proper**.

21. Let's climb Hunter Mountain.
22. That blue dot is Mercy Lake.
23. We can see Franklin County in the distance.
24. Is Edgemere over there?
25. There is the field behind Jackson High School.

Singular and Plural Nouns

(page 76) Write the plural form of each noun in parentheses.

26. Those (family) had a combined yard sale.
27. I carried home four (box) of books.
28. Dad bought two carving (knife).
29. The two (radio) are very old.
30. Look at those portraits of two (woman).

Possessive Nouns (page 78)

Write the correct possessive form of the noun in parentheses.

31. Where did the costumes for the (children) play come from?
32. We found old clothes in (Mrs. James) attic.
33. The (policemen) uniforms were rented.
34. I made the (thieves) masks.
35. For the (donkey) costume, we used an old tent.

UNIT 5: Verbs

Main Verbs and Helping Verbs

(page 144) Write the verb phrase in each sentence. Draw one line under each main verb and two lines under each helping verb.

36. We have formed a club.
37. Our club will explore caves.
38. Old clothes should be worn.
39. Mrs. Akira, our leader, has explored dozens of caves.
40. We may find unusual rocks.
41. This underground lake could have been here for centuries.
42. We can map this cave now.

Direct and Indirect Objects

(page 146) Label the underlined word **direct object** or **indirect object**.

43. Did you buy <u>Ann</u> a birthday present?
44. Don't give <u>her</u> any hints about the surprise party.
45. I mailed her a <u>card</u> today.
46. Can you remind all her <u>friends</u> about the party?
47. Tell <u>them</u> the exact time.
48. I gave everyone my <u>address</u>.
49. My parents gave <u>me</u> permission.

Linking Verbs (page 150) Write each linking verb. Label each **predicate noun** or **predicate adjective**.

50. Jason's vegetable garden is famous.
51. Those tomatoes are delicious.
52. These plants are tomatoes.
53. Jason's lettuce seems fresh.
54. The melons feel ripe.
55. Is that tool a shovel?
56. The garden is pleasant this morning.

Present, Past, and Future Tenses (page 152) Write the verb in each sentence. Label it **present, past,** or **future**.

57. Architects designed this house.
58. Carpenters build it.
59. The masons completed the chimney and fireplace.
60. The plumbers will come tomorrow.
61. Trucks deliver supplies daily.
62. The workers will finish by the end of the month.
63. Then our family will move.

Irregular Verbs (page 156) Write the four principal parts of each irregular verb.

64. choose
65. take
66. speak
67. write
68. teach
69. sing
70. know
71. think
72. do
73. grow
74. sit
75. run

Subject-Verb Agreement (page 160) Write the present tense of the verb in parentheses.

76. Les (come) here often.
77. This book (be) mine.
78. There (be) Ted and Wayne.
79. Either Nita or Bo (study) Spanish.
80. Neither Nadia nor Deirdre (want) to swim.

Commas in a Series (page 164) Add commas to separate the items in each series.

81. We hiked swam and played softball at the picnic.
82. Mr. Santos Aunt Emma and Zoey played the guitar and sang.
83. Annie gathered wood started a fire and grilled hamburgers.
84. We forgot the spoons napkins salt and pickles.
85. Afterwards we cleaned dishes told stories and watched the stars.

Word Choice (page 166) Write the word in parentheses that has a positive connotation.

86. We spent a (peaceful, dull) day at the lake.
87. Mr. Lark is an (ambitious, pushy) young salesman.
88. She is a (dainty, picky) eater.
89. They live in a (shack, cabin).
90. Our neighbors are (curious, nosy).

UNIT 7: Pronouns

Personal Pronouns (page 226) Write each pronoun. Label it **subject** or **object**.

91. Mom and I raise sheep.
92. They graze all summer.
93. We feed sheep hay during the winter.
94. Mom shears them in spring.
95. The lambs play with me.

Pronouns and Antecedents (page 228) Write each pronoun. Then write its antecedent.

96. Dina and Don run every day. They train for the marathon.
97. The marathon is twenty-six miles. It is a long, hard race.
98. Dave went to a marathon. He watched the runners.
99. A doctor measured Don's heartbeat. It was normal.
100. Dina won third place. She is a fine athlete.
101. Afterwards, Dina talked with Dad and Don and gave them some information.

Using Pronouns Correctly (page 230) Write the pronoun in parentheses that correctly completes the sentence.

102. Viet and (I, me) found a puppy.
103. (He and I, Him and me) showed the puppy to Mrs. Dinh.
104. She and (we, us) put up "Lost Dog" signs in our neighborhood.
105. The owners called Viet and (she, her) last night.
106. Their children and (they, them) were very upset.
107. They thanked Mr. Dinh, Viet, and (I, me).

Possessive Pronouns (page 234) Write the sentences. Use the correct pronouns.

108. Is (you're, your) collie in the dog show?
109. That tiny white poodle is (my, mine).
110. Look at (it's, its) ribbon.
111. (They're, Their) boxers have been in many shows.
112. The wolfhound is (our, ours).

Homophones and Homographs (page 242) Write the word that completes each sentence.

113. (They're, There) performing in a play soon.
114. Can you (sew, sow) costumes?
115. Did he (write, right) the script?
116. Which actor has the lead (roll, role)?
117. The cast might take this play on the (road, rode).
118. They will (meet, meat) at the restaurant.

8

Writing Letters

Read the quotation and look at the picture on the opposite page. Beverly Cleary communicates through her writing. What sort of books does she write?

Another way to communicate is through letters. When you write a letter, your purpose and audience are very clear. You may write to a friend or to someone you do not know at all.

Focus A letter is a way of sharing information with an intended audience for an intended purpose.

To whom would you like to send a letter? What will be the purpose of your letter? You can use the letters and photographs in this unit to get ideas for letters you might want to write.

THEME: *COMMUNICATIONS*

*I write the sort of books I wanted to
read when I was a child.*

—Beverly Cleary

LITERATURE

Reading Like a Writer

Have you ever written and received a series of letters? What kinds of things did you find to write about?

Leigh Botts writes letters to his favorite author, Mr. Henshaw. Leigh first wrote because he liked Mr. Henshaw's new book.

As you read "Dear Mr. Henshaw," notice the kinds of things Leigh tells Mr. Henshaw, the questions he asks, and the comments he makes.

from

Dear Mr. Henshaw

by Beverly Cleary

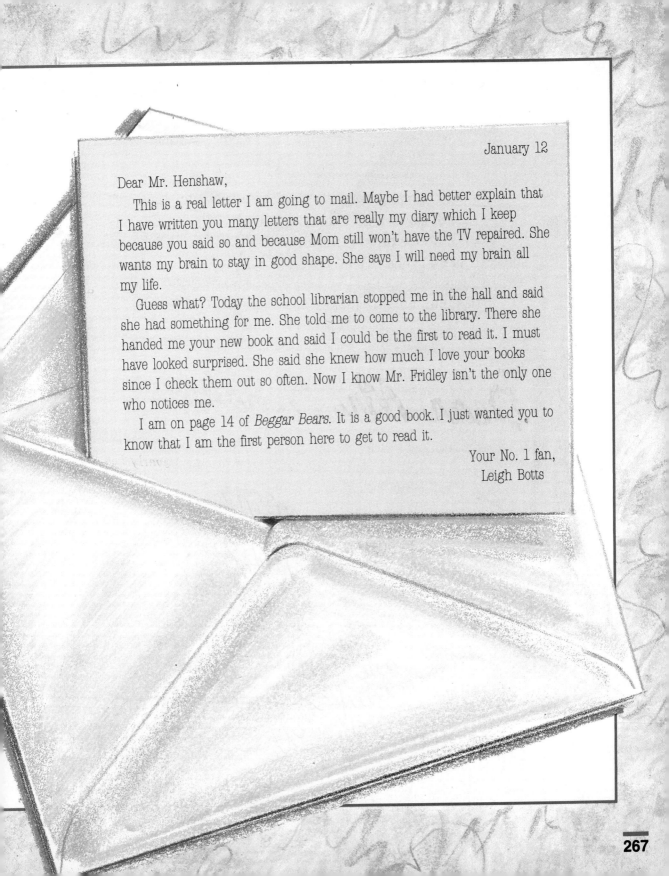

January 12

Dear Mr. Henshaw,

This is a real letter I am going to mail. Maybe I had better explain that I have written you many letters that are really my diary which I keep because you said so and because Mom still won't have the TV repaired. She wants my brain to stay in good shape. She says I will need my brain all my life.

Guess what? Today the school librarian stopped me in the hall and said she had something for me. She told me to come to the library. There she handed me your new book and said I could be the first to read it. I must have looked surprised. She said she knew how much I love your books since I check them out so often. Now I know Mr. Fridley isn't the only one who notices me.

I am on page 14 of *Beggar Bears*. It is a good book. I just wanted you to know that I am the first person here to get to read it.

Your No. 1 fan,
Leigh Botts

January 15

Dear Mr. Henshaw,

I finished *Beggar Bears* in two nights. It is a really good book. At first I was surprised because it wasn't funny like your other books, but then I got to thinking (you said authors should think) and decided a book doesn't have to be funny to be good, although it often helps. This book did not need to be funny.

In the first chapter I thought it was going to be funny. I guess I expected it because of your other books and because the mother bear was teaching her twin cubs to beg from tourists in Yellowstone Park. Then when the mother died because a stupid tourist fed her a cupcake in a plastic bag and she ate the bag, too, I knew this was going to be a sad book. Winter was coming on, tourists were leaving the park and the little bears didn't know how to find food for themselves. When they hibernated and then woke up in the middle of winter because they had eaten all the wrong things and hadn't stored up enough fat, I almost cried. I sure was relieved when the nice ranger and his boy found the young bears and fed them and the next summer taught them to hunt for the right things to eat.

I wonder what happens to the fathers of bears. Do they just go away? Sometimes I lie awake listening to the gas station pinging, and I worry because something might happen to Mom. She is so little compared to most moms, and she works so hard. I don't think Dad is that much interested in me. He didn't phone when he said he would.

I hope your book wins a million awards.

Sincerely,
Leigh Botts

The writer has used informal language. The letter almost seems like dialogue.

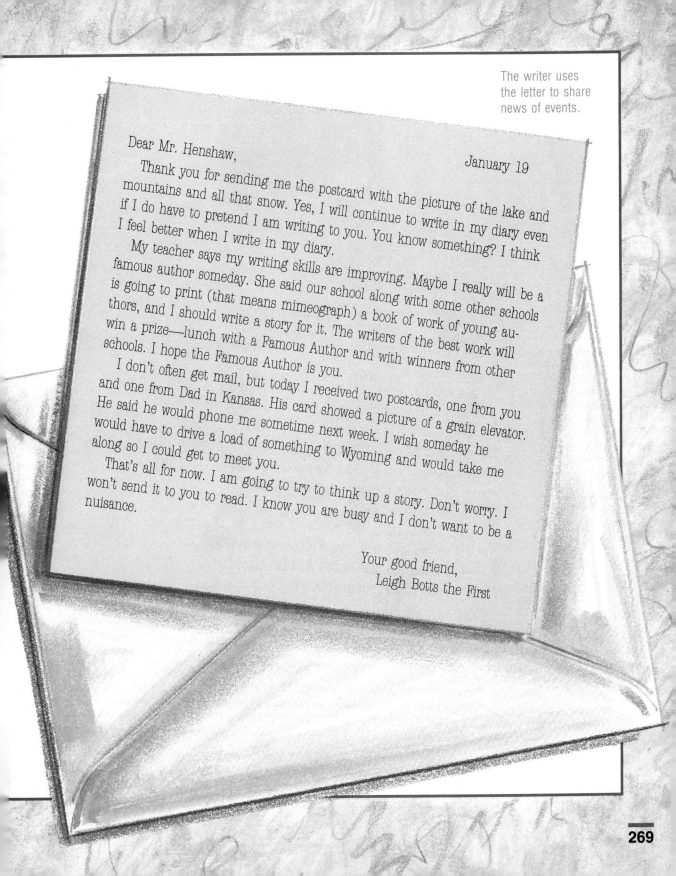

The writer uses
the letter to share
news of events.

Dear Mr. Henshaw,   January 19

Thank you for sending me the postcard with the picture of the lake and mountains and all that snow. Yes, I will continue to write in my diary even if I do have to pretend I am writing to you. You know something? I think I feel better when I write in my diary.

My teacher says my writing skills are improving. Maybe I really will be a famous author someday. She said our school along with some other schools is going to print (that means mimeograph) a book of work of young authors, and I should write a story for it. The writers of the best work will win a prize—lunch with a Famous Author and with winners from other schools. I hope the Famous Author is you.

I don't often get mail, but today I received two postcards, one from you and one from Dad in Kansas. His card showed a picture of a grain elevator. He said he would phone me sometime next week. I wish someday he would have to drive a load of something to Wyoming and would take me along so I could get to meet you.

That's all for now. I am going to try to think up a story. Don't worry. I won't send it to you to read. I know you are busy and I don't want to be a nuisance.

                                              Your good friend,
                                              Leigh Botts the First

Thinking Like a Reader

1. What kinds of things does Leigh Botts write about?

2. What are his reasons for writing to Mr. Henshaw?

Write your responses in your journal.

Thinking Like a Writer

3. How do you know from what Leigh Botts writes that he has received a reply from Mr. Henshaw?

4. Do you think that it is a good idea to mention Mr. Henshaw's having written back? Why or why not?

5. Imagine writing to your favorite author. To whom would you write, and what would you write?

Write your responses in your journal.

Responding to

LITERATURE

Brainstorm *Vocabulary*

In one of his letters to Mr. Henshaw, Leigh Botts says that the school "is going to print (that means mimeograph) a book." *Print* is a general word. *Mimeograph*, on the other hand, is a specific word for a very specific method. Think of something that you might write a letter about—for example, a book, a hobby, or an incident. Then, think of some specific words that go with your idea. For example, if you were writing about a book, specific words might include *novel*, *chapter*, and *plot*. Write your list of specific words in your journal. You can use your personal vocabulary list when you write.

Talk It Over *Tell About an Incident*

In "Dear Mr. Henshaw" Leigh's letters have a conversational tone, as if he were talking to a friend. Leigh tells Mr. Henshaw about daily events, much as you might tell a friend about your day. Work with a partner. Imagine that you are talking to a friend on the telephone. Briefly describe something that happened to you. Keep the incident short, but be sure to include a beginning, a middle, and an end.

Quick Write *Write a Thank-You Note*

One kind of letter is the thank-you note. Thank-you notes may be very short, but they should be sincere and specific. Think of a gift someone has given you or a special favor someone has done for you. Write a note thanking that person. For example, imagine the note that Leigh Botts might have written to the librarian.

Dear Miss Neely,

Thank you for letting me be the first to read *Beggar Bears*. I really enjoyed the book. It was very nice of you to save me the book.

Sincerely,
Leigh Botts

Idea Corner *Think of Topics*

Think of some purpose for writing a business letter of your own, for example, to order something or to ask for information. In your journal, write whatever ideas come to mind. Since business letters are often written on special business stationery, you might want to design a letterhead. A letterhead is the printed top of a sheet of paper. It gives your name and address and may have a design or picture.

PICTURES

![camera icon] *SEEING LIKE A WRITER*

Finding Ideas for Writing

Look at the pictures. Think about what you see.
What ideas for letter writing do the pictures give you?
Write your ideas in your journal.

PICTURES: Ideas for Writing Letters

1 GROUP WRITING: A Business Letter

You know that a friendly letter informs or entertains a friend or a relative. A **business letter** is a letter whose **audience** may be a company or an official. Business letters are written for a specific **purpose**, such as to request information, to place an order, or to make a complaint. What do you need to remember about business letters?

- Correct Letter Form
- Purpose and Audience

Correct Letter Form

Look at the business letter on the opposite page and at the description of each of its parts. Pay special attention to each part, where it is placed, and how it is capitalized and punctuated.

Like a friendly letter, a business letter has several parts.

The **heading** gives the writer's full address and the date. Note that all names are capitalized. The heading is placed just to the right of the middle of the page.

The **inside address** shows the name and address of the person to whom the letter is written. Only the name and address of the business is given if the person's name is not known. The inside address is placed between the heading and the greeting at the left margin.

The **greeting** tells who is being addressed. The correct title is used—*Mr., Miss, Ms.,* or *Mrs.* If you do not know the name of the person you are writing to, use this greeting: *Dear Sir or Madam.* The greeting is followed by a colon.

The **body** of a business letter tells the purpose of the letter—it contains the writer's message. It should be clear, to the point, and polite. Each paragraph is indented.

```
                                    207 Ventura Drive          Heading
                                    Phoenix, AZ 85018
                                    May 4, 1990

Braemore Equipment Company                                     Inside
212 Braemore Drive                                             address
Bay City, MI 48706

Dear Sir or Madam:                                             Greeting
   Last month I ordered a pair of All-Sports shoes, model     Body
number 1571A, from your Spring Catalog. My order
number is B45832.
   The shoes I received do not match. Please send me a new
pair as soon as possible.
   Thank you.

                                    Yours truly,              Closing
                                    Ari Miller                Signature
                                    Ari Miller                Name
```

The **closing** is in the same place as the closing in a friendly letter but is more formal. The usual closing for a business letter is *Sincerely yours, Yours truly,* or a similar phrase. The closing is followed by a comma.

The **signature** includes the writer's full name.

The **writer's name** is typed or printed out in full underneath the signature, to make sure the name can be easily read.

Guided Practice: Correct Letter Form

As a class, talk about the items below and decide where each one belongs in a business letter. Then, write the items in the form of a business letter, using the correct capitalization and punctuation.

Example: dear sir or madam   *Dear Sir or Madam:* greeting

1. wallet photos co.
   P.O. Box 222
   Hackensack, NJ 07606

2. yours truly

3. 123 Elm circle
   Paterson, NJ 07514

4. dear sir

Purpose and Audience

Before you write a letter, make sure that you are very clear about your purpose and audience. Look back at the letter on page 275. Who is Ari's audience? What is Ari's purpose in writing?

The greeting of a business letter identifies your audience. The body of the letter identifies your purpose for writing.

Guided Practice: Selecting a Purpose and an Audience

Read the following list of topics. As a class, decide the purpose and audience of a letter for each topic—whom you would write to and what results you would wish to achieve.

- The local newspaper has made a mistake in a story about your school play.
- Your favorite singer will be performing in the park.
- You are ready to send off the money you have collected for a disaster-relief fund.
- You are planning a bulletin board about the old town hall for the celebration of local history week.

Putting a Business Letter Together

With your classmates you have practiced using the correct form for a business letter. You have talked about various purposes and audiences for business letters. Now, you will write a business letter as a class.

A business letter should be short and to the point; only necessary information is included. The reason for the letter is stated near its beginning. Always be polite in a business letter; use *please* and thank the receiver for help or for attention to the problem.

Business letters are more formal than friendly letters. Look at the examples of formal and informal language. For a business letter, choose the more formal tone.

FORMAL: I am interested in attending your camp.
INFORMAL: I think I'd like to come to your camp.

COOPERATIVE LEARNING: Group Writing

Guided Practice: Writing a Business Letter

Imagine that your class wants to order a model kit by mail. The model kit is number 33012 in the B & G catalog. The kit costs $8.75, and you will enclose a check to pay for it. B & G, Inc., is located at 5544 East Drive, Decatur, Georgia 30033.

Decide with your classmates what your order letter will say and what parts it will have. Then write your own letter, using the current date and your school address. Be sure that your letter is clear and concise, with the correct capitalization and punctuation.

Share your letter with a friend. Ask your friend if the letter follows all the rules for an effective business letter, including correct form.

Checklist: A Business Letter

When you write a business letter, there are some points you will want to keep in mind. A checklist will remind you of the things that you will want to include in your business letter.

Some points need to be added to the checklist below. Make a copy of the checklist and complete it. Keep a copy of it in your writing folder. Check off each item as you write a business letter.

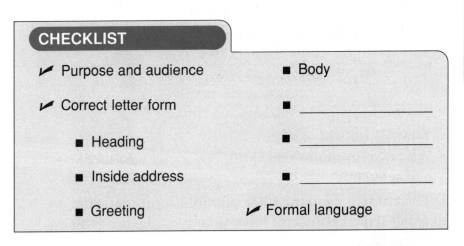

CHECKLIST

✔ Purpose and audience   ■ Body

✔ Correct letter form   ■ _____

   ■ Heading   ■ _____

   ■ Inside address   ■ _____

   ■ Greeting   ✔ Formal language

2 THINKING AND WRITING: Solving Problems

You know that a frequent reason for writing a business letter is to solve a problem. For example, you may write a letter to request information, to order something you need, or to settle a complaint.

You have many problems to solve every day. How can you get information for a project? How should you spend your allowance? What will you do if it rains?

There are steps that you can follow to solve a problem. First, decide what the problem is. Next, think of possible solutions. Then, examine each solution and choose the best one. Finally, carry out the solution that you have chosen.

Look at this page from a student's journal.

> *Problems: Here I am at camp —*
>
> *Dad's birthday next week!*
>
> *What to give him?*
>
> *Make something in crafts?*
>
> *Buy something? (Where)*
>
> *Mail order — Joe's catalog*

Thinking Like a Writer

■ Which solution do you think the writer should choose and why?

The student examined her possible solutions. She decided that she did not have time to make her father a gift. There were no shopping trips scheduled for that week, so she decided that the best solution was to choose a gift from a mail-order catalog. She wrote a business letter to order the gift.

When you have problems to solve, you, too, may find that sometimes a letter will help you solve them.

COOPERATIVE LEARNING

THINKING APPLICATION Solving Problems

Each of the writers named below is planning to write a letter in order to solve a problem. However, every writer has left out an important detail, and without it his or her problem cannot be solved. Help each writer decide which detail should be added. Write your notes on a separate sheet of paper. You may wish to discuss the problems with your classmates.

1. Francisco needs information for a report on forest fires. He will write to the National Forest Service. Read his checklist. What important detail is missing?
   - the address of the National Forest Service
   - his own mailing address
   - an expression of thanks

2. Tanya will write a letter to order a jacket as a present for her cousin. Read her checklist. What important detail is missing?
   - her mailing address
   - the color and size of the jacket
   - the order number of the jacket

3. Binh sent $7.95 to H.B. Specialties for a mini-flashlight and holder. He allowed six weeks for delivery but has not received his flashlight. He will write to complain. Read his checklist. What important detail is missing?
   - the address of H.B. Specialties
   - the order number of the flashlight
   - the amount of money he sent

3 INDEPENDENT WRITING: A Business Letter

Prewrite: Step 1

By now you have learned many important points about writing business letters. Now you will choose a topic and write a letter of your own. Greg chose his topic in this way.

Choosing a Topic

1. First, Greg made a list of situations that might call for the writing of a business letter.
2. Next, he thought about what he might say or ask in each letter.
3. Last, he decided on the best subject for a business letter.

> get my cat into a commercial
>
> order new brakes for my bike
>
> camps for next summer
>
> my computer — find out about new ways to use it

Greg decided to write a letter requesting information about his computer. He explored his topic by **brainstorming** a list of ideas about his computer. He made a list of everything that came to mind about computers. Greg saw that he had many topics on which he wanted more information, which he could obtain with a business letter. A company representative would be his **audience**. The **purpose** of his letter would be to request information. This is what Greg's list looked like.

Exploring Ideas: Brainstorming Strategy

1. What games can I play on my computer?

2. What free information is there about computers?

3. Can I learn to program a computer?

4. A funny thing happened with my computer.

5. What new programs can help with my schoolwork?

6. How does a computer work?

7. Can I get a catalog of computer programs?

Before beginning to write, Greg imagined someone receiving his letter. He wanted to make it clear how that person could help him. Greg narrowed his topic by crossing out items 1, 2, 3, 4, and 6 on his list.

Thinking Like a Writer

- Which items did Greg decide not to include?
- Why do you think he decided to leave those out?

YOUR TURN

JOURNAL

Think of a topic for your own business letter. Use **Pictures** or your journal for ideas. Follow these steps.

- Make a list of topics.
- Choose the one you like best.
- Brainstorm for ideas about your topic.
- Narrow your topic, if necessary.
- Think about your purpose and audience.

Write a First Draft: Step 2

Greg made a planning checklist to help him to remember what to include in his business letter. Greg is now ready to write his first draft.

Part of Greg's First Draft

Dear Sir

I am a sixth grade student. I use an arrow computor. I use it for schoolwork. I am now using Hiwrite. It is you're Word Processing program. The other day I used my computer to write a story and got a great grade on it.

   I would like to know what programs you have in math and sceince. Fairly easy one. Also, how much they are.

   You could send me a catalog, I guess.

While Greg was writing his first draft, he did not worry about making mistakes. He knew that he could go back later to correct his work.

YOUR TURN

Write your first draft. As you prepare to write, ask yourself these questions.

- What information will my audience need?
- What result do I want from my letter?

TIME-OUT You might want to take some time out before you revise. That way you will be able to revise your writing with a fresh eye.

Revise: Step 3

After he finished his first draft, Greg read it to himself. Then he shared his letter with a classmate. He wanted some suggestions for improvement.

Greg then looked back at his planning checklist. He noticed that he had forgotten one other important point. He checked both off so that he would remember them when he revised. Greg now has a checklist to use as he revises.

Greg looked over his letter again and thought of other improvements. Did he use the correct form for a business letter? Was his letter brief and to the point? Then he made changes in his letter. Notice that he did not correct small errors. He knew he could fix them later.

The revisions Greg made changed his letter. Look at his revised draft.

Revising Checklist
- Remember purpose and audience.
- Use correct form.
  - Heading
  - Inside address
  ✔ - Greeting
  - Body
  - Closing
  - Signature
  - Name
✔ - Use formal language.

Part of Greg's Revised Draft

Dear Sir _or Madam_ :

I am a sixth grade student. I use an arrow computor. ~~I use~~
it for schoolwork. I am now using Hiwrite. ~~It is~~ you're
Word Processing program. ~~The other day I used my~~
~~computer to write a story and got a great grade on it.~~

   I would like to know what programs you have in math and
for someone my age   _Please include their prices._
sceince. ~~Fairly easy one.~~ ~~Also, how much they are.~~
Please
~~You could~~ send me a catalog, ~~I guess.~~ _Thank you for your help._

                Yours truly,

                  Greg Butler

Thinking Like a Writer

WISE
WORD
CHOICE

- What parts of a business letter did Greg add?
- Which sentences did he combine? How does combining
  them improve the letter?
- What additions and changes did he make? How do they
  change the tone of the letter?

YOUR TURN

Read your first draft. Look at your checklist. Ask yourself
these questions.

- Have I used the correct form for a business letter?
- How can I make my letter clearer?
- Is my tone formal and polite?

If you wish, ask a friend to read your letter and make
suggestions. Then revise your letter.

Proofread: Step 4

Greg still needed to proofread for mistakes in spelling, grammar, and punctuation. He used a proofreading checklist.

Part of Greg's Proofread Draft

73 Fairview Lane

Andiron, IN 46011

February 28, 1990

Applied Software, Inc.

P.O. Box 42341

Seattle, WA 98115

Dear Sir, *or Madam*:

computer

I am a sixth grade student. I use an arrow ~~computor~~. I use

your

it for schoolwork. I am now using Hiwrite. It is ~~you're~~

YOUR TURN

Proofreading Practice

Below is the beginning of a business letter that you can use to practice your proofreading skills. Find the errors. Write the letter correctly on a separate piece of paper.

Box 87C
Waitfield VT 95673
September 18 1990

R.B. Porter, Inc.
P.O. Box 100
Fall river Massachusets 02720

Dear Sir or madam

Proofreading Checklist
- Did I use the correct form for writing a business letter?
- Did I indent each paragraph?
- Did I spell all words correctly?
- Which punctuation errors do I need to correct?
- Which capitalization errors do I need to fix?

Applying Your Proofreading Skills

Now proofread your business letter. Read your checklist one last time. Review **The Grammar Connection** and **The Mechanics Connection**, too. Use the proofreading marks to make changes.

THE GRAMMAR CONNECTION

Remember these rules about using possessive pronouns.

- Use the possessive pronouns *my, our, your, her, his, its,* and *their* before a noun.
- The possessive pronouns *mine, ours, yours, hers, his, its,* and *theirs* stand alone.
- Do not use an apostrophe in a possessive pronoun.
  This is **her** sweater. (before a noun)
  This sweater is **hers.** (stands alone)
  Where is **your** book? (possessive pronoun)

Check your business letter. Have you used possessive pronouns correctly?

Proofreading Marks
ꟷ Indent
∧ Add
⩓ Add a comma
ᵛᵛ Add quotation marks
⦵ Add a period
⤸ Take out
≡ Capitalize
/ Make a small letter
∿ Reverse the order

THE MECHANICS CONNECTION

Remember these rules about using commas and colons in letters.

- Use a comma to separate the city from the state in an address and the day from the year in a date.
- Use a comma after the closing of a business letter.
- Use a colon after the greeting of a business letter.

Madison, WI	September 11, 1990
Sincerely,	Dear Sir or Madam:

Check your business letter. Have you used commas and colons correctly?

Publish: Step 5

Greg sent his letter to the software company. First, however, he made a copy of it on a photocopier and posted it on the class bulletin board. Several of his friends asked him to let them know what answer he received.

YOUR TURN

Make a final copy of your business letter. Use your best handwriting, or use a typewriter or computer. Think of a way to share your letter. You might use one of the ideas in the **Sharing Suggestions** box below.

SHARING SUGGESTIONS

Exchange letters with a classmate. Write a reply to your classmate's letter.	Send your letter to the person or company for which it was intended. Read the response to the class, and discuss whether it was the response you expected.	With three or four classmates, form a panel. Imagine that you answer mail for a major company. Read and discuss the letters from another group. Decide which are most business-like and why.

4 SPEAKING AND LISTENING: Conducting an Interview

You have just written a business letter. You could think of a letter as one side of a dialogue in which you ask a question or make a request and another person responds. In order to achieve the response you want, you must ask the right question in the right way.

An **interview** follows a similar pattern of questions and answers. To prepare for an interview, first find out about your subject. Do as much research as possible. Then decide what questions to ask. A good way to make an interview flow smoothly is to make a note card. The note card will include only the main questions for the interview.

Look at this note card.

Notes   Interview

1. Purpose: find out about a sportswriter's job

2. How does someone get started as a sportswriter?

3. What preparation is needed?

4. What are the benefits and drawbacks?

What kinds of questions has the writer listed? Notice that the questions cannot be answered by just "yes" or "no."

When you conduct an interview, it will help to keep some guidelines in mind.

- Why is it important to be sure the subject knows the purpose of the interview?
- How will taking notes help you after the interview?

SPEAKING GUIDELINES: An Interview

1. Make a note card of questions. Practice asking questions before the interview.
2. Remember the purpose of the interview and state it clearly.
3. Be courteous to the person whom you interview.
4. Ask questions simply and directly.
5. Listen closely to the answers and take notes about them.
6. Ask questions to get more information about an answer or if new questions occur to you.

SPEAKING APPLICATION An Interview

Think of someone whom you would like to interview. It may be a famous author, a local government official, or even a television or movie star. Use the interview guidelines to help you to prepare. To conduct the interview, work with a partner who will play the part of the person you are interviewing. Your partner will use the following guidelines as he or she is interviewed.

LISTENING GUIDELINES: An Interview

1. Think about the purpose of the interview: What does the interviewer want to know?
2. Listen carefully to each question.
3. Ask the interviewer to explain a question if it is unclear.

5 WRITER'S RESOURCES: Skimming and Scanning

In this unit, you have seen how to get information by writing a letter and by conducting an interview. You also know how to find information in books and articles. When you are reading for information, techniques of skimming and scanning can help you.

Skimming is a way of reading quickly. Skim for an overview of a story or an article. To skim, read the title and any headings. Then, read the first paragraph and the first sentence of other paragraphs. Look for key words. Finally, read the last paragraph. Skimming can help you to decide whether a book or an article has the information you are looking for. You can also skim to review an article after you have read it.

Scanning is a way to find specific information. To scan, decide on key words that will help you to locate the information you need, and look for those words on the page. For example, if you wanted information about computer mail, you might scan for the words *letter*, *mail*, and *computer*. To find a date, look for numerals. When you find a key word, slow down and read carefully to look for the exact information you need.

Practice

Answer the items below on a separate sheet of paper.

1. Skim the following paragraph. Write a sentence that states the main idea.

Computers and the Telephone

You dial a long-distance call from a pay phone. A voice says, "Deposit $1.65 for the first three minutes." A computer is talking to you. When you dial a number, a computer relays the numbers to the correct circuit. When you call Information, an operator punches the name you want into a computer, which tells you the number. Computers also routinely check long-distance lines to be sure that they are clear. You may not realize it, but computers are vital to telephone service.

---

2 Scan the following paragraph. Find out what the initials *CRT* stand for.

When you type information on your computer keyboard, it is transferred to the CRT. From the display on the CRT, you are able to read what you have typed and whatever information the computer supplies. The computer CRT, or cathode-ray tube, is like a television screen. It transmits the picture or letters by highlighting many tiny dots.

WRITING APPLICATION Notes

Skim crafts or how-to books to find an item you would like to make, such as a model or a piece of jewelry. After you have chosen a project, scan to find out what materials are necessary and how to get started. Make notes, and keep them in your writing folder. You will use them in **The Curriculum Connection** on page 292.

Writing About Mathematics

When you think about mathematics, you probably think first of number problems in your arithmetic book. But you are using mathematics all the time—when you plan how to spend your allowance and when you decide whether you have time to go to a movie.

You also often write about mathematics. Many business letters involve mathematics because they mention prices, amounts, or times. Sportswriting requires math about records, distances, batting averages, etc. Writing about mathematics must be clear, direct, and factual.

ACTIVITIES

Visualize an Object to Make   Look at the notes you made when you skimmed and scanned the how-to article for the activity on page 291. Use your notes to draw a diagram of the item you would like to make. Label your diagram with measurements and materials. Then, write a brief explanation of how you would make the item.

Describe a Photograph   Look at the photograph on the following page. Write a letter to a friend describing a billing problem. Include a description of the desk and the bills. Include all the figures your friend will need to understand the problem.

Respond to Literature   The following excerpt is taken from "R.U. There?" by Constance L. Melaro. It illustrates the difficulty of corresponding with a computer. After reading the excerpt, write a letter in response. Your letter may be to the computer, to the woman in the story, or to a friend. Share your response with the class by showing your work or by reading it aloud.

Dear Madam: August 17

Our records show an outstanding balance of $2.98 on your account. If you have already remitted this amount, kindly disregard this notice.

Gentlemen: August 19

I do not have an outstanding balance. I attached a note with my payment advising you that I had been billed twice for the same amount. Please check your records.

Dear Madam: November 17

Our records now show you to be delinquent for four months in the total amount of $17.56 plus $1.87 handling charges. Please remit in full in ten days or your account will be turned over to our Auditing Department for collection.

Dear ANYONE Human: November 19

Will you please take your head out of the computer long enough to read this? I don't owe you this money!!! I don't owe you any money! None!

Dear Madam: February 17

According to our microfilm records, our billing was in error. Your account is clear; you have no balance. We hope there will be no further inconvenience to you.

Dear Madam: March 17

Our records show you to be delinquent in the amount of $2.98, erroneously posted last August to a non-existent account. May we have your remittance at this time?

Dear Machine: March 19

I give up. You win. Here's a check for $2.98. Enjoy yourself.

Dear Madam: April 17

Our records show an overpayment on your part of $2.98. We are crediting this amount to your account.

UNIT CHECKUP

LESSON 1

Group Writing: A Business Letter (page 274) Read this letter. On a separate sheet of paper, rewrite the letter correctly, supplying any missing parts.

100 So. First Street
Ventura, CA 93001
May 1, 1990

Better Vision Institute
230 Park Avenue
New York, NY 10017

Please send me your free kit for schools. Thank you.

Meryl Geehr

LESSON 2

Thinking: Solving Problems (page 278) Imagine that you are writing a letter asking for a refund for an item that did not work properly. What is missing from this list? Write the detail on a separate sheet of paper.

1. a description of the item   **3.** the date of the order
2. your address   **4.** the order number

LESSON 3

Writing a Business Letter (page 280) Imagine that you are looking for a summer job. Write a business letter to possible employers, explaining the kind of job you want and giving your qualifications. Use correct business-letter form.

LESSON 4

Speaking and Listening: An Interview (page 288) Imagine that you are going to interview the mayor. Make a list of the guidelines for conducting an interview.

LESSON 5

Writer's Resources: Skimming and Scanning (page 290) On a separate piece of paper, write whether you would use **skimming** or **scanning** in each situation below.

1. to review the materials for a science test
2. to find a paragraph about tomatoes in a gardening book

THEME PROJECT NEWS PROGRAM

Think about the kinds of communication that you know. Letters, interviews, telephones, telegraphs, radio, and television help to pass information around the world.

Look at the picture below. This picture shows a television news program. Talk with your classmates about the kinds of features a television news program contains.

Imagine that you are the producers and reporters of "Good Morning, Sixth Grade."

- Work with a group of classmates to produce a television news program.
- Begin by brainstorming some ideas for features, such as a survey of students on a school policy or an interview with a member of a sports team.
- Make a list of what you will include.
- Gather the information, and present your program to the class.

UNIT

9

Adjectives

In this unit you will learn about adjectives. Adjectives add flavor and detail to your writing.

Discuss Read the poem on the opposite page. According to the poet, what is the best way to get to know something?

JOURNAL

Creative Expression The unit theme is *Observations*. A good observer takes notes on the activity under study, but remains in the background. Choose a subject to observe, such as a squirrel, a bird, or a child playing, and report your observations to the class. Write your thoughts in your journal.

To look at any thing,
If you would know that thing,
You must look at it long. . . .

—John Moffitt,
    from "To Look at Any Thing"

1 ADJECTIVES

An adjective is a word that modifies, or describes, a noun or a pronoun.

To describe people, places, and things you often use adjectives. Adjectives can tell *what kind*, *which one*, or *how many* about something.

WHAT KIND:	I like Klee's **colorful** paintings.
WHICH ONE(S):	I saw **those** pictures in **this** museum.
HOW MANY:	Kai admired **several** sculptures by **one** artist.

Adjectives can come before or after the word they describe.

That picture shows **three blue** birds.

Klee's paintings, **colorful** and **strange,** amuse me.

A **predicate adjective** follows a linking verb and describes the subject.

The painting is **excellent.** It looks **old.**

Guided Practice

Name the adjective or adjectives in each sentence. Then tell which noun or pronoun each adjective describes.

Example: We saw important pictures.   *important pictures*

1. We liked those paintings by Rousseau.
2. They are famous.
3. Several paintings show wild animals.
4. The animals live in a dense, tropical jungle.
5. That moon, bright and eerie, makes me shiver!

**THINK**

■ How can I use adjectives to improve my writing?

REMEMBER

- An **adjective** is a word that modifies, or describes, a noun or a pronoun.
- A **predicate adjective** follows a linking verb and describes the subject.

More Practice

A. Write each sentence. Then, draw one line under each adjective. Draw two lines under the word that the adjective describes.

Example: Rod posed for the <u>large</u> <u><u>portrait</u></u>.

6. Mrs. Ives painted these pictures.
7. They are original.
8. She has used three colors.
9. This painting is red, yellow, and blue.
10. These shades are called primary colors.
11. These colors, bright and natural, delight the eye.
12. You can mix colors to create secondary colors.
13. Red paint and yellow paint make orange paint.

B. Write each sentence. Fill in each blank with an adjective.

Example: The museum displays _____ sculptures.
 The museum displays modern sculptures.

14. _____ picture shows a room.
15. The picture is by a _____ artist.
16. _____ chairs are in the corner.
17. The door of the room is _____.
18. You can see _____ tapestries on the walls.
19. _____ pictures are of sunflowers.
20. The _____ light makes the room look _____.

Extra Practice, page 316

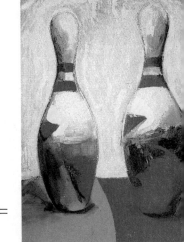

WRITING APPLICATION A Post Card

Imagine that you have just visited a museum. Write a post card to a friend, describing some of the paintings you liked. Identify the adjectives in a classmate's work.

2 ARTICLES AND DEMONSTRATIVES

You often use the words *a*, *an*, and *the* before nouns. These words are special adjectives called **articles.**

The telescope was mounted on **a** large tripod.

Use *the* to refer to a specific item or items.

the sun   **the** eye   **the** stars

Use *a* or *an* to refer to any one item in a group. *A* is used before words beginning with a consonant. *An* is used before words that begin with a vowel sound.

a planet   **an** astronomer   **a** lens   **an** hour

Adjectives that tell *which one* are called **demonstrative adjectives.** They point out specific persons or things.

This planet is nearer to the sun than **that** star.

These telescopes are more powerful than **those** telescopes.

This and *these* point out nearby people or things. *That* and *those* point out people or things that are more distant.

DEMONSTRATIVE ADJECTIVES
Singular   this   that
Plural   these   those

Guided Practice

Tell which word correctly completes each sentence.

Example: I saw (a, an) comet.   *a*

1. The astronomers are observing (a, the) sky.
2. This observatory has (a, an) enormous telescope.
3. We made a visit to (a, an) observatory.
4. The sky was very clear (that, those) evening.
5. (This, These) chart shows the constellation Pisces.

 THINK

■ How do I decide when to use *a* or *an*?

REMEMBER

- *A*, *an*, and *the* are special adjectives called **articles.**
- A **demonstrative adjective** points out something and describes nouns by answering the questions *which one?* or *which ones?*

More Practice

A. Write the article that correctly completes each sentence.

Example: This chart shows (a, an) galaxy near Earth.   *a*

6. (A, An) astronomer gave our class a tour.
7. (A, The) observatory was quiet.
8. Nevertheless, (an, the) scientists were busy.
9. Very few lights shone in (a, the) darkness.
10. One astronomer made notes about (a, an) eclipse.
11. We heard (a, the) hum of several computers.
12. (A, The) ceiling of the room was domelike.
13. Brad and Heather looked through (a, an) telescope.

B. Write the demonstrative adjective that correctly completes each sentence.

Example: (That, Those) planet is visible this week.   *That*

14. (This, These) telescope contains a lens and two mirrors.
15. We will use (that, those) tripod.
16. Can you see the sky through (this, these) lenses?
17. The planet Saturn is now in (that, those) constellation.
18. (That, Those) rings around the planet are fascinating!
19. Particles of water-ice create (that, these) effect.
20. (That, Those) small, bright objects are satellites, or moons.

Extra Practice, page 317

WRITING APPLICATION A Journal Entry

Imagine that you are observing the night sky through a telescope. Write a journal entry to report your observations. Check your writing for correct usage of articles and demonstratives. Share your journal entry with the class.

COOPERATIVE LEARNING

3 ADJECTIVES THAT COMPARE

You often use adjectives to compare two or more people, things, or ideas. Use the **comparative form** of an adjective to compare two things. You form the comparative by adding *er* to most one-syllable and some two-syllable adjectives. Use the **superlative form** of an adjective to compare more than two things. You usually form the superlative by adding *est*.

> COMPARATIVE: The lion is **heavier** than the zebra.
>
> SUPERLATIVE: The elephant is the **heaviest** animal in the jungle.

When you add *er* or *est* to form the comparative or superlative, the spelling of an adjective may change.

heavy

Spelling Changes in Comparative and Superlative Adjectives			
Adjectives ending in *e*: drop the final *e*.	rare	rar**er**	rar**est**
	large	larg**er**	larg**est**
Adjectives ending in a consonant preceded by a single vowel: double the consonant.	flat	flat**ter**	flat**test**
	thin	thin**ner**	thin**nest**
	big	big**ger**	big**gest**
Adjectives ending in *y*: change the *y* to *i*.	angry	angr**ier**	angr**iest**
	tiny	tin**ier**	tin**iest**

Guided Practice

Tell the comparative and superlative forms of each word.

Example: rare   *rarer*   *rarest*

1. cold   **2.** sad   **3.** nice   **4.** busy   **5.** big

?! THINK

■ How do I decide whether to use the comparative or superlative form of an adjective?

heavier

REMEMBER

- The **comparative** form of an adjective compares two nouns.
- The **superlative** form of an adjective compares more than two nouns.

More Practice

A. Write each sentence, using the correct comparative or superlative form of the adjective in parentheses.

Example: Ocelots are (tamer, tamest) than leopards. *tamer*

  6. Leopards have _____ spots than cheetahs. (darker, darkest)
  7. They climb the _____ trees of all. (higher, highest)
  8. Lions are _____ than leopards. (stronger, strongest)
  9. Cheetahs are the _____ of all the big cats. (faster, fastest)
 10. They have _____ tails than leopards. (longer, longest)
 11. They are often _____ than their prey. (swifter, swiftest)
 12. That cub looks _____ than this one. (younger, youngest)
 13. The _____ cub of all looks like a cat. (smaller, smallest)

B. Write these sentences. Use the correct comparative or superlative form of the adjective to complete each sentence.

Example: A rhinoceros is _____ than a lion. (big) *bigger*

 14. Rhinos are some of the _____ beasts of all. (large)
 15. Black rhinos are the _____ of all rhinos. (rare)
 16. Hippos have a _____ temper than rhinos. (nice)
 17. Irritated rhinos may become _____ than lions. (angry)
 18. Is the calf _____ than its mother? (hungry)
 19. This hippopotamus looks _____ than that rhino. (fat)
 20. Those legs are the _____ I have ever seen! (stubby)

Extra Practice, page 318

WRITING APPLICATION A Friendly Letter

Imagine that you are on a safari. Write a letter to a friend, comparing the various wild animals. Identify the comparative and superlative adjectives in a classmate's letter.

4 ADJECTIVES WITH *MORE* AND *MOST*

You have learned to add *er* and *est* to many adjectives to form the comparative and superlative. That rule applies to most one-syllable and some two-syllable adjectives. For most adjectives that have two or more syllables, add the words *more* and *most* to form the comparative and superlative.

Adjective	Comparative	Superlative
difficult	**more** difficult	**most** difficult
colorful	**more** colorful	**most** colorful

Do not combine *more* and *most* with adjectives ending in *er* and *est*.

CORRECT: Herons are **larger** than sea gulls.
INCORRECT: Herons are more larger than sea gulls.

Some adjectives have irregular comparative and superlative forms.

Adjective	Comparative	Superlative
good	better	best
bad	worse	worst
much, many	more	most
little	less	least

Guided Practice

Tell the comparative and superlative form of each adjective.

Example: interesting   *more interesting   most interesting*

1. exciting
2. rewarding
3. good
4. little
5. bad

?! THINK

■ How do I decide when to use *more* and *most* with adjectives?

REMEMBER

- Use *more* and *most* to form the comparative and superlative of most adjectives with two or more syllables.

More Practice

A. Write the correct comparative or superlative form of the adjective in parentheses.

Example: That eagle is ＿＿＿ than this raven. (splendid)
    more splendid

6. Flamingos seem ＿＿＿ than storks. (awkward)

7. Does any bird have ＿＿＿ legs? (delicate)

8. Flamingos have ＿＿＿ necks than swans. (graceful)

9. Their food is ＿＿＿ near the shore. (plentiful)

10. They have the ＿＿＿ bill of any bird. (unusual)

11. That is the ＿＿＿ shade of pink! (attractive)

12. Is this where the birds are ＿＿＿ of all? (numerous)

13. That bird has the ＿＿＿ neck of all. (flexible)

B. Write each sentence, filling in each blank with a comparative or superlative form of an adjective.

Example: The animals are ＿＿＿ varied here.
    The animals are more varied here.

14. The climate here is ＿＿＿ than you might think.

15. There is ＿＿＿ rain in spring than in summer.

16. The ＿＿＿ rain of all falls in November.

17. Summer is the ＿＿＿ time of all for safaris.

18. This is the animals' ＿＿＿ season to find water.

19. You have ＿＿＿ difficulty spotting zebras than leopards.

20. Cheetahs are ＿＿＿ than leopards.

Extra Practice, Practice Plus, pages 319–321

WRITING APPLICATION A Comparison

With a partner choose two different types of animals and compare them. Make up a fact sheet. Check that you have used comparative and superlative adjectives correctly.

COOPERATIVE
LEARNING

5 MECHANICS:
Capitalizing Proper Adjectives

You are studying the English language. The word *English* is a proper adjective that tells *what kind*. A **proper adjective** is an adjective formed from a proper noun. Like a proper noun, a proper adjective begins with a capital letter.

You sometimes need to change the spelling of proper nouns to change them into proper adjectives. Some of the most common spelling changes are shown below.

Proper Noun	Ending	Proper Adjective
Japan	ese	Japan**ese**
America	n	America**n**
Egypt Italy	ian	Egypt**ian** Ital**ian**
England	ish	Engl**ish**

There are also irregular spelling changes in proper adjectives.

France—French   Wales—Welsh   Norway—Norwegian

If needed, use a dictionary to check the correct spelling.

Guided Practice

Tell which word should be capitalized in each sentence.

Example: The delicate lace is irish.   *Irish*

1. That large, old house is victorian.
2. Most of the furniture in this room is asian.
3. On the mantel is a small chinese vase.
4. Are those beads korean?

The American flag

?! THINK

■ How do I decide when an adjective should be capitalized?

REMEMBER

■ A **proper adjective** is formed from a proper noun and begins with a capital letter.

More Practice

A. Correctly write the proper adjective in each sentence.

Example: That navajo blanket is a family heirloom.   *Navajo*

5. The mexican pottery is valuable.
6. The antique table in the dining room is chinese.
7. A large japanese screen stands behind it.
8. Around the table are four french chairs.
9. That colorful rug is made from turkish wool.
10. The beautiful design of the rug is persian.
11. Is that a siamese cat by the open window?
12. Ved told us the teapot was made of indian brass.

B. Write these sentences. Complete each sentence by forming a proper adjective from the noun in parentheses.

Example: We enjoyed the ＿＿＿ tacos (Mexico)
      We enjoyed the Mexican tacos.

13. That restaurant serves ＿＿＿ dishes. (Europe)
14. The ＿＿＿ pasta is always delicious. (Italy)
15. ＿＿＿ sardines are grilled over charcoal. (Portugal)
16. Our class smelled the aroma of ＿＿＿ pudding. (England)
17. You can order gazpacho, a ＿＿＿ soup. (Spain)
18. ＿＿＿ meatballs is a specialty. (Sweden)
19. The ＿＿＿ goulash is always spicy. (Hungary)
20. ＿＿＿ pastries are served for dessert. (France)

Extra Practice, page 322

WRITING APPLICATION Captions

Imagine that you are preparing a photo guide for tourists. Make a list of five countries. Write a caption about each country, using a proper adjective.

VOCABULARY BUILDING:
Synonyms and Antonyms

Good writing has variety and is precise. Using synonyms and antonyms can help you make your writing clearer and more interesting.

A **synonym** is a word that has the same or almost the same meaning as another word.

The ocean looked **calm.**   The ocean looked **placid.**
The beach was **calm.**   The beach was **peaceful.**
I felt **calm.**   I felt **relaxed.**

placid = peaceful = relaxed

Antonyms are words with opposite meanings.

The current was **strong,** but near the shore it was **weak.**

You can often form the antonym of an adjective by using the prefix un, in, or im.

even/**un**even   expensive/**in**expensive   possible/**im**possible

Synonyms and antonyms for many words are given in the Thesaurus on page 510.

Guided Practice

Read each pair of words. Tell which pairs are synonyms and which pairs are antonyms.

Example: fortunate/lucky   synonyms

1. nimble/clumsy   **3.** dark/light   **5.** rough/coarse
2. loud/noisy   **4.** slow/rapid

 THINK

■ How can I use synonyms and antonyms to improve my writing?

REMEMBER

- A **synonym** is a word that has the same or almost the same meaning as another word.
- **Antonyms** are words with opposite meanings.

More Practice

Write a synonym and an antonym for each underlined word in these sentences. Use your dictionary if you need help.

Example: The new clubhouse was <u>comfortable</u>.
            pleasant   uncomfortable

6. The stands on one side of the field were <u>empty</u>.
7. The spectators at the game seemed in a <u>cheerful</u> mood.
8. Some fans waved banners made from <u>bright</u> strips of cloth.
9. The cheers were <u>loud</u> when our team took the field.
10. You could feel the <u>tense</u> excitement in the air.
11. The weather was <u>perfect</u> for a football game.
12. The fans were <u>hopeful</u> about our team's chances.
13. A few fans waved their hats in the <u>cold</u> air.
14. The new stadium looked <u>magnificent</u>.
15. It had been painted a <u>gorgeous</u> shade of blue.
16. The paint was <u>glossy</u>.
17. The floodlights were <u>large</u>.
18. The seats felt <u>soft</u>.
19. The aisles were <u>roomy</u>.
20. The decorations looked <u>showy</u>.

Extra Practice, page 323

WRITING APPLICATION A Descriptive Paragraph

Write brief descriptions of five people or objects in your classroom. Then rewrite your descriptions, replacing as many adjectives as possible with antonyms. Exchange papers with a classmate, and see if you can guess the identity of the original people or objects.

GRAMMAR —AND WRITING CONNECTION

Combining Sentences

You can often combine details from two or three sentences into a single sentence. To combine sentences, you may use possessive nouns and change the position of adjectives.

> **SEPARATE:** Jessica works in a flower shop.
> The shop is owned by her father.
> The shop is colorful.
>
> **COMBINED:** Jessica works in her father's colorful flower shop.

Working Together

COOPERATIVE
LEARNING

Tell how you would combine each group of sentences to make a single sentence. Use an adjective and a possessive noun in each combined sentence.

Example: Jessica ate sandwiches for lunch.
Her mother made the sandwiches.
The sandwiches were delicious.

Jessica ate her mother's delicious sandwiches for lunch.

1. An artist studied the flowers.
   The flowers belonged to Jessica.
   The flowers were red.
2. The artist saw a kitten.
   The kitten was owned by Don.
   The kitten was mischievous.

Revising Sentences

Mark made these notes during a trip to various stores. Help Mark revise his notes by combining the sentences. Make sure you add both an adjective and a possessive noun to your combined sentence.

3. The kitten played with the crayons.
   Crayons were used by the artist.
   The crayons were yellow.

4. Mark passed a sports store.
   The store belonged to Mr. Dent.
   The store was small.

5. Mark spotted a fruit stand.
   The stand was managed by a friend.
   The stand was convenient.

6. Mark had lunch in a coffee shop.
   The coffee shop was owned by his mother.
   The coffee shop felt cozy.

7. Mark stopped at a pizza store.
   It was run by Pietro.
   It was a new store.

8. He saw some children in a toy store.
   The store was managed by an elderly couple.
   The store was crowded.

Write a paragraph about a trip to a store in your neighborhood—a record store, for example. Try to make your paragraph vivid by using adjectives.

When you check over your work, try to combine sentences using possessive nouns.

GRAMMAR AND WRITING CONNECTION: Combining Sentences

UNIT CHECKUP

LESSON

Adjectives (page 298) For each sentence, write the adjective and the word it describes.

1. Alexander Calder is creative.
2. His famous mobiles delight us.
3. He made that mobile.
4. It has eleven units.
5. Each unit is different.
6. His circuses, wonderful and strange, amaze children.
7. They are products of his great genius.

LESSON

Articles and Demonstratives (page 300) Write the correct article or demonstrative to complete each sentence.

8. (An, The) mobile is suspended.
9. It hangs from (this, those) ceiling.
10. All (this, these) units move independently, rising and falling around each other.
11. Do you see (that, those) red triangles?
12. (This, These) mobiles are fascinating.
13. They sway in (an, the) breeze.
14. They make (a, an) unusual tinkling sound as the pieces bump together.

LESSON 3

Adjectives That Compare (page 302) Write each sentence, using the correct comparative or superlative form of the adjective in parentheses.

15. These vegetables are _____ than those. (fresh)
16. This lettuce is the _____ of all. (fine)
17. Have you ever eaten _____ tomatoes? (juicy)
18. That ear of corn is the _____ of all. (sweet)
19. That pumpkin is _____ than this spaghetti squash. (large)
20. Peas are _____ than lima beans. (tasty)
21. That gourd is _____ than this one. (fat)
22. These carrots are the _____ of all. (crunchy)

LESSON

Adjectives with *more* and *most* (page 304) Write each sentence, using the correct comparative or superlative form of the adjective in parentheses.

23. This rug has the _____ pattern. (splendid)
24. The blue carpet has _____ knots than the red one. (many)
25. Which of these two rugs is _____? (expensive)
26. That one shows the _____ wear of all. (little)
27. This is the _____ design of all. (good)
28. That wool carpet is _____ than this one. (good)

LESSON

Mechanics: Capitalizing Proper Adjectives (page 306) Write each group of words. Underline and capitalize each proper adjective.

29. exotic japanese architecture
30. delicate french perfume
31. skilled mexican cooks
32. the english language
33. tasty canadian bacon
34. fine italian leather

LESSON

Vocabulary Building: Synonyms and Antonyms (page 308) Write each sentence. Use a synonym for the underlined word. Then write an antonym for each underlined word.

35. The weather was <u>pleasant</u>.
36. <u>Small</u> flakes of snow fell.
37. <u>Light</u> gusts of wind blew.
38. The wind felt <u>warm</u>.
39. <u>Thin</u> clouds appeared.
40. <u>Large</u> breaks in the clouds formed.

Writing Application: Adjective Usage (pages 298–307) The paragraph below contains 10 errors in adjective usage. Rewrite the paragraph correctly.

41.–50.

   An long road led through the vermont countryside toward the canadian border. A apple orchard lay in the distance. The orchard seemed more larger than I had remembered. To me it was a more beautiful scene in the world. On these day I had the most best times of my vacation.

ENRICHMENT

SWEET AS A SPRING DAY

Scan some magazines and newspapers and cut out interesting pictures. Find five pictures that you especially like. For each picture write one adjective that sums up what you think when you look at it, such as *tall*, *pretty*, *strong*, *scary*, *exciting*. Then, imagine something with which to compare the image. For example, if you have a picture of a skyscraper, you might wish to compare it to a great tree. Now, combine your comparison with your adjective to form a single phrase that describes the picture: "tall as a redwood tree." Create one descriptive phrase for each picture.

TO THE FUTURE—AND BACK

With a small group of classmates, write a story about traveling into the future. Then replace all the adjectives with antonyms.

Change your story as much as possible. You may be able to turn it into a nonsense story.

FUN, FINE, AND FANTASTIC

Play this game with a partner. Make a list of ten subjects you find interesting, such as movie stars, favorite dishes, and special activities. Call out these ten things, one at a time. Tell your partner to call out at least two adjectives that describe each thing. For example, if you call out "meringue," your partner might respond, "tasty!" or "fattening!" Take turns. Try to think of unusual subjects and colorful adjectives.

CREATIVE EXPRESSION

DREAMS

Hold fast to dreams
For if dreams die
Life is a broken-winged bird
That cannot fly.

Hold fast to dreams
For when dreams go
Life is a barren field
Frozen with snow.

—*Langston Hughes*

TRY IT OUT!

"Dreams" is a descriptive poem that uses comparisons to tell how the speaker feels about dreams. Think of a dream or goal you have had. Write a short poem that describes your dream. Try to include a comparison in your poem. Share your poem with a friend.

315

EXTRA PRACTICE

Three levels of practice
Adjectives (page 298)

LEVEL A. Write each sentence. Draw two lines under each adjective that describes each underlined noun.

1. Iron <u>gates</u> stood at the entrance to Cal's house.
2. They opened onto a long <u>driveway</u>.
3. The driveway was made of gray <u>gravel</u>.
4. Tall <u>trees</u> stood by the house.
5. A white <u>porch</u> surrounded the house.
6. Three <u>steps</u> led up to the porch.
7. The <u>house</u> was yellow.
8. There was a <u>chimney</u>, tall and square, on the roof.
9. Dark <u>smoke</u> rose from the chimney.

LEVEL B. Write each sentence. Draw two lines under each adjective. Draw one line under the word the adjective describes.

10. The porch was supported by graceful columns.
11. Pots of pink geraniums were everywhere.
12. Attractive curtains decorated each window.
13. Two gardeners knocked at our door.
14. My elderly aunt answered.
15. They brought these roses.
16. They also cut several tulips.
17. That vase cannot hold the flowers.
18. Roses, both red and white, can be put together.

LEVEL C. Use the following adjectives in sentences. Draw one line under the noun or pronoun that each adjective describes.

19. nine
20. green
21. that
22. six
23. beautiful
24. several
25. those

EXTRA PRACTICE

Three levels of practice
Articles and Demonstratives (page 300)

LEVEL A. Write each article or demonstrative adjective.

1. Italian is an easy language to pronounce.
2. It is one of the most attractive languages.
3. All these vowels should be sounded.
4. That word is pronounced as it is spelled.
5. These consonants are more difficult to pronounce.
6. For example, *ch* always sounds like a *k*.
7. The Italian composer Verdi wrote operas.
8. The Italian language sounds very musical.
9. *Aida* is a famous opera by Verdi.
10. It tells the story of an Ethiopian princess.

LEVEL B. Write each sentence. Draw one line under each article and two lines under each demonstrative adjective.

11. The opera is set in an ancient city.
12. Are these sets for the first act?
13. How tall those columns for the temple are!
14. The students think that the costumes are magnificent.
15. A chariot will be used for the general's entrance.
16. That stage design is splendid.
17. The cast is very excited.
18. Many of these singers are very young.

LEVEL C. Complete each sentence by writing the correct article or demonstrative adjective.

19. (Those, That) costumes will be used in the second act.
20. On (this, these) side is a golden throne.
21. (The, An) tenor must sing a difficult aria.
22. This aria ends with (a, the) very high note.
23. Will (these, this) dancers appear on the stage?
24. (A, The) singing is of high quality.
25. The audience loves (this, those) performances.

EXTRA PRACTICE

Three levels of practice
Adjectives That Compare (page 302)

LEVEL
A. Write the comparative or superlative adjective in each sentence.

1. The teacher said that Mercury is the smallest planet in the solar system.
2. Jupiter is the largest planet.
3. Is Neptune bigger than Uranus?
4. Venus is the planet second nearest to the sun.
5. Are the temperatures on Saturn the coldest of all?
6. It is certainly windier on Mars than on Earth.
7. Mars has icier conditions, too.
8. Pluto takes the longest time to orbit the sun.
9. Which planet has the flatter orbit, Venus or Mars?
10. The temperatures on Mercury are the warmest of all.

LEVEL
B. Choose the form of the adjective in parentheses that correctly completes each sentence.

11. One of the (odder, oddest) mammals of all is the bat.
12. The (older, oldest) bats of all live to be over 20 years old.
13. Some bats can be (smaller, smallest) than your fingernail.
14. Other bats have a wingspan (larger, largest) than five feet.
15. Bats have (shorter, shortest) wings than some birds.
16. They have the (keener, keenest) hearing of any land mammal.
17. Their flight is (jerkier, jerkiest) than that of the eagle.
18. Owls kill the (greater, greatest) number of bats.

LEVEL
C. Write each sentence. Write the form of the adjective in parentheses that correctly completes each sentence.

19. Bats are _____ creatures than I had thought. (cute)
20. They are some of the _____ mammals. (smart)
21. This bat feels _____ than a mouse. (furry)
22. The fur of bats is the _____ of any mammal. (fine)
23. Bats can find their way in the _____ of caves. (dark)
24. Bats are _____ of all when nighttime comes. (happy)
25. It is then that they fly the _____ distances of all. (long)

EXTRA PRACTICE

Three Levels of practice
Adjectives with *more* and *most* (page 304)

LEVEL A. Write the word or words that correctly complete each sentence.

1. Texas is one of the (more interesting, most interesting) of all the states.
2. Few sights are (more historic, most historic) than the Alamo.
3. The Hispanic restaurants there are (better, best) than any others.
4. The shops are (more unusual, most unusual) than you might think.
5. There are (good, better) guides in San Antonio than in Austin.
6. Houston seems (more active, most active) than El Paso.
7. It has the (more exciting, most exciting) events in the state.
8. There are also (more, most) universities there.
9. Dallas is (more commercial, most commercial) than San Antonio.
10. Dallas may be the (more famous, most famous) city in Texas.

LEVEL B. Write the correct comparative or superlative form of the adjective in parentheses to complete each sentence.

11. Which marshland is the _____ of all? (attractive)
12. Are the birds _____ here than there? (numerous)
13. Which of the two cameras is _____? (expensive)
14. Will this camera take the _____ pictures? (beautiful)
15. Those cranes are _____ than I thought. (agile)
16. This species is the _____ of all. (unusual)
17. That pelican is _____ than the cranes. (awkward)
18. This bird is the _____ in the marsh. (colorful)

LEVEL C. Complete each sentence. Use the correct comparative or superlative form of an adjective with *more* or *most.*

19. Those birds have the _____ markings of all.
20. We had _____ trouble finding sea gulls than cranes.
21. The cry of those birds is the _____ I have ever heard.
22. Those photos are the _____ I have ever taken.
23. The photo of the chicks is the _____ one.
24. That picture shows the _____ bird.
25. I had _____ difficulty taking pictures than I had expected.

PRACTICE + PLUS

Three levels of additional practice for a difficult skill

Adjectives with *more* and *most* (page 304)

LEVEL **A.** Write **more** or **most** to complete each sentence.

1. Of all trees, sequoias are the _____ magnificent.
2. Of the two types of sequoias, redwoods and giant sequoias, redwoods are _____ common.
3. Earth's _____ ancient living thing may be a sequoia.
4. The General Sherman tree, the _____ famous sequoia of all, is about 3,500 years old.
5. The 300-foot redwoods are _____ enormous than sequoias.
6. With their gigantic trunks, sequoias are _____ massive in volume than redwoods.
7. Lumber from redwoods is _____ valuable than most wood.
8. Outdoor furniture is its _____ popular use.
9. Giant sequoias are the _____ durable trees of all.
10. They are _____ resistant to disease and insects than any other tree.
11. Of all the places we visited, Redwood National Park was the _____ thrilling.
12. Redwoods like a _____ humid climate than sequoias.
13. California's redwoods are _____ numerous than Oregon's.
14. In the distant past, sequoias were one of the _____ common trees in the Northern Hemisphere.
15. Now, they are _____ localized, growing only in California's high Sierra Nevada Mountains.
16. Today people are _____ concerned about protecting the sequoias than they were in the past.
17. Many citizens have become _____ intelligent about the environment than they were in the past.

PRACTICE + PLUS

Write each sentence, using the correct comparative or superlative form of each adjective.

18. This bowl is (beautifuller, more beautiful) than that one.
19. Cut the apples into (more manageable, manageabler) pieces.
20. Be (carefuller, more careful) with that knife.
21. Pears are (expensiver, more expensive) this year than last.
22. The season was the (most productive, productivest) in several years.
23. Fruit is one of the (nutritiousest, most nutritious) foods.
24. Oranges are (plentifuller, more plentiful) than grapefruit.
25. Is watermelon the (most popular, popularest) fruit in summer?
26. Aren't these the (delicious, most delicious) strawberries you've ever tasted?
27. I never tasted a (bitterer, more bitter) lime.
28. You'll be (comfortabler, more comfortable) in the shade.
29. That is the (most glorious, gloriousest) tree on the farm.
30. What is the (flavorfullest, most flavorful) fruit you ever ate?
31. Plant the (most robust, robustest) bushes you can buy.
32. We had a (difficulter, more difficult) time picking the fruit today than yesterday.
33. The labor was the (demandingest, most demanding) we've ever experienced.
34. Last year's work was (enjoyabler, more enjoyable).

Write a sentence using the comparative or superlative form of each adjective listed below.

35. dangerous
36. likable
37. unusual
38. vigorous
39. expensive
40. flavorful
41. convenient
42. important

43. consistent
44. appropriate
45. difficult
46. comfortable
47. valuable
48. exciting
49. fortunate
50. remarkable

EXTRA PRACTICE

Three levels of practice
Mechanics: Capitalizing Proper Adjectives (page 306)

LEVEL A. Write the proper adjective in each phrase. Be sure that you capitalize it.

1. english antiques
2. french toast
3. persian rug
4. african carving
5. irish heirloom
6. spanish omelet
7. yorkshire pudding
8. italian salami
9. swiss cheese

LEVEL B. Write these sentences. Underline and capitalize each proper adjective.

10. The curtains are made of danish fabric.
11. The flowered pattern is swedish.
12. italian crystal was used for the chandelier.
13. That small table is made of haitian mahogany wood.
14. An american rocking chair sways back and forth.
15. The hand-made kitchen tiles are mexican.
16. The antique french china is kept in the sideboard.
17. Embroidered cushions of peruvian llama wool lie on the floor.

LEVEL C. For each proper noun write a proper adjective. Then write a sentence that uses the new word as a proper adjective. Use a dictionary if you need one.

18. Scotland
19. Venezuela
20. Cambodia
21. Norway
22. China
23. Alaska
24. Portugal
25. Spain

EXTRA PRACTICE

Three levels of practice
Vocabulary Building: Synonyms and Antonyms (page 308)

LEVEL A. Replace the underlined word with a synonym from the box.

excited	shrill	gorgeous	frisky	unhurried
quiet	solemn	rapid	booming	

1. The orchestra played a <u>slow</u> introduction.
2. The flutes in the orchestra sounded <u>lively</u>.
3. The violins started to play a <u>fast</u> passage.
4. Soon the drums sounded a <u>deep</u> thud.
5. A solo trumpet played a <u>sharp</u> note.
6. The trombones added a <u>serious</u> tone.
7. The last notes of the first movement were <u>peaceful</u>.
8. The music reminded me of a <u>splendid</u> sunset.
9. The applause of the audience was <u>eager</u>.

LEVEL B. Write an antonym for each underlined word in these sentences.

10. Miguel and I sat on a <u>quiet</u> beach.
11. The ocean was <u>calm</u>.
12. I felt the <u>warm</u> sand under my feet.
13. The breeze was <u>gentle</u>.
14. I could see <u>small</u> clouds in the sky.
15. Soon I discovered two <u>tiny</u> shells.
16. They were striped with <u>bright</u> colors.
17. The edges of the shells were very <u>rough</u>.
18. It was a <u>perfect</u> morning for Miguel and me.

LEVEL C. Write each sentence twice. First, use a synonym for the underlined word. Then, use an antonym for it.

19. It was an <u>excellent</u> day for fishing.
20. The water had reached the <u>right</u> temperature for the fish.
21. I chose a <u>strong</u> fishing rod.
22. My cousin handled the <u>sharp</u> hooks carefully.
23. On the first cast I caused a <u>terrible</u> tangle.
24. A <u>huge</u> fish took my hook.
25. The fish put up a <u>tough</u> fight.

UNIT
10

Writing Descriptions

Read the quotation and look at the picture on the opposite page. The child is observing the effect of casting light through prisms. What do the lights look like to you?

Descriptive writing provides a clear picture of a person, place, or thing for your audience. You will want your audience to be able to see an image of what you have described.

Focus A description creates a clear and vivid picture of a person, place, or thing.

What would you like to describe? In this unit you will read a vivid description and look at many photographs to give you ideas for writing descriptions.

We shall not cease from exploration
And the end of all our exploring
Will be to arrive where we started
And know the place for the first time.

—T. S. Eliot, from "Little Gidding"

Have you ever waited for an important event to begin?

Anne Morrow Lindbergh tells about waiting for the launch of *Apollo 8*, the first manned space flight to orbit the moon. The huge rocket carried three astronauts and was launched from Cape Canaveral on the eastern coast of Florida on the morning of December 21, 1968.

As you read about the launch, look for the details that help you see and hear what the author observed.

"MORNING—

'*The Bird Perched for Flight*'"

from *Earth Shine* by Anne Morrow Lindbergh

We wake to the alarm at four thirty and leave our motel at five fifteen. The three astronauts must be already climbing into their seats at the top of their "thirty-six-story" rocket, poised for flight. The pilgrimage of sightseers has started to the Cape. Already the buses have left and lines of cars are on the roads. It is dark, a little chilly, with a sky full of stars. As we approach the Cape we see again the rocket and its launching tower from far off over the lagoon. It is still illumined with searchlights, but last night's vision has vanished. It is no longer tender or biological but simply a machine, the newest and most perfected creation of a scientific age—hard, weighty metal.

We watch the launching with some of the astronauts and their families, from a site near the Vehicle Assembly Building. Our cars are parked on a slight rise of ground. People get out, walk about restlessly, set up cameras and adjust their binoculars. The launch pad is about three miles away, near the beach. We look across Florida marsh grass and palmettos. A cabbage palm stands up black against a shadowy sky, just left of the rocket and its launching tower. As dawn flushes the horizon, an egret rises and lazily glides across the flats between us and the pad. It is a still morning. Ducks call from nearby inlets. Vapor trails of a high-flying plane turn pink in an almost cloudless sky. Stars pale in the blue.

The overall impression is clearly stated.

With the morning light, *Apollo 8* and its launching tower become clearer, harder, and more defined. One can see the details of installation. The dark sections on the smooth sides of the rocket, marking its stages, cut up the single fluid line. Vapor steams furiously off its side. No longer stark and simple, this morning the rocket is complicated, mechanical, earth-bound. Too weighty for flight, one feels.

People stop talking, stand in front of their cars, and raise binoculars to their eyes. We peer nervously at the launch site and then at our wrist watches. Radio voices blare unnaturally loud from car windows. "Now only thirty minutes to launch time . . .
fifteen minutes . . . six minutes . . .
thirty seconds to go . . .
twenty . . . T minus fifteen . . .
fourteen . . . thirteen . . .
twelve . . . eleven . . .
ten . . . nine . . .
Ignition!"

329

A jet of steam shoots from the pad below the rocket. "Ahhh!" The crowd gasps, almost in unison. Now great flames spurt, leap, belch out across the horizon. Clouds of smoke billow up on either side of the rocket, completely hiding its base. From the midst of this holocaust, the rocket begins to rise—slowly, as in a dream, so slowly it seems to hang suspended on the cloud of fire and smoke. It's impossible—it can't rise. Yes, it rises, but heavily, as if the giant weight is pulled by an invisible hand out of the atmosphere, like the lead on a plumb line from the depths of the sea. Slowly it rises and—because of our distance—silently, as in a dream.

The sound, sight, and sensation of the launch are vividly described.

Suddenly the noise breaks, jumps across our three separating miles—a shattering roar of explosions, a trip hammer over one's head, under one's feet, through one's body. The earth shakes; cars rattle; vibrations beat in the chest. A roll of thunder, prolonged, prolonged, prolonged.

I drop the binoculars and put my hands to my ears, holding my head to keep it steady. My throat tightens—am I going to cry?—my eyes are fixed on the rocket, mesmerized by its slow ascent.

The foreground is now full of birds; a great flock of ducks, herons, small birds, rise pell-mell from the marshes at the noise. Fluttering in alarm and confusion, they scatter in all directions as if it were the end of the world. In the seconds I take to look at them, the rocket has left the tower.

It is up and away, a comet boring through the sky, no longer the vulnerable untried child, no longer the earthbound machine, or the weight at the end of a line, but sheer terrifying force, blasting upward on its own titanic power.

It has gone miles into the sky. It is blurred by a cloud. No, it has made its own cloud—a huge vapor trail, which hides it. Out of the cloud something falls, cartwheeling down, smoking. "The first-stage cutoff," someone says. Where is the rocket itself?

There, above the cloud now, reappears the rocket, only a very bright star, diminishing every second. Soon out of sight, off to lunar space.

One looks earthward again. It is curiously still and empty. A cloud of brown smoke hangs motionless on the horizon. Its long shadow reaches us across the grass. The launch pad is empty. The abandoned launching tower is being sprayed with jets of water to cool it down. It steams in the bright morning air. Still dazed, people stumble into cars and start the slow, jammed trek back to town. The monotone of radio voices continues. One clings to this last thread of contact with something incredibly beautiful that has vanished.

The author describes the scene from far to near.

"Where are they—where are they now?" In eleven minutes we get word. They are in earth orbit. They "look good" in the laconic space talk that comes down from over a hundred miles above earth. And one realizes again that it is the men above all that matter, the individuals who run the

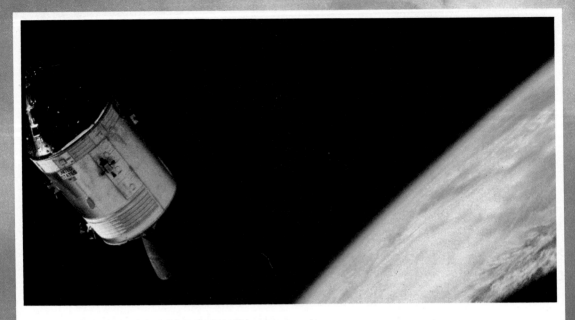

machine, give it heart, sight, speech, intelligence, and direction; and the people on earth who are backing them up, monitoring their every move, even to their heartbeats. This is not sheer power, it is power under control of people.

We drive slowly back to town. Above us the white vapor trail of the rocket is being scattered by wind into feathery shapes of heron's wings—the only mark in the sky of the morning's launching.

Thinking Like a Reader

1. What is Anne Morrow Lindbergh's reaction to the enormous power of the rocket?

2. In what ways do you think you might have reacted if you had been present at the launch of *Apollo 8*?

Write your responses in your journal.

Thinking Like a Writer

3. How does the writer let you know how the rocket looked?

4. Which details does she use?

5. Which details do you like best?

6. If you were writing about a rocket launch or space flight, how would you describe it?

Write your responses in your journal.

Brainstorm *Vocabulary*

In "Morning—The Bird Perched for Flight,' " Anne Morrow Lindbergh mentions a cabbage palm that "stands up black against a shadowy sky." Think of a place you know. It might be in your neighborhood. In your journal write all the images that come to mind as you think about the place. Use words or phrases to create a personal vocabulary list. You can use these words and phrases in your writing.

Talk It Over
Describe a Machine

In her description, Anne Morrow Lindbergh mentions the "dark sections on the smooth sides of the rocket" that mark its stages. This detail helps her to explain how the rocket looks. Imagine that you want to describe the appearance of a machine, such as a computer, to a friend who has never seen one. Pretend that you are describing the machine in a telephone conversation. Use a few familiar images to describe it as clearly as you can.

Quick Write *Write a Poster*

Write a description of an exotic place for a travel poster. Include specific details in your description. Try to persuade people to visit the place. For example, imagine that you are writing about a beach.

The endless white sands stretch to the horizon. The water of the ocean is clear and cool. Small waves lap at the fine sand and colorful shells. Palm leaves sway in the warm breeze. The bright sun burns in the clear, blue sky.

Keep your description in your folder.

Idea Corner
Think of Places

Think of some ideas for writing a paragraph that describes a place. In your journal, write whatever ideas and observations come to mind. You might write topic ideas such as "My Neighbor's Garage" or "The Skyscraper." You might also write a comparison, or you might sketch a small picture and label certain parts of it.

Finding Ideas for Writing

Look at the pictures. Think about what you see.
What ideas for descriptive writing do the pictures give you?
Write your ideas in your journal.

Kilauea Volcano, Hawaii

PICTURES: Ideas for Descriptive Writing

South African Astronomical Observatory, Southland

1 GROUP WRITING: A Description

COOPERATIVE
LEARNING

The **purpose** of a description is to create a clear, vivid picture of a person, place, or thing for a particular **audience**. Your audience might be your classmates or a younger reader. What other elements help to make a description clear and vivid?

- Overall Impression
- Sensory Details
- Order of Details

Overall Impression

Read this paragraph. Notice the underlined sentence.

> On our way up to the dome-shaped observatory, we heard eerie sounds through the dark night. At the bottom of the hill, the hoot of an owl startled us. The crickets made a ghostly melody. Moonlight cast a faint glow on the chalky, jagged boulders. At each step, the gravel crunched loudly under our feet. Halfway up the hill, we could dimly make out the dark, domelike building. Finally, we arrived at the summit and reached the observatory.

The underlined sentence tells you the topic of the paragraph and the mood. It gives you an overall impression of the trip to the observatory. The details throughout the paragraph support the overall impression.

Guided Practice: Stating an Overall Impression

As a class, choose a place from this list, or think of other places, and explore ideas about it. Then write one sentence that gives an overall impression of that place.

a city street   a school cafeteria   a vacant lot
a local park   a school playing field   the beach

Example: When the trees were in bloom, the park
looked like a colorful tapestry.

Sensory Details

The details in a descriptive paragraph often appeal to the five senses; they tell about how things look, sound, taste, feel, or smell.

In the paragraph that describes the walk to the observatory, the sensory details help to give you an overall impression. Look back at that paragraph.

- Which details help you to see the dark night or hear its sounds?
- Which details could you add that relate to other senses?

Guided Practice: Charting Sensory Details

Think of sensory details that might apply to the place you have chosen to describe. As a class, make a chart like the one below, about the walk to the observatory. Write sensory words that tell about the overall impression of the place.

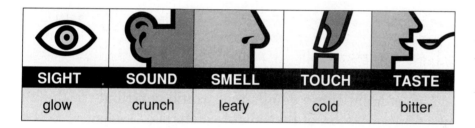

SIGHT	SOUND	SMELL	TOUCH	TASTE
glow	crunch	leafy	cold	bitter

Order of Details

Review the paragraph about the observatory. Notice how it is organized. The sensory details used describe the subject from bottom to top. The clear organization makes the description effective. Find the words in the paragraph that show its organization.

Other ways to organize a description include near-to-far, left-to-right, and inside-to-outside. Alternatively, a description can be organized by the order of importance of each detail and by grouping similar types of details together. Think about the paragraph. In what other ways could it be organized?

Putting a Description Together

As a class you have written a sentence that gives an overall impression of a place. You have also listed some sensory words about that place.

Think about your overall impression sentence. Then, look at your chart of sensory words. It is time for you to decide which sensory details best support the overall impression.

Here is how one student decided. Read the overall impression sentence. Then, look at the sensory words that are checked.

The school cafeteria was like a busy crossroads.

SIGHT	SOUND	SMELL	TOUCH	TASTE
✔ trays	✔ clatter	chicken	hot	sour
✔ friends	✔ bang	onions	smooth	salty
red	hum	bacon	silky	lemony
signs	swish	paint	rough	sweet

This student chose details that would contribute to the overall impression of the school cafeteria as a busy crossroads.

Guided Practice: Writing a Description

With your class, add more sensory details to your chart and cross out any details that do not support the overall impression. Then, write three detail sentences using sensory words from your chart. Choose the best words to express your overall impression of the place to your audience. Discuss different ways of organizing the paragraph, and decide on the most effective order.

Share your description with a classmate. Ask your classmate if he or she thinks your description is clear and vivid.

Checklist: A Description

When you write a description, you will want to keep some points in mind. To help yourself remember the points, you can make a checklist.

Look at this checklist. Some points need to be added. Make a copy of the checklist and finish it. Keep a copy of it in your writing folder. You can use the checklist when you write your description.

CHECKLIST

✔ Purpose and audience   ■ Smell

✔ Overall impression   ■ Touch

✔ Sensory details   ■ _____

   ■ Sound   ✔ Order of details

   ■ _____

2 THINKING AND WRITING: Classifying

You have learned that you can make descriptive writing more vivid by carefully choosing sensory words. Once you have chosen your descriptive details, think about the best order for them.

Classifying can help you both to select and to organize details. **Classifying** is grouping together items that have something in common. For example, you could classify a basket of fruit into groups of apples, pears, oranges, and so on.

This index card shows a writer's notes for a description of a beach at sunset. The overall impression is the beauty of the sunset, which looked like a picture.

purple bands of light	honks of sea gulls
fluffy pink clouds	white foam of waves
the smell of seaweed	silver crescent moon
oily mud	salty air
	cool breeze

The writer decided to classify the details on the index card. The writer classified each detail according to the sense to which it appealed.

SIGHT	SOUND	SMELL	TOUCH	TASTE
purple bands white foam silver moon fluffy pink clouds	honks of sea gulls	seaweed	oily mud cool breeze	salty air

W R I T I N G

TOGETHER

Thinking Like a Writer

■ Which details support the overall impression?

The writer realized that the overall impression of the description was how the sunset looked. Only those details classified under "Sight" support the overall impression.

THINKING APPLICATION Classifying Descriptive Details

COOPERATIVE LEARNING

Gloria is planning to write a description of eating out in a restaurant. In one paragraph she wants to describe how comfortable and inviting the restaurant was. In a second paragraph she wants to describe the delicious meal she ate. Gloria has made a list of sensory details about eating out. Help her to decide which details to include in which paragraph. Classify the details into categories. Then, write on a separate piece of paper the details to include in each paragraph. You may wish to discuss your thinking with other students. In your discussions, explain your choices to each other.

soft, cushioned chairs
dim lighting
the smell of burning wood
spicy noodles
thick carpet
pretty paintings

buttery corn on the cob
pleasant music
glittering china
tall candles
lemony chicken
peppery sauce

3 INDEPENDENT WRITING: A Description

Prewrite: Step 1

By now, you know about the elements that contribute to a clear, vivid description. You are ready to choose your own topic for descriptive writing. José, a student your age, chose a topic in this way.

Choosing a Topic

1. First, José wrote a list of places to describe.
2. Next, he thought about describing each place.
3. Last, he decided on the best place.

José liked the last place on his list best. He decided, however, to

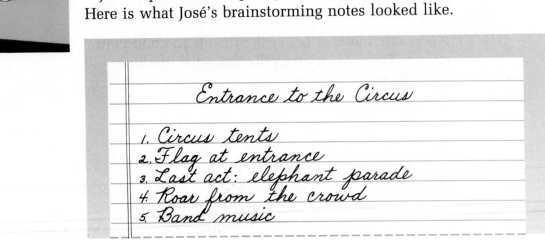

the woods

my room

the parade on July 4

the circus

narrow the topic to a description of his arrival at the circus. The **purpose** for his description would be to describe his arrival so vividly that an **audience** of his classmates could share his excitement.

José explored his topic by **brainstorming** a list of details. Here is what José's brainstorming notes looked like.

Entrance to the Circus

1. Circus tents
2. Flag at entrance
3. Last act: elephant parade
4. Roar from the crowd
5. Band music

Exploring Ideas: Charting Strategy

Before he began to write, José closed his eyes and tried to remember his visit to the circus several months ago. He did this to get a clear picture of his subject. At this point, he used his brainstorming notes to make an observation chart. He also changed some details.

Observation Chart			
Subject:	Arriving at the circus		
Purpose:	To describe		
Audience:	My classmates		
Sight	**Sound**	**Smell/Taste**	**Touch**
circus tents	roar of crowd	candied apples	canvas
flag	band music		breeze
acrobats			
Overall impression: Thrill, excitement			

Thinking Like a Writer

- Which details did José add?
- Which detail did he decide to cross out?
- Why do you think he crossed out that part?

Think of a place that you would like to describe. Use **Pictures** or your journal to help you find ideas. Follow these steps.

- Make a list of places.
- Choose the topic you like best.
- Narrow your topic if it is too broad.
- Brainstorm for details and make a list.
- Think of an overall impression of your place.
- Think about your purpose and audience.

Use your notes to make an observation chart. Remember, you can change the observation chart at any time.

Write a First Draft: Step 2

José made a checklist to help him. He used his checklist as he wrote his first draft.

José's *First Draft*

From a distance the circus tents looked like colurful umbrellas. we got out of the car. We heard cheerful band music and a roar from the crowd. We passed near the Gate. The air became more sweeter with the smell of candied apples. Over the entrance the american flag waved in the breeze. In our excitement we could hardly wait to draw aside the canvas of the tent flap. Once inside the Big Top, we held our breath as we watched the acrobats go through the air on the flying trapeze.

José concentrated on getting his ideas down on paper. He knew he could go back later to revise and correct errors.

YOUR TURN

Write the first draft of your description. As you prepare to write, ask yourself these questions.

- What will my audience need to know to form a clear picture of my subject?
- What overall impression do I want to create?
- How can I best arrange the details?

Planning Checklist
- Remember purpose and audience.
- Include an overall impression.
- Use sensory words and details.
- Order the details.

🕐 **TIME-OUT** You might want to take some time out before you revise. That way you will be able to revise your writing with a fresh eye.

Revise: Step 3

When he had finished writing his first draft, José read it over to himself. Then he asked one of his classmates to read it and make some suggestions for improvement.

> Your paragraph is good, but I wanted to know more details to see exactly what you saw.

> I see what you mean. Thanks for the suggestion.

José then looked back at his planning checklist. He asked himself several questions about his draft. Was the overall impression clear? Did he use sensory details? Did he arrange the details in a clear order? He noticed that he had forgotten one point. He checked it off so that he would remember it when he revised his description. José now had a checklist to use as he revised.

José made changes in his paragraph. Notice that he did not correct errors in punctuation and spelling. He knew he could fix them later.

The revisions José made improved his paragraph. Look at José's revised draft on the next page.

Revising Checklist
- Remember purpose and audience.
- Include an overall impression.
✔ Use sensory words and details.
- Order the details.

From a distance the circus tents looked like colurful *red and yellow* *striped*
umbrellas. *As piled* we got out of the car, We heard cheerful
band music and a roar from the crowd. ~~We passed~~ near
the Gate, The air became more sweeter with the smell
of candied apples. Over the entrance the american flag
flapped lazily
waved in the breeze. In our excitement we could hardly
rough
wait to draw aside the canvas of the tent flap. Once
inside the Big Top, we held our breath as we watched
whiz
the acrobats go through the air on the flying trapeze.

Thinking Like a Writer

WISE
WORD
CHOICE

- Which words did José change or add?
- How do the added words improve his paragraph?
- Which sentences did he combine? How does combining them improve the paragraph?

YOUR TURN

Read your first draft. Ask yourself these questions.

- Do I use exact sensory words to make my description clear and vivid?
- Can I improve my writing by combining sentences?
- Can I make the order of my details clearer and more effective?

If you wish, ask a friend to read your paragraph and to make suggestions. Then revise your paragraph.

WRITING PROCESS

Proofread: Step 4

José knew that his work was not complete until he proofread his paragraph. While proofreading, José checked for errors in grammar and mechanics. He used a proofreading checklist and corrected errors with proofreading marks.

Part of José's Proofread Draft

¶ From a distance, the circus tents looked like ~~colorful~~

~~red and yellow~~   *colorful striped*

umbrellas. ~~we~~ got out of the car. We heard cheerful

As piled

band music and a roar from the crowd. ~~We passed~~ near

the gate. The air became ~~more~~ sweeter with the smell

of candied apples. Over the entrance the american flag

flapped lazily

~~waved~~ in the breeze. In our excitement we could hardly

YOUR TURN

Proofreading Practice

Below is a paragraph that you can use to practice your proofreading skills. Find the errors. Write the paragraph correctly on a separate piece of paper.

Outside the back door is a small Brick patio. In summer the bricks feel warm and rough under our bare feet. Along the fense are trailing branches of rose bushes. I do not think any uther flower has a more richer smell. Behind the patio are several tables with colorful portuguese tiles.

Proofreading Checklist
- Did I indent my paragraph?
- Did I spell any words incorrectly?
- Which punctuation errors do I need to correct?
- Which capitalization errors do I need to correct?
- What errors in the use of adjectives do I need to correct?

Applying Your Proofreading Skills

Now proofread your description. Also look at your checklist for the last time. Review **The Grammar Connection** and **The Mechanics Connection**, too. Use the proofreading marks to mark changes.

THE GRAMMAR CONNECTION

Remember these rules about adjectives.

■ Add *er* and *est* to most adjectives to make the comparative and superlative forms.

■ Use *more* or *most* before most adjectives that have two or more syllables.

■ Do not use *more* and *most* with adjectives ending in *er* and *est*.

CORRECT: Peaches are **larger** than apricots.
INCORRECT: Peaches are **more larger** than apricots.

Check your description. Have you correctly used adjectives that compare?

THE MECHANICS CONNECTION

Remember these rules about proper adjectives.

■ A proper adjective is formed from a proper noun.

■ Always capitalize proper adjectives.
     The observatory is near the **Canadian** border.

Review your writing. Have you capitalized all proper adjectives?

Proofreading Marks

⌐ Indent
∧ Add
⋏ Add a comma
⌄⌄ Add quotation marks
⊙ Add a period
⌿ Take out
≡ Capitalize
/ Make a small letter
∿ Reverse the order

Publish: Step 5

José copied his paragraph in his best handwriting on a large sheet of paper. Then, he asked a friend to illustrate his paragraph with a colorful drawing of the entrance to the circus. He posted his writing for the class to read. Several of his classmates who had never been to a circus asked him to share more details about his experience.

YOUR TURN

Make a final, neat copy of your description. Think of a way to share your description. You might find some ideas in the **Sharing Suggestions** box below.

SHARING SUGGESTIONS

Use your description to create a poster.	Include your description in a letter to a friend.	Read your description to your family or friends.

4 SPEAKING AND LISTENING: Giving a Talk

You have just written a description about a place that you know. Your description included an overall impression of the place and vivid, sensory details that you organized carefully. Now you can use what you have learned about writing a description to give a short talk. In your talk you will also give your overall impression of a place. In addition, you will include vivid details to help your listeners "see" the place you are describing.

First, you will want to make a note card to use for your talk. You do not have to write everything on your note card. The note card should include only the main points and some details. Look at this note card.

Notes	Impressions of a Place
1. lake at sunrise, smooth as glass	
2. tall, motionless reeds	
3. moist air	
4. warm shaft of light from rising sun	
5. faint splashes of swans	
6. lake like an oasis of calm	

Notice that the overall impression is listed last on the note card. What other points are listed? How do the sensory details support the overall impression?

When you give a talk, it will help you to keep some guidelines in mind. These speaking guidelines will help you to focus your talk.

SPEAKING GUIDELINES: A Short Talk

1. Remember that your **purpose** is to describe.
2. Think about what your **audience** wants to know.
3. Make a note card. Practice using your note card.
4. Focus on an overall impression. Include sensory details. Plan the ordering of details.
5. Look at your listeners.
6. Speak in a loud, clear voice.

- Why are sensory details important when I am telling about a place?
- How can I organize my description to help my audience form a picture of the place?
- How can I make sure that my purpose is clear to my audience?

SPEAKING APPLICATION A Short Talk

Think of a place that is special to you. It may be at home, at school, or in the area where you live. Prepare a note card to use to give a short talk about this place. Use the speaking guidelines to help you to prepare. Your classmates will be using the following guidelines as they listen to your description.

LISTENING GUIDELINES: A Short Talk

1. Listen to "see" the image.
2. Listen for sensory details.
3. Listen for an overall impression.
4. Listen for the order of the description.

5 WRITER'S RESOURCES: Tables and Graphs

In this unit you have written descriptions of places. You have used many resources, including photographs, stories, and your own imagination, to find ideas for writing. Other useful resources for a writer include tables and graphs.

A **table** organizes information in an orderly arrangement that is easy to read. A table usually contains **rows** (lines that go across the table) and **columns** (lines that go up and down). This table shows the names and locations of some national parks in the United States.

NATIONAL PARKS

State	National Park	Area (in acres)
Arizona	Grand Canyon	1,218,375
Arkansas	Hot Springs	5,839
California	Redwood	110,178
	Sequoia	402,482
	Yosemite	761,170
Colorado	Mesa Verde	52,085
	Rocky Mountain	265,200

Notice that the table has a title and has a caption above each column. These help to show you how the table is organized. In addition, the captions tell you the unit of any measurements. Here, area is given in acres. Notice also that the table is organized in alphabetical order—both states and parks are listed alphabetically.

A **graph** uses bars, lines, or dots to show comparisons between similar things. The bar graph on page 353 shows the depth of five of the deepest lakes in the world.

Notice that the graph is labeled to make it easy to read. The caption at the bottom tells you that the graph shows depth in feet.

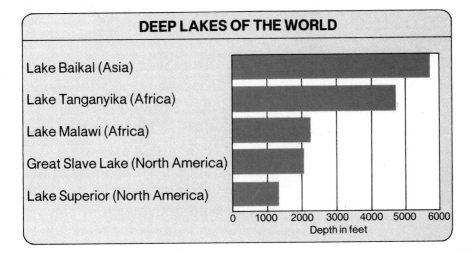

DEEP LAKES OF THE WORLD

Lake Baikal (Asia)

Lake Tanganyika (Africa)

Lake Malawi (Africa)

Great Slave Lake (North America)

Lake Superior (North America)

0   1000 2000 3000 4000 5000 6000
Depth in feet

Practice

Answer the questions below by referring to the table and
the graph.

1. In which state is Hot Springs National Park located?
2. Which national park has the largest area?
3. Which two national parks are located in Colorado?
4. Which state listed in the table has the most national parks?
5. How many acres are in the smallest park listed?
6. According to the graph, which is the world's deepest lake?
7. Which lake has a depth of more than four thousand feet but
   less than five thousand feet?
8. According to the graph, which three continents contain very
   deep lakes?
9. About how much deeper is Lake Tanganyika than Lake
   Malawi?
10. Which lake is the shallowest, according to the graph?

WRITING APPLICATION A Graph

Use an **almanac** or an **atlas** to identify the five
largest cities or towns in your state. Determine the
population of each city or town. Then, create a bar graph
(like the one in the lesson) that presents the information
you have found.

6 WRITER'S RESOURCES: Maps

Maps are another useful resource for writing descriptions of places. A **map** shows a specific geographical area. Maps show the relative size and location of places. Most maps have symbols that give more information about an area.

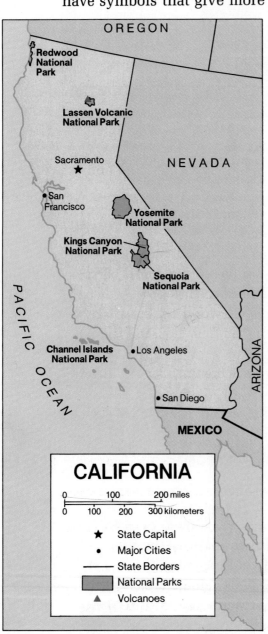

OREGON
Redwood National Park
Lassen Volcanic National Park
Sacramento ★
NEVADA
● San Francisco
Yosemite National Park
Kings Canyon National Park
Sequoia National Park
PACIFIC OCEAN
Channel Islands National Park
● Los Angeles
ARIZONA
● San Diego
MEXICO

CALIFORNIA

0   100   200 miles
0   100   200   300 kilometers

★   State Capital
●   Major Cities
──   State Borders
▭   National Parks
▲   Volcanoes

Look at this map of California. To understand the symbols on the map, read the **legend** underneath it. The legend shows the marks that identify the state capital, the major cities, the state borders, the national parks, and volcanoes.

Also, notice the **distance scale** on the map. You can use the distance scale to figure out the number of miles or kilometers between points on the map. To find out the distance between San Francisco and Sacramento, for example, first line up the edge of a sheet of paper with the dots that represent those cities on the map. Mark your paper with two dots. Then, lay your sheet of paper next to the distance scale on the map, with the first dot lined up with 0 on the scale. Read the number on the scale next to the second dot. The distance scale shows that the two cities are about 75 miles, or 120 kilometers, apart.

Practice

Answer these questions by referring to the map opposite.

1. Which city is the capital of California?
2. Which large city in California is closest to Mexico?
3. According to the map, which mainland national park in California lies closest to the Pacific Ocean?
4. Which national park is nearest to Los Angeles?
5. About how many miles separate Redwood National Park from Yosemite National Park?
6. Which two national parks in California are located near the Nevada border?
7. Which national parks in California are nearest to each other?
8. Which national park in California has the largest area?
9. Which national park might you visit if you were interested in volcanoes?
10. What is the approximate distance between San Francisco and Yosemite National Park?

WRITING APPLICATION A Description

Use a map to find information about your state. Write a brief description of a place in your state, using the information you found as the details in your paragraph. Keep your description in your writing folder. You will use it in **The Curriculum Connection** on page 356.

Writing About Geography

The word *geography* comes from a Greek word that means "writing about the earth." When you think of geography, you probably think about maps. But geography is more than the making and reading of maps. It is the study of the earth's features and of the ways that people live in different places.

Geographers use a number of methods to describe the earth. They draw maps to show where places are located and to give additional information about an area. They also take photographs and interview people. Finally, geographers write descriptions for encyclopedias, magazines, textbooks, almanacs, and government reports to give us an accurate picture of the world.

ACTIVITIES

Visualize a Place   Look at the description you wrote about a place in your state. Based on the information in your description, draw a picture of the place. Under the picture, write sentences that describe the place.

Describe a Photograph   Look at the photograph on the opposite page. It shows some of the treasure found in the tomb of King Tutankhamen. Think of how you would describe the treasure. Write a letter to someone who has never seen the photograph. Remember to use sensory words.

Respond to Literature   The following description is taken from a book by Howard Carter, who discovered the tomb of King Tutankhamen in Egypt. This tomb was one of the

most important modern finds. After reading the description, write a response. Your response may be a letter to Howard Carter, a poem about King Tutankhamen, or a descriptive paragraph about a future discovery you would like to make.

The Tomb of Tutankhamen (tü'täng kä'mən)

Carter describes the scene as he first opened the door to King Tutankhamen's tomb.

"The day following . . . was the day of days, the most wonderful that I have ever lived through, and certainly one whose like I can never hope to see again. Throughout the morning the work of clearing continued. . . . Then, in the middle of the afternoon . . . we came upon a second sealed doorway. . . . With trembling hands I made a tiny breach in the upper left-hand corner. Darkness and blank space, as far as an iron testing-rod could reach, showed that whatever lay beyond was empty. . . . I inserted the candle and peered in. . . . At first I could see nothing, the hot air escaping from the chamber causing the candle flame to flicker, but presently, as my eyes grew accustomed to the light, details of the room within emerged slowly from the mist, strange animals, statues, and gold—everywhere the glint of gold."

UNIT CHECKUP

LESSON 1

Group Writing: A Description (page 336) Read the paragraph below. On a separate sheet of paper, write a sentence that states the overall impression. Then add other sensory details to the description.

A bright glow identified the heart of the downtown area. The lights of highways formed delicate threads branching out from the center. At the edge of a wide circle around the city, these threads faded into inky darkness.

LESSON 2

Thinking: Classifying (page 340) The details below are for a description of a hiking trip. Classify them into categories.

- slippery branches
- thick, black mud
- cold night
- unsteady feet
- firm sand
- bird song
- blazing sun
- roaring waterfall
- brown leaves

LESSON 3

Writing a Description (page 342) Imagine that you are an explorer. Write a description of your latest discovery. Remember to include a main impression.

LESSON 4

Speaking and Listening: Giving a Talk (page 350) Imagine you are going to give a talk to describe your school. You will prepare a note card to use for your talk. First, make a list of what kinds of points you should include on your note card and why. Then, write notes for the note card.

LESSON 5

Writer's Resources: Tables and Graphs (page 352) Select a sport and prepare a table or graph that shows information relating to it. For example, make a table showing baseball teams, scores, and division placings.

LESSON 6

Writer's Resources: Maps (page 354) Select a geographical area of your choice. Use a map to find information about the area. Write a short summary of the information.

THEME PROJECT ASTRONOMY FAIR

In this unit you have learned how to create word pictures by observing with your senses.

Writers use their observations to help their readers to visualize a person, place, or thing. Think about other ways of describing observations.

Astronomers observe the skies to learn more about our universe. Think about the kinds of observations that astronomers make.

Look at the picture below. This picture shows astronomers at work in an observatory. Talk with your classmates about all the things you see in the photograph.

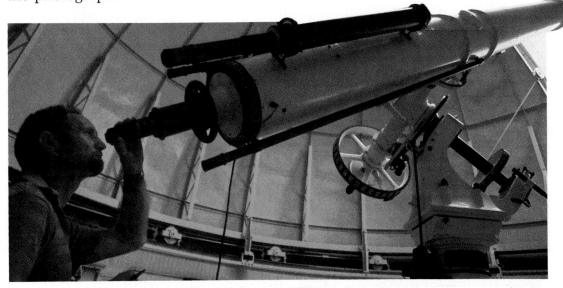

Plan an astronomy fair with your classmates. Think of different ways of observing or presenting astronomers' observations.

- Plan a slide show.
- Write a script.
- Draw pictures and diagrams.
- Prepare a talk.
- Design an exhibit.

UNIT

11

Adverbs

In Unit 11 you will learn about adverbs. Adverbs add detail to your writing by telling how, where, when, and to what extent something is done.

Discuss Read the poem on the opposite page. What do you think the difference between the two roads might be? Discuss your ideas with a partner.

Creative Expression The unit theme is *Crossroads*. It is often more difficult to choose the unknown than the familiar. Write about a time when you made a difficult choice. Write your thoughts in your journal.

JOURNAL

*Two roads diverged in a wood, and I—
I took the one less traveled by,
And that has made all the difference.*

—Robert Frost,
from "The Road Not Taken"

1 ADVERBS THAT MODIFY VERBS

An adverb is a word that modifies a verb, an adjective, or another adverb.

You know that adjectives are words that describe nouns. Adverbs are also words that describe other words. Often adverbs are used to describe verbs.

Adverbs that modify verbs may tell *how*, *where*, *when*, or *to what extent* about the verb. Many adverbs end in the letters *ly*.

An adverb that modifies a verb may be placed before the verb, after the verb, or at the very beginning of a sentence.

HOW:	Maria spoke **slowly.**
WHERE:	She stood **there.**
WHEN:	**Then** she sat in a chair.
TO WHAT EXTENT:	She **completely** convinced us.

Guided Practice

Tell which word in each sentence is an adverb. Then name the verb that each adverb modifies.

Example: Maria and her staff work quickly.   *quickly   work*

1. Maria often presents reports on television.
2. She studied hard for this job.
3. Frequently, Maria reads the evening news.
4. She usually reports from the local station.
5. She works there with a staff of reporters.
6. Maria usually reports on environmental issues.

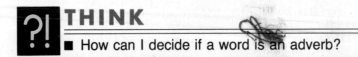

?! THINK

■ How can I decide if a word is an adverb?

REMEMBER

- Many adverbs modify verbs.
- Adverbs can tell *how, where, when,* or *to what extent* about a verb.

More Practice

A. Write each sentence. Underline the adverb. Then draw two lines under the verb that the adverb modifies.

Example: Maria really likes her job.
    Maria <u>really</u> <u>likes</u> her job.

7. She investigates issues thoroughly.
8. She interviews people courteously.
9. Then, she checks all her facts.
10. Finally, she writes her report.
11. She arrives at the television studio early.
12. Maria practices her delivery there.
13. A producer warmly encourages Maria.

B. Write each sentence. Use an adverb in each blank.

Example: A television journalist must dress _____.
    A television journalist must dress smartly.

14. Television journalists must speak _____.
15. They must talk _____ into the camera.
16. Journalists must check their facts _____.
17. _____ they are ready to go on the air.
18. To be persuasive, a journalist must act _____.
19. Journalists should explore the issues _____.
20. They should _____ try to be fair.

Extra Practice, page 382

WRITING APPLICATION A Review

Imagine that a newspaper has assigned to you the job of reviewing a television news show. Write at least five sentences for the review. Exchange your review with a classmate. Identify the adverbs in each other's work.

COOPERATIVE
LEARNING

2 ADVERBS THAT MODIFY ADJECTIVES AND ADVERBS

You have learned that adverbs often modify verbs. Adverbs can also modify adjectives or other adverbs. Adverbs that modify adjectives and adverbs answer the questions *how* and *to what extent.*

ADVERB MODIFYING AN ADJECTIVE:

Highway safety is a **very** serious problem.

ADVERB MODIFYING AN ADVERB:

We should think about it **extremely** carefully.

Guided Practice

Tell which word each underlined adverb modifies. Then tell whether the word you name is an adjective or an adverb.

Example: You speak <u>quite</u> clearly.   *clearly   adverb*

1. This article states the facts <u>very</u> strongly.
2. Do you know about this <u>dreadfully</u> important problem?
3. We don't drive <u>too</u> fast.
4. The city needs an <u>almost</u> immediate solution.
5. The mayor acted <u>extremely</u> quickly.

 THINK

■ How can I decide which word an adverb modifies?

REMEMBER

- Adverbs can modify adjectives or other adverbs.
- Adverbs that modify adjectives or other adverbs answer the questions *how* or *to what extent.*

More Practice

A. Write each underlined adverb and the word it modifies. Label the modified word an **adjective** or an **adverb.**

Example: Seat belts are <u>really</u> useful. *really   useful   adjective*

6. Why are seat belts <u>so</u> important?
7. They are <u>very</u> helpful in preventing injuries.
8. Isn't that theory regarded <u>somewhat</u> doubtfully?
9. No, it is <u>completely</u> true!
10. The mechanism works <u>extremely</u> simply.
11. Make sure that the belt is <u>thoroughly</u> tight.
12. Some drivers behave <u>quite</u> carelessly.
13. Most states <u>very</u> strongly encourage seat belts.
14. I am <u>totally</u> sure they are a good idea.

B. Write each sentence. Draw one line under each adverb and two lines under the word it modifies. Label the modified word a **verb**, an **adjective**, or an **adverb.**

Example: Our van recently received seat belts.

Our van <u>recently</u> <u>received</u> seat belts.   *verb*

15. Our bus driver always wears his seat belt.
16. Mr. Garcia sets a very good example.
17. Sometimes we forget to use our belts.
18. Mr. Garcia reminds us politely.
19. He tells us to be extremely careful.
20. The bus can stop quite unexpectedly.

Extra Practice, page 383

WRITING APPLICATION An Advertisement

Create five or six phrases that advertise the services of an airline. Identify the adverbs in a classmate's work.

3 ADVERBS THAT COMPARE

The **comparative** form of an adverb compares two actions. The **superlative** form compares more than two actions.

In the debate, Julie spoke **longer** than Carla.
Tanya spoke the **longest** of all.

Add *er* or *est* to all adverbs with one syllable and to some adverbs with two syllables. Use *more* or *most* with most adverbs with two syllables and with all adverbs with more than two syllables.

Adverb	Comparative	Superlative
long	longer	longest
early	earlier	earliest
keenly	more keenly	most keenly

Do not combine *more* or *most* with *er* or *est*.

CORRECT: Tanya spoke **longer** than Carlo.
INCORRECT: Tanya spoke more longer than Carlo.

Some adverbs have irregular forms.

successfully

Adverb	Comparative	Superlative
well	better	best
badly	worse	worst
little	less	least
much	more	most

more successfully

Guided Practice

Tell the correct comparative and superlative forms.

Example: frequently   *more frequently*   *most frequently*

1. late **2.** busily **3.** fast **4.** peacefully **5.** successfully

most successfully

THINK

■ How can I decide the correct form of an adverb?

REMEMBER

- To form the **comparative** of an adverb, add *er* or use *more* with the adverb. To form the **superlative**, add *est* or use *most* with the adverb.

More Practice

A. Write the adverb form that correctly completes each sentence.

Example: The audience listened (more carefully, most carefully) than before.   *more carefully*

6. Tanya spoke (more late, later) than Cody.

7. She looked at us (more regularly, most regularly) than he.

8. We listened to her the (eagerliest, most eagerly) of all.

9. Tanya had prepared (better, more better) than Cody.

10. We understood her the (clearest, most clearly) of all.

11. You listened to Ed (more attentively, most attentively) than I.

12. Did he speak (more skillfully, skillfuller) than she?

13. Did he speak (more accurately, most accurately) than Tanya?

B. Write each sentence. Use the correct adverb.

Example: The contest went _____ than expected. (well)
The contest went better than expected.

14. Tanya did _____ than Rick in the contest. (badly)

15. Rick answered _____ than Tanya. (fast)

16. His spelling was correct _____ often than hers. (much)

17. Bob spelled his words _____ than anyone else. (slowly)

18. However, Bob spelled the _____ of all. (accurately)

19. Sadly, our team prepared _____ than usual. (little)

20. It was the _____ fought contest ever. (intensely)

Extra Practice, page 384

WRITING APPLICATION A Magazine Article

Write a brief sports article that compares the actions of three athletes. Identify the adverbs in a classmate's article.

4 ADVERB OR ADJECTIVE?

Some words can be used both as adjectives and as adverbs, and these words may be easily confused. Remember that an **adjective** modifies a noun or a pronoun. An **adverb** modifies a verb, an adjective, or another adverb.

ADJECTIVE:
Oak is a **hard** wood.
The journey was **long**.

ADVERB:
We studied **hard**.
I worked **long** into the night.

Some adverbs have an *ly* ending, which makes them easy to recognize.

ADJECTIVE:	quick	slow	loud	soft
ADVERB:	quickly	slowly	loudly	softly

The words *good* and *well* are sometimes confused. The word *good* is always used as an adjective. The word *well* is usually used as an adverb. When *well* means "healthy," it is used as an adjective.

That was a **good** decision   (adjective)
You spoke **well**.   (adverb)
You felt **well** this morning. (adjective)

Guided Practice

Tell which word in parentheses correctly completes each sentence.

Example: The presentation was (good, well).   *good*

1. Gwen is a (good, well) salesperson.
2. She is always (polite, politely) to her customers.
3. She treats everyone (helpful, helpfully).
4. Her presentations of new products are (good, well).
5. They are planned especially (good, well).

THINK
■ How can I tell whether to use an adjective or an adverb?

REMEMBER

- Use adjectives, including *good*, to modify nouns.
- Use adverbs to modify verbs, adjectives, or other adverbs.

More Practice

A. Write the word in parentheses that correctly completes each sentence.

Example: Gwen (usual, usually) likes selling.   *usually*

6. How does someone do (good, well) in sales?

7. A (good, well) salesperson should be confident.

8. Salespeople must relate to others (easy, easily).

9. They must know their facts (thorough, thoroughly).

10. They should also speak (clear, clearly).

11. A presentation must be (persuasive, persuasively).

12. Are you (real, really) interested in sales?

13. I think it is a (wonderful, wonderfully) career.

B. Write each sentence, using the correct word in parentheses. Write whether the word is an **adverb** or an **adjective**, and underline the word it modifies.

Example: It can be (particular, particularly) interesting.
        It can be particularly <u>interesting</u>.   adverb

14. Salespeople have (interesting, interestingly) careers.

15. They often travel (wide, widely).

16. They learn about (different, differently) products.

17. Maybe you would make a (good, well) salesperson.

18. Could you behave (helpful, helpfully) to customers?

19. Usually, salespeople behave (courteous, courteously).

20. They must look (good, well) and work (hard, hardly).

Extra Practice, Practice Plus, pages 385–386

WRITING APPLICATION A Job Application

Imagine that you are preparing to interview for a job selling electronic toys. Write five statements to persuade the interviewer to give you the job.

5 AVOIDING DOUBLE NEGATIVES

Some negative words are used as adverbs. A **negative** is a word that means "no."

It was **not** easy for women to enter medical school.

Most negative words have several opposites. These opposites, called **positive** words, express the idea of "yes."

Negative	Positive	Negative	Positive
never	ever, always	nothing	anything, something
none	one, some, all	no one	everyone, someone
no	any	nowhere	anywhere, somewhere
hardly	almost	neither	either

Use only one negative word to give a negative meaning. Using two negatives together in a sentence makes a **double negative** and is incorrect. To correct a double negative, you can usually substitute a matching positive word, or you can drop one of the negatives.

INCORRECT:	I won't never give up.
CORRECT:	I won't **ever** give up.
CORRECT:	I **will** never give up.

Guided Practice

Tell which word correctly completes each sentence.

Example: Yoko hadn't read (anything, nothing) about Elizabeth Blackwell.   *anything*

1. Yoko hadn't (never, ever) heard the story of Blackwell's life.
2. Elizabeth Blackwell never wanted to be (anything, nothing) other than a doctor.
3. In 1845 medical schools did not admit (no, any) women.
4. Blackwell never (did, didn't) accept rejection.

 **THINK**

■ How can I correct a double negative?

REMEMBER

■ Correct a double negative by substituting a positive word for one negative or by dropping *not* or *n't*.

More Practice

A. Write the word that correctly completes each sentence.

Example: Nobody (never, ever) had a more interesting
career.   *ever*

5. (Hardly, Almost) no one supported Blackwell's plans.
6. Her family didn't agree with her, (neither, either).
7. Elizabeth Blackwell (wouldn't, would) never accept defeat.
8. However, (almost, hardly) none of her friends approved.
9. Blackwell didn't think (any, no) career was more important.
10. No graduate of Geneva College (is, isn't) more famous!
11. At first, she was not accepted by (no, any) other doctor.

B. Rewrite each sentence. Correct each double negative.

Example: No text isn't as great as the Constitution.
No text is as great as the Constitution.

12. Haven't you never studied the Philadelphia Convention?
13. In 1787 people thought America wouldn't never survive.
14. Madison said nothing wasn't more vital than agreement.
15. Some states like Georgia had hardly no population.
16. They weren't as rich as the larger states, neither.
17. Large states did not want to give up no votes.
18. No progress wasn't made until Roger Sherman spoke.
19. Hardly none of the states rejected his proposal.
20. It said no state wouldn't lose its say in government.

Extra Practice, page 387

WRITING APPLICATION A Story

Write a brief story of a day when everything seemed to go wrong for you. For example, you slept late and missed the school bus. Try to use a negative word in each sentence. Make sure you do not use any double negatives.

6 MECHANICS: Using Commas to Set Off Words

You already know how to use **commas** to punctuate dates, to join compound sentences, and to separate words in a list. Study these additional uses of commas.

- Use a comma to show a pause after an **introductory word**.

    Yes, I think that the new law is needed.

- Use commas to set off words called **interrupters** that interrupt the flow of thought in a sentence.

    Senator Perillo, **of course,** is campaigning hard.

- Use commas to set off **nouns of direct address** (the name of someone who is being spoken to directly).

    Are you in favor of the parkland bill**, Sam**?
    What do you think**, Chuck,** about the issue?

- Use commas to set off an **appositive**. An appositive is a word or group of words that immediately follows a noun and identifies or explains it. If an appositive is necessary for the meaning of a sentence, do not use commas.

    This bill, **a tax measure**, failed to pass.
    The word *senate* comes from Latin.

Guided Practice

Tell where to use commas in the following sentences.

Example: What are you looking for Ms. Nguyen? *after for*

1. My computer an out-of-date model needs to be replaced.
2. These computers are highly praised I believe.
3. Do you have the newest model Mr. Sato?
4. Yes it is over here.
5. It costs more money I imagine.
6. Would you like to see this computer Ms. Nguyen?

 THINK

- How do I decide where to use commas to set off words?

REMEMBER

- Use a comma to set off an introductory word.
- Use commas to set off words that interrupt the flow of thought.
- Use commas to set off some appositives.
- Use commas to set off nouns of direct address.

More Practice

A. Write these sentences. Add commas where needed.

Example: This store the biggest in town has good prices.

This store, the biggest in town, has good prices.

7. Well I do not know anything about that brand.
8. This machine a new model might interest you.
9. It is easy to use I expect.
10. You will have no trouble learning it of course.
11. Mr. Simpson can you give me a good price?
12. Yes we will give you a special discount.

B. Write this dialogue. Add commas where needed.

Example: Earl: Here is our special guest Mike Gittings.

Earl: Here is our special guest, Mike Gittings.

13. Earl: This is Mike Gittings World Series champion.
14. Mike: It's a pleasure to speak with you Earl.
15. Earl: Mike what can kids learn from baseball?
16. Mike: Baseball a team sport encourages team spirit.
17. Earl: You train hard all year I imagine.
18. Mike: Yes it's important to keep in shape.
19. Earl: What diet do you suggest for youngsters Mike?
20. Mike: A good diet of course should be well balanced.

Extra Practice, page 388

WRITING APPLICATION An Interview

Imagine that you have interviewed an astronaut.
Write a brief script for the questions and answers.
Remember to use commas to set off words.

VOCABULARY BUILDING: Prefixes

A **prefix** is a word part added to the beginning of a base word. Once you know the meaning of a prefix, you can figure out the meaning of a familiar base word that has that prefix. Your vocabulary will grow, and you can vary your writing.

This chart gives examples of some common prefixes.

Prefix	Meaning	Example
re	again, back	rethink, replace
un	not, the opposite of	unknown, unhappy
dis	not, the opposite of, lack of	dislike, disinfect, disorder
mis	wrongly, badly	misplace, misbehave
in	not, without, in, into	incomplete, inexperience, indoors
im	not, without, in, into	impatient, imbalance, imprison
ir, il	not, without	irregular, illogical
non	not, the opposite of, without	nonworking, nonsense, nonstop
pre	before, in preparation for	preview, preschool
post	after, later, behind	postscript, postoperative, postnasal
inter	between or among, together	international, interlace
bi	having two of, twice	bicycle, biweekly
ex	out of or from, previous	excavate, ex-president

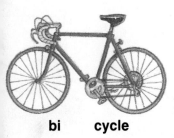

bi   cycle

Guided Practice

Tell the prefix and give the meaning of each word.

Example: nonreturnable   *non   cannot be returned*

1. impossible   **2.** interaction   **3.** recopy

THINK

■ How can I make a new word with a prefix?

REMEMBER

- A **prefix** is a word part added to the beginning of a base word.
- A prefix changes the meaning of the base word to which it is added.

More Practice

A. Write each word, and underline its prefix. Then write the meaning of the word. Use a dictionary if necessary.

Example: misbehave   _misbehave_   _behave badly_

4. informal
5. untidy
6. replace
7. disapprove

8 nonmetal
9. implant
10. postproduction
11. interchange

B. Write each sentence, adding a prefix to each underlined word so that it makes sense in the sentence.

Example: The council <u>considered</u> their new decision.
The council reconsidered their new decision.

12. Dog owners demonstrated against the <u>popular</u> decision.
13. They complained that they <u>liked</u> the new rule.
14. Although he had retired, they even wrote to the <u>mayor</u>.
15. He <u>claimed</u> all responsibility.
16. He said that a judge should make a decision <u>dependently</u>.
17. Until the hearing, many people continued their <u>stop</u> protest.
18. The judge declared the council's decision poor and <u>guided</u>.
19. She said the new rule was both unacceptable and <u>moderate</u>.
20. Finally, the judge <u>covered</u> the picture of her dog on her desk!

Extra Practice, page 389

WRITING APPLICATION A List

Choose five prefixes from this lesson. Then, using a dictionary, add the prefixes to five new base words. Exchange lists of words with a classmate. Try to identify the meanings of each other's words.

COOPERATIVE LEARNING

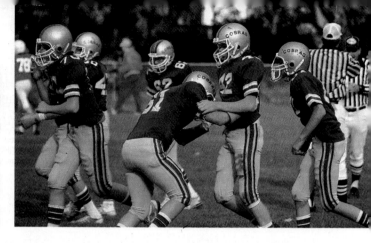

GRAMMAR ——AND—— WRITING CONNECTION

Combining Sentences

As you write, you may often want to show how ideas in two separate sentences are related. Combining sentences can make your writing more interesting.

Separate: We must make a decision. Time is running out.

Combined: We must make a decision *because time is running out.*

Or: *Because time is running out,* we must make a decision.

When you combine sentences, you can change the order of the words in the new sentence. Notice that a comma follows a clause when it begins a sentence.

Working Together

Read each group of sentences. Then tell how you would combine them into a single sentence, using such joining words as *although, because, even though, until,* and *when.*

Example: I practiced daily. My writing improved.
I practiced daily until my writing improved.
Because I practiced daily, my writing improved.

1. I will go out for the team. I might not make it.
2. The International Club is her favorite.
   She has never been outside the country.
3. We joined the science club. We want to be doctors.

Revising Sentences

Maria must decide whether to join the journalism club. Imagine that you are her adviser, and help her to combine the following pairs of sentences by using adverb clauses. Remember to punctuate correctly with commas, depending on the placement of the adverb clauses.

4. In my opinion journalism is worthwhile and important.
   It helps you to think about many issues.
5. I could wait to join later.
   I will be going to high school.
6. I can write about many different things now.
   I am in junior high school.
7. My favorite subject now is classical music.
   I play several different kinds of instruments.
8. I would like to join the journalism club.
   I may be too busy.
9. Combining interests is a good idea.
   Each subject can feed the other.
10. I will join the club.
    I can write about my love of music.

Think about a decision you must make soon. Write a paragraph that gives your reasons for making the decision. When you revise, work with a partner to find pairs of sentences to combine. Experiment with adverb clauses by changing the word order in the combined sentences.

UNIT CHECKUP

LESSON

Adverbs That Modify Verbs (page 362) Write each adverb and the verb it modifies.

1. Alma prepared her speech perfectly.
2. She logically identified the main idea.
3. She practiced her speech often.
4. She seldom made a mistake.
5. She stood there with her notes.
6. Then she gave her speech.

LESSON

Adverbs That Modify Adjectives and Adverbs (page 364) Write each adverb and the word it modifies. Then write whether the modified word is an **adjective** or another **adverb**.

7. A fact is thoroughly reliable.
8. Facts can be checked rather easily.
9. Facts make very good support for opinions.
10. Opinions are quite personal.
11. Opinions can be completely different.
12. They are quite unreliable.

LESSON

Adverbs That Compare (page 366) Write the adverb that correctly completes each sentence.

13. Jim writes (clearlier, more clearly) than Pat.
14. His editorials read (better, more better) than Pat's.
15. He states the issues (completer, more completely) than anyone.
16. He writes (more easily, easier) than Ed.
17. We read his editorials the (carefulest, most carefully).
18. We think (deeper, more deeply) after reading him.

LESSON

Adverb or Adjective? (page 368) Write the correct adjective or adverb to complete each sentence.

19. That editorial explores the issues (good, well).
20. The writer has a (good, well) grasp of the facts.

21. The writer favors a (tough, toughly) policy.
22. Pollution is a (serious, seriously) problem.
23. It (bad, badly) endangers our lives.
24. The writer must feel (strong, strongly) about it.

LESSON 5

Avoiding Double Negatives (page 370) Write the word in parentheses that correctly completes each sentence.

25. Abe Lincoln didn't (never, ever) study public speaking.
26. He hadn't (no, any) degree from college.
27. Yet, no president (wasn't, was) a better speaker.
28. (Almost, Hardly) no one heard him without being moved.
29. There is not (anything, nothing) better than the Gettysburg Address.
30. None (couldn't, could) hear it without shedding a tear.

LESSON 6

Mechanics: Using Commas to Set Off Words (page 372) Write these sentences. Use commas where needed.

31. Our decision I think is important.
32. What is your opinion Meg?
33. The mayor Mr. Simon called for a vote.
34. We should cast our ballots I believe.
35. What will you do now Mr. Mayor?
36. I shall of course rethink the issues.

LESSON 7

Vocabulary Building: Prefixes (page 374) Write the prefix in each word. Then write the meaning of the word.

37. prepaid
38. unlimited
39. nonfiction

40. disfigure to
41. reprint
42. postdate

Writing Application: Adverb Usage (pages 362–370) The following paragraph contains 8 errors with adverbs. Rewrite the paragraph correctly.

43.–50.

A few students at Munro High came to an unexpectedly decision last month. They voted overwhelming to reintroduce school uniforms. Hardly none of the other students agreed with them. Many students said the decision was unlikeliest to be upheld. Another meeting was called quick. The newly decision was complete different. The first vote was swift overturned.

Skating Away

Imagine that you are a judge at an ice-skating contest. For each of the three ice-skating contestants, think of an adverb in each category below that describes the skating.

How	Where	When	To What Extent

Poster Time

Think of a famous important decision—for example, Christopher Columbus's refusing to turn back for home and continuing to America. Draw a poster showing the decision being made. Then, write captions about the decision, using adverbs. For example, **Columbus sailed on bravely**.

Ten Seconds . . .

Play this game in a small group. Choose someone to begin; then choose for that person a topic from the list. He or she must speak about that topic, using at least one adverb in each sentence. If the speaker pauses for more than 10 seconds or does not use an adverb, it becomes someone else's turn. Repeat the activity with everyone in the group, taking turns.

TOPICS

moving to a new city
becoming an astronaut
winning a race

CREATIVE EXPRESSION

On the Mountain Pass
Here on the mountain pass,
somehow they draw one's heart so—
violets in the grass.

—Bashō

Try It Out!

A *haiku* is a traditional Japanese poem that has three lines. Haiku often show a scene from nature. Write a haiku of your own. Try to describe a scene from nature. At the same time, express a strong feeling that you have about life.

EXTRA PRACTICE

Three levels of practice
Adverbs That Modify Verbs (page 362)

LEVEL A. Write the adverb in each sentence.

1. Today we will discuss writing.
2. We will write persuasively.
3. Persuasive writing can powerfully influence people.
4. It can add greatly to a person's career.
5. Persuasion contributes usefully to our system of government.
6. We often experience persuasion in advertising.
7. Newspaper editorials always employ persuasion.
8. We see examples of such persuasion daily.

LEVEL B. Write each sentence. Underline the adverb. Then draw two lines under the verb that the adverb modifies.

9. We should think carefully about persuasive writing.
10. Persuasion may be used thoughtlessly.
11. Persuasion often influences people.
12. Writers sometimes provoke their audiences.
13. Candidates rarely ignore their voters.
14. Advertisers usually sell a product.
15. Persuasion always tries influencing a point of view.

LEVEL C. Use the following adverbs in sentences. Underline the verb that each adverb modifies.

16. greatly
17. often
18. always
19. there
20. completely
21. nearly
22. then
23. never
24. occasionally
25. softly

EXTRA PRACTICE

Three levels of practice
Adverbs That Modify Adjectives and Adverbs (page 364)

LEVEL A. Write each underlined adverb and the word that it modifies.

1. Kerry is planning his paragraph <u>extremely</u> carefully.
2. He started work <u>rather</u> early.
3. His <u>very</u> first task was to find a topic.
4. An opinion is a <u>fairly</u> common topic for a paragraph.
5. Think about your opinion <u>quite</u> thoroughly.
6. Your opinion should not be <u>too</u> general.
7. Factual statements are not <u>so</u> suitable for an opinion.
8. People do not disagree <u>very</u> much about facts.

LEVEL B. Write each sentence. Draw one line under each adverb. Draw two lines under the word it modifies.

9. Kerry decided on his topic very quickly.
10. It states that the new road proposal needs relatively careful study.
11. Kerry now thought about his audience.
12. This kind of preparation is especially important.
13. What does your audience already know?
14. Can you immediately catch your readers' attention?
15. Your readers have a fairly sophisticated point of view.

LEVEL C. Write each sentence. Draw one line under each adverb. Draw two lines under the modified word. Label the word a **verb**, an **adjective**, or an **adverb**.

16. Solid arguments are very persuasive.
17. Some readers might be totally opposed.
18. Kerry can persuade people effectively.
19. His topic was quite suitably persuasive for an editorial.
20. His readers would then decide for themselves.
21. Kerry organized his reasons particularly well.
22. Suddenly, he thought of a mistake.
23. The error seemed extremely obvious.
24. He quickly corrected it.
25. Often Kerry found small errors quickly.

EXTRA PRACTICE

Three levels of Practice
Adverbs That Compare (page 366)

LEVEL A. Write the adverb that correctly completes each sentence.

1. Facts convince readers (better, best) than opinions.
2. Facts are (more thoroughly, most thoroughly) reliable than feelings.
3. Of all the writers, Susan worked the (harder, hardest).
4. The new road would go through the (more densely, most densely) settled area of any in town.
5. It would cost (much, more) than a bypass.
6. It was designed (worse, worst) than citizens had thought.
7. The plan appealed (little, less) over time.

LEVEL B. Write the form of the adverb in parentheses that correctly completes each sentence.

8. Luke organized his reasons _____ this year than last. (well)
9. He began _____ than before. (skillfully)
10. He wrote _____ of all toward the end. (well)
11. Luke wrote _____ than he did last year. (easily)
12. He referred _____ to facts than to opinions. (often)
13. He quoted Mr. Roth _____ of all the experts. (frequently)
14. He asked that the project be studied _____ than before. (well)
15. He wrote his conclusion _____ of all. (forcefully)

LEVEL C. Write complete sentences using the phrases below. Identify each **comparative** and **superlative adverb**.

16. answered most accurately
17. wrote more skillfully
18. studied this issue most thoughtfully
19. asked more often
20. argued more persuasively
21. spoke the most clearly
22. sprints the fastest
23. looks healthier
24. marked harder
25. worked best

EXTRA PRACTICE

Three levels of practice
Adverb or Adjective? (page 368)

LEVEL A. Write the correct word to complete each sentence.

1. James (careful, carefully) wrote his paragraph.
2. His topic seemed (reasonable, reasonably).
3. He stated his opinion (clear, clearly).
4. He checked his facts (accurate, accurately).
5. His facts were also balanced (well, good).
6. Mr. Ruiz was a (famous, famously) expert on highways.
7. His opinions were (sound, soundly).
8. James used (suitable, suitably) language.
9. He avoided (emotional, emotionally) charged words.

LEVEL B. Write each sentence by choosing the correct word in parentheses. Write whether the word is an **adjective** or an **adverb.**

10. James criticized the road proposal (good, well).
11. He dealt with (different, differently) opinions.
12. He arranged his reasons (smooth, smoothly).
13. Hardship for many families was (clear, clearly) first among the issues.
14. Cost was also an (important, importantly) concern.
15. We read his report (hopeful, hopefully).
16. James's ideas were (good, well).

LEVEL C. Write two sentences, one for each phrase in the pair. Make the sentences mean almost the same thing. Identify each **adjective** and **adverb.**

17. poor design   planned poorly
18. high cost   highly expensive
19. looked bad   presented badly
20. incomplete study   researched incompletely
21. final suggestion   recommended finally
22. good writing   write well
23. fast action   act fast
24. more details   more fully
25. extreme heat   extremely hot

PRACTICE + PLUS

Three levels of additional practice for a difficult skill
Adverb or Adjective? (page 368)

LEVEL A. Label the underlined word **adjective** or **adverb**.

1. The mayor worked <u>hard</u> to set up a recycling program.
2. Townspeople were <u>neighborly</u> and cooperated fully.
3. One <u>early</u> step was to sort out all newspapers.
4. Paper dealers paid a <u>good</u> price for the old paper.
5. Next, aluminum and glass were collected <u>separately</u>.
6. These materials are <u>easy</u> to reuse.
7. <u>Lately</u>, metal and wooden trash are being separated.
8. The program has reduced the town's garbage <u>fast</u>.
9. Everyone agrees that the program has worked <u>well</u>.
10. It won't be <u>long</u> before all communities recycle.

LEVEL B. Write the word in parentheses that correctly completes each sentence. Write whether the word is an **adjective** or **adverb**.

11. Our garbage problem seems more (serious, seriously) now than it ever did before.
12. People are producing garbage (rapid, rapidly).
13. Burning garbage smells (bad, badly).
14. It is also (real, really) dangerous to breathe.
15. How (slow, slowly) plastics decay!
16. It isn't (good, well) to waste these resources.
17. Spare land is filling up (quick, quickly).
18. Finding new dump sites won't be (easy, easily).
19. Recycling garbage works (good, well).

LEVEL C. Write one sentence, using both the adjective and the adverb from each pair.

20. sure/surely
21. bad/ badly
22. easy/ easily
23. sudden/ suddenly
24. well (adjective)/ well (adverb)
25. hard (adjective)/ hard (adverb)

EXTRA PRACTICE

Three levels of practice
Avoiding Double Negatives (page 370)

LEVEL
A. Write the negative word from each sentence.

1. Nothing is more effective than persuasion.
2. Hardly anyone ignores a sound argument.
3. No paragraph should lack a topic sentence.
4. Never choose an overly broad topic.
5. No one debates these facts.
6. Of these opinions, none seems believable.
7. Never give an opinion without evidence.
8. Slanted facts are appropriate nowhere.
9. Neither are charged words suitable.
10. Nobody can be convinced without good reasons.

LEVEL
B. Write each sentence, using the correct word in parentheses.

11. Nobody (was, wasn't) convinced by that speaker.
12. Didn't he give (any, no) support for his opinion?
13. He (had, hadn't) no strong reasons.
14. Nothing he said (was, wasn't) based on facts.
15. He did not make (no, any) practical suggestions for action.
16. He didn't show (no, any) understanding of the issue.
17. Hardly (nobody, anybody) understood his statements.
18. His speech wasn't (nothing, anything) like yours.

LEVEL
C. Rewrite each sentence. Correct the double negatives.

19. There wasn't no applause when he finished.
20. Hardly no one had listened.
21. Didn't you do no research for the debate?
22. I couldn't find no sound facts in these books.
23. Didn't you never think of the library?
24. You can't find a better source of information nowhere.
25. There is hardly no book you can't locate if you try.

EXTRA PRACTICE

Three levels of practice
Mechanics: Using Commas to Set Off Words (page 372)

LEVEL A. Write **introductory word, interrupter**, **appositive,** or **direct address** to show why commas are used in these sentences.

1. Can you help me, Mr. Gonzalez?
2. Lucy, what would you like to know?
3. Well, I have to write a persuasive paragraph for school.
4. I need some information for my topic, water resources.
5. Mr. Gonzalez, didn't you do a survey of the reservoirs?
6. Yes, I completed it last year for the governor.
7. It was, as you might imagine, a long project.
8. Oh, you probably learned a great many facts.

LEVEL B. Write each sentence. Add commas where needed.

9. Of course we spent more than three months writing the report.
10. Would you mind if I took notes sir?
11. I need accurate facts as you can see for my assignment.
12. I would be happy to help you Lucy.
13. Water supply a complicated subject is important.
14. What point of view Lucy are you supporting?
15. I think the mayor our highest official should build a new reservoir.

LEVEL C. Write this dialogue. Add commas where needed. Explain why you added commas.

16. Mr. G: Yes the present reservoir is too far away.
17. Lucy: I have also learned sir that the water mains are old.
18. Mr. G: Well you certainly seem to have done some research!
19. Lucy: The present reservoir our only source is inadequate.
20. Mr. G: I want to help you of course with your topic.
21. Lucy: Mr. Gonzalez I want to know how much water an average person uses.
22. Mr. G: I should be able to tell you that I think.
23. Lucy: The usage figures Mr. Gonzalez should be daily ones.
24. Mr. G: Unfortunately they may not be broken down that way.
25. Lucy: I will be grateful sir for any help you can give me.

EXTRA PRACTICE

Three levels of practice
Vocabulary Building: Prefixes (page 374)

LEVEL A. Write each underlined word. Draw a line under the prefix.

1. The lawyer <u>re</u>viewed her client's case.
2. She considered some facts to be <u>in</u>significant.
3. She checked and <u>pre</u>planned her argument.
4. Her client should not seem <u>un</u>convincing.
5. Some arguments seemed <u>dis</u>couraging.
6. The court was <u>non</u>partisan.

LEVEL B. Write each sentence. Draw a line under the prefix of the underlined word. Then write the meaning of the word.

7. The lawyer knew the judge would be <u>impartial</u>.
8. The judge accepted her <u>pretrial</u> motion.
9. The lawyer needed to <u>postpone</u> the trial.
10. She tried for an <u>unlimited</u> extension.
11. She didn't want the jury to be <u>misled</u>.

LEVEL C. Write each word. Underline its prefix. Then write the meaning of each word and use it in a sentence. Use a dictionary if needed.

12. mistrial
13. impersonal
14. intervene
15. unskilled
16. disappear
17. incapable
18. postwar
19. repossess
20. presoak
21. ex-judge
22. nonviolent
23. unemotional
24. irrational
25. bifocal

UNIT
12

Writing Persuasive Paragraphs

Read the quotation and look at the picture on the opposite page. The picture shows a kind of crossroads in a part of the world filled with the excitement that Diane Wolkstein speaks of. Why does she think stories are wonderful?

When you write to persuade, you will want to present facts and your own ideas to persuade your audience to take a certain action or to feel the way you do. In a way, you have to imagine your audience at a crossroads. You must persuade them to choose a certain path.

Focus Persuasive writing encourages an audience to accept an opinion or to take an action.

What subject could you use for persuasive writing? The folk tale and photographs in this unit may give you some ideas.

THEME: *CROSSROADS*

Machu Picchu, a prehistoric Inca site, Peru

Part of what's wonderful about stories is the excitement and suspense of not knowing what will happen next.

—Diane Wolkstein

LITERATURE

Reading Like a Writer

AWARD
WINNING
SELECTION

Have you ever felt that someone was being unfair to you? What reasons or arguments did you use to try to persuade that person to be fair?

The poor Haitian woman in this folk tale must convince a judge that she is right about an important issue.

As you read the selection, look for the reasons that were used to settle the issue.

THE CASE OF THE UNCOOKED EGGS

a Haitian folk tale, collected by Diane Wolkstein

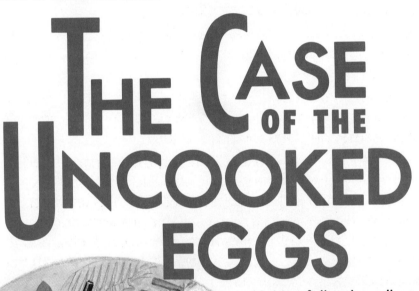

A poor woman in Kenscoff once offered lodging to a soldier, and before he left he gave her a gift of three eggs. She looked at the eggs. They were longer on one end. She decided not to cook them but to put them under the hen to hatch.

Soon three fat red roosters peeped out of the shells. The woman raised the roosters and took them to market and sold them for five dollars. With the money, she bought two small pigs. She nourished the pigs on banana peels and corn and sold them for a goat. She sold the goat for a calf, and when the calf had grown into a strong ox, she sold it and bought land.

The writer tells the facts in logical order.

Some years later, the same soldier was again passing through Kenscoff and asked for lodging at the woman's house.

"Oh, don't you recognize me?" she cried. "When you were here last you gave me three eggs. I never forget when someone does me a good turn."

She was so happy to see him she made him a large meal, and as they ate together, she told him what she had done with the three eggs. After they had finished their coffee, she took him around her property and showed him her fields of carrots, tomatoes, leeks, and radishes; her cattle; even her flowers. He stayed with her for five days. She treated him royally and then he left.

Eight days later she received a summons to appear in court. As she had never done any harm to anyone in her life, she did not go. A week later, she received a second summons. She ignored this one as well. But when the third summons came, she woke at two in the morning and walked five hours to town.

Both the woman and the soldier use facts and reasons to support their opinions.

Waiting for her in the courthouse was the soldier. He declared that because of his gift to her of three eggs, she was able to buy livestock, fields, and even roses and violets. Now it was only correct that she share her goods with him.

"But the soldier did not give me roosters," she told the judge, "he only gave me eggs!"

"Yes, and those eggs, did they not give you all that you have?" the soldier insisted.

The woman left the courthouse. She hired a lawyer. The soldier hired a lawyer. The case went on and on, the two lawyers deliberating endlessly. As the case came to a close the woman was so exhausted, she was nearly willing to divide her property with the soldier.

Then, on the Thursday evening before the final decision was to be made on Monday, an old ragged beggar knocked on her door.

"Charity for a poor man," he said. "A little something to eat."

"Not at this moment," she said. "I am not giving out charity. I do not even know what I will have tomorrow." And she explained the case to him.

"Madame, don't you worry; nothing serious will happen!"

"Nothing serious! It's almost all over!" But she relented and offered him some bread and rice and beans.

Then he said, "Madame, here is some advice. Eat well on Saturday and Sunday. Get up early Monday, make yourself coffee, walk to town, and I will be waiting for you in the court."

The woman looked at him. "*You* will be waiting for me. But what can you do?"

"You shall see."

Sunday, just before midnight, the woman woke up. She prepared coffee for herself and started down to Port-au-Prince. The beggar was already seated on one of the benches. The woman sat down. The lawyers arrived and the final speeches were made. They talked and talked and talked. The woman felt so tired she was certain that if someone dropped a handkerchief on her, she would fall to the floor and not be able to get up.

The writer uses persuasive language to appeal to the reader.

Just then the old beggar called out: "Judge!"

"What is it, old vagabond?"

"I have come to hear the verdict."

"Why should an old beggar like you concern yourself with the verdict of this case?"

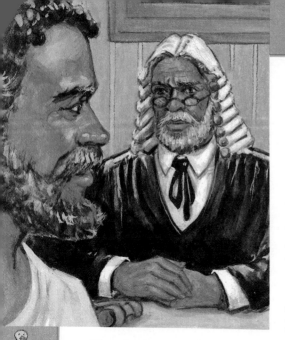

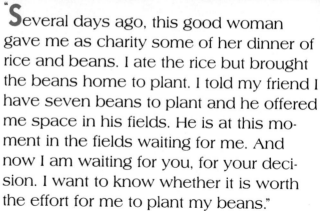

"Several days ago, this good woman gave me as charity some of her dinner of rice and beans. I ate the rice but brought the beans home to plant. I told my friend I have seven beans to plant and he offered me space in his fields. He is at this moment in the fields waiting for me. And now I am waiting for you, for your decision. I want to know whether it is worth the effort for me to plant my beans."

The people in the courthouse laughed and shouted. The lawyers stood up to look at the man.

The judge said, "Whoever heard of cooked beans being planted?"

"Thank you, judge," said the beggar. "When this good woman told me it was believed in court that eggs could provide flowers and pigs and goats, I thought, perhaps I, too, should make the effort. After all, if the laws have been changed, and eggs can give all that, what can beans do?"

Everyone shouted, "Bravo!"

The case was dismissed. The woman had won.

Thinking Like a Reader

1. Why did the judge decide that the woman should win the case?

2. Have you ever been in a situation where your opinion has been proved right? Why was your opinion proved right? Explain the situation.

Write your responses in your journal.

Thinking Like a Writer

3. How does the writer let you know that the woman deserved to win?

4. What reason does the beggar use to convince the judge at the end of the trial? Do *you* find this reason convincing? Why or why not?

Write your responses in your journal.

BRAINSTORM *Vocabulary*

In "The Case of the Uncooked Eggs," the beggar refers to the woman twice as "this good woman." He also says that the woman gave him some of her dinner "as charity." Imagine that you are the woman's lawyer. In your journal, write words or phrases that describe the woman favorably. You might want to include some positive comparisons in the phrases that you write. Add your words to your personal vocabulary list and try to use them in your writing.

Talk It Over
Taking Another Point of View

When you speak persuasively, you try to persuade your audience to accept your opinion. In "The Case of the Uncooked Eggs," the beggar convinces the judge that the woman is right. Imagine that you are the lawyer for the soldier. Prepare a speech from the soldier's point of view that might have persuaded the judge to rule for him and against the woman in the story.

Quick Write *Write an Ad*

Now that you have imagined yourself as a lawyer, try writing a newspaper ad describing your services. In your advertisement, tell your readers why they should hire you to represent them if they have to go to court to plead a case. Write your advertisement on a separate sheet of paper.

Your advertisement might look like this.

Doris Kane, Lawyer
Courteous Service
Reasonable Fees
Never Lost a Case!
125 North Street   555-7208

IDEA CORNER *Think of Opinions*

Think of ideas for writing a persuasive paragraph. In your journal, write whatever opinions come to mind. You might write opinions about community issues, such as "Why we should support the museum" or "Why riding buses should be free." You might also write about more personal opinions, like "Why everyone should love the poetry of Sandburg."

Finding Ideas for Writing
Look at the photographs. Think about what you see.
What ideas for persuasive writing do the pictures give you?
Write your ideas in your journal.

The Granger Collection

1 GROUP WRITING: Persuasive Paragraphs

COOPERATIVE LEARNING

The **purpose** of persuasive writing is to persuade your **audience** to accept an opinion or to do something. What does an effective persuasive paragraph include?

- Topic Sentence
- Supporting Reasons
- Order of Reasons

Topic Sentence

Read the following paragraph. Notice the underlined sentence.

> We should all take advantage of the chance to join the Zoo Society. First, members can save money because they receive free admission to the zoo and tickets for free rides. Secondly, members automatically receive a free, one-year subscription to the society's educational magazine, *Animal Kingdom*. Most importantly, membership in the society helps to finance wildlife protection programs throughout the world. I urge readers to sign up for membership in this worthwhile organization today.

The topic sentence, which is underlined, states the writer's opinion. The supporting sentences give reasons that support that opinion.

Guided Practice: Writing a Topic Sentence

As a class, choose a topic from the list below, or think of one on which you all agree. Explore some ideas with your classmates. Write a topic sentence that states your opinion.

Example: Every state should pass a law requiring drivers and their passengers to wear seat belts.

- smoking in public places
- shortening the school year
- television advertising
- lowering the speed limit

Supporting Reasons

To be convincing, the opinion expressed in persuasive paragraphs must be supported by **reasons**—facts and opinions. A **fact** is a statement that is known to be true. An **opinion** is a personal judgment about something a person feels or believes to be true.

Look back at the paragraph about the Zoo Society.

- What opinion is expressed?
- What supporting facts or opinions are given?

Guided Practice: Supporting Reasons

Recall the opinion you have already stated in a topic sentence. Think of reasons to support your opinion. As a class, make a list like the one below, containing facts and opinions that support the topic sentence.

Topic: Every state should pass a law requiring drivers and their passengers to wear seat belts.

Facts	Opinions
■ Seat belts save lives.	■ Seat belts are fun to use.
■ Belts are standard equipment in cars.	■ Belts are easy to use.

Order of Reasons

Review the paragraph on page 400. Notice that the writer presented the most important reason last. When you organize your reasons in persuasive paragraphs, use a **logical order.** Either present your most important reason first, or save it for last as you build up to it.

Look at the paragraph again. Notice that the writer has used **persuasive language** to appeal to the audience. Using words like "free," "automatically," and "worthwhile" helps to persuade your readers to accept your point of view.

Also, notice that the writer has ended with a strong **concluding sentence** that urges readers to join the Zoo Society. Your persuasive writing will be more convincing if you end with a strong concluding sentence.

Putting Persuasive Paragraphs Together

As a class you have written a sentence that states an opinion. You have also listed some reasons that support your opinion.

Now think about your topic sentence. Look at your list of facts and opinions. Which reasons will you include?

Look at how one student chose which reasons to include. First, read the topic sentence stating an opinion. Then, look at the chart that lists the student's reasons. Notice the reasons that are checked.

Topic Sentence: The speed limit should be lowered nationwide to 50 miles per hour.

Reasons: ✔ Lower speed shown to save lives and cut down on accidents.
I personally prefer riding at a lower speed.
✔ Studies have proved energy savings.
✔ Fewer accidents will mean better traffic flow.

This student chose reasons that directly support the opinion that the speed limit should be lowered. The student did not choose a personal opinion to support the topic sentence.

Guided Practice: Writing Persuasive Paragraphs

Now, write your persuasive paragraph. Write three detail sentences that give reasons supporting your opinion. In your detail sentences, include facts and opinions from your list. Choose the best persuasive words to convince your readers of your opinion. Be sure to use a logical order for your detail sentences. End with a strong concluding sentence.

Share your persuasive paragraph with a classmate. Ask your classmate if he or she has been convinced that your opinion is correct.

COOPERATIVE LEARNING: Group Writing

Checklist: Persuasive Paragraphs

When you write persuasive paragraphs, you can help yourself to remember points by making a checklist. A checklist will remind you of the elements that you will want to include in your paragraphs.

Look at the checklist below. Some points need to be added. Make a copy of this checklist and complete it. Keep a copy of it in your writing folder. You can use the checklist when you write your persuasive paragraphs.

CHECKLIST

✔ Purpose and audience

✔ Topic sentence that states your opinion

✔ Supporting reasons

✔ Persuasive language

■ _____ order

■ Strong _____ sentence

2 THINKING AND WRITING: Distinguishing Fact from Opinion

Think about what you have learned about persuasive writing. You know that you should use sound reasons to persuade your audience to accept your opinion or to take action. Reasons can include both facts and opinions.

The ability to distinguish between fact and opinion can make you a better writer and a better judge of the information that you read, hear, or use.

A **fact** is something known to be true or something that can be checked or proved. For example, it is a fact that each state is represented by two senators in Congress.

An **opinion** cannot be proved because it expresses a personal judgment, feeling, or belief. The following sentence is an opinion: I believe Senator Chandler should be reelected because she is the best candidate.

Opinions often contain **judgment words** like *believe*, *best*, *better*, *worse*, *worst*, *should*, and *probably*. These words signal that a writer is expressing an opinion.

Look at this page from a writer's notebook.

> Chandler votes for lower taxes
> by far the best speaker
> seems younger than her opponent
> issued foreign policy report
> supports clean air bill
> endorsed by the governor
> believed to be fair
> will probably win

The writer plans to write a paragraph whose purpose is to persuade readers to reelect Senator Chandler. On the page, many facts and opinions are listed.

Thinking Like a Writer

■ Which reasons do you think are important in supporting the writer's opinion?

Although many reasons are listed on the notebook page, the writer needs to make a choice and include only those reasons that contribute directly to the argument. Here, two reasons do not fit—the opinion that Senator Chandler seems younger than her opponent and the opinion that she will probably win.

When you write persuasively, you will have to make choices, too. You will have to decide which reasons are important and support your opinion.

THINKING APPLICATION Distinguishing Fact from Opinion

COOPERATIVE
LEARNING

Each of the writers named below is planning to write a persuasive paragraph. Help each writer to decide which reasons best support his or her opinion. On a separate sheet of paper, write the reasons that should be included. You may wish to discuss your thinking with other students. In your discussions, explain your choices to each other.

1. Marion's paragraph will try to persuade her readers to set up a regular exercise program. Which reasons should she include?

   exercise reduces stress   best exercise in walking
   exercise can be fun   proven link with good health

2. Milt's paragraph will support a four-day school week. Which reasons should he include?

   more free time   time for independent study
   time to earn extra money   five days is too long

3. In her paragraph, Yolanda will argue in favor of more computer courses at school. Which reasons should she include?

   computers important for   computers are fun
     jobs
   help students with   machines are expensive
     homework

3 INDEPENDENT WRITING: Persuasive Paragraphs

Prewrite: Step 1

You have learned a good deal about persuasive writing. Now you are ready to choose a topic. Derek, a student your age, chose a topic in this way. He decided that his **audience** would be the people who lived in his town. His **purpose** would be to convince them of his opinion on some local issue.

Choosing a Topic

1. First, Derek wrote a list of opinions.
2. Next, he thought about supporting each opinion with reasons.
3. Last, he decided on the best opinion.

Derek chose his last topic, but he decided to narrow it to an argument against building a new shopping center.

> • planting more trees on our town streets
> • banning smoking on all local public transportation
> • starting a chess club at the library
> • limiting new construction in our town

Exploring Ideas: Freewriting Strategy

Derek explored his topic by freewriting.

> New shopping center is a bad idea. The town board should reject the application. What about traffic on the highway? More accidents from the traffic? Shopping center might be ugly. And I think parkland is more important. Board meeting is next Thursday night.

Before he began to write, Derek used his freewriting notes to brainstorm a list of supporting facts and opinions for his position on the shopping center. He included some new facts and opinions on his brainstorming chart.

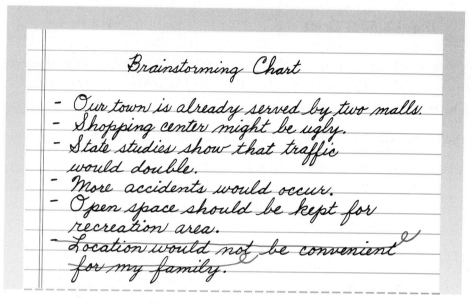

Brainstorming Chart

- *Our town is already served by two malls.*
- *Shopping center might be ugly.*
- *State studies show that traffic would double.*
- *More accidents would occur.*
- *Open space should be kept for recreation area.*
- ~~*Location would not be convenient for my family.*~~

Thinking Like a Writer

- What information did Derek add on his chart?
- What did he decide to cross out?
- Why do you think he crossed out that part?

YOUR TURN

Think of a topic that you would like to use for a persuasive paragraph. Follow these steps. Use **Pictures** or your journal to find ideas.

- Make a list of opinions about different topics.
- Choose one about which you feel strongly.
- Narrow your topic if it is too broad.
- Think about your purpose and audience.

Freewrite to think of ideas. Then make a brainstorming chart of reasons that support your opinion. Remember, you can add to or take away from the chart at any time.

Write a First Draft: Step 2

Before he started to write his first draft, Derek made a planning checklist. Then he was ready to write his first draft.

Derek's First Draft

The board should worry about the aplication to build a new shopping center on Highway 27. a new center is unnecessary I believe. Our Town is already served by two malls. Next, the state has made studies. They have shown that a new center would increase the traffic on the highway. Car accidents would therefore happen more oftener. Most importantly, the new center would occupy land that we should preserve as a recreation area for our town's citizens.

While Derek was writing his first draft, he did not worry about making errors. He was interested in getting his ideas down on paper.

YOUR TURN

Write the first draft of your persuasive paragraph. As you prepare to write, ask yourself these questions.

- What does my audience need to know?
- What opinion do I want to express?
- How can I best support my opinion?

TIME-OUT You might want to take some time out before you revise. That way you will be able to revise your writing with a fresh eye.

Planning Checklist
- Begin with a topic sentence that states your opinion.
- Include supporting facts and reasons.
- Use persuasive language.
- Use logical order.
- End with a concluding sentence.

Revise: Step 3

After he had finished his first draft, Derek read it over to himself. Then he asked one of his classmates to read it and make some suggestions for improvement.

After he met with his friend, Derek took out his checklist. He checked off the point his friend had mentioned so that he would remember it when he revised his paragraph.

Derek used this checklist when he revised his paragraph. As he revised, he made several changes. Notice that he did not correct small errors. He knew he could fix them later.

The revisions Derek made improved his paragraph. Look at Derek's revised draft on the next page.

Revising Checklist
- ■ Begin with a topic sentence that states your opinion.
- ■ Include supporting facts and reasons.
- ■ Use persuasive language.
- ■ Use logical order.
- ✔ ■ End with a concluding sentence.

Derek's Revised Draft

Our
~~The~~ board should ~~worry about~~ _reject_ the aplication to build a new

shopping center on Highway 27. a new center is unnecessary

I believe, _since_ Our Town is already served by two malls. _well_ Next,

studies by
~~the state has made studies. They~~ have shown that a new _clearly_

center would ~~increase~~ _double_ the traffic on the highway. _at rush hour_ Car

accidents would therefore happen more oftener. Most

importantly, the new center would occupy land that we should

all
preserve as a recreation area for our town's citizens. _For these reasons, I urge all board members to vote "no" on the proposal._

Thinking Like a Writer

WISE
WORD
CHOICE

- What sentence did Derek add? Why do you think he added it?
- Where did Derek add persuasive language? How does the addition improve his paragraph?
- Which sentences did he combine? How does combining them improve his writing?

YOUR TURN

Read your first draft. Make a checklist. Ask yourself these questions.

- How can I state my opinion more clearly?
- How can I make my supporting reasons stronger?
- How would combining sentences improve my writing?
- How could my concluding sentence be more effective?

If you wish, ask a friend to read your paragraph and make suggestions. Then revise your paragraph.

Proofread: Step 4

Derek knew that his work was not complete until he proofread his paragraph. He used a proofreading checklist while he proofread, and he checked for errors in grammar and mechanics. He used proofreading marks to correct the errors he found.

Part of Derek's Proofread Draft

¶ The board should worry about the ~~aplication~~ [Our] [reject] [application] to build a new

shopping center on Highway 27. a new center is unnecessary,

I believe. Our Town is already served by two malls. Next, [since] [well]

the state has made studies. They have shown that a new [studies by] [clearly]

center would increase the traffic on the highway. Car [double] [at rush hour]

accidents would therefore happen more ~~oftener~~. Most [often]

YOUR TURN

Proofreading Practice.

Below is a paragraph that you can use to practice your proofreading skills. Find the errors. Write the paragraph correctly on a separate piece of paper.

> Our community should pass a Law forbidding people to drive on the beech. oil stains and exhaust fumes cause pollution. In addition drivers are eroding sand dunes. Most importantly local police reported three serious accidents involving beach buggies last summer. For these reasons voters should support a bill that will keep drivers off our beach.

Proofreading Checklist
- Did I indent my paragraph?
- Did I spell each word correctly?
- Which punctuation errors do I need to correct?
- Which capitalization errors do I need to correct?
- What errors in adverb usage do I need to correct?

WRITING PROCESS

Applying Your Proofreading Skills

Now proofread your persuasive paragraph. Also, read your checklist one last time. Then review **The Grammar Connection** and **The Mechanics Connection** below. Use the proofreading marks to make changes.

THE GRAMMAR CONNECTION

Remember these rules about adjectives and adverbs.

- Use adjectives, including *good,* to modify nouns or pronouns.
- Use adverbs, including *well*, to modify verbs, adjectives, or other adverbs.
- Use *well* as an adjective meaning *healthy.*

  She does not feel **well**. She writes very **well**.
- Use *more* or *most* before most adverbs that have two or more syllables.

  John exercises **more frequently** than I do.
- Do not combine *more* or *most* with *er* or *est*.

Check your writing. Have you correctly used adjectives and adverbs?

THE MECHANICS CONNECTION

Remember this rule about using commas to set off words.

- Use a comma to set off introductory words, words that interrupt the flow of thought, and nouns of direct address.

  Yes, Inez, your suggestion, I believe, is being considered.

Check your writing. Have you used commas correctly?

Proofreading Marks

- ¶ Indent
- ∧ Add
- ⩘ Add a comma
- ⸌⸍ Add quotation marks
- ⨀ Add a period
- ⌿ Take out
- ≡ Capitalize
- / Make a small letter
- ∿ Reverse the order

Publish: Step 5

Derek wanted to share his persuasive paragraph with the people in his town. He typed out his paragraph, made photocopies of it, and distributed it to the board members and others in the community. Several of his classmates and neighbors told him that his arguments had convinced them that the new shopping center should not be built.

YOUR TURN

Make a final copy of your persuasive paragraph. Use your best handwriting or type it neatly. Think of a way to share your opinion and the reasons supporting it. You may find some ideas in the **Sharing Suggestions** box below.

SHARING SUGGESTIONS

| Send your writing to your local radio station. | Post your para-graph on the class bulletin board. | Read your work to an interested friend or relative. |

4 SPEAKING AND LISTENING: Listening for Point of View and Bias

You have just written persuasive paragraphs to convince an audience of your opinion about a topic. Your paragraphs included facts and opinions, persuasive language, logical order, and a strong concluding sentence.

Now you can use what you know about persuasion to become a more careful listener.

Look at these illustrations.

A person's **point of view** is his or her position on a particular issue. In the illustration on the left, the voter's point of view is that the current mayor has done a good job and should be elected again. Voters with another point of view, however, might disagree.

Bias is a highly personal distortion of judgment which prevents a person from looking fairly at an opposing argument. The runner in the illustration on the right is biased when she tries to persuade you that jogging is the best form of exercise.

When you listen to speeches, commercials, or discussions, it will help you to keep some guidelines in mind. These listening guidelines will help you as you form your opinions about what you hear.

LISTENING GUIDELINES: Point of View and Bias

1. Listen for the speaker's point of view.
2. Listen for the reasons the speaker uses to support his or her point of view.
3. Think about whether the speaker's opinion could be considered from another point of view.
4. Listen for any bias in the speaker's opinions.

- In what kinds of situations is it important to listen for a speaker's point of view?
- What is bias?
- How can personal bias affect a speaker's opinion?

LISTENING APPLICATION Point of View and Bias

Listen to the coverage of an issue as it is presented on a local news program. Listen for the presentation of various points of view. Think about whether any opinions are biased. Then give a short talk giving your own opinion about the issue. Use the speaking guidelines below. Make sure that your own point of view is fair and not biased.

SPEAKING GUIDELINES: Persuasive Speaking

1. Present your point of view clearly.
2. Allow for different points of view, and use reasons to show that your opinion is best.
3. Avoid bias in forming and supporting your opinion.
4. Summarize your opinion in your conclusion.
5. Remember your **purpose** and **audience.**

5 WRITER'S RESOURCES: Parts of a Book

In this unit, you have used many resources in writing a persuasive paragraph to persuade your audience to do something or to accept your opinion.

Books are also a useful resource for a writer. It will help you to know the various parts of a book so that you can use books more effectively.

The **title page** tells you the title of the book, the author's name, the company that published the book, and the place of publication. On the back of the title page, the **copyright page** tells you the year the book was published.

The **table of contents** in the front of a book lists the titles of the chapters or main sections and the page numbers on which they begin. Look at part of the table of contents from a book about American government.

You will also often find useful sections at the back of a book. An **appendix** gives more information about one of the topics covered in the main body of the book. A **glossary** is a list of words arranged in alphabetical order with their meanings—like a small dictionary.

At the very end of a book, you may find an index. An **index** is an alphabetical listing of all the topics in the book. The **main topics** are capitalized. Sometimes an entry for a main topic will include several **subtopics**.

Election campaigns
    effect of media on, 200
    and independent groups, 242-43
    and media, 190-91, 240-42
    strategy in, 235-37
    winning, 133-143
Election districts, 221, 276
Elections
    meaning in, 253-260
    participating in, 242-253
    popular rule and, 256-259
    structure of, 248-253
Elections, congressional
    financing of, 287
    during wartime, 92

Practice

Answer the questions below by referring to the examples on the opposite page and above.

1. On what page does Chapter 8 of the book begin?
2. On what page does this chapter begin discussing differences in public opinion?
3. Does Chapter 8 include a discussion of different kinds of mass media?
4. On what page is there a discussion of opinion polls?
5. According to the index, on what page does the book discuss congressional elections during wartime?
6. How many page references does the index list for the main topic, Election Districts?
7. Which subtopics are listed in the index under the main topic, Election Campaigns?

WRITING APPLICATION Parts of a Book

In your school or local library, find a book about newspapers. Use the card catalog to help you. Then make notes about the book using information you find in different parts of the book, including the title page, the copyright page, the table of contents, and the index. Keep your notes in your writing folder. You will use them in **The Curriculum Connection** on page 418.

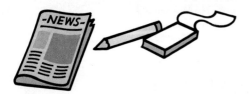

Writing About Journalism

You know that a journal is a daily record, or diary, of observations, experiences, thoughts, and feelings.

The word *journalism* also comes from a word that means "day." Journalists report and comment on daily events in all forms of mass communication: newspapers, magazines, books, television, and radio.

Journalists give the *facts* about news events in articles and broadcasts. They may also comment on these events by giving their *opinions*, most often in editorials. Remember that facts are statements that can be checked and verified as true. Opinions are personal judgments about something the writer feels or believes to be true.

ACTIVITIES

Create a Front Page Look at the notes you made on a book about newspapers. Then, try to imagine what a newspaper in the year 2050 might look like. What would the newspaper be named? Where would it be published? What language would it use? What might the front page look like? Draw a picture of the front page of the newspaper, and write headlines for the leading articles.

Describe a Cartoon Look at the cartoon on page 419. What issue is presented in the cartoon? What is the artist trying to say? Write about how you think the cartoon might affect people's thoughts or actions. Include reasons to support your opinion. If you wish, write a caption for the cartoon, or draw a cartoon to illustrate a similar issue.

Respond to Literature The following selection is taken from an essay by Andy Rooney, who comments about American life in magazine articles and on television programs. After reading Rooney's opinion, write a response—a letter to Rooney or a persuasive speech that supports another opinion or point of view. Share your response with the class.

All the Fixings

You can buy a new one but you can't get the old one fixed. That's the crisis in America.

If your car needs a new engine, they'll do that for you, but if the window on the passenger's side is sticking, forget it . . . .

If you want your old kitchen torn out and done over, there are contractors who'll do that, but don't spend any time trying to have the broken toaster fixed. . . .

We can't even get anyone to repair the minor things wrong with our bodies. You can find a doctor to do a heart bypass operation but if you have a bad cold or a flu virus and a 101-degree fever, learn to live with it. What we need is a group of doctors who specialize in ordinary illness. We could call them "general practitioners."

We have to do one of two things in this country. We've got to make things that can be fixed or start making them good enough in the first place so they don't always need fixing.

UNIT CHECKUP

LESSON 1

Group Writing: Persuasive Paragraphs (page 400) Read this paragraph. Write the topic sentence that states the writer's opinion. Then list the reasons that support the opinion.

Students at our school should become more involved in the hospital volunteer program. The hospital administration has said it could use between 35 and 40 more volunteers each week. Volunteers can run errands, work in the kitchen, or just sit and talk with patients. Working at the hospital can be a wonderful experience, since students can make new friends of different ages.

LESSON 2

Thinking: Distinguishing Fact from Opinion (page 404) Write whether each statement is a fact or an opinion.

1. Abraham Lincoln was born in 1809 in Kentucky.
2. Lincoln was probably one of our nation's greatest presidents.
3. I believe his best speech was the Gettysburg Address.
4. Lincoln worked to keep the union together.
5. The Lincoln Memorial was built during World War I.

LESSON 3

Writing Persuasive Paragraphs (page 406) Imagine that you are a successful author. Write a radio advertisement in which you try to persuade people to buy and read your book.

LESSON 4

Speaking and Listening: Listening for Point of View and Bias (page 414) Imagine that you are about to listen to a speech about the benefits of television advertising. Make a list of the four main listening guidelines you should bear in mind to judge point of view and bias in the speech.

LESSON 5

Writer's Resources: Parts of a Book (page 416) Use the school or local library to find a book on a topic that interests you. Write the author, the publisher, the date and place of publication, and the number of chapters.

THEME PROJECT · CAMPAIGN POSTER

In an election campaign, posters are designed to send a persuasive message to voters. Try to remember posters you have seen. They may have had a photograph of the candidate and a slogan that summed up the campaign theme.

Look at the photograph below. This campaign poster was used by famous political candidates for president and vice-president in an important election. Talk with your classmates about the poster you see in the photograph and the different images it includes.

With a group of classmates or by yourself, make an election campaign poster for yourself or for an actual politician.

- Think about the persuasive message you want to communicate.
- Brainstorm for a list of possible slogans.
- Then create your campaign poster and write on it the slogan you have chosen.

UNIT

13

Prepositions, Conjunctions, and Interjections

In this unit you will learn about prepositions, conjunctions, and interjections. These words add detail to your writing and help you to join related ideas.

Discuss Read the poem on the opposite page. According to the poet, who or what may have already been at the edge of the world?

Creative Expression The unit theme is *Explorations*. What part of the world would you like to explore? Imagine that you are the leader of an expedition. Write a travel plan. Write your plan in your journal.

JOURNAL

THEME: *EXPLORATIONS*

What will you find at the edge of the world?
A footprint,
a feather,
desert sand swirled?

—Eve Merriam, from "Landscape"

1 PREPOSITIONS AND PREPOSITIONAL PHRASES

A preposition is a word that relates a noun or pronoun to another word in a sentence.

This book **about** rockets is Juan's.

A **prepositional phrase** is a group of words that begins with a preposition and ends with a noun or pronoun. A prepositional phrase may include a modifier.

The rocket rose **above the gray clouds**.

The noun or pronoun that follows the preposition is called the **object of the preposition**.

Prepositions			
about	before	during	through
above	behind	for	to
across	below	from	toward
after	beside	in	under
against	between	into	until
around	beyond	of	up
as	by	on	with
at	down	over	within

Guided Practice

Tell the preposition or prepositions in each sentence.

Example: The engines in the spacecraft are powerful.   in

1. Space exploration is full of challenges.
2. A spacecraft travels across vast distances.
3. On the moon, astronauts gathered samples.
4. Voyager 2 sent pictures from Saturn.
5. Some satellites travel in orbit around the earth.

 THINK

■ How can I identify a prepositional phrase?

REMEMBER

- A **preposition** relates a noun or pronoun to another word in a sentence.
- A **prepositional phrase** is a group of words that begins with a preposition and ends with a noun or pronoun.

More Practice

A. Write the preposition in each sentence.

Example: America has sent men into space.   *into*

   6. After much planning, orbital flights took place.
   7. The docking of two spacecraft was accomplished.
   8. In 1968 the Apollo program began.
   9. Astronauts made journeys around the moon.
   10. The next year they landed on the lunar surface.
   11. The moment of the landing was unforgettable.
   12. It was the climax of much research.

B. Write each prepositional phrase. Draw one line under the preposition and two lines under its object.

Example: Many space probes function without crews.
            without crews

   13. Ten years after its launch, *Voyager 2* still travels.
   14. Its cameras are operated by remote control.
   15. They have photographed satellites of Jupiter.
   16. The space probe flew near Saturn's rings.
   17. The cameras relayed pictures to Earth.
   18. Scientists studied these pictures with great interest.
   19. *Voyager 2* has succeeded beyond people's expectations.
   20. In 1989, *Voyager 2* headed toward Neptune.

Extra Practice, page 448

WRITING APPLICATION A Descriptive Paragraph

Imagine that you are an astronaut in a spacecraft. Describe to Mission Control what you see. Identify the prepositional phrases in your work.

2 PREPOSITIONAL PHRASES AS ADJECTIVES

You know that a prepositional phrase contains a preposition, the object of the preposition, and any modifiers of the object. When prepositional phrases modify or describe a noun or pronoun, they act as adjectives. These phrases are called **adjective phrases.**

Someone **from our team** identified that mineral.
The surface **of that rock** is rough.
The rock **with jagged edges** is very old.

Unlike most adjectives, adjective phrases come after the words they modify. Adjective phrases answer such questions as *What kind?* or *Which one?*

We found a rock **with a strange fossil**. (What kind?)
The rocks **on the left** are called *mica*. (Which ones?)

Guided Practice

Tell which noun or pronoun each underlined adjective phrase modifies.

Example: The sand <u>on the ground</u> covers solid rock.   *sand*

1. Geologists study the structure <u>of the earth</u>.
2. They collect information <u>about minerals</u>.
3. Do you know anything <u>about geology</u>?
4. The shaft <u>under the rock</u> is deep.
5. Scientists record the distances <u>between the earth's plates</u>.

THINK

■ How can I decide if a prepositional phrase is acting as an adjective phrase?

REMEMBER

- An **adjective phrase** is a prepositional phrase that modifies, or describes, a noun or pronoun.
- Adjective phrases can tell *what kind* or *which one*.

More Practice

A. Write the noun or pronoun that each underlined adjective phrase modifies.

Example: Here is the collection of fossils.   *collection*

6. The fossils at the museum are ancient.
7. Fossils preserve traces of ancient life.
8. Some fossils contain the bones of huge dinosaurs.
9. Those near the entrance display tiny insect remains.
10. The formation of fossils is fascinating.
11. Deposits along the ocean floor may form fossils.
12. Many fossils preserve parts of extinct fish.
13. Fossils of ancient plants are relatively common.

B. Write the adjective phrase in each sentence. Then write the noun or pronoun that it modifies.

Example: The Museum of Natural History is a wonderful place.   *of Natural History*   *Museum*

14. Its exhibition of dinosaurs is famous.
15. It includes the huge skeleton of a stegosaur.
16. The weight of this beast was more than three tons.
17. Stegosaurs ate the leaves on treetops.
18. The muscles in their tails were extremely strong.
19. The bony prongs on their tails helped them to balance.
20. These prongs resembled the runners on a sled.

Extra Practice, page 449

WRITING APPLICATION A Post Card

Imagine that you have discovered a prehistoric fossil. Write a post card to a friend describing your find. Identify the adjective phrases in your work.

3 PREPOSITIONAL PHRASES AS ADVERBS

You have learned that a prepositional phrase can act as an adjective when it modifies a noun or pronoun. Prepositional phrases can also modify, or tell more about, verbs, adjectives, or adverbs. When they modify these words, they are called **adverb phrases.** Adverb phrases tell *where*, *how*, or *when*.

Dr. Fleming *worked* **in the laboratory.** (modifies a verb)
He was *eager* **for results**. (modifies an adjective)
He stayed *late* **into the night.** (modifies an adverb)

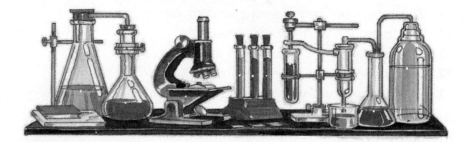

Guided Practice

Tell the word that each underlined adverb phrase modifies. Say whether the word is a **verb,** an **adjective,** or an **adverb.**

Example: Dr. Fleming read <u>about a new drug</u>. *read   verb*

1. Many diseases were once common <u>throughout the world</u>.
2. They were dangerous <u>to millions</u>.
3. Doctors sometimes worked <u>in teams</u>.
4. They experimented <u>with different drugs</u>.
5. Cures developed slowly <u>over the years</u>.
6. Yellow fever was common <u>in the nineteenth century</u>.
7. This disease is dangerous <u>to humans</u>.

 THINK

■ How can I decide if a prepositional phrase is acting as an adverb phrase?

REMEMBER

- An **adverb phrase** is a prepositional phrase that modifies, or tells more about, a verb, an adjective, or an adverb.
- Adverb phrases tell *where*, *how*, or *when*.

More Practice

A. Write the word or words that each underlined adverb phrase modifies. Label the word or words a **verb,** an **adjective**, or an **adverb.**

Example: Several diseases are carried <u>by mosquitoes.</u>
         are carried   verb

8. Dr. Walter Reed traveled far <u>into Panama.</u>
9. He studied the virus <u>for many months.</u>
10. He proved it was carried <u>by mosquitoes.</u>
11. Health programs began <u>in many countries.</u>
12. Yellow fever was eliminated <u>in most areas.</u>
13. Dr. Reed became famous <u>for his important work.</u>

B. Write the adverb phrase in each sentence. Then write the word or words that the phrase modifies.

Example: Medical research advances in sudden leaps.
         in sudden leaps   *advances*

14. Dr. Alexander Fleming lived in London.
15. The drug penicillin was discovered in Fleming's lab.
16. The discovery happened by accident.
17. A strange mold developed in a lab dish.
18. It killed germs with remarkable speed.
19. Penicillin now helps us in many ways.
20. For his discovery, Fleming won the Nobel Prize in 1945.

Extra Practice, page 450

WRITING APPLICATION A News Article

Write a brief news article describing a new discovery in medicine. Exchange articles with a partner and identify the adverb phrases in each other's work.

USING VERBS AFTER PREPOSITIONAL PHRASES

A verb must always agree, or work, with its subject. A singular subject needs a singular verb. A plural subject needs a plural verb.

Sometimes a prepositional phrase comes between the subject and the verb in a sentence. When you write, make sure that the verb agrees with the subject of the sentence and not with the object of the preposition.

The **purpose** (of these stones) **is** unknown.

The **monuments** (on the plain) **are** impressive.

Guided Practice

For each sentence, tell the subject and the verb.

Example: The remains of Stonehenge are in England.

remains   *are*

1. This monument of the Druids remains a puzzle.
2. Experts on the subject have different opinions.
3. Questions about it remain unanswered.
4. The history of these stones is mysterious.
5. The ruins of Stonehenge are on Salisbury Plain.

THINK

- How can I decide if the verb in a sentence should be singular or plural?

REMEMBER

■ The verb must always agree, or work, with the subject of the sentence, not with the object of a preposition.

More Practice

A. Write each sentence. Draw one line under the subject and two lines under the verb.

Example: These monuments of stone are ancient.

These <u>monuments</u> of stone <u>are</u> ancient.

6. This group of stones forms a circle.

7. The height of these stones exceeds 24 feet.

8. Just one of these pillars weighs 50 tons.

9. Parts of the monument date from 1900 B.C.

10. Additions to the circle were made later.

11. Ditches around the entrance were constructed.

12. An inner circle of bluestone was built.

B. Write the correct form of the verb in parentheses.

Example: The size of these monuments (is, are) impressive.   *is*

13. The purposes of Stonehenge (remain, remains) uncertain.

14. (Was, were) the function of these stones linked to religion?

15. Some scholars of early history (have, has) thought so.

16. Surveys of the site (suggests, suggest) another purpose.

17. The builders of this circle (was, were) probably astronomers.

18. The stones in that row (was, were) possibly marker stones.

19. Movements of the sun and moon (were, was) observed.

20. (Was, Were) predictions of an eclipse possible?

Extra Practice, Practice Plus, pages 451–452

WRITING APPLICATION A Journal Entry

Imagine that you are an archaeologist who has just discovered a mysterious set of ruins from an ancient civilization. Write a journal entry about the discovery. Check for subject-verb agreement in your work.

CONJUNCTIONS

When you join words or sentences to make your writing smoother, you use a conjunction. A **conjunction** is a word that joins words or groups of words in a sentence. Three common conjunctions are *and*, *or*, and *but*. *And* adds information. *Or* gives a choice. *But* shows contrast.

Conjunctions can join two simple subjects to form a compound subject or two verbs to form a compound predicate. They can also join two simple sentences to form a compound sentence. Remember to use a comma before the conjunction in a compound sentence.

COMPOUND SUBJECT:
Dolphins **and** whales are common here.
COMPOUND PREDICATE:
We map their movements **or** photograph them.
COMPOUND SENTENCE:
We know they can communicate with each other, **but** their language is hard to understand.

Guided Practice

Tell which word in each sentence is a conjunction.

Example: Can dolphins or porpoises communicate?   *or*

1. We often confuse dolphins and porpoises.
2. A dolphin's head is beaked, but a porpoise's head is round.
3. Are porpoises or dolphins common in these waters?
4. Dolphins swim and play together.
5. They are small whales, but they are friendly to humans.
6. They look fishlike, but they are actually mammals.

 THINK

■ How can I decide which conjunction to use?

REMEMBER

■ A **conjunction** joins words or groups of words. *And* adds information. *Or* gives a choice. *But* shows contrast.

More Practice

A. Write each sentence and underline the conjunction. Then write whether the conjunction helps form a **compound subject, predicate,** or **sentence.**

Example: Humans <u>and</u> animals share features.   *subject*

7. Dolphins and porpoises are playful creatures.
8. Occasionally, they come to the surface and breathe.
9. Dolphins steer and navigate skillfully.
10. Echoes and vibrations tell them their location.
11. They bend or flap their powerful tails.
12. Dolphins and other whales can be trained in captivity.
13. Scientists observe and study them carefully.

B. Write each sentence. Complete the sentence with the conjunction that best fits the blank.

Example: The clicks _____ squeaks may be a language.   *and*

14. Do dolphins recognize pitch, _____ are they more sensitive to volume?
15. Dolphins _____ whales use language for many purposes.
16. They locate food _____ avoid danger.
17. We can hear their signals, _____ they are hard to understand.
18. There are recordings of their clicks _____ squeaks.
19. Both the sound waves _____ echoes may have meanings.
20. Does oceanography _____ zoology interest you as a career?

Extra Practice, page 453

WRITING APPLICATION A Post Card

Imagine that you are part of a team of scientists that is studying the ocean floor. Write a post card to a friend describing some of your observations. Exchange post cards with a classmate and identify the conjunctions.

MORE ABOUT CONJUNCTIONS

You can vary your writing by using conjunctions other than *and*, *or*, or *but* to combine sentences.

SEPARATE: Vikings lived near the sea. They became sailors.

COMBINED: **Since** Vikings lived near the sea, they became sailors.

Some conjunctions tell *where*, *when*, *why*, *how*, or *under what conditions* an action takes place.

Where:	where, wherever
When:	when, before, after, while, since, until
Why:	as, because, since
How:	as, as if, as though
Under What Conditions:	although, if, though, unless

A sentence that contains two closely related ideas joined by a conjunction other than *and*, *or*, or *but* is called a **complex sentence**.

Although their ships were small, they explored widely.

Guided Practice

Name the conjunction in each sentence.

Example: The Vikings arrived in the New World before Columbus sailed to America.   *before*

1. Although they lived over 1000 years ago, the Viking sailors explored far and wide.
2. The Vikings came from a region where farmland was scarce.
3. When their homeland grew crowded, many Vikings left.
4. They could sail far away since their ships were fast.
5. After they settled Iceland, some moved to Greenland.

THINK

■ How can I use conjunctions to combine sentences?

REMEMBER

■ Use conjunctions that tell *where*, *when*, *why*, *how*, or *under what conditions* an action takes place to join sentences.

More Practice

A. Write the conjunction in each sentence.

Example: Because the winters were hard, the Vikings often sailed southward.   *Because*

6. When one Viking got lost in 985, he found North America.

7. He told about it after he returned to Greenland.

8. Because they were still in need of good farmland, the Vikings sailed to North America in about 1000.

9. They called it Vinland, since grape vines grew there.

10. Wherever the colonies were located, they did not survive.

B. Use the conjunctions in parentheses to combine each pair of sentences into a complex sentence.

Example: Europe was raided by Vikings. The Vikings expanded their territory.   (when)
When Europe was raided by Vikings, the Vikings expanded their territory.

11. Some Vikings explored westward. Others attacked their neighbors to the south and east. (while)

12. The Vikings were feared throughout Europe. They were fierce raiders. (since)

13. Vikings even reached Italy. Few realize it. (though)

14. The Vikings conquered England in 1016. They ruled there until 1042. (after)

15. The English first united as a people. They wanted to fight off these invaders. (because)

Extra Practice, page 454

WRITING APPLICATION A Narrative Paragraph

Imagine that you accompanied the Vikings to the New World. Write a paragraph describing the journey.

7 INTERJECTIONS

An **interjection** is a word or group of words that expresses strong feeling.

Study the following list of common interjections.

amazing   *My*

Aha	Hey	Oh	Phew
Yikes	Hooray	Oh, dear	Well
Good grief	My goodness	Oh, no	Wow
Great	Gee	Oops	Ugh

Oh my

An interjection that expresses a very strong feeling is followed by an exclamation mark. Interjections like these stand alone, either before or after a sentence.

> **Oh, no!** I lost my notes.
> Did you find them? **Phew!**

When an interjection expresses a milder feeling, it is used at the beginning of a sentence and is set off by a comma.

> **Gee,** are you certain of that fact?
> **Oh,** I forgot to check it in the encyclopedia.

Guided Practice

Tell which word in each sentence listed below is an interjection.

Example: Oh, I need a good grade on this report.   *Oh*

1. Hooray! I found a terrific topic for my report.
2. Great! What topic have you chosen?
3. Gee, I'd like to research industrial robots.
4. Wow! That sounds really interesting.
5. My, you have learned quite a bit.

HEY! WOW! GREAT! HOORAY!

 THINK

■ How do I decide how to punctuate interjections?

REMEMBER

■ An **interjection** is a word or group of words that expresses strong feeling.

■ Strong interjections are followed by exclamation marks, and milder ones are followed by commas.

More Practice

A. Write each sentence. Underline the interjection.

Example: Oh, language is interesting.

   Oh, language is interesting.

6. Wow! Did you know that the word "robot" means "work"?
7. Aha! It is not an English word, is it?
8. Oh, no! It comes from the Czech word *robota*.
9. Hey, did you find out when robots were invented?
10. Was the first mention of a robot in 1921? My goodness!
11. Wow! Did you know robots have memories?
12. They are often operated by computers. Amazing!

B. Write each sentence. Add the correct punctuation.

Example: Good grief The robots are taking over. *Good Grief!*

13. Aha Robots can be used to assemble machine parts.
14. Goodness You can also program them to weld car bodies.
15. Are they more accurate than humans? Good grief
16. Gee you have to give them directions.
17. Oh but they never get tired, as we do.
18. Wow The eye of that robot is an electric cell.
19. Hey which country uses robots the most?
20. Aha The answer is Japan. Goodness

Extra Practice, page 455

WRITING APPLICATION A Dialogue

COOPERATIVE
LEARNING

With a partner write a short, lively, excited dialogue between two classmates at a sports event. Then, act out your dialogue for the class. Have other students identify the interjections in your dialogue.

MECHANICS: Using Commas in Compound Sentences

You have learned that a conjunction is a word that joins words or groups of words in a sentence. Three of the most common conjunctions are *and*, *or*, and *but*.

You can often prevent your writing from sounding choppy by using a conjunction to join two simple sentences into a compound sentence. Use a comma before the conjunction.

And adds information.

You researched Galileo. I reported on Copernicus.
You researched Galileo, **and** I reported on Copernicus.

Or gives a choice.

I must check those facts. My report may be inaccurate.
I must check those facts, **or** my report may be inaccurate.

But shows contrast.

Copernicus was Polish. Galileo was Italian.
Copernicus was Polish, **but** Galileo was Italian.

Guided Practice

Tell which word is the conjunction in each sentence.

Example: Does the earth revolve around the sun, or is it the other way around? or

1. Copernicus studied law, but he won fame in science.
2. He observed the planets, and he stated that the planets revolve around the sun.
3. Many people challenged him, but Copernicus was stubborn.
4. He paved the way for modern astronomy, and Galileo was one of his followers.
5. Was Galileo mainly an astronomer, or did his work also involve mathematics?

 THINK

■ How can I tell when to use a comma before a conjunction?

REMEMBER

■ Always use a comma before the conjunction in a compound sentence.

More Practice

A. Write the conjunction in each sentence.

Example: Copernicus was brilliant, and his ideas changed our view of the universe.   *and*

6. Copernicus studied ancient records, and his theory was based on centuries of observations.
7. He knew that the movements of planets should be regular, but Mars's movement often seemed backward.
8. This motion puzzled Copernicus, and he studied it.
9. The earth could not be fixed, or the motion would not occur.
10. Both planets orbit the sun, and the illusion occurs when the earth passes Mars.

B. Write each sentence. Add the correct punctuation.

Example: Tom discussed Copernicus and we listened.
Tom discussed Copernicus, and we listened.

11. His telescope was small but he saw many of the planets.
12. Copernicus observed the satellites of Jupiter and he described them clearly.
13. Isaac Newton was a mathematician but his theories had great importance in astronomy.
14. His laws of gravity are famous but his interests covered many other fields as well.
15. People called him a philosopher but he was really a scientist.

Extra Practice, page 456

The Granger Collection

WRITING APPLICATION A Biographical Sketch

Write a paragraph about a scientist whom you admire. Then, exchange papers with a classmate. See if you can combine pairs of simple sentences in each other's work. Remember to use commas correctly.

VOCABULARY BUILDING: Suffixes

A **suffix** is a word part added to the end of a base word. The addition of a suffix often changes a word's meaning or part of speech.

Noun-forming Suffixes		
Suffix	**Meaning**	**Example**
an	one who is of or from	Puerto Ric**an**
er, or	one who or that which	sing**er**, sail**or**
ian	one skilled in	music**ian**
ist	one who works at, practices, or adheres to	chem**ist**
ment	act, condition, or result of	state**ment**
ness	quality, state, or condition of	good**ness**

Adjective-forming Suffixes		
able, ible	able to, capable of being	read**able**, vis**ible**
an	of or belonging to	Caribbe**an**
ful	full of, marked by	joy**ful**
less	lacking, without	help**less**
ly	like in nature or manner	king**ly**
ward	moving or tending toward	back**ward**
y	showing, suggesting	speed**y**

violin

violinist

Guided Practice

Tell the suffix in each of the following words.

Example: cupful   *ful*

1. geologist
2. restful
3. messy
4. actor
5. changeable

THINK

■ How can knowing suffixes help me to understand new words?

REMEMBER

■ A **suffix** is a word part added to the end of a base word.

More Practice

A. Write each underlined word. Draw one line under the suffix. Then write the meaning of the word.

Example: The city was defense<u>less</u>.

        defense<u>less</u>   without defense

6. Homer told of the Trojan War in his <u>notable</u> work, the *Iliad*.

7. In this poem, a <u>powerful</u> Greek army attacked Troy.

8. The city did not seem <u>destructible</u>.

9. However, the <u>fierceness</u> of the Greek army proved too great.

10. Many <u>historians</u> thought the story of Troy was a myth.

11. In 1871, a German <u>archaeologist</u> proved it was fact.

12. He began digging at a <u>rocky</u> site in Turkey.

13. Soon, the foundations of walls became <u>visible</u>.

14. He had discovered an ancient <u>settlement</u>.

15. <u>Specialists</u> confirmed that it was the city of Troy.

B. Write each word and underline its suffix. Write the meaning of each word. Use a dictionary if needed.

Example: sorrowful   *sorrow<u>ful</u>   full of sorrow*

16. politician
17. hopeful
18. slowly
19. reliable
20. queenly

21. collectible
22. seriousness
23. disappointment
24. affordable
25. theorist

Extra Practice, page 457

WRITING APPLICATION A Word List

Choose five suffixes from this lesson and use a dictionary to find a new word with each suffix. Exchange your list of new words with a classmate. Try to identify the meanings of each other's words.

COOPERATIVE
LEARNING

GRAMMAR —AND WRITING CONNECTION

Placing Prepositional Phrases Correctly

Place a prepositional phrase as near as possible to the word it modifies. A misplaced prepositional phrase can make your meaning unclear.

Confusing: The painting is on the far wall with many different colors.

Clear: The painting **with many different colors** is on the far wall.

Confusing: They built a house by a river with a front porch.

Clear: They built a house **with a front porch** by a river.

Sometimes an adverb phrase works best at the beginning of a sentence.

Confusing: The teacher read us a story about horse races during recess.

Clear: **During recess,** the teacher read us a story about horse races.

Working Together

COOPERATIVE
LEARNING

Tell how you would place the prepositional phrase to make the meaning of each sentence clear.

Example: A boy held a book about caves on the sidewalk.
A boy on the sidewalk held a book about caves.

1. We read about historical cave discoveries on Monday.
2. One student described a cave in our class.
3. Someone had looked for a cave entrance in his family.

Revising Sentences

Maria wrote these sentences about a television program. Help Maria revise her sentences to make her meaning clearer by repositioning a prepositional phrase.

4. My family and I watched an exciting television show in our living room about the desert.

5. Several frantic explorers searched for water in white suits.

6. They showed men on camels between laundry soap commercials.

7. They pitched a tent near an oasis with mosquito netting.

8. Their exact distance was concealed by sun glare from the oasis.

9. The immense heat made the explorers nervous in the desert.

10. Constant interruptions told us of exciting future adventures on this program in the desert.

11. A large snake crawled during the credits on the sand.

12. The programs were boring compared to this one on other channels.

Write a paragraph about going to a theater. Describe the occasion, using the four prepositional phrases below. Be sure to place them correctly.

> toward our seats
> from the applause
> into the bright light
> out of the theater

UNIT CHECKUP

LESSON 1

Prepositions and Prepositional Phrases (page 424) Write each prepositional phrase. Underline the object of the preposition.

1. Sunspots are dark areas on the sun.
2. The temperature of these areas is lower.
3. Sunspots are caused by magnetic storms.
4. Astronomers with special telescopes study sunspots.
5. Can you see a sunspot with the naked eye?

LESSON 2

Prepositional Phrases as Adjectives (page 426) Write the adjective phrase in each sentence. Then write the noun or pronoun it modifies.

6. Decibels are measurements of sound.
7. A noise of zero decibels is scarcely audible.
8. The level of normal conversation is 60 decibels.
9. Sounds of over 150 decibels are painful.

LESSON 3

Prepositional Phrases as Adverbs (page 428) Write the adverb phrase in each sentence. Then write the word that the phrase modifies.

10. Elephants live on the African plain.
11. They travel in large herds.
12. Usually, they walk at a steady pace.
13. They can run quickly for their size.

LESSON 4

Using Verbs After Prepositional Phrases (page 430) Write the sentence. Complete each sentence with the correct form of the verb.

14. An interesting fact about supernovas (is, are) in our science book.
15. Matter inside these stars (explode, explodes).
16. Supernovas in that galaxy (is, are) rare.
17. The traces of one supernova (form, forms) the Crab Nebula.

LESSONS 5-6

Conjunctions and More About Conjunctions (pages 432–434) Write each sentence and underline the conjunction.

18. With binoculars, you can see and study Mercury.
19. At night it is invisible, but it can be seen at dusk.
20. Hydrogen or helium may exist in its atmosphere.
21. When I grow up, I want a career in astronomy.
22. I chose astronomy because it is a fascinating field.
23. Although you may doubt it, we will likely travel to Mars.
24. Mars will be selected since it is near our own planet.

LESSON 7

Interjections (page 436) Add the correct punctuation.

25. Wow Did you know those facts about quasars?
26. Some are eight billion light years away. Goodness
27. Gee they travel nearly at the speed of light.
28. They are brighter than some whole galaxies. My

LESSON 8

Mechanics: Using Commas in Compound Sentences (page 438) Add the correct punctuation.

29. You researched the Greeks but I worked on the Incas.
30. Make notes carefully or your facts will be wrong.
31. I checked books and Liz made a list of articles.
32. We prepared the charts and you drew the diagrams.

LESSON 9

Vocabulary Building: Suffixes (page 440) Write the suffix in each of the following words.

33. hopeful
34. homeward
35. exactness
36. senseless

37. historian
38. geographer
39. navigator
40. pharmacist

41. establishment
42. brainy
43. understandable
44. Texan

Writing Application: Usage of Prepositions, Conjunctions, and Interjections (pages 424–438). The following paragraph contains 6 errors with prepositions, conjunctions, and interjections. Rewrite the paragraph correctly.

45.–50.

The measurements of the universe is not known. Not only is space curved but it has no beginning. When you think about the problem it seems hard. No one can measure but gauge those vast spaces. One expert described the difficulties on the subject of space exploration. Gee it hardly seems worth pursuing.

WHAT'S THAT WORD?

Play this game with a partner. Find an article in a newspaper or magazine. Read your partner a paragraph from the article. Ask your partner to identify all the prepositions, conjunctions, and interjections in the paragraph. Take turns at reading aloud and identifying.

MAKE THE HEADLINES!

Create headlines for a fictitious newspaper. Look through discarded newspapers for examples. Write your headlines as dramatically as possible, using interjections and exclamatory sentences. If you wish, write a brief news story to accompany one of your headlines.

AUTHOR, AUTHOR

Think about a story or book you have read. Imagine that you have submitted the story to a publishing company and the publisher has asked you to write a different ending. Write a paragraph proposing a revised ending. Use conjunctions in your sentences, and identify the purpose of each one.

WORD FAMILY TREE

Begin with a simple word; for example, *word*. See how many prefixes and suffixes you can add to the word to make new, related words.

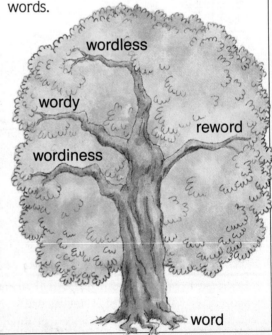

CREATIVE EXPRESSION

•

The Sidewalk Racer
or
On the Skateboard

Skimming
an asphalt sea
I swerve, I curve, I
sway, I speed to whirring
sound an inch above the
ground; I'm the sailor
and the sail, I'm the
driver and the wheel
I'm the one and only
single engine
human auto
mobile.

•

—Lillian Morrison

TRY IT OUT!

A **concrete poem** is a poem whose shape on the page suggests its meaning. In the poem above, the speaker is describing what it feels like to be moving on a skateboard at a fast speed. Notice that the poem is the shape of a skateboard. Now, write a concrete poem of your own. First, think of a subject that you would like to describe. Then, imagine a simple shape that would show the subject of your poem. Position the lines of your poem in that shape on your paper.

EXTRA PRACTICE

Three levels of practice
Prepositions and Prepositional Phrases (page 424)

LEVEL A. Write the preposition in each sentence.

1. Butterflies develop in several stages.
2. This process is a wonder of nature.
3. First, the eggs of butterflies hatch.
4. Young butterflies have the form of caterpillars.
5. The caterpillars then cover themselves with a cocoon.
6. In this stage, the insects are called *pupa.*
7. Finally, a butterfly emerges into its adult stage.
8. The life span for most species is one month.

LEVEL B. Write the prepositional phrase in each sentence. Underline the object of each preposition.

9. How are moths different from butterflies?
10. Both groups of insects look similar.
11. Both moths and butterflies feed on plants.
12. They both have two pairs of wings.
13. These wings function as a single pair.
14. Moths, however, are protected by their color.
15. This color is often similar to their habitat.
16. In contrast, butterflies are brightly colored.

LEVEL C. Write the prepositional phrase in each sentence. Draw one line under the preposition and two lines under the object of the preposition.

17. The wings of butterflies are delicate.
18. They are covered with dustlike scales.
19. These insects love the nectar from flowers.
20. Their antennae have knobs at the tips.
21. Butterflies are active by day.
22. They rest with upright wings.
23. Moths usually are active at night.
24. At rest, their wings are outspread.
25. There are many species of butterflies and moths.

EXTRA PRACTICE

Three levels of practice
Prepositional Phrases as Adjectives (page 426)

LEVEL A. Write the noun or pronoun that each of the underlined adjective phrases modifies.

1. Acoustics is the science of sound.
2. Our teacher said that research into sound is exciting.
3. Experts in acoustics design concert halls.
4. A knowledge of sound waves is needed.
5. The reflection from hard surfaces causes an echo.
6. Many echoes in an enclosed space cause reverberation.
7. Some reverberation in a hall is desirable.
8. This reverberation avoids deadening the sound of music.
9. The shape of the walls affects acoustics.
10. The materials in the walls also affect sound.

LEVEL B. Write the adjective phrase in each sentence. Then write the noun or pronoun that it modifies.

11. Different kinds of wood alter the sound waves.
12. Panels on the ceiling have the same effect.
13. The size of the auditorium is also a factor.
14. Experts achieve a balance of factors.
15. The design of a concert hall is complicated.
16. Tina gave an interesting report about volcanoes.
17. Volcanoes are openings in the earth's crust.
18. They are cone-shaped mountains with a central crater.
19. Pressures inside the earth cause these openings.

LEVEL C. Write a sentence using each prepositional phrase below as an adjective phrase.

20. under the surface
21. from volcanoes
22. in the ocean
23. of spectacular fame
24. inside the earth
25. near the top

EXTRA PRACTICE

Three Levels of practice
Prepositional Phrases as Adverbs (page 428)

LEVEL A. Write the adverb phrase that modifies the underlined word.

1. Wolves are often <u>frightening</u> to humans.
2. These animals have been <u>misunderstood</u> for centuries.
3. Wolves are <u>remarkable</u> in many ways.
4. Wolves usually <u>travel</u> in packs.
5. They <u>journey</u> for many miles every day.
6. Wolf packs <u>live</u> like a family.
7. Wolves are <u>affectionate</u> toward each other.
8. They <u>care</u> deeply for their cubs.
9. The animals <u>share</u> food with each other.
10. They <u>survive</u> in a difficult environment.

LEVEL B. Write the adverb phrase in each sentence. Then write the word that the phrase modifies. Write whether the word is a **verb**, an **adjective**, or an **adverb**.

11. Wolves communicate with each other.
12. Scientists study their language with great interest.
13. Wolves make signals in three ways.
14. A wolf's howl is familiar to most people.
15. Wolves howl for several reasons.
16. By their howls they signal danger.
17. They also communicate across great distances.
18. A wolf's howl carries far over the land.
19. Wolves do not really howl at the moon.
20. Wolves also communicate with scent.

LEVEL C. Write a sentence using each prepositional phrase as an adverb phrase. Underline the word that the phrase modifies.

21. by an eclipse of the sun
22. with a wild animal
23. to a species of flower
24. in a science lab
25. about someone you admire

EXTRA PRACTICE

Three levels of practice

Using Verbs After Prepositional Phrases (page 430)

LEVEL A. Write each sentence. Draw one line under the subject and two lines under the verb.

1. The color of tropical seas is blue.
2. The absence of green plants causes this color.
3. The clarity of these waters is amazing.
4. Many shades of blue dazzle the eye.
5. Plants in the sea prefer cooler waters.
6. The plant life in cool areas is more plentiful.
7. The color of colder waters appears greener.
8. The energy of sea plants depends on the sun.
9. The structure of coral reefs is remarkable.

LEVEL B. Complete each sentence by choosing the correct form of the verb in parentheses.

10. This article on reefs (is, are) informative.
11. The study of coral reefs (is, are) fascinating.
12. Corals on a reef (is, are) more numerous in deep water.
13. Boulders of coral (is, are) sometimes six feet high.
14. The top of these masses often (show, shows) cavities.
15. The fingers of coral (seem, seems) delicate.
16. Different types of organisms (live, lives) on the reef.
17. An anemone with its tentacles (is, are) typical.
18. The colors of coral (is, are) brilliant.

LEVEL C. Write each sentence using the correct present-tense form of the verb in parentheses.

19. An urchin with its spines (be) dangerous.
20. The sting from their spines (resemble) a hornet's.
21. Colonies of coral (project) from the sand.
22. The arms of a starfish (move) it around.
23. Young colonies of coral often (look) purple.
24. The shells of tulip snails (be) graceful.
25. The surface of these snails (appear) reddish.

PRACTICE + PLUS

Three levels of additional practice for a difficult skill
Using Verbs After Prepositional Phrases (page 430)

LEVEL
A. Write the verb form in parentheses that correctly completes each sentence.

1. The worker bees in a colony (is, are) explorers.
2. A bee during its flights (looks, look) for flowers.
3. The nectar of flowers (is, are) a favorite food.
4. Water located in easy-to-reach spots (is, are) also needed.
5. Chemicals in a bee's stomach (changes, change) the nectar to honey.
6. A bee, in most cases, (uses, use) landmarks to fly home.
7. Workers with nectar (reenters, reenter) the hive.
8. Workers from another hive cannot (enters, enter) it.
9. The life of workers (lasts, last) two months.

LEVEL
B. Write the subject of each sentence. Then write the verb in parentheses that agrees with the subject.

10. A colony with too many bees (has, have) a problem.
11. The workers of the colony (leaves, leave) the hive.
12. Bees in a swarm (number, numbers) in the thousands.
13. Explorers from the group (return, returns) to the others.
14. The others in a cluster (waits, wait) on a branch.
15. Scouting for new hive locations (has, have) occurred.
16. Bees in a new location (builds, build) a hive quickly.
17. The remaining workers in the old hive (work, works) as usual.

LEVEL
C. Complete each sentence correctly with a present-tense verb.

18. A colony of bees _____ for many years.
19. A number of products _____ from beeswax.
20. People around the world _____ honey.
21. The bees near an orchard _____ fruit trees.
22. The people around bees often _____ a bee sting.
23. Bees, in fact, _____ only when hurt or afraid.
24. Bees at all times _____ hard work and cooperation.
25. The hard work of bees _____ people.

EXTRA PRACTICE

Three levels of practice
Conjunctions (page 432)

LEVEL
A. Write each sentence. Underline the conjunction.

1. Plants and flowers grow in the garden.
2. Do you know how they develop and grow?
3. Sunlight and rain are both necessary.
4. A plant needs sunlight, or it will die.
5. The plant absorbs and stores energy from the sun.
6. Some shrubs or trees turn their leaves toward the sun.
7. You saw those plants, but I did not.
8. Plants absorb the energy of light, and they convert it into food.
9. Water and sunlight combine to produce healthy plants.

LEVEL
B. Underline the conjunction in each sentence. Then, write whether it helps to form a **compound subject**, a **compound predicate**, or a **compound sentence**.

10. Soil conditions and care are also important.
11. Plants and flowers use chlorophyll.
12. This substance traps and stores the sun's energy.
13. Chlorophyll is a compound, and plants cannot live without it.
14. Chlorophyll absorbs and uses sunlight.
15. Certain rays of the spectrum are absorbed, but the green portion is reflected.
16. As a result, plants and shrubs look green.
17. The plants receive energy, and photosynthesis occurs.
18. Direct light and water are necessary for this process.
19. Hydrogen and oxygen are changed into compounds.

LEVEL
C. Use the conjunction that best completes each sentence.

20. The compounds feed the plant, _____ it grows.
21. Daisies have chlorophyll, _____ mushrooms do not.
22. Fir trees _____ pine trees produce their seeds in cones.
23. Leaves may breathe air _____ trap sunlight.
24. We study healthy plants, _____ plant pathologists study diseases.
25. I planted _____ watered those fruit trees.

Three levels of practice
More About Conjunctions (page 434)

LEVEL
A. Write **Yes** if the underlined word is a conjunction. Write **No** if it is not.

1. Albert Einstein was one <u>of</u> the world's great scientists.
2. <u>If</u> someone is very bright, we might call him or her an "Einstein."
3. Strangely, however, Einstein's genius was <u>not</u> always obvious.
4. Einstein did not talk <u>until</u> he was three years old.
5. <u>Whenever</u> he was in class, he answered questions slowly.
6. One school expelled him <u>because</u> he didn't behave well.
7. Would Einstein <u>ever</u> be a success at anything?

LEVEL
B. Write each conjunction in each sentence.

8. Einstein thought about physics while he went to school.
9. When he was only 26, he presented a theory of relativity.
10. This theory was critical because it explored the connection between matter and energy.
11. Atomic energy became possible after he wrote this work.
12. Although the following fact is less well known, Einstein also revolutionized our understanding of light.
13. As if that were not enough, he developed theories about space and time.

LEVEL
C. Combine each pair of sentences. Use the conjunction in parentheses.

14. Einstein moved permanently to the United States in 1933. He lived in Germany and Switzerland. (before)
15. He became an American. He liked life here. (since)
16. He had many unanswered scientific questions. He worked long and hard. (because)
17. Einstein was a scientist. He was concerned about people and world affairs. (although)
18. People were oppressed. Einstein supported them. (if)
19. Einstein wanted to relax. He played the violin. (when)
20. Einstein continued to work. He died at age 76. (until)

EXTRA PRACTICE

Three levels of practice
Interjections (page 436)

LEVEL A. Write each sentence. Underline the interjection.

1. Wow! The solar system seems like a good report topic.
2. Oh, no! That topic is much too broad.
3. Gee, how about focusing on one planet?
4. Well, that sounds like a better idea.
5. Hey! I think I will research the planet Mars.
6. Great! However, you still need a more limited topic.
7. Aha! I can report on the canals on Mars.
8. That topic sounds good. Hooray!
9. Oh, there are many theories about the canals.

LEVEL B. Write each sentence. Underline the interjection and add the correct punctuation.

10. Hey can these canals be seen through a telescope?
11. Wow We also have pictures of them from *Mariner 4.*
12. Look at these photographs! Goodness
13. Gee the canals are still mysterious.
14. Aha What other sources can you use for your report?
15. Here is an encyclopedia article. Hooray
16. Good grief Does Mars have volcanoes as well?
17. One is the largest in the solar system. Yikes

LEVEL C. Write each sentence. Add an interjection and punctuate the sentence correctly.

18. These pictures of the satellites are exciting.
19. Look at the size of that satellite!
20. How far they travel!
21. I can't wait to visit the planetarium.
22. We're going next week.
23. I forgot I'll be on vacation.
24. It's too late to change my plans.
25. You'll collect some pamphlets for me?

GRAMMAR

Three levels of practice
Using Commas in Compound Sentences (page 438)

LEVEL
A. Write each sentence. Add the correct punctuation.

1. The library was open late and Ramona went there.
2. She needed sources for her report and the librarian helped her.
3. She read some articles but books were hard to locate.
4. Ramona considered a change of topic but the librarian suggested she look in the encyclopedia.
5. This source listed several books and Ramona consulted them.
6. Her topic was the Golden Gate Bridge and she spent an hour taking notes.
7. The bridge is 4,200 feet long and construction lasted four years.
8. Ramona liked the topic and she was very thorough.

LEVEL
B. Write each sentence and underline the conjunction. Add the correct punctuation.

9. She reviewed her notes but one card was missing.
10. Had she left it in a book or did it fall off the desk?
11. Ramona found the card and the library then closed.
12. She worked at home and her outline was soon completed.
13. She sorted her note cards but a topic sentence did not occur to her.
14. She then thought a bit and her topic sentence became clear.
15. The Golden Gate is a wonder but its construction required great courage.

LEVEL
C. Combine each pair of sentences into a compound sentence. Use one of the conjunctions *and*, *or*, or *but*. Use commas correctly.

16. Ramona's report opened with a topic sentence. It continued with an account of the engineers' problems.
17. First Ramona outlined her ideas in a logical order. Then she concentrated on revising the report.
18. Ramona worked hard. Her report was terrific.
19. The topic was difficult. The text was interesting.
20. Ramona practiced in front of a mirror. Then she presented her report in class.

EXTRA PRACTICE

Three levels of practice
Vocabulary Building: Suffixes (page 440)

LEVEL
A. Write each underlined word. Draw a line under the suffix.

1. Whales are the most <u>powerful</u> of all sea creatures.
2. Humpback whales are quite <u>recognizable</u>.
3. They have <u>lengthy</u> fins.
4. Most humpbacks are slow <u>swimmers</u>.
5. They move <u>northward</u> in late spring and summer.
6. Humpbacks are <u>visible</u> in all the oceans.
7. They sense their <u>environment</u> through sonar.
8. Humpbacks dive with a <u>graceful</u> motion.
9. Their songs have an eerie <u>strangeness</u>.
10. Is their music <u>ghostly</u>?

LEVEL
B. Write each word and underline its suffix. Write the meaning of each word. Use a dictionary if needed.

11. weightless
12. readiness
13. dentist
14. lawful
15. brotherly
16. changeable
17. cellist
18. resentment

LEVEL
C. Write each word and underline the suffix. Then use each word in a sentence that shows its meaning.

19. shapely
20. outward
21. conductor
22. hefty
23. sentiment
24. pediatrician
25. tangible

MAINTENANCE

UNIT 1: Sentences

Four Kinds of Sentences

(page 2) Write each sentence. Add end punctuation. Label each sentence **declarative, interrogative, imperative,** or **exclamatory.**

1. Is that a black bear
2. How fast it runs
3. Bears can run 25 miles per hour
4. Tell me more about bears
5. Please do not feed the bears

Complete Subjects and Predicates

(page 4) Write each sentence. Draw one line under the complete subject and two lines under the complete predicate.

6. A flash of lightning appeared.
7. Thunder rumbled in the valley.
8. Some raindrops hit the ground.
9. The people in town raced for cover.
10. Our street was soon a river.

Simple Subjects and Predicates

(page 6) Write the simple subject and the simple predicate of each sentence.

11. This old house has a secret.
12. The back of this wall is really a door.
13. Very narrow steps lead upward.
14. You reach the attic by way of these stairs.
15. Watch your step.

UNIT 3: Nouns

Singular and Plural Nouns

(page 76) Write the plural form of each noun.

16. studio
17. country
18. goose
19. salmon
20. loaf
21. man
22. valley
23. dish

Possessive Nouns (page 78)

Write the possessive form of each noun in parentheses.

24. The (women) coats are here.
25. (Charles) story won a prize.
26. Are the (ponies) saddles new?
27. Did you see the (turkey) food?
28. Is this the (Joneses) house?

UNIT 5: Verbs

Action and Linking Verbs

(pages 142 and 150) Write the verb in each sentence. Label it **action verb** or **linking verb**.

29. The new library is ready.
30. The mayor appears happy.
31. He delivers a fine speech.
32. The doors finally open.
33. The crowd seems cheerful.
34. The rooms are magnificent.

Direct and Indirect Objects

(page 146) Write the sentences. Underline any indirect objects. Draw two lines under any direct objects.

35. I told Don the story.
36. Did Chad sell her the boat?
37. Give Edward the key.
38. Matt saw the movie yesterday.
39. Anita hit the ball to Cory.

40. My grandmother in Utah sent Aldo the ring one summer.

Irregular Verbs (page 156)

Write the four principal parts of each irregular verb.

41. make
42. draw
43. drive
44. see
45. choose
46. teach
47. write
48. sit

Subject-Verb Agreement (page 160)

Write the correct present-tense form of the verb in parentheses.

49. Your fork (be) here.
50. Pots and pans (belong) there.
51. The men and women (be) hungry.
52. Does Rita (cook) well?
53. Here (be) the dishes.
54. (Be) the spoons clean?

UNIT 7: Pronouns

Using Pronouns Correctly

(page 230) Write the pronoun in parentheses that correctly completes each sentence.

55. Dad and (me, I) read the note.
56. Mr. Pei hired Doris and (I, me).
57. Stan and (he, him) like chess.
58. Arnie and (they, them) left.
59. Did you see Mom and (we, us)?
60. (Her, She) is the girl in the newspaper photo.

Possessive Pronouns (page 234)

Write the pronoun in parentheses that correctly completes each sentence.

61. (Your, You're) new house is so beautiful.
62. I love (it's, its) location.
63. Do the twins like (their, theirs) new yard?
64. This bedroom is (hers, her).
65. (Ours, Our) is downstairs.

UNIT 9: Adjectives

Adjectives, Articles, and Demonstratives (pages 298–300) Write each sentence. Draw one line under each adjective, two lines under each article, and three lines under each demonstrative.

66. That remarkable dinosaur is an allosaur.
67. This fierce beast was a powerful reptile.
68. These sharp teeth and curved claws made it a fearsome enemy.
69. The allosaurs lived before the famous tyrannosaurs.
70. Those old drawings show a harmless apatosaurus.
71. This huge beast could only eat soft plants.

Adjectives That Compare (page 302) Write the adjective in parentheses that correctly completes each sentence.

72. On the (hotter, hottest) day of the summer, we went to the mountains.
73. The air was (cooler, coolest) there than in the city.
74. We picnicked in the (shadier, shadiest) spot we could find.
75. The night sky was (clearer, clearest) there than at home.
76. It was the (finer, finest) night of the whole summer.

Adjectives with *more* and *most* (page 304) Write the form of the adjective in parentheses that correctly completes the sentence.

77. Our balloon ride was the (more exciting, most exciting) event of this whole summer.
78. Of the two balloons, ours was (more colorful, most colorful).
79. We floated over the (more beautiful, most beautiful) area of all in the state.
80. My photographs were (more interesting, most interesting) than Mom's.
81. Ballooning was the (more satisfying, most satisfying) experience I have ever had.

Proper Adjectives (page 306) Write the proper adjective or adjectives in each sentence correctly.

82. We had eggs, canadian bacon, and english muffins for breakfast.
83. We ate chinese food for our lunch.
84. The norwegian sardines and swiss cheese made a tasty snack.
85. For dinner we had alaskan crab.
86. These french pastries were a delicious dessert.

UNIT 11: Adverbs

Adverbs That Modify Verbs

(page 362) Write each sentence. Underline each adverb. Then draw two lines under the verb it modifies.

87. Cary goes skating there.
88. The tall girl skates gracefully.
89. She takes skating lessons daily.
90. Cary already took several lessons.
91. The lessons helped her immensely.
92. Yesterday she practiced for two hours.
93. Her mother frequently watches Cary's practice exercises.
94. She may soon enter a competition in Chicago.

Adverbs That Modify Adjectives and Adverbs

(page 364) Write each adverb. Then write whether it modifies a **verb**, an **adjective**, or an **adverb.**

95. A rather large crowd gathered for the public auction.
96. The contents of a very large home would be sold to the highest bidders.
97. The auctioneer spoke quite fast.
98. The prices of items we bid on rose rapidly.

99. Truly unusual items were bought for large sums of money.
100. Many people worked quite hard in the enormous storerooms.
101. Soon they emptied the whole house.
102. All the people quickly took away the items that they had bought.
103. We felt very happy with all of our purchases.

Adverbs That Compare

(page 366) Write the form of the adverb in parentheses that completes each sentence correctly.

104. Of all the runners, Thomas ran the (fast).
105. He even ran (gracefully) than Alfred.
106. Of the three athletes who were the main competitors, Raymond ran the (bad).
107. He was the (badly) prepared of all of us.
108. We all trained (regularly) than he did.
109. The enthusiastic crowd applauded Jesse the (loudly) of all.
110. Clearly, he had performed the (good) at the international meet.

Adverb or Adjective? (page 368) Write the word in parentheses that completes the sentence correctly.

111. Gina crawled (slow, slowly) into the cave.

112. She cut her knee (bad, badly) on a sharp rock.

113. As a result, she did not feel (good, well).

114. Suddenly, she saw some (beautiful, beautifully) paintings.

115. They (sure, surely) were done thousands of years ago!

116. Experts soon checked the site (thorough, thoroughly).

117. They said Gina had done a (good, well) deed.

Avoiding Double Negatives (page 370) Rewrite each sentence to avoid the double negative.

118. Nobody can't remember the blizzard of 1888.

119. It hardly never stopped snowing for four days and nights.

120. Because of twenty-foot drifts, you could not go nowhere.

121. People didn't have no big snowplows then, either.

122. None of the authorities didn't know what to do to solve all of the problems.

123. Hardly nothing moved for days.

Using Commas to Set off Words (page 372) Write each sentence. Add commas where needed.

124. Did Lee come in from practice yet Alan?

125. No Mr. Cobb our teacher is outside.

126. When you walk Greg try not to slouch.

127. Well I'll try harder Larry.

128. Yes friends I am here.

129. No I did not hear Frank tell the story Sandy.

Prefixes (page 374) Write the prefix of each underlined word. Then, write the meaning of the word.

130. He seemed <u>unconcerned</u> about our fate.

131. You can <u>reapply</u> for the job next month, if you are still interested in it.

132. Did you remember to <u>preheat</u> the oven to 350°?

133. He was <u>impatient</u> with Denise because she was late again.

134. As usual, all of his papers are completely <u>disorganized</u>.

135. The <u>international</u> meeting begins tomorrow.

136. During the <u>postwar</u> years, our standard of living rose.

137. Arriving without a reservation is <u>inadvisable</u>.

UNIT 13: Prepositions, Conjunctions, and Interjections

Prepositions and Prepositional Phrases (page 424) Write the prepositional phrase or phrases in each sentence. Underline the object of each preposition.

138. The howl of the coyote cut through the night.

139. Most coyotes rest by day.

140. Families of coyotes often live underground in dens.

141. The female guards her pups with great care.

142. Coyotes were once found only west of the Mississippi.

143. Now, they live in many eastern areas of our country.

Using Verbs After Prepositional Phrases (page 430) Write the verb in parentheses that completes each sentence correctly.

144. The plants in this garden (is, are) delightful.

145. The flowers on that bush (is, are) red.

146. The tomatoes in this row (gets, get) more sunlight.

147. That row of raspberries (is, are) almost ripe.

148. The peas on this side (tastes, taste) the sweetest.

149. The loveliest gardens in this section (look, looks) pretty.

Conjunctions (page 432) Write the conjunction in each sentence.

150. Did you go to the movie or to the play?

151. The house, small but comfortable, was ideal for us.

152. We saw Lotte and Anna at the ice-skating rink.

153. The girls hopped, skipped, and jumped around the field.

154. You or Sabrina will have to stay here for a while.

Interjections (page 436) Write each interjection.

155. Whew! We finally made it.

156. Hey, I found my watch.

157. Ugh! What is that?

158. Wow! What a beautiful sight!

159. That pot is hot! Ouch!

Suffixes (page 440) Write the suffix in each underlined word and the meaning of the word.

160. It has been an eventful day.

161. Did the homeless family find a place to live?

162. This computer program is user-friendly.

163. The tourist liked the Greek islands best.

164. Tired and hungry, we drifted homeward.

165. He treated the children with great tenderness.

UNIT
14

Writing Research Reports

Read the quotation and look at the picture on the opposite page. George Laycock has written several books about caves. Why do you think he makes an outline before he begins to write?

When you write a research report, you will want to summarize the information you have gathered from different sources. Your purpose will be to inform.

Focus A research report provides information about a limited topic based on facts obtained from different sources.

What would you like to research? The article and the photographs in this unit may give you some ideas for topics to research.

THEME: *EXPLORATIONS*

When I first begin to consider a book subject, I find it a good plan to make an outline of the chapters it will contain. This helps tell you whether you have a book or not. . . .

—George Laycock

Have you ever explored a new area? What did it feel like to explore, and how did you go about it?

This selection recounts the exploration of several famous caves. Some caves are famous because of their spectacular formations; they are usually discovered by experts. Other caves, often discovered by accident, are famous for the prehistoric art within them.

As you read the selection, look for the ways in which the author describes how the caves were discovered.

Famous Caves
Worldwide

from *Caves* by George Laycock

If you mark locations of known caves on a map of the world, you soon discover that there are caverns in almost every country, though they are more concentrated in some places than others. One reason for this is that some countries have more people interested in caves, more underground explorers searching out the hidden recesses of the earth. Especially famous for their caves, in addition to the United States, are France, Spain, Great Britain, Mexico, and Venezuela, as well as parts of Africa and Australia and a number of countries in eastern Europe.

Some caves are not known beyond their own local neighborhoods. Others are famous around the world. One famous cave lies in the heart of France. Its visitors come by the hundreds and travel into the cave by elevator and boats to see its hidden lakes.

This cavern, the cave of Padirac, is reached either by highway or railroad up a limestone mountain. The route leads through a gray and barren countryside, a desert land in spite of the abundant rainfall. As fast as water falls upon this part of France it vanishes deep into the earth, leaving

the surface of the land dry and thirsty. Because of this dryness, the rocky, gray land grows only scattered plants. There is little to support people or their livestock. Only occasionally along the way does one see a house where a local family is struggling to survive on the harsh arid land.

But cavers who understand the nature of limestone study the landscape beyond the road. They see sinkholes and the absence of streams, and this tells them they are traveling over a karst landscape. They know that somewhere beneath them lie strangely shaped caverns steeped in mysterious blackness.

Three hundred feet below the surface of this land a stream flows through a tunnel 15 to 30 feet wide. The roof is 30 feet above the water in some places, elsewhere 150 feet high. Only the first stage of the descent into Padirac is made by elevator. From there, visitors walk down to water level, where small boats await them. After about a quarter of a mile the little boat arrives on the Lake of the Raindrops. On the walls there are deposits of calcite that sparkle like raindrops as they catch and reflect the light. The subterranean river flows on for more than three miles, sometimes widening into lakes. One of the famous views that visitors remember is the Great Dome, 280 feet high. But this cave is not famous for delicate formations. Instead, the rocky scenery here is bold and impressive for its ruggedness.

Two other caves known around the world are famous because ancient artists, working under flickering yellow flares, painted magnificent pictures on their walls. The first of these was found beneath the hills of northern Spain.

Near the coast of Spain, in a region known for its old castles, a man and his dog went out one afternoon to hunt rabbits. This hunter worked as the head gamekeeper for the owner of an estate, Don Marcelino de Sautuola, and he had hunted these fields many times. He believed that he knew every feature of the landscape. But on this day the dog was sniffing at the grass in the rocky hillside when suddenly he disappeared completely. It was as if the dog had simply vanished through a hole in the earth.

The man hurried to where he had last seen the dog and found, to his amazement, that it had indeed fallen into a deep hole. As the man alternately dug at the entrance and whistled for his pet, the dog crawled up to him out of the mouth of the cave.

Then the gamekeeper, keeping the dog close beside him, hurried back to the castle to report his discovery to Don Marcelino. Together they returned for a closer look at the cave. It was not the only cave known in the community. There were many others, and to Don Marcelino there seemed, on this first day, to be nothing special about the new cave found by the gamekeeper and the little dog.

But Don Marcelino never forgot the cave. Nine years later he went to Paris to attend the World's Fair of 1878. There he spent many hours studying the collections of Stone Age tools made and used by ancient people who occupied Europe thousands of years before. There were tools of bone and even drawings of strange wild beasts that had since vanished from Europe. Don Marcelino was deeply interested in these ancient people. He wondered if there might be more evidence of their way of life in the new cave on the hillside of his estate, and he began spending long hours in the cave, exploring its rooms and passages. There he discovered stone tools that had lain untouched for thousands of years.

Often, on these cave visits, Don Marcelino took along his nine-year-old daughter Maria. And it was Maria who made the greatest discovery of all. The November day was dark and cloudy, but the dim light of the cave was another world. Maria, carrying a candle, was experimenting with

Each paragraph covers one main topic, and the paragraphs are arranged in logical order.

the shapes of the shadows formed by the light it cast on the uneven stone walls of the cave.

Suddenly she stopped, staring in disbelief. Never before had Maria seen shapes such as the one now revealed by her light. It was almost as if the huge creature actually moved with the flickering of the light. She cried out to her father. He heard her in the distance shouting, "Bulls, Bulls," and came quickly to see what Maria had found. In a low space, previously hidden, a giant wild bison had been painted in bold red and black. And as father and daughter looked around they saw other beasts, including horses and boars.

In this way the ancient cave paintings of Altamira, perhaps the finest display anywhere of prehistoric art, were discovered thousands of years after some long-forgotten, but highly skilled artists had drawn them there. Among

the famous visitors to come to Altamira in the following years was Alphonsus XII, the king of Spain. With the other visitors, the king squeezed and crawled through the tight places, moving from one remarkable painting to the next, admiring the skill of those ancient artists.

But even more impressive to some is the cave found on September 12, 1940, in the south of France on a hill named Lascaux. Again a curious dog played the role of cave discoverer. Four of the neighborhood boys were out exploring the countryside as they often did. They were headed for one of their favorite places, where they liked to hike through the forest and run over the slopes of the Lascaux hill. With them was Robot, a small terrier belonging to Simon, the youngest of the boys.

All went well until someone noticed that Robot had suddenly disappeared. Simon whistled as loud as he could. He kept on whistling. But Robot did not come. They began searching where the dog was last seen, and there they found a small hole in the hill. It was half hidden by grass and roots. The boys soon realized that they had discovered a large cave. No matter how loudly they whistled, Robot neither came nor answered. Sadly they turned homeward.

The next morning, equipped with ropes, they returned and went into the cave. They found Robot, uninjured, and led the joyous dog back out into daylight.

But the world would soon know that the four boys had found much more than a lost and frightened dog. The light of the matches they carried showed them walls and ceilings rich in ancient cave art. Deer, horses, lions, rhinoceroses, and bison, painted centuries ago, were still in perfect condition on the dark, dry cave walls. Ancient artists, painting with fingers, sticks, and paint blown through hollow reeds, had decorated the cave with animals in rich reds, oranges, yellows, and black. Scientists determined

All the details and information that the writer gives are based on research and facts.

that they had worked in the cave about seventeen thousand years before Robot fell through the hillside.

This splendid primitive art gallery was opened to visitors, and thousands of people journeyed to Lascaux to see the wonders of its caverns.

Thinking Like a Reader

1. Why do you think the accidental discovery of the caves at Altamira and at Lascaux was so significant?

2. Have you ever discovered anything that was important to you? What was it? How did you happen to discover it?

Write your responses in your journal.

Thinking Like a Writer

3. What facts and details does the author use?

4. How does his presentation of information hold your interest?

5. If you were writing about why the artists decorated the caves, how would you gather more information?

Write your responses in your journal.

Brainstorm *Vocabulary*

In "Famous Caves Worldwide," George Laycock mentions that cave explorers use clues such as sinkholes and the absence of streams to identify a karst landscape—a limestone area where caves are located. The word *karst* is a technical term from the science of geology. Technical terms are frequently used in nonfiction writing such as research reports. Technical phrases are useful when giving additional details about science and processes. In your journal, write some other scientific terms you know. These words and phrases may give you some ideas to explore in a research report.

Talk It Over *A Process*

When you explain a topic or a process, you give facts about it in a logical order. Imagine that you are Maria in "Famous Caves Worldwide," and that you are reporting your discovery of the cave paintings at Altamira to a friend who was not present. Explain the facts of your discovery in a logical order.

Quick Write *Write Notes*

Now that you have been thinking of a topic you might like to explore in a research report, try writing one or two notes about the topic. Each note you write should contain a fact. For example, if your topic is the solar system, your notes might look like this:

—sun and nine planets
—Mercury closest to sun
—Jupiter is largest planet
—Mars is nearest to Earth
—Pluto is farthest away
—asteroid Ceres discovered in 1801

Write your notes on a separate sheet of paper.

Idea Corner *Think of Topics to Explore*

Think about topics you would like to explore in a research report. You probably already have some ideas. In your journal, write whatever ideas come to mind. You could write ideas in the form of questions such as these: What makes waves form? Why do leaves turn green in spring and yellow in fall? What causes a hurricane?

PICTURES

SEEING LIKE A WRITER

Finding Ideas for Writing
Look at the pictures. Think about what you see.
What ideas for a research report do the pictures give you?
Write your ideas in your journal.

A diving suit with robotic-type hand extensions, EPCOT, Florida

PICTURES: Ideas for Writing a Research Report

Lindbergh with his airplane, the *Spirit of St. Louis*

The Granger Collection

DREADCO

PERPETUAL
MOTION
?

COOPERATIVE
LEARNING

GROUP WRITING: A Research Report

You know that a research report is a report based on outside sources of information. Its **purpose** is to inform an **audience** about a topic. The following steps will help you to write an effective research report.

- Finding Facts and Taking Notes
- Making an Outline
- Writing Paragraphs from an Outline

Finding Facts and Taking Notes

One student decided to write a research report about submarines. She went to the library and found several sources of information. She found this passage in a book.

> When a submarine dives, pumps fill its large ballast tanks with seawater. Water is heavier than empty tanks, so the submarine sinks. At the desired depth, pumps force out some of the water, and the sub stops. Finally, to rise to the surface again, the pumps empty the tanks and lighten the sub.

The writer took some notes. She also wrote information about where she had found her facts, so she could go back to it later if she needed to.

title	Underwater World
author	Jay Duggan
subject	how submarines dive
summary	ballast tanks make sub dive
	--pumps fill tanks with seawater
	--water heavier than empty tanks
page	27

Guided Practice: Finding Facts and Taking Notes

As a class, choose a topic from the list below, or think of one on which you all agree. Each of you should find one source on your topic and make a note card using that source.

solar energy   the life of a butterfly   robots

microscopes   clouds and rain   space flight

Making an Outline

You can use your note cards to make an outline. First, group your note cards into categories. In your outline, each category will be a **main topic**, indicated by a Roman numeral. **Subtopics,** marked with capital letters, support the main topic. **Details** give information about subtopics and are indicated by numbers. Discard any cards that do not fit a category. Look at the example. Notice where the Roman numerals, capital letters, and numbers are placed.

How a Submarine Works

I. Construction of submarines
    A. Inner and outer hull
    B. Function of ballast tanks
       1. Diving
       2. Remaining at desired depth
       3. Rising to surface
    C. Other systems
       1. Heating and ventilation
       2. Communications
II. Uses of submarines
    A. Underwater research
    B. Defense

- What are the main topics of this report?
- How many paragraphs will the whole report have?

Guided Practice: Outlining

Recall your topic and group your note cards into categories. Then use your note cards to write your outline. Be sure that your outline has at least three main topics.

Writing Paragraphs from an Outline

A research report has three parts: an introduction, a body, and a conclusion. The introduction attracts the reader's attention and tells what the subject is. The body develops the subject, and the conclusion summarizes the information in the report.

Your outline is a guide from which to write your report. The main topics in the outline become topic sentences for the paragraphs of your report. The subtopics become supporting sentences, in which you use the details.

Begin with an introductory sentence that tells what your subject will be. Next, write a topic sentence for the first main topic in your outline. Then, write a sentence for each subtopic that appeared under that main topic in your outline. When you come to a new main topic, begin a new paragraph. The body of the report will contain the facts and information you have learned from your research. At the end of the last paragraph, write a conclusion that summarizes the main points of your report.

Putting a Research Report Together

With your classmates you have selected a topic for a research report. You have discovered facts about the topic and organized your facts in an outline.

Guided Practice: Writing a Research Report

Turn your outline into a research report at least three paragraphs long. Begin with an introductory sentence. Make sure your introduction attracts the reader's attention. Then write the first main topic of your outline as a topic sentence. Write supporting sentences, including details, for the subtopics. Use details from the notes you have gathered. Then begin your next paragraph. Write a conclusion at the end. Try to summarize your findings.

Share your report with a friend. Ask your friend what he or she learned about the subject from reading your report.

Checklist: A Research Report

When you write a research report, you will want to keep in mind some important points.

One way to remember the important elements of a research report is to make a checklist. The checklist will remind you of the things you need to include in your research report.

Look at this checklist. Make a copy of the checklist and complete it. Keep a copy of it in your writing folder. You can use it when you write your own research report.

CHECKLIST

- ✔ Find information and take notes.
- ✔ Organize note cards into groups.
- ✔ Make an outline.
- ✔ Write paragraphs from the outline.
- ✔ Include an introduction, a body, and

_____ .

2 THINKING AND WRITING: Summarizing

Think about the steps in writing a research report. Taking notes, outlining, and writing a conclusion all require summarizing. **Summarizing** is stating in your own words the main points of something you have read or heard.

Read this paragraph from a magazine article.

> Robots may be operated by any one of three different kinds of power systems. Some run on electricity, either by battery or by being attached with wires to an electrical outlet. Other, usually larger, robots may be operated by hydraulic, or water, power. A third kind of robot may be operated by a pneumatic power system, which uses forced air.

To summarize the information in this paragraph, one student first thought about the main idea of the paragraph. He decided that it was "power systems used in robots."

Next, the student looked for the most important facts about the main idea. He decided that they were the three kinds of power systems for robots—electric, hydraulic, and pneumatic. He wrote those facts on his note card. Later, he summarized the information in his own words, like this:

Three power systems that can operate robots are electric, hydraulic, and pneumatic power.

Thinking Like a Writer

- How has the student summarized the information in the paragraph?

To summarize information, first find the subject. If you are making a note card, write the subject first. Then, give the main facts that relate directly to the subject. Use as few words as possible, but be accurate. Be sure to summarize in your own words.

COOPERATIVE
LEARNING

THINKING APPLICATION Summarizing Information

Two students, Vera and Sam, have found the following paragraphs. Help each writer decide how to summarize the information in the paragraphs. On a separate piece of paper, write a one- or two-sentence summary of each paragraph. You may wish to discuss your thinking with other students. In your discussion, explain why you summarized in the way that you did.

1. When a liquid changes to a gas, it absorbs heat. That knowledge is used to cool refrigerators. In a refrigerator, a pump forces a gas through a condenser. Under pressure, the gas becomes liquid and loses heat. The heat is then blown out of the refrigerator. Once it leaves the condenser, the liquid changes back to gas, again absorbing heat and cooling the refrigerator.

2. Most archaeologists agree that the ancient Egyptians used an inclined plane, or ramp, to build the pyramids. As the pyramid rose, gently sloping earthen ramps were built along its walls. Up these ramps, slaves pushed and pulled the huge stone blocks that formed the walls. When the pyramid was finished, the ramps were removed from the top, and the earth carted away.

WRITING

PROCESS

Prewrite: Step 1

You have learned quite a bit about the elements of a research report. Now you are ready to choose a topic of your own. Heather, a student your age, chose a topic in this way.

Choosing a Topic

1. First, Heather wrote a list of topics that interested her.
2. Next, she narrowed her topic when she discussed it with a small group of classmates.
3. Last, she decided on the facts she needed to find to get started on her report.

> -- how rain clouds form
> -- the eruption of a volcano
> -- how to program a robot
> -- Mars
> -- aviation ------- airplanes

Heather liked the last topic on her list best. She thought she would narrow the topic of aviation to a topic connected with airplanes. Her **purpose** would be to present a clear explanation of her topic to an **audience** of her classmates.

Exploring Ideas: Outlining Strategy

Heather began by finding facts and taking notes on her subject. She kept her information on note cards. She wrote the name of the book, the author, and the page number on every note card, so she could find the source again later if she needed to. Heather grouped her cards by subject and used them to make an outline.

How Airplanes Fly

I. History of flight
   A. The Wright brothers
   B. The first true flight
   C. Balloons and blimps
II. Three elements of flight
   A. Power
   B. Lift
      1. Shape of wings
      2. Movement of air over wings
   C. Control
III. Methods of control
   A. Parts of the plane
   B. Starting, stopping, and steering

Before writing, Heather imagined that she was teaching a class of beginning fliers. She decided that they would want to know less about the history of flight and more about the process. At this point, she revised her outline.

Thinking Like a Writer

- Heather took out a subtopic. Which subtopic do you think she took out, and why?

YOUR TURN

JOURNAL

Think of a topic that you would like to develop in a research report. Follow these steps. Use **Pictures** or your journal to find ideas.

- Make a list of topics. Choose one that interests you most.
- Narrow your topic if it is too broad.
- Collect information, take notes, and create an outline for your report.
- Think about your purpose and audience.

You can add or take away from your outline at any time.

Write a First Draft: Step 2

Heather's planning checklist was very helpful.

Part of Heather's First Draft

On December 17, 1903, the wright brothers in history became the first true aveators. They invented the first heavier-than-air aircraft. The Wright brothers succeeded. They were the first to understand the basic, fundamental principles of what makes an airplane fly.

In his book The First to Fly, sherwood Harris explains that there are three essential elements of flight. A power plant such as an engine and a propeller must move the plane fast enough to overcome drag. The wings of the plane are designed to be more curved on the top than on the bottom.

While Heather was writing her first draft, she concentrated only on getting her ideas down on paper.

Planning Checklist
■ Remember purpose and audience.
■ Find information and take notes.
■ Make an outline.
■ Write paragraphs from the outline.
■ Include a good introduction and conclusion.

YOUR TURN

Write the first draft of your research report. As you prepare to write, ask yourself these questions.

■ What does my audience need to know?
■ What facts should I include to explain my topic clearly?
■ How can I make my introduction and conclusion strong?

TIME-OUT You might want to take some time out before you revise. That way you will be able to revise your writing with a fresh eye.

Revise: Step 3

When she had finished her first draft, Heather read it over to herself. Then she asked one of her classmates to read it and make some suggestions for improvement.

Heather looked back at her planning checklist. She put a check mark beside the point her classmate had mentioned so that she would remember it when she revised her research report.

Heather used this checklist when she revised her report. She asked herself several questions. Had she included enough information in her report so that her audience would find the report informative? Had she organized the information clearly? Were her introduction and conclusion effective? As she revised, she made several changes. She did not correct small errors. She knew she could fix them later.

The revisions Heather made improved her report. Look at part of Heather's revised draft on the next page.

Revising Checklist
- ■ Remember purpose and audience.
- ✔■ Find information and take notes.
- ■ Make an outline.
- ■ Write paragraphs from the outline.
- ■ Include a good introduction and conclusion.

WRITING

PROCESS

On December 17, 1903, the wright brothers in history became the first true aveators. They invented the first heavier–than–air aircraft. The Wright brothers succeeded *e* *because* They were the first to understand the basic, fundamental *e* principles of what makes an airplane fly.

In his book The First to Fly, sherwood Harris explains that there are three essential elements of flight. *First,* A power plant such as an engine and a propeller must move the plane fast enough to overcome drag. *or air resistance* The wings of the plane are designed to be more curved on the top than on the bottom.

Thinking Like a Writer

WISE
WORD
CHOICE

- What detail did Heather add? Why?
- Why do you think Heather added a transition word?
- Why do you think Heather combined sentences?

YOUR TURN

Read your first draft. Ask yourself these questions.

- What facts can I add to make my subject clearer to my audience?
- How can I make my introduction and conclusion stronger?
- How can combining sentences improve my writing?

If you wish, ask a friend to read your work and make suggestions for improvements. Then revise your report.

Proofread: Step 4

Heather knew that her work was not complete until she proofread her report. In the proofreading stage, she checked for errors in grammar and mechanics. She used proofreading marks to correct the errors she found.

Part of Heather's Proofread Draft

On December 17, 1903, the wright brothers *in history* became the first true *aveators.* They invented the first heavier-than-air aircraft. The Wright brothers succeeded. *because* They were the first to understand the basic, fundamental principles of what makes an airplane fly.

In his book The First to Fly, sherwood Harris explains that there are three essential elements of flight. *First,* A power plant, such as an engine and a propeller must move the plane fast

YOUR TURN

Proofreading Practice

Below is a paragraph that you can use to practice your proofreading skills. Find the errors. Write the paragraph correctly on a separate piece of paper.

In the process Called photosynthesis, green plants use the energy from the sun for growth and development. first, the chlorophyll in plants traps the energy from sunlight. The result is to break down water into hydrogen and oxyjen. These elements then mix with carbon and oxygen to create plant tissue

Proofreading Checklist
■ Did I indent each new paragraph?
■ Did I spell all words correctly?
■ Which punctuation errors do I need to correct?
■ Which capitalization errors do I need to correct?

W R I T I N G

PROCESS

Applying Your Proofreading Skills

Now proofread your research report. Also read your checklist one last time. Then review **The Grammar Connection** and **The Mechanics Connection**. Use the proofreading marks to make changes.

THE GRAMMAR CONNECTION

Remember this rule about placing prepositional phrases.

- Place a prepositional phrase as close as possible to the word it modifies.

CORRECT: We saw photographs of birds **in flight.**
INCORRECT: **In flight** we saw photographs of birds.

Check your writing. Have you placed prepositional phrases correctly?

THE MECHANICS CONNECTION

Remember these rules about quotation marks and italics.

- Use quotation marks before and after the words of a direct quotation.

  "Solar energy is the only alternative," says Dr. Hay.

- Use quotation marks for the title of a story, essay, poem, song, magazine or newspaper article, or book chapter.

  Chapter 6 is titled "Plant Care" and begins on page 60.

- Use italics (underlining) to identify the title of a book, play, film, TV series, magazine, or newspaper.

  The article appeared in Discover magazine.

Check your research report. Have you used quotation marks correctly?

Proofreading Marks

- ¶ Indent
- ∧ Add
- ∧, Add a comma
- ∨∨ Add quotation marks
- ⊙ Add a period
- ℓ Take out
- ≡ Capitalize
- / Make a small letter
- ∿ Reverse the order

Publish: Step 5

Heather made a neat final copy of her research report. At the end of the report, she added a bibliography—an alphabetical listing by author of all of her sources. She illustrated the report with photographs of the first flight of the Wright brothers, which she had found in a magazine. Heather posted her illustrated report on the class bulletin board. Several of her classmates told her that they wanted to know more about flying.

YOUR TURN

Make a neat final copy of your research report. Think of a way to share your report. You might find some ideas in the **Sharing Suggestions** box below.

SHARING SUGGESTIONS

Illustrate your report with a drawing, graph, or chart and begin a class encyclopedia.	Present your information as an oral report to younger students.	Enter your research report in a school or local writing contest.

4 SPEAKING AND LISTENING: Giving an Oral Report

You have just written a research report that explains a topic. Your report included facts, logical order, and a strong introduction and conclusion.

Now you can use what you have learned about research to give an oral report. In your report you will explain a topic to your classmates.

First, you will want to make an outline to use for your oral report. Your outline should include only the main points and some important details.

Look at this outline.

Ocean Tides

I. Tides caused by force of gravity
   A. Gravity from sun
   B. Gravity from moon (twice as strong as sun's)
II. High tide
   A. Moon causes high tide at two points on opposite sides of Earth
   B. Moon's rotation around Earth causes two high tides in every 24-hour period, roughly 12 hours apart
III. Low tide
   A. Occurs halfway between two locations of high tide
   B. Caused by movement of water toward area of high tide

Notice that the topic of the report is included, as well as the important supporting details that the speaker will need to include to explain the topic.

When you give an oral report, keep the following guidelines in mind. They will help you to prepare and deliver your report effectively.

SPEAKING GUIDELINES: An Oral Report

1. Remember your **purpose** and **audience**. Try to think of questions your audience might ask.
2. Make an outline with the main points of your report. Practice speaking from the outline.
3. Be sure that your report has a good introduction and conclusion.
4. Begin each new topic with a topic sentence. Be sure that the details are in logical order.
5. Look at your listeners and speak in a strong, clear voice.

■ Why is it important to make an outline for an oral report?

SPEAKING APPLICATION An Oral Report

Think of a topic that interests you, for example, how a refrigerator works or what causes autumn leaves to change colors. Prepare an outline to use to give a short oral report about this process. Use the speaking guidelines to help you prepare. Your classmates will be using the following guidelines as they listen to your report.

LISTENING GUIDELINES: An Oral Report

1. Look directly at the person who is speaking.
2. Listen for the topic of the report. The topic will usually be stated at the beginning.
3. Try to remember the facts the speaker gives. Take notes on important points.
4. Ask questions about information you missed or did not understand.

5 WRITER'S RESOURCES: The Encyclopedia

In this unit you have written a research report. You have used many resources to find ideas for your writing, including photographs, reports, and your own imagination. Another useful resource for writers is the encyclopedia.

An encyclopedia is a set of books containing articles about people, places, things, events, and ideas. The articles are arranged in alphabetical order in volumes.

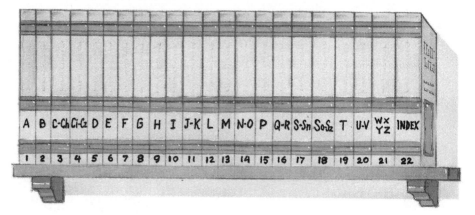

When Heather wrote her research report on how an airplane flies, she began her research by reading an encyclopedia article in the school library. In the article entitled "Airplane," she found many facts about how planes are designed to fly. When you are assigned a research report, an encyclopedia article can provide you with a general discussion of your topic.

When you use an encyclopedia to find facts about a topic, you must have a **key word** in mind. For example, when Heather consulted an encyclopedia, she first looked under the key word *flight*. She found several cross-references that looked like this:

FLIGHT. See AIRPLANE, BIRDS, SPACE FLIGHT.

The cross-references helped Heather to locate the article on her specific topic.

Practice

Use the encyclopedia volumes shown on the opposite page. Write each subject below. Then write the number of the volume of the encyclopedia that would include an article about that subject.

1. how batteries work
2. the parts of a radio
3. building a telescope
4. kangaroos
5. pollution from acid rain
6. reptiles
7. the process of photosynthesis
8. how malaria epidemics are controlled
9. weather satellites
10. what causes earthquakes
11. robots
12. the life cycle of yellow jackets
13. the history of skydiving
14. stage sets
15. volcanoes
16. what causes lunar eclipses
17. famous tombs
18. American aviators
19. Nobel Peace Prize winners
20. woodwind instruments

WRITING APPLICATION A Summary

Use an encyclopedia article to research facts about a scientific topic that interests you. For example, you might write about the weather, plant life, or space exploration. Be sure to check any cross references to your topic. Write a short summary of the information you find. Remember to use your own words when you write your summary. Keep your summary in your writing folder. You will use it in **The Curriculum Connection.**

THE CURRICULUM CONNECTION

Writing About Science

The word *science* comes from a Latin word for *knowledge*. Scientific knowledge gives a clear, factual explanation of the physical world around us.

Scientists try to be as accurate, objective, and systematic as they can. They use observations and experiments to increase our knowledge about everything from the tiniest cells in the human body to the largest galaxies in the universe. Scientists work in laboratories, in universities, and in business. They also write articles and reports for many different types of publications: textbooks, magazines, encyclopedias, and government pamphlets.

ACTIVITIES

Create a Visual Aid Look at the summary you wrote about the scientific topic you looked up in the encyclopedia. Draw a visual aid such as a chart, a graph, or a diagram that you think will help your classmates to understand the information you have summarized.

Be a Scientist Think about an occurrence in nature that intrigues you, for example, how a snake sheds its skin or how an eclipse is caused. Then do some research, take notes, and write a paragraph that could be used as part of an exhibit at a science museum.

Respond to Literature The following passage from a book about weather explains a natural event nearly everyone has seen—lightning. After you read the selection, write your response to the ideas in it. Your response might be a poem, a description, or a research report.

What Is Lightning?

Lightning is a giant electric spark that leaps from cloud to ground or from cloud to cloud. No one knows for certain just what happens, but lightning might occur like this. In a thunderstorm, drafts of warm, moist air rush up inside a thundercloud. Moisture in the rising air condenses to form billions of water drops and ice crystals. These pick up tiny electric charges as they move through the air, but the amount they pick up depends on their size and shape. The violent air currents in thunderclouds move different-sized particles at different speeds. So particles of similar size and with a similar amount of electricity become concentrated in the same part of the cloud.

The bottom of a thundercloud builds up a very powerful negative charge, while the earth below the cloud is normally positively charged. This difference in charges often creates a voltage powerful enough for a giant spark to flash between the cloud and the ground.

A lightning flash always takes the easiest path to earth. It zigzags downward in the wettest regions of the air, because it travels more easily through moist air. The downstroke blasts a kind of invisible channel through the air to the ground. Almost instantly, a return stroke leaves the ground and flashes up through the same channel.

UNIT CHECKUP

LESSON 1

Group Writing: A Research Report (page 476) Read this paragraph. Jot down the topic and make notes on the important points of information.

Blood travels from the left side of the heart through the main artery, called the aorta, to lesser arteries and veins. This blood is rich in oxygen. In the tiny capillary veins of our body tissues, the blood feeds the cells with nutrients and oxygen and receives carbon dioxide. Now oxygen-poor, it returns to the right side of the heart, which contracts to pump it through the lungs. After receiving new oxygen and eliminating carbon dioxide, the blood returns again to the left side of the heart.

LESSON 2

Thinking: Summarizing (page 480) Read the paragraph below. Write a two-sentence summary of it.

Liquids expand when they are heated. To make a thermometer, a liquid that expands easily, such as mercury or alcohol, is sealed in a tube with a bulb at the bottom. When the thermometer is warmed, the liquid inside expands and moves up the tube, where it can be measured to show temperature.

LESSON 3

Writing a Research Report (page 482) Imagine that you are an undersea explorer and that you have just made an exciting discovery. Do some research on the topic. Then write a short research report.

LESSON 4

Speaking and Listening: Giving an Oral Report (page 490) In a paragraph, summarize the guidelines for giving an effective oral report. You may also list the listening guidelines for an oral report.

LESSON 5

Writer's Resources: The Encyclopedia (page 492) Choose a topic that interests you. Find information about your topic in an encyclopedia. Write a brief summary of the information you find.

THEME PROJECT ✏️ TECHNOLOGY FAIR

You have just written a research report that used facts to explain and explore a topic.

Exploration is important for scientists because it often also has many practical results that affect our everyday lives. The practical applications of scientific exploration are called *technology*. For example, scientific discoveries about recording sounds and pictures led to the invention of the videocassette recorder (VCR), which millions of people now use in their homes.

Look at the picture below. This picture shows a computer that will write spoken words on the screen. In a few years, handicapped people who cannot type may be able to "write" without having to use a keyboard. With your classmates, discuss other recent inventions that have improved the quality of our lives.

As a class project, hold a technology fair.

- Give oral reports on recent advances in technology.
- Create exhibits about new inventions.
- Use props, slides, films, and recordings.
- Invite other classes to attend your technology fair.

Writer's Reference

CONTENTS

GRAMMAR

Sentences

A **sentence** is a group of words that expresses a complete thought. The **complete subject** of a sentence includes all the words that tell whom or what the sentence is about. The **simple subject** is the main word or words in the complete subject.

> **The <u>fox</u>** runs quickly.   **The quick brown <u>fox</u>** runs quickly.

The **complete predicate** of a sentence includes all the words that tell what the subject does or is. The **simple predicate** is the main word or words in the complete predicate.

> The fox **was <u>running</u> away very quickly**.

A **compound subject** has two or more simple subjects with the same predicate. The simple subjects are joined by *and* or *or*.

> The **fox** and the **dog** were running fast.

A **compound predicate** is two or more simple predicates that have the same subject. The predicates are joined by *and* or *or*.

> The fox **runs, jumps,** and **hides**.

A **compound sentence** contains two or more simple sentences joined by *and, but,* or *or*.

> Holly washed the dishes. Bill swept the kitchen floor.
> Holly washed the dishes, and Bill swept the kitchen floor.

A **run-on sentence** joins together two or more sentences that should be written separately.

> The doorbell rang the guests were early and I answered the door.

Divide a run-on sentence into several sentences.

> The doorbell rang. The guests were early. I answered the door.

A **sentence fragment** is a group of words that does not express a complete thought. Add a subject or predicate to make a complete sentence.

> Many bright new flags. (fragment—no predicate)
> Snapped smartly in the breeze. (fragment—no subject)

Nouns

A **noun** is a word that names a person, place, thing, or idea. A **proper noun** names a particular person, place, thing, or idea.

> boy   city   bridge   happiness
> Fred   Oklahoma City   Tower Bridge

A **singular possessive noun** shows what one person or thing owns. Usually, **'s** is added to singular nouns to form a singular possessive.

> June**'s** sculpture   the dog**'s** tail

A **plural possessive noun** shows what more than one person or thing owns. If a plural noun ends in **s**, an **apostrophe** is added to form the plural possessive.

> boys**'** home   foxes**'** teeth

If a plural noun does not end in **s**, **'s** is added to form the plural possessive.

> women**'s** clothes   moose**'s** antlers

Verbs

An **action verb** is a word that expresses action. A verb may be one word, or the **main verb** may have a **helping verb** that helps show an action.

> want   have wanted   helps   has helped

A **linking verb** is a verb that links the subject of a sentence to a noun or adjective in the predicate.

> She **is** clever.

Present tense shows that action is happening now.

> We **spell** the words correctly. (present)

Past tense shows action that has already happened.

> We **spelled** the words correctly. (past)

Future tense shows action that will happen in the future.

We **will spell** the words correctly. (future)

> You must memorize the **irregular verb** forms. Here are some examples of irregular verbs.
>
> | Verb | Past | Past Participle |
> |------|------|-----------------|
> | be | was | been |
> | bring | brought | brought |
> | choose | chose | chosen |
> | come | came | come |
> | give | gave | given |
> | know | knew | known |
> | ring | rang | rung |

Pronouns

A **pronoun** is a word that takes the place of one or more nouns and the words that go with the nouns.

A **subject pronoun** is used as the subject of a sentence. A subject pronoun can also be used after forms of the linking verb **be**.

Subject pronouns: I, you, he, she, it, we, they

An **object pronoun** is used as the object of a verb or as the object of a preposition.

Object pronouns: me, you, him, her, it, us, them

A **possessive pronoun** is a pronoun that shows who or what owns something.

Possessive pronouns: my, your, his, her, its, our, their, mine, yours, hers, ours, theirs

An **indefinite pronoun** does not refer to a particular person, place, or thing.

Indefinite pronouns: all, any, anyone, each, every, few, nobody

An **antecedent** is a word or group of words to which a pronoun refers.

<u>Ken</u> called **his** mother from the school.

Adjectives

An **adjective** is a word that modifies, or describes, a noun or a pronoun.

> **famous** leader   **three** advisors   **that** opinion

The words **a**, **an**, and **the** are special adjectives called **articles**.

> **a** chicken   **an** egg   **the** golden egg

A **demonstrative adjective** points out something and describes nouns by answering the question **which one**? or **which ones**?

> **This** airport is closer to my destination than **that** one.

Adverbs

An **adverb** is a word that modifies a verb, an adjective, or another adverb. An adverb tells **how**, **where**, **when** or **to what extent**.

> We sang the chorus **very** loudly.　　　(how, modifies adverb)
> We practiced **everywhere**.　　　　　(where, modifies verb)
> Our concert is **tomorrow**.　　　　　(when, modifies verb)
> The choir is **extremely** large. (to what extent, modifies adjective)

Prepositions

A **preposition** is a word that relates a noun or pronoun to another word in a sentence.

> Carol noticed a rabbit **in** the garden.

A **prepositional phrase** is a group of words that begins with a preposition and ends with a noun or a pronoun.

> Carol noticed a rabbit **in the garden**.

The noun or pronoun that follows a preposition is called the **object of the preposition**.

> The rabbit hopped up the **path**.

When the **object of a preposition** is a pronoun, use an object pronoun.

> The rabbit hopped toward **her**.

Conjunctions

A **conjunction** is a word that joins words or groups of words.

Three common conjunctions are **and**, **or**, and **but**. **And** adds information.

Or gives a choice. **But** shows contrast. Some conjunctions tell **where, when, why, how,** or **under what conditions** an action takes place.

Interjections

An **interjection** is a word or group of words that expresses strong feeling.

> **Hooray!** Our team won the football game. **Great!**

MECHANICS

End Punctuation

Use **end punctuation** to end a sentence.

A **period** (.) ends a **statement** or a **command**.

A **question mark** (?) ends a **question**.

An **exclamation mark** (!) ends an **exclamation**.

Periods

Use a period to show the end of an abbreviation.

> Ms.   Sr.   Rev.   Ave.

Use a period after an initial.

> P. T. Barnum   Susan B. Anthony

Colons

Use a colon after the greeting in a business letter.

> Dear Madam: Dear Mr. Stein:

Commas

Use a comma between the name of a city and a state.

> Fort Wayne, Indiana   Austin, Texas

Use a comma between the day and the year in a date.

> November 11, 1918   April 1, 1988

Use commas to separate words in a series.

> Rainbows are red, yellow, green, blue, and purple.

Use a comma after the greeting in a friendly letter. Use a comma after the closing in all letters.

Dear Ronald,   Sincerely,

Use commas to set off introductory words, nouns in direct address, some appositives, and interrupters.

Well, Gettysburg was a famous battle.
This, Jane, is the site of the battle of Gettysburg.
At that time, the 1860s, there was a civil war.
In the battle, as you must know, many people were killed.

Use a comma before a direct quotation.

Tim asked, "Where are we going?"

Use commas to separate a direct quotation from the other words in a sentence.

"I always knew," she said, "that I would be a great writer."

Use a comma before **and**, **but**, or **or** when you form a compound sentence.

He wanted to leave, but he agreed to stay.

Apostrophes

Use an apostrophe (**'**) in contractions to show where letters are missing.

wouldn't   o'clock   you'll

Use an apostrophe with nouns to show possession.

doctor**'s** office   men**'s** shirts   ships**'** lanterns

Quotation Marks

Put quotation marks before and after a direct quotation. **Do not** use quotation marks unless you use the speaker's exact words.

"Next year I will go to summer camp," said Rose.
Rose said that next year she will go to summer camp.

Do not put quotation marks around explanatory words.

"Next year," said Rose, "I will go to summer camp."

Put quotation marks before and after the title of a short story, a song, a poem, or a chapter title.

"White Gardens"   "The Star-Spangled Banner"   "The Dance"

Italics (Underlining)

Use italics or underline the titles of books, newspapers, magazines, and movies.

<u>War and Peace</u>   <u>The Wall Street Journal</u>   <u>Mary Poppins</u>

Capitalization

Capitalize the names of specific persons, pets, places, or things.

Harry **S.** Truman   **F**reckles   **R**hode **I**sland   Lincoln **M**emorial

Capitalize initials.

Robert **E.** Lee   Ulysses **S.** Grant

Capitalize titles of respect when they are part of a specific name.

General Washington   **D**octor Albert Schweitzer

Always capitalize the first-person pronoun **I**.

Capitalize the first word and all important words in the title of a book, newspaper, song, poem, play, short story, movie, or television show.

Pride and Prejudice   "Casey at the **B**at"   "Who's the **B**oss?"

Capitalize family names if they refer to specific people.

I asked **F**ather for advice.   I asked my father for advice.

Capitalize the days of the week and the months of the year.

Monday   **F**riday   **J**une   **D**ecember

Capitalize names of holidays and religious days.

Fourth of **J**uly   Labor **D**ay   Christmas

Capitalize the names of streets and avenues.

Elm **S**treet   Fifth **A**venue

Capitalize names of specific clubs, organizations, and companies.

Sierra **C**lub   Internal **R**evenue Service   **X**erox Corporation

Capitalize the names of important historical events and documents.

Declaration of Independence   American **R**evolution

Capitalize proper adjectives.

French   American   African   Chinese

Capitalize the first word of a quotation. **Do not** capitalize an explanatory word unless it begins a sentence. **Do not** capitalize the second part of an interrupted quotation unless it begins a new sentence.

"**There is**," she said, "**no** food in this house."

Capitalize all words in the greeting of a letter, and the first word in a letter's closing.

My Dear Friend: **Your friend,**

Capitalize the first word of each main topic and subtopic in an outline.

I. **Types of letters**
    A. **Business letters**
    B. **Friendly letters**

Abbreviations

Capitalize and put a period after abbreviations of addresses.

    St.   Dr.   Blvd.

Use the **United States Postal Service** abbreviations for state names. Notice that each abbreviation consists of two capital letters. No period follows these abbreviations.

AL (Alabama)	LA (Louisiana)	OH (Ohio)
AK (Alaska)	ME (Maine)	OK (Oklahoma)
AZ (Arizona)	MD (Maryland)	OR (Oregon)
AR (Arkansas)	MA (Massachusetts)	PA (Pennsylvania)
CA (California)	MI (Michigan)	RI (Rhode Island)
CO (Colorado)	MN (Minnesota)	SC (South Carolina)
CT (Connecticut)	MS (Mississippi)	SD (South Dakota)
DE (Delaware)	MO (Missouri)	TN (Tennessee)
FL (Florida)	MT (Montana)	TX (Texas)
GA (Georgia)	NE (Nebraska)	UT (Utah)
HI (Hawaii)	NV (Nevada)	VT (Vermont)
ID (Idaho)	NH (New Hampshire)	VA (Virginia)
IL (Illinois)	NJ (New Jersey)	WA (Washington)
IN (Indiana)	NM (New Mexico)	WV (West Virginia)
IA (Iowa)	NY (New York)	WI (Wisconsin)
KS (Kansas)	NC (North Carolina)	WY (Wyoming)
KY (Kentucky)	ND (North Dakota)	

Capitalize and put a period after **abbreviations** used in titles of respect.

    Rep. Carl Jones   **Ms.** Nina Lee   **Prof.** Renalda Luiz

Capitalize and put a period after abbreviations of days and months.

Tues.   **Sat.**   **Feb.**   **Oct.**

Capitalize and put a period after abbreviations of company names.

Co. (company)   **Corp.** (corporation)   **Inc.** (incorporated)

Capitalize and put a period after all letters in some abbreviations.

A.M.   **B.C.**   **B.A.**

USAGE

Verbs

A verb must agree with the subject of a sentence. If a subject is singular, the verb must be singular. If a subject is plural, the verb must be plural.

The **woman drives**. (singular)   The **women drive**. (plural)

Pronouns

Use a **subject pronoun** as the subject of a sentence.

She noticed the dark clouds.

Use an **object pronoun** as the object of a verb or as the object of a preposition.

I saw **her** at the library. She spoke to **me**.

Use a **subject pronoun** in a compound subject. Use an **object pronoun** in a compound object.

Ed and **I** won. (subject)   The prize was given to Ed and **me**. (object)

When you use the pronouns **I** or **me** with another pronoun or a noun, always name yourself last.

He and **I** are friends. Tom waved to Dave and **me**.

A pronoun **must agree** with the noun to which it refers.

Tony found the **wallet** and returned **it** to the owner.
The **cats** sharpened **their** claws.

Adjectives

If an adjective compares **two nouns**, the adjective usually ends in **er**.

Tom was **older** than Anthony.

If an adjective compares **three or more** nouns, it usually ends in **est.**

The **largest** of the states is Texas.

Some adjectives use the word **more** or **most** to show comparison. These are usually adjectives of more than two syllables. Use **more** to compare two nouns.

These slippers are **more comfortable** than those shoes.

Use **most** to compare more than two nouns.

We avoided the **most difficult** trail up the mountain.

Do not combine **er** or **est** with the word **more** or **most**.

Some adjectives are **irregular**. That is, they do not form their comparison forms in the usual way. Here are some **irregular adjectives**.

Adjectives	Comparative	Superlative
good	better	best
bad	worse	worst
much	more	most
little	less	least

Adverbs

The **comparative form** of an adverb compares two actions. You usually add **er** or **more** to an adverb to make the comparative form.

Sue works **harder** than Al. Al writes **more carefully** than Sue does.

The **superlative form** of an adverb compares more than two actions. You usually add **est** or **most** to an adverb to make the superlative form.

Greta ran the **fastest** in the race. She is **most frequently** the winner.

Do not combine **er** or **est** with **more** or **most**.

Double Negatives

Negatives are words that mean **no**. Some examples of negatives are **no**, **never**, **none**, **not**, and **nothing**. Use only one negative in a sentence.

I did **not** get **anything**. (correct)   I did **not** get **nothing**. (incorrect)

Prepositions

Sometimes a prepositional phrase comes between the subject and the verb of a sentence. Make sure that the verb agrees with the subject of the sentence and not with the object of the preposition.

The **purpose** (of these experiments) **is** well known.
The **discoveries** (in this field) **are** important.

Troublesome Words

Some words or word pairs are easy to confuse. Look at the rules below.

good–well   bad–badly
Good and *bad* are adjectives. They describe nouns.

I wanted a **good** beginning, but I am off to a **bad** start.

Well and *badly* are adverbs. They tell about verbs.

Pam swims **well**.   Jack skates **badly**.

When *well* means "healthy," it is used as an adjective.

Maria does not feel **well** today.

lie–lay
Lie, an intransitive verb, means "to rest or to stretch out."

We used to **lie** in the shade of the old maple tree.

Lay, a transitive verb, means "to put or set something down."

Will you **lay** that book on the table?

borrow–lend
Borrow means "to take something for a short time."

He wanted to **borrow** my bike.

Lend means "to give for a short time."

I decided to **lend** him my bike.

whose-who's, its-it's, your-you're, their-they're
Do not confuse possessive pronouns and contractions. A possessive pronoun does not have an apostrophe.

Possessive pronouns: whose, its, your, their
Contractions: who's, it's, you're, they're

THESAURUS FOR WRITING

What Is a Thesaurus?

A **thesaurus** is a reference that can be very useful in your writing. It provides synonyms for many common words. A **synonym** is a word that has the same or almost the same meaning as another word.

The thesaurus can help you choose more interesting words and more exact words to use in your writing. For example, look at this sentence:

> Perry *ran* to the nearest fire alarm.

Ran is not an interesting word, and it says little about Perry. If you look up the word *run* in the thesaurus, you will find these synonyms: *dash, race, scurry, sprint*. Each of these words means "to run," but each one suggests a certain way of running. Replacing *ran* with one of these words would make the sentence more interesting and more exact.

Using the Thesaurus

The words in a thesaurus are listed in alphabetical order. If you want to find a word, look it up as you would in a dictionary. For example, if you looked up the word *proud*, you would find this entry:

> **proud** *adj.* having a sense of one's own worth, usually in a positive way. Hannah was *proud* to be in the Junior Olympics.
>   **conceited** having too high an opinion of oneself. A lot of kids think Nancy is *conceited* because she is smart.
>   **haughty** having or showing much pride in oneself. The king was too *haughty* to speak to his subjects.
>   **vain** overly concerned with or proud of oneself. Elsa is *vain* about her long hair.
>   **antonym**: humble

The word *proud* is called an **entry word.** The entry for *proud* gives the part of speech, a definition of the word, and an example sentence. Below that are indented synonyms. Each synonym is also defined and used in an example sentence. In some entries you will find words listed as "other synonyms" and **antonyms**, words with opposite meanings.

In some cases you will find cross-references. For example, if you look up the word *allow*, you will find this cross-reference: "See *let.*" This means that you should look up the word *let;* the word *allow* will be listed under *let.* You may also find a cross-reference within an entry.

A

agree *v.* to say "yes"; to have the same opinion; to be in harmony. He didn't *agree* with her.
assent to express acceptance (of an idea, proposal, etc.). Ms. Yee *assented* to the architect's plan.
concur to have the same opinion. Everyone in the group *concurred*.
consent to give permission or approval. I won't *consent* to such an action.

allow *See* let.

angry *adj.* feeling or showing anger. Cal's lie made Fay *angry*.
enraged filled with rage; angry beyond control. The *enraged* animal attacked the hunters.
furious extremely angry. Dad was *furious* that we got home so late.
resentful feeling bitter or indignant. Is he *resentful* about her success?

answer *v.* to give a spoken or written response. *Answer* the new question.
reply to say in response. Kevin *replied*, "Fine, thank you."
respond to give an answer. The mayor *responded* to my letter.
retort to reply, usually sharply, to criticism or a remark. "That's not true!" *retorted* Pamela.
antonyms: ask, inquire

ask *v.* to put a question to. *Ask* Kim if she wants to go with us.

inquire to seek information by asking questions. The woman *inquired* about job openings.
query to seek a formal answer to a question. The editor *queried* the author about her meaning.
question to try to get information (from someone). The police *questioned* the man.
antonyms: *See* answer.

awful *adj.* causing fear, dread, or awe. Ana gave an *awful* shriek.
dreadful causing great fear. I had a *dreadful* nightmare.
frightful causing fear. The dancers wore *frightful* masks.
terrible causing terror or awe. The tyrannosaurus was terrible.
Other synonyms: dire, shocking, ominous, horrifying

B

beautiful *adj.* full of beauty; having pleasing qualities. Look at that *beautiful* magnolia tree.
attractive appealing or pleasing, but not in an exceptional way. Tom is an *attractive* man.
gorgeous extremely beautiful or richly colored. She wore a *gorgeous* red silk dress.
lovely beautiful in a comforting way. He played a *lovely* tune.
antonyms: ugly, hideous, unattractive
Other synonyms: stunning, striking, appealing

big *adj.* of great size. This is a *big* room.
  enormous much greater than the usual size. I have an *enormous* amount of homework tonight.
  huge extremely big. The explosion tore a huge *hole* in the wall.
  large of great size; big. German shepherds are usually *large* dogs.
  antonyms: *See* little.
  Other synonyms: monstrous, massive, titanic

brave *adj.* willing to face danger; without fear. The *brave* prince captured the dragon.
  bold showing courage; fearless. A *bold* band of explorers set out across the wilderness.
  courageous having courage. His *courageous* act earned him a medal.
  daring willing to take risks. The firm hired a *daring* new president.
  antonyms: afraid, fearful

break *v.* to come apart; to separate into pieces. My glasses *broke*.
  crack to break without fully separating. The cup fell and *cracked*.
  fracture to break or split a bone. He *fractured* a rib.
  shatter to break suddenly into many pieces. The glass *shattered* when I dropped it.

bright *adj.* filled with light; shining. The kitchen is *bright*.
  brilliant shining or sparkling with light. The diamonds were *brilliant*.
  glistening shining with reflected light. Moonlight danced across the *glistening* water.
  antonyms: dark, dull

C

clean *adj.* without dirt or stain. We folded the *clean* clothes.
  immaculate perfectly clean. His fingernails are *immaculate*.
  pure free from contamination. The mountain air was fresh and *pure*.
  spotless extremely clean. "I want the room *spotless*," said Dad.
  antonyms: dirty, filthy, messy

cold *adj.* having a low temperature; lacking warmth or heat. It's *cold* in this room.
  chilly uncomfortably cool. It was a gray and *chilly* November day.
  icy very cold. He enjoyed a glass of *icy* milk with his lunch.
  antonyms: *See* hot.

cook *v.* to prepare food for eating, using heat. Can you *cook* dinner?
  bake to cook in an oven. The cake has to *bake* at 350 degrees.
  broil to cook by exposing to a flame or other source of intense heat. We *broiled* fish for dinner.
  roast to cook with very little moisture, in an oven or over an open fire. They *roasted* chestnuts.
  Other synonyms: sauté, boil

collect *v.* to gather or bring (things) together. He *collected* coins.
assemble to gather or bring together, especially people. Father *assembled* the family in the living room.
compile to collect and put together (information), as in a list or report. We *compiled* a list of customers.
gather to bring together in one place or group. "Let's *gather* the kids and go home," said Mr. Chan.

cry *v.* to shed tears. The little boy *cried* when he fell down.
sob to cry with short gasps. Lynn *sobbed* when her cat died.
weep to show grief, joy, or other strong emotions by crying. Safe at last, Tony *wept* with relief.
whine to make a high-pitched, mournful cry of pain or distress. The new puppy *whined* all night.
antonyms: *See* laugh.

D

do *v.* to carry out. We will *do* our skit right after the piano solo.
achieve to bring about an intended result. He *achieved* his goals.
execute to complete, often when told to do so; to put into effect. Who is going to *execute* the plan?
perform to carry out to completion. Ms. Lewis asked her aide to *perform* a difficult task.

dry *adj.* not wet; free of moisture. Our swimsuits were soon *dry*.
arid dry as a result of having little rainfall. Parts of the southwestern U.S. are quite *arid*.
parched dried out by heat. A cool drink relieved her *parched* throat.
antonyms: *See* wet.

E

easy *adj.* requiring little mental or physical effort; not difficult. The test questions were *easy*.
facile not hard to do or achieve; done easily and quickly. Sorting the office mail is a *facile* task.
simple not complicated. Checkers is a *simple* game.
antonyms: difficult, hard

F

far *adj.* a long way off; not near. Is the park too *far* to walk to?
distant extremely far. Her cousins lived in a *distant* city.
remote far away, in an out-of-the-way place. They live on a *remote* dirt road.
antonyms: near, close

fast *adj.* moving or done with speed. He is a *fast* reader.
quick done in a very short time. Mrs. Mann made a *quick* phone call.
rapid with great speed, often in a continuing way. We had to make some *rapid* decisions.

swift moving with great speed. Be careful of the *swift* current.
antonym: slow

funny *adj.* causing laughter. All the party guests wore *funny* hats.
amusing causing smiles of enjoyment or laughter. The clowns were *amusing*.
comical causing laughter through actions. The frolicking dog was a *comical* sight.
hilarious very funny and usually noisy. That Marx Brothers movie has some *hilarious* scenes.

G

get *v.* to go for and return with. Will you *get* me a drink of water?
acquire to come into possession of through effort. The collector *acquired* many famous paintings.
obtain to get as one's own, often with some difficulty. You must *obtain* your parents' permission.

give *v.* to turn over possession or control of; to make a present of. Please *give* this note to Amelia.
confer to give as an honor. The club *conferred* an award on Jaime.
contribute to give or supply in common with others. Will you *contribute* to the Animal Fund?
grant to give in response to a request. I will *grant* your wish.
present to give in a formal way, usually something of value. She

was *presented* with the award.
antonyms: See take.

good *adj.* above average in quality; not bad. She is a *good* speller.
excellent extremely good. Mr. Ramirez is an *excellent* teacher.
fair somewhat good; slightly better than average. That is a *fair* price.
fine of high quality; very good. Her dress was made of *fine* linen.
antonyms: bad, poor
See *also* great.

great *adj.* of unusual quality or ability. Beethoven was a *great* composer.
remarkable having unusual qualities. The weather was *remarkable* for the time of year.
superb A greater quality than most. He won a prize for his *superb* essay.
See *also* good.

H

happy *adj.* having, showing, or bringing pleasure. "I am *happy* to be here," the speaker began.
glad feeling or expressing joy or pleasure. Henry was *glad* to help.
joyful very happy; filled with *joy*. The wedding was *joyful*.
merry happy and cheerful. We always have a *merry* time together.
pleased satisfied or content. Are you *pleased* with your new haircut?
antonyms: See sad.

Other synonyms: delighted, contented, ecstatic

hard *adj.* not easy to do or deal with. That was a *hard* test.
difficult hard to do; requiring effort. The puzzle was *difficult*.
strenuous requiring great effort. Handball is a *strenuous* sport.
tough difficult to do, often in a physical sense. Digging the garden was *tough* work.
antonyms: *See* easy.

help *v.* to provide with support; be of service to. We *helped* Mr. Larsen with his yard work.
aid to give help to (someone in trouble). She *aids* the homeless.
assist to help, often in a cooperative way. The librarian *assisted* Margie with her research.

high *adj.* located or extending a great distance above the ground. The kite was very *high* in the sky.
lofty very high; of grand or inspiring height. Castle guards kept watch from four *lofty* towers.
tall having a height greater than average, but with a relatively narrow width. He is quite *tall*.
towering of great or imposing height. The canyon's walls were *towering*.
antonyms: low, short

hot *adj.* having a high temperature; having much heat. The sun is *hot*.

fiery as hot as fire; burning. Mickey had a *fiery* sunburn.
scalding hot enough to burn, often said of liquids. Don't touch that *scalding* water!
scorching intensely hot, enough to cause burning or drying. The *scorching* sun killed the grass.
torrid extremely hot, often said of weather. Light-colored clothes are the best for *torrid* regions.
antonyms: *See* cold.
Other synonyms: blistering, blazing

hurt *v.* to cause pain or damage. Be careful not to *hurt* the kitten.
harm to do damage to. Will driving on bad roads *harm* the car?
injure to cause physical damage. Gary *injured* his foot.

I

interesting *adj.* arousing or holding interest or attention. History is an *interesting* subject.
captivating capturing and holding the attention of by beauty or excellence. Dolley Madison is said to have been a *captivating* woman.
fascinating causing and holding interest of through a special quality or charm. Kerry has had some *fascinating* adventures.
inspiring having a rousing effect; arousing interest. Nate gave an *inspiring* speech.
antonyms: dull, boring

L

large *See* big.

laugh *v.* to make the sounds and facial movements that show amusement. Dale makes me *laugh*.
chortle to chuckle gleefully. "I fooled you!" Andy *chortled*.
chuckle to laugh softly, especially to oneself. Something she was reading made Liz *chuckle*.
giggle to laugh in a silly, high-pitched, or nervous way. Rudy *giggled* at the silly songs.
guffaw to laugh loudly. Theo *guffawed* at the joke.
antonyms: *See* cry.

let *v.* to give permission to. Will your parents *let* you sleep over?
allow to grant permission to or for, usually in relation to rules. No one is *allowed* to visit him.
permit to allow (a person) to do something. Please *permit* me to go.
antonyms: deny, refuse, forbid

like *v.* to take pleasure in (something); to feel affection for (someone). Do you *like* pizza?
admire to have affection and respect for (someone). Many people *admire* Senator Jeffries.
enjoy to take pleasure in (something). I *enjoy* dancing.
love to like (something) a lot; to feel great affection for (someone). She *loves* the sound of the ocean.
antonyms: dislike, hate

little *adj.* small in size; not big. The box held a *little* toy train.
small not large. Chihuahuas are very *small* dogs.
tiny extremely small. Those *tiny* insects are called mites.
wee very small. Look at the baby's *wee* fingernails!
antonyms: *See* big.
Other synonyms: puny, minute, minuscule, miniature

look *v.* to see with one's eyes. Let me *look* at the map with you.
glance to look quickly. Jim *glanced* at the headlines.
peer to look closely. I *peered* into the fog but saw nothing.
stare to look at for a long time with eyes wide open. People *stared* at the woman's strange outfit.
Other synonyms: behold, discern, inspect, scan
See also see.

loud *adj.* having a strong sound. Is this music too *loud* for you?
deafening loud enough to make one deaf. The rock music was *deafening*.
noisy full of sounds, often unpleasant. The old car was very *noisy*.
raucous loud and rowdy. The kids next door had a *raucous* party.
antonyms: *See* quiet.

M

mad *See* angry.

many *adj.* consisting of a large number. *Many* people like cats.
numerous a great many. The plant sprouted *numerous* new leaves.
plenty (of) enough, or more than enough, suggesting a large number. We had *plenty* of help getting the gym ready for the dance.
several more than a few but less than many. Greg ate *several* figs.
antonym: few

mean *adj.* lacking in kindness or understanding. I warned Ike not to be *mean* to that dog.
nasty resulting from hate. Linda said some *nasty* things about me.
selfish concerned only about oneself. Howie was *selfish* and kept the best piece for himself.
spiteful filled with ill feelings toward others. Why is Sharon being so *spiteful* today?
antonyms: *See* nice.

N

neat *adj.* clean and orderly. She likes to keep her room *neat*.
meticulous extremely concerned about details. Andy is *meticulous* about his appearance.
tidy neat and clean, often said of a place. The desk was *tidy*.
well-groomed carefully dressed and groomed. Curt manages to look *well-groomed* even in blue jeans.
antonyms: messy, untidy, sloppy

new *adj.* having just come into being, use, or possession. What color is your family's *new* car?
fresh new or seeming new and unaffected by time or use. Get me a head of *fresh* lettuce.
modern having to do with the present time; up-to-date. *Modern* homes depend on electricity.
recent referring to a time just before the present. The Chous are *recent* immigrants to this country.
antonyms: *See* old.

nice *adj.* agreeable or pleasing. The new teacher is *nice*.
agreeable to one's liking; pleasant. He was quite *agreeable*.
gentle mild and kindly in manner. The veterinarian was *gentle*.
kind gentle and friendly; good-hearted. An old woman with a *kindly* face answered the door.
pleasant agreeable; giving pleasure to. Ellie had a *pleasant* visit.
sweet having or marked by agreeable or pleasing qualities. Their son is a *sweet* little boy.
antonyms: *See* mean.

O

often *adv.* many times; again and again. I *often* forget my lunch.
frequently happening again and again. Gina *frequently* saw Tim.

regularly happening at fixed times. See your dentist *regularly*.
repeatedly over and over again. Mom told the kids *repeatedly* to wipe their feet.
antonyms: seldom, rarely

old *adj.* having lived or existed for a long time. The fossil was *old*.
aged having grown old. Her *aged* grandmother is still very active.
ancient of great age; very old; of times long past. The castle is *ancient*.
antonyms: young; See *also* new.
other synonyms: archaic, elder, venerable, senior, antique

P

plain *adj.* not distinguished from others in any way. Without her makeup, she was quite *plain*.
common average or standard; not distinguished. The dandelion is a *common* weed.
ordinary plain; average; everyday. It's just an *ordinary* paper bag.
antonyms: special; See *also* unusual.

proud *adj.* having a sense of one's own worth, usually in a positive way. Hannah was *proud* to be in the Junior Olympics.
conceited having too high an opinion of oneself. A lot of kids think Nancy is *conceited* because she is smart.

haughty having or showing much pride in oneself. The king was too *haughty* to speak to his subjects.
vain overly concerned with or proud of oneself. Elsa is *vain* about her long hair.
antonym: humble

Q

quiet *adj.* with little or no noise. We heard the cat's *quiet* footsteps.
calm free of excitement or strong feeling; quiet. When giving first aid, try to keep the victim *calm*.
peaceful calm; undisturbed. The house seemed very *peaceful* after the kids left for school.
silent completely quiet; without noise. The library was *silent*.
still without sound; silent. Be *still* so I can hear the news.
tranquil of a calm or peaceful nature. We spent a *tranquil* morning at the lake.
antonyms: loud, noisy

R

ready *adj.* fit for use or action. Are you *ready* to go?
alert watchful and ready. The ranger was *alert* for any sign of a fire.
prepared ready or fit for a particular purpose. Jacob was not *prepared* for Mr. Bauer's question.
set ready or prepared to do something. Is everyone *set* to go?

really *adv.* in fact. Are you *really* moving to Alaska?
actually in fact; really. The ape was *actually* a man in a costume.
indeed really; truly. This is *indeed* a surprise!
truly in fact; really. I am *truly* sorry that I doubted you.

rich *adj.* having great wealth. The duchess is a *rich* woman.
affluent wealthy; prosperous. These expensive stores are geared toward *affluent* customers.
opulent showing wealth or affluence. Their *opulent* mansion even had silver doorknobs.
wealthy having many material goods or riches. Mr. Harris's successful invention made him a *wealthy* man.
antonym: poor

right *adj.* free from error; true. Which is the *right* answer?
accurate without errors or mistakes. Are your sums *accurate*?
correct agreeing with fact or truth. That clock rarely shows the *correct* time.
exact very accurate; completely correct. The doctor needed to know my *exact* weight.
antonyms: wrong, mistaken

rude *adj.* not polite; ill-mannered. The salesperson was *rude* to me.
discourteous without good manners. It was *discourteous* of him

to start eating without us.
impolite not showing good manners. Dan was so *impolite* that Mrs. Fisk never invited him back.
uncouth lacking social polish or culture. Margie was surprised by her friend's *uncouth* behavior.
antonyms: polite, courteous

run *v.* to go quickly on foot. *Run* and tell Dad he has a phone call.
dash to go very fast; to run with sudden speed. He *dashed* to catch the bus.
race to run very fast; to run in competition. The dog *raced* across the field after the rabbit.
scurry to move hurriedly. People *scurried* out of the rain.
sprint to run at top speed for a short distance. Hank had to *sprint* to catch the train.

S

sad *adj.* feeling or showing unhappiness or sorrow. Beth was *sad* because her friend was sick.
downcast low in spirits; sad. Why does Bob look so *downcast*?
miserable extremely unhappy. The boy was *miserable* about missing the school play.
wretched very unhappy; deeply distressed. Ellen felt *wretched* when she was homesick.
antonyms: *See* happy.

same *adj.* being just like something else in kind, quantity, or degree.

We have the *same* middle name.

alike similar, showing a resemblance. Some twins do not look *alike* at all.

equal the same in size, amount, quality, or value. Mr. Hill cut the melon into ten *equal* pieces.

identical the same in every detail. My grandmother has a painting *identical* to that one.

antonym: different

say *v.* to make known or express in words. *Say* hello to Meg for me.

declare to make known publicly or formally. Ed Frost *declared* that he would run for office.

pronounce to say formally or officially that something is so. The chairperson *pronounced* the meeting over.

speak to express an idea, fact, or feeling. She will *speak* to the Maurers about Hal's behavior.

state to express or explain fully in words. *State* your full name.

talk to express ideas or information by means of speech; to speak. Can the baby *talk* yet? See *also* tell.

Other synonyms: proclaim, exclaim

scared *adj.* afraid; alarmed. She is *scared* of moving to a new city.

afraid feeling fear, often in a continuing way or for a long time. Many people are *afraid* of snakes.

fearful filled with fear. Cruel treatment made the dog *fearful*.

frightened scared suddenly, or for a short time. The *frightened* deer ran back into the woods.

terrified extremely scared; filled with terror. Lucy is *terrified* of thunderstorms.

Other synonyms: petrified, aghast, awestruck

see *v.* to receive information, impressions, etc. through use of the eyes. Did you *see* the parade?

observe to notice. The police are trained to *observe* details.

perceive to become aware of through sight or other senses. Do you *perceive* anything unusual?

view to see or look at, usually for some purpose. Tourists climb the tower to *view* the landscape. See *also* look.

shy *adj.* uncomfortable in the presence of others. We saw a *shy* little face peeking out at us.

bashful easily embarrassed; very shy. Ben is *bashful* and turns red when the teacher calls on him.

retiring avoiding society or publicity. The poet became more *retiring* as he got older.

timid showing a lack of courage; easily frightened. The *timid* boy spoke in a tiny voice.

antonym: bold

sick *adj.* having poor health. We took our *sick* dog to the vet.

ill not healthy; sick. The patient was very *ill*.

unwell not feeling well. Dan was *unwell* and asked to be excused.

antonyms: well, healthy

small *See* little.

smart *adj.* intelligent; bright; having learned a lot. Collies are supposed to be *smart* dogs.

clever mentally sharp; quick-witted. Liz is *clever* at games.

intelligent able to learn, understand, and reason. Humans are the most *intelligent* mammals.

shrewd clever or sharp in practical matters. The manager made a *shrewd* bargain.

wise able to know or judge what is right, good, or true; often describing a person with good sense rather than one who knows a lot of facts. The family often sought Aunt Mary's *wise* advice.

antonym: stupid

smile *v.* to have, show, or give a smile, in a happy or friendly way. *Smile* for the camera!

beam to smile joyfully. The girl *beamed* as she received her prize.

grin to smile broadly, with great happiness or amusement. Glen *grinned* at himself in the mirror.

smirk to smile in a silly or self-satisfied way. Fran *smirked* when Olga got into trouble.

antonyms: frown, scowl

strange *adj.* differing from the usual or the ordinary. Do you hear something *strange*?

odd not ordinary. What an *odd* thing to say!

peculiar strange or odd, but in an interesting or curious way. Listen to this *peculiar* story.

weird strange or odd, in a frightening or mysterious way. *Weird* noises came from the closet. *See also* unusual.

strong *adj.* having great strength or physical power. Oxen are *strong* animals.

brawny strong and muscular. Working in the garden all summer made Lee *brawny*.

muscular having well-developed muscles; strong. All the athletes were *muscular* and fit.

powerful having great strength, influence, or authority. Senator Cruz is a *powerful* leader.

antonym: weak

sure *adj.* firmly believing in something. Are you *sure* of the time?

certain free from doubt; very sure. Greg was *certain* he knew who the mysterious visitor was.

confident firmly trusting; sure of oneself or of another. Leon was *confident* he would get the job.

definite positive or certain, often in a factual way. The boys were *definite* about their plans.

antonyms: doubtful, unsure

surprised *adj.* feeling sudden wonder. I'm *surprised* to see you.
amazed overwhelmed with wonder or surprise. Isaac was *amazed* to learn he had slept for twelve hours.
astonished greatly surprised; shocked. Meg was *astonished* by the surprise party.
astounded greatly surprised; stunned. The crowd was *astounded* by the team's victory.
awestruck filled with awe or wonder. We were *awestruck* by the incredible fireworks display.

T

take *v.* to get into one's hands or possession; to obtain. Please *take* some of these apples.
grab to take roughly or rudely. Children must learn not to *grab*.
seize to take suddenly and by force. The police officer *seized* the gun.
snatch to take suddenly and quickly, often in secret. A man tried to *snatch* Myra's purse.
antonyms: *See* give.

talk *See* say.

tell *v.* to put or express in written or spoken words. *Tell* me your name.
announce to state or make known publicly. Kyle *announced* that he was quitting the club.

narrate to tell about events, especially in a story. Mrs. Owens *narrated* a fairy story.
relate to tell or report events or details. Cora *related* what happened at school that day.
See also say.

thin *adj.* not fat. She is not fat, but she is not *thin* either.
lean with little or no fat, but often strong. A greyhound is *lean*.
slim thin, in a good or healthy way. It is healthy to be *slim*.
antonyms: fat, plump, chubby

think *v.* to occupy one's thoughts (with). Be quiet so I can *think*.
believe to accept as true or real. Lora couldn't *believe* she had won.
consider to regard; to believe. I *consider* myself lucky.

U

unusual *adj.* not usual, common, or ordinary. We've had *unusual* weather for this time of year.
extraordinary very unusual; beyond the ordinary. No one should miss this *extraordinary* event.
rare seldom happening, seen, or found. Eclipses are *rare*.
uncommon rare or unusual. Snow is *uncommon* in April. *See also* strange.
antonyms: usual, common; *See also* plain.
Other synonyms: abnormal, queer, singular, irregular

upset *adj.* feeling uneasy; distressed. Her failure *upset* her.
anxious uneasy or fearful of what may happen. Are you *anxious* about tomorrow's test?
concerned troubled or worried. She is *concerned* about her health.
worried uneasy or troubled about something. I was late, and my parents were quite *worried*.
antonym: calm
Other synonyms: agitated, distraught

V

very *adv.* to a great extent. Alaska is a *very* large state.
considerably to a large or important degree. Her brother is *considerably* older than she is.
extremely greatly or intensely. The soup was *extremely* hot.
somewhat a little, to some extent. The book was *somewhat* boring.

W

walk *v.* to move or travel on foot. Harry and Lynn *walk* to school.
march to walk with regular steps. Soldiers *march* in parades.
stride to walk with long steps, usually with a purpose. The principal *strode* down the hall.
stroll to walk in a relaxed or leisurely manner. The couple *strolled* through the museum.
Other synonyms: ramble, saunter, hike, parade, tread, step, pace

want *v.* to have a desire or wish for. Frankie *wanted* a new bicycle.
crave to want badly, often in an uncontrollable way. I *crave* a good, crunchy apple.
desire to have a strong wish for. The child *desired* a good grade.
wish to have a longing or strong need for. We *wish* we could go, too.
yearn to feel a strong and deep desire. The sailors *yearned* for the sight of land.

wet *adj.* covered or soaked with water or other liquid. We got *wet* when it started to rain.
damp slightly wet. The laundry was still *damp*.
moist slightly wet; damp. Keep the plant's soil *moist*.
soggy damp and heavy. The bread was just a *soggy* lump of dough.
sopping extremely wet; dripping. The *sopping* towel dripped.
antonyms: See dry.
Other synonyms: drenched, dank

whole *adj.* made up of the entire amount, quantity, or number. The *whole* family came to dinner.
complete having all its parts. We bought a *complete* set of dishes.
entire whole; having all its parts. The *entire* team was sick.
total whole, full, or entire, often referring to numbers. The town's *total* population is 762.

THESAURUS

LETTER MODELS

A friendly letter, a thank-you letter, and an invitation all have the same parts. The **heading** contains the address of the letter writer and the date. The **greeting** greets the reader of the letter with *Dear* and his or her name. The greeting ends with a comma. The **body** of the letter contains your message. The **closing** is a friendly way of saying good-bye. It always ends with a comma. The **signature** is the signed name of the writer.

HEADING

> 167 English Road
> Cambridge, MA 02121
> July 18, 1991

GREETING

Dear Chuck,

BODY

Boy, do I miss you! I hope you're having a good summer. Say hi to your mom and dad from me. Write soon and let me know what is going on with you.

CLOSING

Your friend,

SIGNATURE

Jeff

HEADING

> 22 Court Street
> Stratford, CT 06491
> February 17, 1991

GREETING

Dear Alice,

BODY

Thank you for the beautiful gift. How did you know that I wanted a pink sweater? I tried it on this morning and I just love it.

CLOSING

Your friend,

SIGNATURE

Jessica

SPELLING STRATEGIES

In your writing, it is very important to spell every word correctly. Otherwise, the meaning of what you write may not be clear. Follow the steps below to help improve your spelling.

1. Learn the basic spelling rules.
2. Learn the correct spellings of some commonly misspelled words.
3. Learn to spell words by syllables.
4. Check your work carefully when you have finished writing.
5. Check your spelling in a dictionary whenever you are unsure.

Spelling Rules

Here are some rules to help you spell certain kinds of words correctly.

Words with *ie* and *ei*
Spell the word with *ie* when the sound is ē, except after *c*.

Sound is ē: chief, relief, field, niece
Except after *c*: receipt, ceiling, perceive

Spell the word with *ei* when the sound is not ē, especially if the sound is ā.

Sound is ā: neigh, freight, eighty, sleigh

There are some exceptions to this rule.

Exceptions: either, seize, weird, friend

Adding *s* and *es*
In most cases, *s* can be added to a noun without changing the spelling.

Examples: lock + s = locks   sign + s = signs

If the word ends in *ch*, *s*, *sh*, *x*, or *z*, add *es*.

Examples: beach/beaches   genius/geniuses
flash/flashes   six/sixes

Changing *f* to *v*
For most words ending in *f* or *fe*, change the *f* to *v* when adding *s* or *es*.

Examples: loaf/loaves   wharf/wharves

There are some exceptions to this rule.

Exceptions: roof/roofs   chief/chiefs

Words ending in *o*

For most words that end in *o* following a vowel, add *s* to form the plural.

Examples: rodeo + s = rodeos   studio + s = studios

For most words that end in *o* following a consonant, add *es* to form the plural.

Examples: zero + es = zeroes   potato + es = potatoes

For some words from the Italian language that refer to music, add *s:*

Examples: piano/pianos   solo/solos
cello/cellos   alto/altos

Irregular nouns

Some nouns become plural in irregular ways.

Examples: ox/oxen   child/children
mouse/mice   tooth/teeth
goose/geese

Some words stay the same when singular or plural.

Examples: deer/deer   series/series
fish/fish   sheep/sheep

Adding *es, ed, ing, er,* and *est*

If the word ends in a consonant and *y*, change the *y* to *i* before any ending that does not begin with *i*.

Examples: study/studies   carry/carried

However, for most words that end in a vowel and *y*, keep the *y* when adding an ending.

Examples: employ/employed   relay/relaying

In most cases, if a one-syllable word ends in one vowel and one consonant, double the consonant when adding an ending that begins with a vowel.

Examples: step/stepped   trim/trimmer
shop/shopping   thin/thinnest

For most two-syllable words ending in one vowel and one consonant, double the consonant only if the accent is on the second syllable.

Examples: refer/referred   begin/beginning

If the word ends in a silent *e*, drop the *e* when adding an ending that begins with a vowel.

Examples: safe/safer   write/writing
                tame/tamest   daze/dazed

Adding prefixes and suffixes

When a prefix is added to a word, the spelling of the base word stays the same.

Examples: pre + plan = preplan
                mis + behave = misbehave

When a suffix is added to a word, the spelling of the base word may change. If the word ends in silent *e*, drop the *e* when adding a suffix that begins with a vowel.

Examples: wiggle + y = wiggly
                machine + ist = machinist

However, for most words ending in silent *e*, keep the *e* when adding a suffix that begins with a consonant.

Example: hope + ful = hopeful

When adding the suffix **ness** or **ly**, the spelling of the base word usually does not change.

Example: fine + ness = fineness

However, if the word ends in *y* and has more than one syllable, change the *y* to *i*.

Examples: silly + ness = silliness
                crazy + ness = craziness

Homophones

Homophones are often misspelled. Knowing the meanings of homophones will help you choose and spell them correctly.

Examples: beat   beet   bough   bow
                groan   grown   pain   pane

Contractions and possessives

Use an apostrophe in a contraction.

Examples: he + is = he's   was + not = wasn't

Do not use an apostrophe with a possessive pronoun.

Examples: hers   ours   yours   its

OVERVIEW OF THE WRITING PROCESS

You have learned that writing is a process. When you write, you follow certain steps. Sometimes you follow the steps in a different order, but basically you proceed from the beginning to the end of the process.

Prewriting

- Decide on a **purpose** and **audience** for your writing.
- Choose a topic that would be suitable for your purpose and audience.
- Explore ideas by brainstorming, clustering, or listing.
- Narrow your topic if it is too broad to cover well.

Writing a First Draft

- Use your prewriting ideas to write your draft.
- Do not be too concerned about making errors. Get your ideas on paper.

Revising

- Read your draft. Then share it with someone else to get a response.
- Ask yourself these questions about your draft.

   What else will my audience want to know? What details can I add?
   How can I make my purpose clearer?
   How can I make my writing easier to understand?
   How can I improve the organization of my writing?

Proofreading

- Read your revised draft.
- Ask yourself these questions about your revised draft.

   Have I followed correct paragraph form?
   Have I used complete sentences?
   Have I used capitalization and punctuation correctly?
   Have I spelled all words correctly?

Publishing

- Make a clean copy of your revised and proofread draft.
- Share your writing with the audience for whom you wrote it.

STUDY STRATEGIES

Studying is an important part of learning. When you study, plan your time carefully. Decide how much time to spend on each assignment. Find a quiet, comfortable place to work. Keep study materials handy—paper, pens, and pencils, and reference works such as dictionaries.

The SQ3R Method

There are many different ways to study. One method, useful for reading a chapter or an article, is called "SQ3R." The name stands for the five steps you should follow.

1. **Survey** Survey or scan the whole chapter or article you are going to read to get a general idea of what it covers.
2. **Question** Prepare questions to help you understand the work. Use the title and any important headings to make up the questions.
3. **Read** Read the chapter or article. Look for answers to the questions you made up, and look for important points in what you read.
4. **Record** Note important points and the answers to the questions.
5. **Review** Look back over the article and the notes you have written.

The Proto Method

The PROTO Method can be used in studying all kinds of material.

1. **Preview** First, preview the material to identify the general idea. Look at the title of the selection. Look at the major headings.
2. **Read** Second, read the material. Look at the headings again before you read each part. Identify the most important points in each section. If you don't understand, look for clues in the headings and read the material again.
3. **Organize** After you have read the material once, figure out how you can organize the important points. Information may be organized by sequential order, classification, cause-effect, or comparison-contrast.
4. **Take Notes** Use your chosen method of organization to take notes on the important points. You may want to write down each major idea or title, and then write notes under each idea. Or you may want to use an outline, a time line, or a flow chart.
5. **Overview** Finally, read through your notes and the list of important ideas to form an overview or summary of what you have read.

Special Study Tips

Following Directions For many assignments, your teacher will give you directions before you begin. Pay close attention to the directions.

1. Identify the steps you should follow.
2. Ask questions about any steps that are unclear to you.
3. Collect the materials you will need for the assignment.
4. Follow the directions step by step.

Setting a Purpose Before you begin studying, identify the purpose of your work. For example, your goal might be to identify the causes of an event. Use the directions to help you identify the purpose for your study. Then keep to the purpose as you work.

Outlining An outline helps you decide what is most important and helps you put each note in the right place. You can organize an outline by sequential order, classification, cause-effect, or comparison-contrast.

Mapping Mapping is similar to outlining, but it uses a diagram or picture to organize ideas. You may choose to outline information by using a map, a time line (listing things in the order in which they happened), a diagram (a picture of how all the parts work together), or a flow chart (a diagram showing how each event leads to the next one).

Using Graphic Aids Many selections include graphic aids, such as maps, charts, tables, graphs, and diagrams. In many cases, the graphic aid provides a summary of important points in the selection. Look at the graphic aid carefully to figure out what it means, how the information relates to the selection, and why it is important.

Memorizing When you study something, you will want to remember it. Here are some ways to help you memorize important information.

1. **Speak and write**. First, say it out loud. Then write it down. Hearing and seeing what you want to remember will help you memorize it.
2. **Classify ideas**. Think of a way to classify information you want to remember. For example, you might list important events in chronological order. You might list important facts in alphabetical order or in groups related to categories such as causes and effects.
3. **Invent memory joggers**. A "memory jogger" might be a word or a funny sentence that helps you remember things. For example, in

music there are five lines on a staff, and each one represents a different note. In order, the five notes are E, G, B, D, and F. Many people learning to read music memorize these with the sentence, *"Every Good Boy Does Fine."* The first letter of each word is the note.

4. **Repeat** things as many times as you can. Repeating information often will help you remember it.

Taking Tests

Taking tests is an important part of schoolwork. You can use many of the study skills you have learned to make test taking easier.

1. **Preview the test**. Look through the test quickly to see what it covers and how long it is.

2. **Plan your time**. Your teacher will tell you how much time you have to finish the test. Decide how much time to spend on each part of the test. Some parts may take longer than others. Reading stories, for example, will usually take longer than answering vocabulary questions. Keep track of the time as you work.

3. **Follow directions**. Listen to any directions your teacher gives you. Then read the test directions carefully before you begin the test. As you work through the test, read any directions you see at the beginning of each new section.

4. **Read questions carefully**. Figure out exactly what the question means. Use key words to figure out what kind of answer is required. (Key words might include "why," "when," "who," "because," "after," and "what.") Then decide on your answer.

5. **Do easy questions first**. Work through the test and finish every question for which you know the answer. Leave the difficult questions for last. Then go back and work on each difficult question.

6. **Mark your answers carefully**. If you are taking a multiple-choice test, fill in only one bubble for each question and fill it in completely. If you are writing your answers, write each one clearly and neatly so the teacher can read it.

7. **Check your work**. When you have answered all the questions, use the time you have left to go back and check your work. Make sure you have answered each question.

SENTENCE STRUCTURE: Diagraming Guide

A sentence diagram is a set of lines that shows how the words in a sentence go together. You will begin by diagraming the most important words in a sentence. As you study these lessons, you will learn how to diagram the other words. Finally, you will be able to diagram every word in a sentence.

Simple Subjects and Simple Predicates (pp. 6-7)

The simple subject and simple predicate are written on a horizontal line called a **base line**. The simple subject and simple predicate are separated by a vertical line that cuts through the base line.

Find the simple subject and simple predicate in this sentence.

The class is planning a field trip.

Study this diagram. See how the simple subject and simple predicate are diagramed.

| class | is planning |

In imperative sentences, the subject does not appear. The subject *you* is understood. It always appears in parentheses when you diagram an imperative sentence.

Raise your hand.

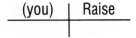

Practice Diagram only the simple subjects and simple predicates in these sentences.

1. Students are asking many questions.
2. Museums are on the list.
3. Some students want a picnic.
4. The teacher has voted for the zoo.
5. Vote for the picnic.

Compound Subjects and Compound Predicates (pp. 10-11)

Each part of a compound subject or predicate is written on a separate line. The conjunction *or*, *and*, or *but* is written on a dotted line connecting the separate parts.

Find the parts of the compound subject and predicate in this sentence.

Lewis and Clark walked and canoed across America.

See how the compound subject and compound predicate are diagramed.

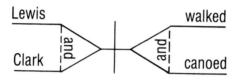

There may be more than two words in a compound subject or a compound predicate.

Soldiers, trappers, and guides climbed and explored.

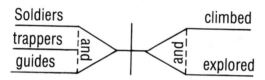

Practice Diagram only the subjects and predicates in these sentences. Subjects and predicates may be compound.

1. Sacajawea and her husband guided the explorers.
2. She knew English and spoke Indian languages.
3. She and her husband hunted and trapped wild game.
4. The woman thought quickly and acted wisely.
5. Lewis and Clark liked and trusted Sacajawea.

Predicate Nouns (pp. 150-151)

A predicate noun is written on the base line after the verb. A slanting line separates the predicate noun from the verb.

Read this sentence and find the predicate noun.

My brother is a collector.

See how a predicate noun is diagramed.

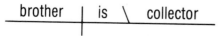

Some sentences have more than one predicate noun.

His favorites are stamps and seashells.

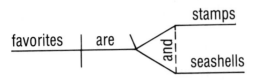

Practice Diagram only the subjects, the verbs, and the predicate nouns in these sentences.

1. The conch is a large pink shell.
2. Cowries are also common shells.
3. His best shells are a triton and a sundial.
4. Our vacations are shell expeditions.
5. I become an explorer and a collector.
6. This common shell is a mussel.
7. A razor clam is a long narrow shell.

Predicate Adjectives (pp. 150-151)

A predicate adjective is written the same way as a predicate noun in a diagram. It is placed on the base line. A slanted line separates it from the verb.

Predicate nouns and predicate adjectives follow common linking verbs such as *seem*, *taste*, *feel*, *smell*, *become*, *appear*, and forms of *be*.

Find the predicate adjective in this sentence.

Some animals seem very strange.

See how a predicate adjective is diagramed.

animals | seem \ strange

Some sentences have a compound predicate adjective.

A platypus is rare and unusual.

See how the compound predicate adjective is diagramed. Notice the word *and* on the dotted line.

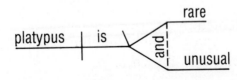

Practice Diagram the subjects, the verbs, and the predicate adjectives in these sentences.

1. Platypus eggs are small and white.
2. Its beak appears artificial.
3. Its toes seem sharp and tiny.
4. The female is small and delicate.
5. The animal seems harmless.

Direct Objects (pp. 146-147)

A direct object appears on the base line after the verb. A vertical line separates the verb from the direct object. This line does not go beneath the base line.

Find the direct object in this sentence.

The students chose library books.

Now look at the diagram of this sentence.

students	chose	books

Some sentences have a compound direct object.

Some authors write books and poems.

See how a compound direct object is diagramed.

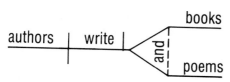

Practice Diagram the subjects, the verbs, and the direct objects in these sentences.

1. I wanted an adventure story.
2. Sandy collected stories and poems by Anna Soong.
3. My friend selected a long, complicated fable.
4. Lin prefers legends.
5. Luis and Ana wanted plays or film scripts.

Indirect Objects (pp. 146-147)

An indirect object is written on a horizontal line below the base line. A slanting line connects the indirect object to the verb.

Find the indirect object in this sentence.

The teacher gave us a surprise.

See how this sentence is diagramed.

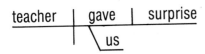

Practice Diagram the subjects, verbs, direct objects, and indirect objects.

1. She handed the students a quiz.
2. She offered us blank paper.
3. She told us the joke.
4. She showed us April Fools' Day on the calendar.

Adjectives (pp. 298-301)

An adjective is diagramed by placing it on a slanted line under the word it modifies. Don't forget that *a*, *an*, and *the* are special adjectives.

Find all the adjectives in this sentence.

Many countries have beautiful flags.

See how adjectives are diagramed.

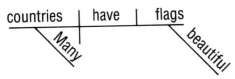

Adjectives in a series are connected by the word *and* on a dotted line.

The United States uses a red, white, and blue flag.

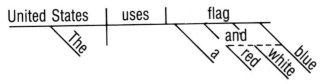

Practice Diagram all the words in these sentences.

1. The Danish flag is the oldest banner.
2. The American flag is red, white, and blue.
3. The famous old design uses thirteen stripes.
4. The modern British flag combines three old flags.
5. One old, beautiful, and famous design uses a yellow dragon.

Adverbs (pp. 362-365)

An adverb may modify a verb, an adjective, or another adverb. It is diagramed on a slanted line below a verb. It is diagramed on a parallel line beside an adjective or an adverb. Another line connects the two parallel lines.

Find the adverbs and the words they modify in this sentence.

A very tired student works quite slowly and quietly.

Look at this sentence diagram. Notice how the word *and* is written on the dotted line.

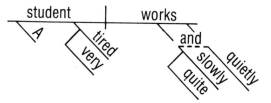

Adverbs may be used between a main verb and a helping verb. Sometimes adverbs may not appear beside the words they modify.

Find the adverbs in this sentence.

She reviews the notes often.

Practice Diagram all the words in these sentences.

1. Tests sometimes contain difficult questions.
2. Frequently you guess the correct answer.
3. Other questions are very hard.
4. Very often, word clues tell you an answer.
5. I can never forget a very important answer.

Prepositional Phrases (pp. 424-429)

Prepositional phrases modify other words in a sentence. In a sentence diagram, write the preposition on a slanted line under the word it modifies. Write the object of the preposition on a line parallel to the base line. Write modifiers of the object as you would any other modifiers.

Find the two prepositional phrases in this sentence.

My cousin performed in a concert for young people.

See how the second prepositional phrase is diagramed.

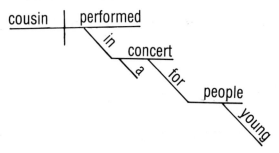

Practice Diagram every word in these sentences.

1. Music by many composers was played at the concert.
2. A choir of students sang a folk song from France.
3. The song at the end brought tears to many eyes.

Compound Sentences (pp. 12-15)

Each part of a compound sentence is diagramed as a separate sentence. The **conjunction**, usually or, and, or but, is written on a horizontal line between the two parts. Dotted lines connect the conjunction to the verbs in each part of the compound sentence.

Read this compound sentence.

I may play baseball, or I may go to a movie.

See how the compound sentence is diagramed.

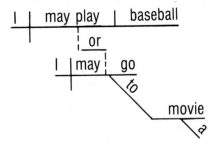

Practice Diagram each word in these compound sentences.

1. I like the movies, but I prefer a good book.
2. Read this book, and people will listen to you.
3. He gave me this book, but I gave him nothing.

G L O S S A R Y

OF WRITING, GRAMMAR, AND LITERARY TERMS

WRITING TERMS

audience	the reader or readers for whom a composition is written
chronological order	the arrangement of events in the order in which they happen in time
detail sentences	sentences that tell more about the main idea of a paragraph
first draft	the first version of a composition, in which the writer gets his or her basic ideas down on paper
main-idea sentence	the sentence that states the overall point of a paragraph
overall impression	the general idea or feeling expressed in a description
personal narrative	a piece of writing in which the writer tells about something that has happened in his or her life
prewriting	the stage in the writing process in which the writer chooses a topic, explores ideas, gathers information, and organizes his or her material before writing a first draft
prewriting strategies	particular ways of gathering, exploring, planning, and organizing ideas before writing the first draft of a composition

- **brainstorming**   a way to select a writing topic by listing ideas

> 1. What games can I play on my computer?
>
> 2. What free information is there about computers?
>
> 3. Can I learn to program a computer?
>
> 4. A funny thing happened with my computer.
>
> 5. What new programs can help with my schoolwork?
>
> 6. How does a computer work?
>
> 7. Can I get a catalog of computer programs?

- **charting**   a way to gather ideas under different headings—especially useful in comparing and contrasting

Comparision Chart		
Points to compare and contrast	Jogging	Running
Purpose	relaxing exercise	competitive recreation
Benefits	physical fitness	physical fitness
Equipment	running shoes; shorts; T-shirt	running shoes; shorts; T-shirt

- **clustering**   a way to explore ideas by gathering details related to the writing topic

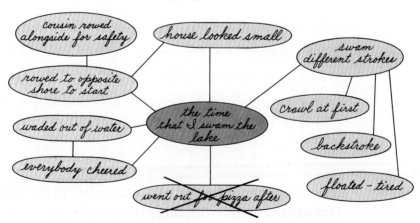

- **freewriting**   a way to generate ideas by simply writing continuously for a specified time, without stopping to correct errors

> *New shopping center is a bad idea. The town board should reject the application. What about traffic on the highway? More accidents from the traffic? Shopping center might be ugly. And I think parkland is more important. Board meeting is next Thursday night.*

- **outline**   a way to organize topic-related ideas in the order in which they will be discussed—especially useful in drafting a research report

> **How Airplanes Fly**
> I. History of flight
>   A. The Wright brothers
>   B. The first true flight
>   C. Balloons and blimps
> II. Three elements of flight
>   A. Power
>   B. Lift
>   1. Shape of wings
>   2. Movement of air over wings
>   C. Control
> III. Methods of control
>   A. Parts of the plane
>   B. Starting, stopping, and steering

proofread   to correct errors in punctuation, capitalization, spelling, and grammar in a writing draft

publish   to share a composition with an audience

purpose   the writer's reason for writing a composition—for example, to explain, to entertain, or to persuade

revise   to improve the first draft of a composition by adding or taking out information, combining and reordering sentences, or changing word choice according to the purpose and audience

sensory details   in a description, the details that appeal to the reader's five senses—sight, hearing, touch, taste, and smell

supporting details	facts, examples, or sensory details that give more information about the main idea of a paragraph
time order	the arrangement of events in a composition according to when they occur in time
topic sentence	another name for the **main-idea sentence**
transition words	words or phrases that may help writers to compare and contrast, such as *on one hand* and *on the other hand;* also, words that link sentences in a narrative, such as *finally* and *in the meantime*
writing conference	a meeting in which a writer asks and answers questions about his or her writing with the purpose of improving it
writing process	the steps for writing a composition, including prewriting, writing a first draft, revising, proofreading, and publishing

GRAMMAR TERMS

action verb	a word that expresses action Minnows *swim* in fresh water.
adjective	a word that modifies, or describes, a noun or pronoun The Pacific is the *largest* ocean in the world.
adjective phrase	a prepositional phrase that modifies, or describes, a noun or a pronoun The study *of insects* is called entomology.
adverb	a word that modifies a verb, an adjective, or another adverb Did you read the newspaper *today?*
adverb phrase	a prepositional phrase that modifies, or tells more about, a verb, an adjective, or an adverb Robin swam *to the raft.*

antecedent	a word or group of words to which a pronoun refers Charles Babbage designed a *calculating machine* in the nineteenth century, but *it* was not widely used.
appositive	a word or group of words that follows and identifies a noun The Amazon, *a river in South America,* is approximately 4,000 miles long.
article	the special adjective *a, an,* or *the* *The* zipper was invented in 1891.
common noun	a noun that names any person, place, thing, or idea When will the *speaker* arrive?
complete predicate	all the words that tell what the subject of a sentence does or is The workers *measured the perimeter of the garden.*
complete subject	all the words that tell whom or what a sentence is about *A monarch butterfly* can fly twenty miles per hour.
compound sentence	a sentence that contains two sentences joined by a comma and the word *and, or,* or *but* *The last dinosaur died long ago, but scientists are still fascinated by these creatures.*
conjunction	a word that joins other words or groups of words in a sentence Will you read the fiction *or* the nonfiction book?
demonstrative adjective	an adjective that points out something or describes a noun by answering the question *which one?* or *which ones?* *That* redwood is the oldest tree in the forest.
direct object	a noun or pronoun that receives the action of a verb Galileo studied the *stars.*
helping verb	a verb that helps the main verb to show an action I *have* looked for the book.

indefinite pronoun a pronoun that does not refer to a particular person, place, or thing
>   *Everyone* likes the rebuilt city park.

indirect object a noun or pronoun that answers the question *to whom? for whom? to what?* or *for what?* after an action verb
>   The porpoise brought *Maria* the ball.

interjection a word or group of words that expresses strong feeling
>   *Oh!* We must finish the race!

irregular verb a verb that does not form the past tense by adding *d* or *ed*
>   Jules Verne *wrote* many science fiction stories.

linking verb a verb that connects the subject of a sentence to a noun or an adjective in the predicate
>   Venus *is* the planet nearest to Earth.

noun a word that names a person, place, thing, or idea
>   Where is the *engineer* going?

object of a preposition the noun or pronoun that follows the preposition in a prepositional phrase
>   There are eight national parks in *Alaska*.

object pronoun a pronoun that is used as the object of an action verb or as the object of a preposition
>   The whole crowd watched *her*.

possessive noun a noun that shows ownership
>   Are you *John's* sister?

possessive pronoun a pronoun that shows who or what owns something
>   *Our* nation has fifty states.

predicate adjective an adjective that follows a linking verb and describes the subject
>   The map seemed *clear*.

predicate noun a noun that follows a linking verb and renames or identifies the subject
>   The present was a *sweater*.

preposition	a word that relates a noun or pronoun to another word in a sentence Columbus left Spain *in* a wooden ship.
prepositional phrase	a group of words that begins with a preposition and ends with a noun or pronoun They built a birdhouse *near the gate.*
pronoun	a word that takes the place of one or more nouns and the words that go with the nouns *He* read a book by Charles Dickens.
proper adjective	an adjective formed from a proper noun Claire brought *French* bread to the party.
proper noun	a noun that names a particular person, place, thing, or idea The *Washington Monument* is taller than the *Statue of Liberty.*
run-on sentence	two or more sentences that have been joined together incorrectly *The first flight by the Wright brothers was in 1903 it occurred in Kitty Hawk, North Carolina.*
sentence	a group of words that expresses a complete thought *Marigolds planted around a garden will help discourage insects.*
sentence fragment	a group of words that does not express a complete thought *The old mansion at the top of the hill.*
simple predicate	the main word or words in the complete predicate of a sentence A zebra *lives* for approximately fifteen years.
simple subject	the main word or words in the complete subject of a sentence The old and valuable *violin* was handled carefully.
subject pronoun	a pronoun that is used as the subject of a sentence *We* choose the freshest vegetables.

LITERARY TERMS

alliteration	the repetition of the same first letter or initial sound in a series of words—for example, "Sally sings simple songs."
characters	the people in a story or play
concrete poem	a poem whose shape suggests the subject of the poem
dialogue	the conversations that people have in a story or a play
fiction	written works such as novels and short stories that tell about imaginary characters and events
free verse	a poem that sounds like ordinary speech and has no regular rhythm or rhyme
haiku	a poem that has three lines and usually seventeen syllables, and that frequently describes something in nature
metaphor	a figure of speech in which a comparison is made without using the word *like* or *as*—for example, "The field was a green blanket."
meter	the regular pattern of beats in a poem
nonfiction	written works that deal with real situations, people, or events, such as biographies
personification	a description in which human qualities are given to something that is not human—for example, "The leaves danced across the ground."
plot	the sequence of events in a story
setting	the time and place in which the events of a story happen
simile	a figure of speech in which a comparison is made using the word *like* or *as*—for example, "The kite soars like a bird."

INDEX

Business letters
(continued)
    problem solving with,
        278–279
    proofreading, 285–286
    publishing, 287
    punctuation in, 286
    purpose of, 274, 276
    putting together, 276–277
    revising, 283–284
    topics for, 280
but
    in compound sentences,
        12–13, 20–21, 438–439
    as conjunction, 432–433

C

Call number, 218–219
Capitalization
    of abbreviations, 240–241
    of proper adjectives,
        306–307, 322, 460
    of proper nouns, 74–75,
        82–83, 94, 98
    of sentences, 16–17, 34, 102
Captions, writing, 307
Card catalog, 218–219
Characters, story, 117
Charting, 122, 206, 337, 343
Charts, 134, 241
Chronological order,
    120–121
Classifying, 340–341
Cleary, Beverly ("Dear
    Mr. Henshaw"), 266–270
Climax, of story, 117
Clipped words, 86–87
Closing, of letter, 275
Colon, 286
Columns, in tables, 352
Combining sentences
    with adjectives and
        possessive nouns,
        310–311
    with adverb clauses,
        367–377
    with conjunctions,
        434–435
    with pronouns, 244–245
Comma
    in appositive, 80–81, 103

in compound sentences,
    12–13, 20–21, 186,
    438–439, 456
with conjunction,
    432–433
with interjection,
    436–437
in letters, 286
rules about, 212, 286
in series, 164–165,
    186, 262
to set off words,
    372–373, 388, 412, 462
Common nouns, 74–75, 94,
    103, 261
Comparative forms,
    302–305, 318–321,
    366–367, 384, 460
**Comparing and
    contrasting,** 204–205
**Comparison and contrast
    paragraphs**
    audience for, 200, 206
    draft of, 208
    order of details in, 201
    prewriting, 206–207
    proofreading, 211–212
    publishing, 213
    purpose of, 200, 206
    putting together, 202–203
    revising, 209–210
    topic sentence for, 200,
        202
    topics for, 206
    transition words in, 201
Comparison, writing, 217,
    235, 305, 366–367
Complete predicates, 4–5,
    27, 102, 458
Complete subjects, 4–5, 27,
    102, 260, 458
Compound objects,
    232–233
Compound predicates,
    10–11, 30, 260,
    432–433, 453
Compound sentences
    commas in, 31, 438–439
    conjunctions in, 31,
        432–435, 453–454
    creating, 12–13, 20–21

Compound subjects, 10–11,
    30, 232–233, 432–433,
    453
Compound words, 86–87, 101
Concluding sentences, 401
Conjunctions, 432–435,
    453–454, 463
Connotations, 166–167, 187, 262
Contents, 416
Context clues, 18–19, 35, 103
Contractions, 234–237
Copyright page, 416
Curriculum Connections
    geography, 356–357
    health, 220–221
    journalism, 418–419
    literature, 136–137
    mathematics, 292–293
    science, 494–495
    social studies, 68–69

D

Days of the week, 82–83
Declarative sentences,
    2–3, 8, 26, 260, 458
Demonstratives, 300–301,
    317, 460
Descriptions. *See also*
    Descriptive paragraphs
    audience for, 336
    classifying for, 340–341
    draft of, 344
    prewriting, 342–343
    proofreading, 347–348
    publishing, 349
    purpose of, 336
    putting together, 338–339
    revising, 345–346
    sensory details for, 337
    topics for, 336, 342
    writing, 355
**Descriptive paragraphs,
    writing,** 309, 425.
    See also Descriptions
Details
    narrative, 117
    order of, 201, 337
    sensory, 53, 337
    in sentences, 48–49
    supporting, 49

Detail sentences, 48–49
Diagraming, 532–538
Dialogue
    in story, 117
    writing, 231, 437
Diary entries, writing,
    5, 61, 229
Diction, 166–167
Dictionary
    definitions in, 19
    in library, 216
    use of, 64–65
Directions. *See also*
    Instructions
    explaining, 223
    writing, 143, 151
Direct objects, 146–149,
    176, 261, 459
Discussion, class, 62–63
Double negatives, 370–371,
    387, 462
Drafts
    of business letters, 282
    of comparison and
        contrast paragraphs, 208
    of descriptions, 344
    of personal narratives, 56
    of persuasive writing, 408
    of research reports, 484
    of stories, 124

E

either. . .or, 162–163
Encyclopedia, 216,
    492–493
End marks, 2–3, 16–17, 102
    See also Punctuation
Enrichment, 24–25, 92,
    172, 248, 314, 380, 446
Entry words, 64–65
Exclamation mark
    with interjections, 436–437
    in sentences, 2–3, 16–17, 60
Exclamatory sentences,
    2–3, 26, 260, 458

F

Facts
    and opinions, 401, 404–405
    for research reports, 476–477

Fiction in the library,
    216–217
Folk tales, writing, 77
Fragments, sentence, 14–15,
    32–33, 60
Freewriting, 406–407
Future tense, 152–153, 179,
    262

G

Geography connection,
    356–357
good, 368–369
Grammar, Mechanics, and
    Usage Handbook,
    499–509
Grammar and Writing
    Connections. *See also*
    Grammar Connections
    combining sentences
        with adjectives and
        possessive nouns,
        310–311
        with adverb clauses,
        376–377
        into compound sentences,
        20–21
        with pronouns, 244–245
    revising sentences
        with prepositional
        phrases, 442–443
        and tenses, 168–169
        with words in a series,
        88–89
Grammar Connections.
    See also Grammar and
    Writing Connections
    adjectives, 348, 412
    adverbs, 412
    possessive nouns, 128
    possessive pronouns, 286
    prepositional phrases,
        488
    run-on sentences, 60
    sentence fragments, 60
    subject-verb agreement,
        212
Graphs, 352–353
Greeting, of letter, 274
Guide words, 64–65

H

Heading, of letter, 274
Health connection, 220–221
Helping verbs, 144–145,
    154–155, 175, 180–181, 261
here, 8–9
Holidays, 82–83
Homographs, 242–243,
    259, 263
Homophones, 242–243,
    259, 263
How-to paragraphs, 153

I

I, 232–233
Imperative sentences,
    2–3, 8–9, 26, 260, 458
Indefinite pronouns,
    238–239, 257
Index
    in almanac, 134–135
    in atlas, 132–133
    in books, 417
    in thesaurus, 66
Indirect objects, 146–147,
    176, 261, 459
Initials, 82–83
Inside address, of letter, 274
Instructions, giving,
    214–215. *See also*
    Directions
Interjections, 436–437, 455,
    463
Interrogative sentences,
    2–3, 8–9, 26, 260, 458
Interrupters, 372–373, 388
Interviews
    conducting, 288–289
    question-and-answer
        formats for, 147, 237, 373
    writing questions for, 11
Intransitive verbs,
    148–149, 177
Introductory words,
    372–373, 388
Irregular nouns, 76–77, 95
Irregular verbs, 156–159,
    181–182, 262, 459
Italics, 488

proper, 74–75, 82–83, 94, 98, 103, 261
singular, 76–77, 95, 458

O

Object pronouns, 226–227, 230–231, 253
Objects
compound, 232–233
direct, 146–149, 176, 261, 459
indirect, 146–147, 176, 261, 459
of prepositions, 424–425, 448
pronouns as, 226–227, 230–231, 253
Opinions, 401, 404–405
or
in compound sentences, 12–13, 20–21, 438–439
in compound subjects and objects, 232–233
as conjunction, 432–433
in series, 88–89
and subject-verb agreement, 162–163
Oral reports, 490–491
Order. *See also* Sequence
of details, 201, 337
of reasons, 401
Outlines
for research reports, 477–478, 482–483
for stories, 123

P

Paragraphs. *See also*
Comparison and contrast paragraphs; Descriptive paragraphs; Narrative paragraphs; Persuasive paragraphs
how-to, 153
writing, 17, 81, 153
Parts of speech. *See*
specific types of
Past participle, 154–155, 158–159, 180–182
Past tense, 152–153, 179–182, 262

Period
in abbreviations, 240–241
rules about, 2, 60
in sentences, 2–3, 16–17
Periodicals, 216
Personal narratives. *See also* Narrative paragraphs
audience for, 48
draft of, 56
main idea for, 48, 52
prewriting, 54–55
proofreading, 59–60
publishing, 61
purpose of, 48, 55
putting together, 50–51
revising, 57–58
sensory details for, 53
supporting details for, 49, 52
time order in, 49
topics for, 54
writing, 227
Personal pronouns, 226–227, 250, 263
Personification, 25
Persuasive language, 401, 414
Persuasive paragraphs
audience for, 400, 406
draft of, 408
facts and opinions in, 401, 404–405
order of reasons in, 401
prewriting, 406–407
proofreading, 411–412
publishing, 413
purpose of, 400, 406
putting together, 402–403
revising, 409–410
topic sentences for, 400–401, 406
Phrases
adjective, 426–427, 449
adverb, 428–429, 450
prepositional
as adjectives, 426–427
as adverbs, 428–429
correct use of, 442–443
and prepositions, 424–425, 448, 463
rules about, 488

verbs after, 430–431, 451–452, 463
verb, 144–145, 175
Pictures, 46–47, 114–115, 198–199, 272–273, 334–335, 398–399, 474–475
Plot, of story, 116
Plural nouns, 76–79, 84–85, 94, 103, 458
Plurals
antecedents, 228–229
indefinite pronouns, 238–239
nouns, 76–79, 84–85, 95, 458
possessive nouns, 78–79, 84–85, 128
possessive pronouns
apostrophes with, 234–237
in combining sentences, 310–311
forming, 78–79, 128
and subject-verb agreement, 160–163
verbs, 160–163, 238–239
Poetry
"Dreams" (Langston Hughes), 315
"On the Mountain Pass" (Bashō), 381
"Paula the Cat" (Nikki Giovanni), 25
"The Sidewalk Racer or On the Skateboard" (Lillian Morrison), 447
"This Is Just To Say" (William Carlos Williams), 249
Point of view, 414–415
Point-by-point method, 201
Positives, 370–371
Possessive nouns
apostrophes with, 84–85, 99, 103, 261, 458
forming, 78–79, 96, 103, 128, 261, 458
in sentence combining, 310–311

of descriptions, 336
of personal narratives, 48, 55
of persuasive paragraphs, 400, 406
of research reports, 476, 483
of stories, 116

Q

R

S

INDEX